2021

International Fire Code®

STUDY
COMPANION

From the publisher of the IFC®

Features:
- 18 study sessions and quizzes
- 630 total questions and answers
- Fully illustrated

A great learning tool for:
- Fire inspectors
- Plans examiners
- Fire officials

ICC

INTERNATIONAL
CODE COUNCIL®

2021 *International Fire Code*® Study Companion:
Based on the 2021 *International Fire Code*®

International Code Council Staff:

Executive Vice President and Director of Business Development:
Mark A. Johnson

Senior Vice President, Business and Product Development:
Hamid Naderi

Vice President and Technical Director, Products and Services:
Doug Thornburg

Senior Marketing Specialist:
Dianna Hallmark

Manager of Product Development:
Mary Lou Luif

Project Manager:
Doug Thornburg

Publications Manager:
Anne F. Kerr

Manager of Publications Production:
Jen Fitzsimmons

Project Editor:
Valerie Necka

Production Technician:
Cheryl Smith

Cover Design:
Ricky Razo

T027808

TABLE OF CONTENTS

INTRODUCTION

This study companion provides practical learning assignments for independent study of the provisions of the 2021 *International Fire Code*® (IFC®). The independent study format affords a method for the student to complete the study program in an unregulated time period. Progressing through the workbook, the learner can measure their level of knowledge by using the exercises and quizzes provided for each study session.

The workbook is also valuable for instructor-led programs. In jurisdictional training sessions, community college classes, vocational training programs and other structured educational offerings, the study guide and the IFC can be the basis for classroom instruction.

All study sessions begin with a general learning objective, the specific code sections or chapters of the code under consideration, and a list of questions summarizing the key points of study. Each session addresses selected topics from the IFC and includes code text, a commentary on the code provisions, illustrations representing the provisions under discussion and multiple choice questions that can be used to evaluate the student's knowledge. Before beginning the quizzes, the student should thoroughly review the IFC, focusing on the key points identified at the beginning of each study session.

The workbook is structured so that after every question the student has an opportunity to record their response and the corresponding code reference. The correct answers are located in the back of the workbook in the answer key.

Questions or comments concerning this workbook are encouraged. Please direct your comments to ICC at studycompanion@iccsafe.org.

Acknowledgements

Grateful appreciation is due to the following people for their assistance in reviewing this updated publication. Buddy Showalter, P.E. of the International Code Council provided expert review and comments improving the clarity of the review sessions and questions. Jacob Stocke of TE Apprenticeship, Bryan Castles of Western Technologies Inc., Chris Kimball of West Coast Code Consultants and Russell Ensslin all provided thoughtful review for the original edition of study sessions in their specialty areas and on general special inspection requirements.

About the International Code Council

The International Code Council is the leading global source of model codes and standards and building safety solutions that include product evaluation, accreditation, technology, codification, training and certification. The Code Council's codes, standards and solutions are used to ensure safe, affordable and sustainable communities and buildings worldwide. The International Code Council family of solutions includes the ICC Evaluation Service, the International Accreditation Service, General Code, S. K. Ghosh Associates, NTA Inc., ICC Community Development Solutions and the Alliance for National & Community Resilience. The Code Council is the largest international association of building safety professionals and is the trusted source of model codes and standards, establishing the baseline for building safety globally and creating a level playing field for designers, builders and manufacturers.

Washington, DC Headquarters:

500 New Jersey Avenue, NW, 6th Floor, Washington, DC 20001

Regional Offices:

Eastern Regional Office (BIR)

Central Regional Office (CH)

Western Regional Office (LA)

Distribution Center (Lenexa, KS)

888-ICC-SAFE (888-422-7233)

www.iccsafe.org

Family of Solutions:

About the Author

Kevin H. Scott

President

KH Scott & Associates LLC

Kevin Scott is President of KH Scott & Associates LLC. Kevin has extensive experience in the development of fire safety, building safety and hazardous materials regulations. Kevin has actively worked for over 30 years in the development of fire code, building code and fire safety regulations at the local, state, national and international levels. Kevin previously worked as a Senior Regional Manager with the International Code Council, and before that, he was Deputy Chief for the Kern County Fire Department, California, where he worked for 30 years. He has developed and presented many seminars on a variety of technical subjects including means of egress, high-piled combustible storage, hazardous materials, and plan review and inspection practices.

Kevin was a member of the original IFC Drafting Committee that worked to create the first edition of the IFC. He served for 7 years on the IFC Code Development Committee and was chairperson for the committee from 2001 to 2004. Kevin has actively participated in numerous technical committees to evaluate specific hazards and technologies, and to create regulations specific to those hazards.

Some of the more significant committees are:

- High-piled Combustible Storage Committee
- Hydrogen Gas Ad Hoc Committee
- Task Group 400
- Technical Advisory Committee on Retail Storage of Group 'A' Plastic Commodities
- UL Laboratories Fire Council

Kevin's constant work to improve fire and life safety has been recognized on many levels. His contributions have been acknowledged by various organizations when they presented him with the following awards:

- William Goss Award in 2021—presented by the California State Firefighters Association
- Mary Eriksen-Rattan Award in 2013—presented by the Southern California State Fire Prevention Officers' Association
- William Goss Award in 2009—presented by the California State Firefighters Association
- Fire Official of the Year Award in 2005—presented by the California Building Officials
- Robert W. Gain Award in 2003—presented by the International Fire Code Institute

2021 IFC Chapters 1, 11 and Appendix A
Administration

OBJECTIVE: To obtain an understanding of the administrative provisions of the *International Fire Code*® (IFC®), including the scope and purpose of the code, duties of the fire code official, application to new and existing facilities, requirements for permits, inspection practices, definitions, referenced standards and establishment of a Board of Appeals.

REFERENCE: Chapters 1, 11 and Appendix A, 2021 IFC

KEY POINTS:
- What is the purpose and scope of the IFC?
- When do the provisions of the appendices apply?
- What are some important points to remember about the intent of the IFC?
- When do the construction and design provisions of the code apply to new buildings and facilities?
- What requirements in the code apply to existing buildings?
- Do any of the construction provisions apply to existing buildings and facilities?
- How is the scope of the IFC similar to that of the *International Building Code*® (IBC®)? How does the scope of the IFC differ from that of the IBC?
- What provisions of the IFC are applicable to one- and two-family dwellings regulated by the *International Residential Code for One- and Two-Family Dwellings*® (IRC®)?
- How are historic buildings dealt with in the International Codes?
- Which provisions apply when there are differences between the IFC and its referenced codes and standards?
- When do other nationally recognized fire safety standards come into play?
- Which requirements are to be determined by the fire code official?
- Who is the fire code official?

KEY POINTS: (Cont'd)

- When there is a conflict between a general requirement and a specific requirement, which one applies?
- How is the code compliance agency established, and how is it organized?
- What types of actions is the fire code official authorized to perform?
- What is the fire code official authorized to do regarding applications and permits?
- Under what circumstances does the fire code official have the right to enter a building or premises?
- How long are official records to be retained?
- After a building is constructed, can the owner change the use of a building? What provisions apply when this occurs?
- What determines whether materials and equipment are approved?
- What are the criteria and procedures for evaluating and approving modifications and alternate materials and equipment, and when may additional technical assistance be required?
- What is the fire code official's role in fire investigations, and what authority does he or she have at fires and other emergencies?
- What are the two main types of permits issued under the IFC?
- What administrative processes, requirements and conditions are involved with the issuance of permits?
- What are the specific activities, systems or facilities that require permits?
- What is the role of the Board of Appeals?
- What provisions that are available to govern the establishment and operation of a Board of Appeals?
- What are the procedures for taking action against violations of the IFC?
- How does the *International Fire Code* authorize the fire code official to deal with unsafe buildings?
- When and how may a stop work order be issued?
- Why are definitions an important part of the IFC, and where can they be found?
- What are referenced standards? How may they be utilized in conjunction with the IFC?

Code Text: *This code establishes regulations affecting or relating to structures, processes, premises and safeguards regarding all of the following: (1) The hazard of fire and explosion arising from the storage, handling or use of structures, materials or devices; (2) Conditions hazardous to life, property or public welfare in the occupancy of structures or premises; (3) Fire hazards in the structure or on the premises from occupancy or operation; (4) Matters related to the construction, extension, repair, alteration or removal of fire protection systems; (5) Conditions affecting the safety of fire fighters and emergency responders during emergency operations.*

Discussion and Commentary: This section of the IFC lays out the scope of the code. It addresses activities that create a fire or life safety hazard. The code is not limited to only "fire" hazards. It includes regulations for the safe use and handling of hazardous materials, construction of building components and egress systems that affect the safety of employees and occupants, proper installation and repair of fire protection systems and smoke control systems, equipment and services in a building such as refrigeration systems and elevators, and other processes that pose various hazards such as dry cleaning and fuel-dispensing. The code also considers the safety and needs of emergency response personnel.

The IFC is used as a design document for new construction and remodels. It also contains requirements for maintaining fire protection systems, safely handling hazardous materials, and conducting business operations in a safe manner.

Code Text: *Provisions in the appendices shall not apply unless specifically adopted.*

Discussion and Commentary: The appendices contain nonmandatory provisions and are provided in part to assist the fire code official in establishing a Board of Appeals or provide a method for determining fire flow requirements, as well as provide requirements for fire department access in addition to the requirements in IFC Chapter 5.

Some of the appendices are designed to be adopted and others are provided for information only. Appendices E, F and G are provided for information only and are not intended to be adopted. Specifically, Appendix E contains hazardous material categories with various chemicals listed under each category which are only meant to be a representative sample; it is not a complete classification of hazardous materials found in each chemical category. Appendix F is a crosswalk between the IFC hazardous material classifications and the NFPA terminology and is to be used as a resource to create an NFPA 704 placard. Appendix G provides a conversion of pounds to volume for certain common cryogenic fluids; this appendix does not provide any regulations, only information.

The appendices designed for adoption are:

- Appendix A – Board of Appeals
- Appendix B – Fire-flow Requirements for Buildings
- Appendix C – Fire Hydrant Locations and Distribution
- Appendix D – Fire Apparatus Access Roads
- Appendix H – Hazardous Materials Management Plan (HMMP) and Hazardous Materials Inventory Statement (HMIS) Instructions
- Appendix I – Fire Protection Systems—Noncompliant Conditions
- Appendix J – Building Information Sign
- Appendix K – Construction Requirements for Existing Ambulatory Care Facilities
- Appendix L – Requirements for Fire Fighter Air Replenishment Systems
- Appendix M – High-rise Buildings—Retroactive Automatic Sprinkler Requirements
- Appendix N – Indoor Trade Shows and Exhibitions

Section 101.2.1 clearly states that the appendices are only applicable and enforceable when they are specifically named in the adopting ordinance or rule.

(Photograph courtesy of Professional Development Incorporated, San Antonio, Texas.)

The photograph illustrates a fire-flow test. The requirements in Appendix B, "Fire-flow Requirements for Buildings," set forth the minimum fire-flow requirements, when the appendix is adopted.

Code Text: *The purpose of this code is to establish the minimum requirements consistent with nationally recognized good practice for providing a reasonable level of life safety and property protection from the hazards of fire, explosion or dangerous conditions in new and existing buildings, structures and premises and to provide a reasonable level of safety to fire fighters and emergency responders during emergency operations.*

Discussion and Commentary: There are four primary concepts in this section:

1. The provisions in the IFC are *minimum* requirements. Although additional measures are not required by the code, higher levels of safety may be reached and maintained. The acceptable minimum level of the code requirements has been set through an open, public consensus process.

2. The IFC and standards referenced in the code are nationally recognized, as opposed to provisions that may have been developed at the local level without a similar amount of discussion, statistical evidence, knowledge and consensus. As such, the model code provisions and referenced standards tend to have much more legal validity than local requirements, which may be developed without the same level of national and international input.

3. Even the strictest adherence to all of the requirements of the IFC will not make a building or premises fire proof, explosion proof or otherwise free of all potential hazards. The stated intent of the IFC is to provide *a reasonable level of life safety and property protection.* The "reasonable level" is determined by the governmental voting members who vote on changes and revisions to the code after the issues have been evaluated and re-evaluated in two separate public hearings.

4. The IFC includes in its intent statement the goal to provide for the safety of emergency responders. This is a natural extension of the intent to protect occupants and premises, as providing for the safety of fire fighters and emergency responders greatly increases the likelihood that lives and property are protected.

This section could be considered a mission statement for the IFC. The IFC recognizes the importance of providing for the safety of occupants as well as fire fighters and emergency responders during emergency operations.

Code Text: *Construction and design provisions. The construction and design provisions of this code shall apply to: (1) Structures, facilities and conditions arising after the adoption of this code, (2) Existing structures, facilities and conditions not legally in existence at the time of adoption of this code, (3) Existing structures, facilities and conditions when required in Chapter 11, (4) Existing structures, facilities and conditions that, in the opinion of the fire code official, constitute a distinct hazard to life or property.*

Administrative, operational and maintenance provisions. The administrative, operational and maintenance provisions of this code shall apply to: (1) Conditions and operations arising after the adoption of this code, (2) Existing conditions and operations.

Discussion and Commentary: This section of the IFC states that, unlike the IBC and most of the other International Codes which focus primarily on regulating new construction, the IFC includes regulations applicable to new and existing buildings, and new and existing activities, operations and processes.

These sections specify the circumstances under which the IFC may be applied to new buildings or facilities and to existing buildings and facilities. The applicability of its provisions are divided into two categories:

- Construction and design, and
- Administrative, operational and maintenance.

The construction provisions in the IFC apply in four specific circumstances: (1) The building or facility is new and development or construction commences after the code is adopted. This timing for application of the new code is typically based on the date of application for permit; the code in force at the date of application is applicable, (2) Existing buildings or operations that are not legal. In other words, they did not comply with the code when they were constructed. Perhaps a permit was not obtained, or the construction and design did not comply with the code in force at the time of construction, (3) Chapter 11 contains specific construction requirements for existing buildings. These requirements are retroactive even though the building complied with the code in force at the time the building was built. The intent of Chapter 11 is to establish a minimum level of safety in buildings that were constructed decades ago. (4) Existing buildings or facilities where the fire code official determines that a distinct hazard exists.

The administrative, operational and maintenance provisions apply to new facilities as well as to facilities that have been in operation for several years.

Both new and existing buildings must comply with the administrative, operational and maintenance requirements in the code.

Code Text: *A change of occupancy shall not be made unless the use or occupancy is made to comply with the requirements of this code and the* International Existing Building Code. ***Exception:*** *Where approved by the fire code official, a change of occupancy shall be permitted without complying with the requirements of this code and the* International Existing Building Code, *provided that the new or proposed use or occupancy is less hazardous, based on life and fire risk, than the existing use or occupancy.*

Discussion and Commentary: A change of use can result in a change of the occupancy classification of a building. When a change of use occurs, the use must comply with the requirements of the *International Existing Building Code*® (IEBC®) and the requirements of the IFC. When a new use or operation occurs, the code regulates it as if it is new. As a new operation, it must comply with the current IBC. If the jurisdiction has adopted the IEBC, then the change of occupancy can comply with either the IBC or IEBC. This section allows a change of use without requiring the entire building or lease space to comply with all of the requirements of the IFC and the IEBC when the new or proposed use is less hazardous. This evaluation is based on the life safety and fire risk of the proposed new use.

For example, consider an existing retail store with an occupancy classification of Group M. The owner decides to change from retail to business management, and the building is now an office. This is a change of occupancy, but changing from Group M to Group B does not create a more hazardous occupancy. This change could be allowed if approved by the fire code official.

An example of a change of occupancy that is less hazardous would be changing a Group S-1 occupancy to a Group S-2 occupancy. Materials stored in a Group S-2 occupancy do not exhibit the high heat release and burning rates found in materials stored in a Group S-1 occupancy.

Code Text: *Where structures are designed and constructed in accordance with the* International Residential Code, *the provisions of this code shall apply as follows: (1) Construction and design provisions of this code pertaining to the exterior of the structure shall apply including, but not limited to, premises identification, fire apparatus access and water supplies. Where interior or exterior systems or devices are installed, construction permits required by Section 105.6 shall apply, (2) Administrative, operational and maintenance provisions of this code shall apply.*

Discussion and Commentary: The IFC contains construction requirements as well as operational and maintenance requirements. All new commercial buildings must comply with the construction requirements in the IFC and the IBC. Detached one- and two-family dwellings can be constructed under the IRC rather than the IBC. The IFC contains requirements that are applicable to one- and two-family dwellings and townhouses. For construction and design, the building is constructed to meet the provisions in the IRC, and the applicable IFC requirements include fire department access, water supplies, premises identification and LP-gas tank location. The administration, operational and maintenance provisions also apply such as the allowed quantity of black powder.

The IRC requires the installation of dwelling fire sprinkler systems in one- and two-family dwellings and in townhouses, and the IFC requires a construction permit for their installation.

Topic: Historic Buildings	**Category:** Scope and Administration
Reference: IFC 102.6, 1103.1.1	**Subject:** Applicability

Code Text: *Historic buildings. The provisions of this code relating to the construction, alteration, repair, enlargement, restoration, relocation or moving of buildings or structures shall not be mandatory for existing buildings or structures identified and classified by the state or local jurisdiction as historic buildings where such buildings or structures do not constitute a distinct hazard to life or property. Fire protection in designated historic buildings shall be provided with an approved fire protection plan as required in Section 1103.1.1.*

Historic buildings. Facilities designated as historic buildings shall develop a fire protection plan in accordance with NFPA 914. The fire protection plans shall comply with the maintenance and availability provisions in Sections 404.3 and 404.4.

Discussion and Commentary: Historic buildings are treated differently than other buildings to maintain the historic value of the structure. The most important principle for application of this special treatment is that the building must be recognized as having historic significance.

Historic buildings were built under previous codes, or possibly constructed prior to any building code. The intent is to provide a minimum level of safety while still retaining the historic value as much as possible. These sections together require the development of a fire protection plan in accordance with NFPA 914 *Code for Protection of Historic Structures.*

NFPA 914 provides guidance on the development of a fire protection plan specific to the facility. The fire protection plan will not bring the building up to current code but will provide for alternate methods for protecting life and property.

Once developed, the fire protection plan becomes an operational guide for the continued use of the building. The fire code official will enforce the requirements in the fire protection plan rather than the contents in the IFC.

HISTORIC BUILDINGS. Any building or structure that is one or more of the following: (1) listed, or certified as eligible for listing by the state historic preservation officer or the Keeper of the National Register of Historic Places, in the National Register of Historic Places, (2) designated as historic under an applicable state or local law, or (3) certified as a contributing resource within a national register, state designated or locally designated historic district (IFC Section 202).

Code Text: *The codes and standards referenced in this code shall be those that are listed in Chapter 80, and such codes and standards shall be considered part of the requirements of this code to the prescribed extent of each such reference and as further regulated in Sections 102.7.1 and 102.7.2.*

Discussion and Commentary: Section 102.7 includes a reference to Chapter 80, which contains over 280 referenced standards. Many standards contain more detailed and specific requirements than are typically found in the body of the code. An example is ASTM Standard E1537—2016, the *Test Method for Fire Testing of Upholstered Furniture.*

The standard listing also includes a date or edition for the referenced standard, as in UL Standard 2245—2006. The specific edition can be critical. Note that the 2006 edition of NFPA 1124 is referenced in addition to the 2017 edition. This occurs because there are provisions in the 2006 edition which do not appear in the 2017 edition. The IFC code section referencing NFPA 1124 will specify which edition applies to the hazard.

Other standards provide detail on the proper design and installation of devices or equipment. An example is NFPA 13, *Standard for the Installation of Sprinkler Systems.* In this case, the code specifies where automatic sprinkler systems are required, and the standard specifies how to design and install the automatic sprinkler system.

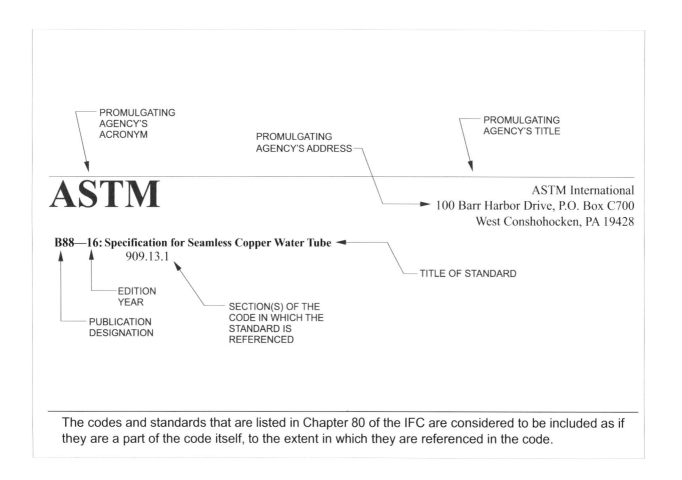

The codes and standards that are listed in Chapter 80 of the IFC are considered to be included as if they are a part of the code itself, to the extent in which they are referenced in the code.

Code Text: *Conflicts. Where conflicts occur between provisions of this code and referenced codes and standards, the provisions of this code shall apply.*

Provisions in referenced codes and standards. Where the extent of the reference to a referenced code or standard includes subject matter that is within the scope of this code, the provisions of this code, as applicable, shall take precedence over the provisions in the referenced code or standard.

Conflicting provisions. Where there is a conflict between a general requirement and a specific requirement, the specific requirement shall be applicable. Where, in a specific case, different sections of this code specify different materials, methods of construction or other requirements, the most restrictive shall govern.

Discussion and Commentary: Conflicts can and do occur between the code requirements and the requirements in some of the referenced standards. When this occurs, as indicated in Sections 102.7.1 and 102.7.2, the code language takes precedence over the language in the standard. These "conflicts" are intentional and modify, or amend, the requirements in the standard. Consider the different requirement in the code as an amendment to the requirement in the standard. In some cases, the code language is more restrictive than the standard, but it does not need to be. The hierarchy of the application of the code specifies that the code language takes precedence even when it is less restrictive.

There are also requirements within the code that appear to conflict with one another. In this case, the requirement that is more specific to the application is the requirement that takes precedence. For example, there are general hazardous materials requirements, and Chapter 12 includes requirements for electrical energy storage systems which contain hazardous materials. The requirements in Chapter 12 are specific to energy storage and would be the appropriate requirements rather than the general requirements for all hazardous materials. Some of the requirements in Chapter 12 are more restrictive and some are less restrictive than the general hazardous materials requirements, but they are designed specifically for electrical energy storage systems.

There is a specific hierarchy for application of conflicting requirements in the code or between the code and referenced standards. Applicability is not based on the most restrictive requirement.

Code Text: *The fire code official is hereby authorized to enforce the provisions of this code. The fire code official shall have the authority to render interpretations of this code, and to adopt policies, procedures, rules and regulations in order to clarify the application of its provisions. Such interpretations, policies, procedures, rules and regulations shall be in compliance with the intent and purpose of this code. Such policies, procedures, rules and regulations shall not have the effect of waiving requirements specifically provided for in this code.*

Discussion and Commentary: It is important that fire code officials use a knowledge-based approach to administering the IFC, utilizing all the available and accurate information they can bring to bear in interpreting the code and making decisions regarding its application. These determinations are to be based upon the intent and purpose of the IFC as stated in Section 101.

The fire code official is given full authority to interpret the code and develop policies on its application. For example, Section 507.1 specifies that the location and type of water supply for fire-fighting shall be approved. The fire code official could develop a policy to explain in further detail what locations would be approved, such as: fire hydrants located at street intersections; fire hydrants located at the start of a cul-de-sac curve rather than at the center of the cul-de-sac; or fire hydrants no further than 20 feet away from a driveway entrance onto the protected property. This policy does not need to go through the official adoption process because it is explaining what "approved" means to the fire code official.

Along with the broad authority given by the IFC, the fire code official also has a responsibility to make decisions in concert with the intent and purpose of the code. Note that IFC Section 104.1 states that any actions by the fire code official shall not waive any requirements of the code.

Code Text: *Right of entry. Where it is necessary to make an inspection to enforce the provisions of this code, or where the fire code official has reasonable cause to believe that there exists in a building or upon any premises any conditions or violations of this code that make the building or premises unsafe, dangerous or hazardous, the fire code official shall have the authority to enter the building or premises at all reasonable times to inspect or to perform the duties imposed upon the fire code official by this code. If such building or premises is occupied, the fire code official shall present credentials to the occupant and request entry. If such building or premises is unoccupied, the fire code official shall first make a reasonable effort to locate the owner, the owner's authorized agent or other person having charge or control of the building or premises and request entry. If entry is refused, the fire code official has recourse to every remedy provided by law to secure entry.*

Warrant. Where the fire code official has first obtained a proper inspection warrant or other remedy provided by law to secure entry, an owner, the owner's authorized agent or occupant or person having charge, care or control of the building or premises shall not fail or neglect, after proper request is made as herein provided, to permit entry therein by the fire code official for the purpose of inspection and examination pursuant to this code.

Discussion and Commentary: These are extremely important provisions and are based upon the Fourth Amendment to the US Constitution, which prohibits the search or seizure of any property unless permission has been granted by the building owner or occupant, the hazard is in plain sight and on a public right of way, or a search warrant has been issued. Failure to strictly follow the correct procedures can result in the fire code official not being able to enforce the provisions of the IFC, i.e., having an enforcement action nullified due to a violation of the Fourth Amendment. If there is any doubt regarding the legal ability to enter a property, the fire code official should always consult with legal counsel before entering the premises.

This section allows the fire code official to conduct an inspection, however, it also acknowledges the business owner's right to refuse. Notice that the section states the fire code official is to "request" permission to enter for inspection.

This section does not mean that the business never is inspected. Rather, this section recognizes the rights of the business owner and guides the fire code official in the fulfillment of his or her duties.

For additional information and resources regarding legal issues, ICC publishes *Legal Aspects of Code Administration*. The legal portions of code enforcement or law enforcement training programs may also be helpful.

Code Text: *Official records. The fire code official shall keep official records as required by Sections 104.6.1 through 104.6.4. Such official records shall be retained for not less than five years or for as long as the structure or activity to which such records relate remains in existence, unless otherwise provided by other regulations.*

Approvals. A record of approvals shall be maintained by the fire code official and shall be available for public inspection during business hours in accordance with applicable laws.

Inspections. The fire code official shall keep a record of each inspection made, including notices and orders issued, showing the findings and disposition of each.

Fire records. The fire department shall keep a record of fires occurring within its jurisdiction and of facts concerning the same, including statistics as to the extent of such fires and the damage caused thereby, together with other information as required by the fire code official.

Administrative. Application for modification, alternative methods or materials and the final decision of the fire code official shall be in writing and shall be officially recorded in the permanent records of the fire code official.

Discussion and Commentary: It has been said that the basic duties of a code official can be summarized as observe and document. Documentation, or the maintenance of official records, is an extremely important function, especially when an enforcement action enters the judicial system. To the best extent possible, the code compliance agency should establish record keeping and filing systems that make good documentation automatic and a basic part of daily activities.

Documentation includes plans reviewed, permits issued, inspections conducted, and any alternatives approved by the fire code official. This document is often needed for review of additional plans or additions to a facility, or to document a repeat violation occurring at a location.

The last phrase in the first paragraph of IFC Section 104.6 acknowledges that government entities have differing requirements for the maintenance and archiving of public records.

Code Text: *To determine the acceptability of technologies, processes, products, facilities, materials and uses attending the design, operation or use of a building or premises subject to inspection by the fire code official, the fire code official is authorized to require the owner or owner's authorized agent to provide, without charge to the jurisdiction, a technical opinion and report. The opinion and report shall be prepared by a qualified engineer, specialist, laboratory or fire safety specialty organization acceptable to the fire code official and shall analyze the fire safety properties of the design, operation or use of the building or premises and the facilities and appurtenances situated thereon, to recommend necessary changes. The fire code official is authorized to require design submittals to be prepared by, and bear the stamp of, a registered design professional.*

Discussion and Commentary: This section recognizes that the application of the IFC has become increasingly complex owing to rapid technological changes in building designs and manufacturing processes. Examples of this increased complexity include smoke control systems, the design of automatic sprinkler systems for the protection of high-piled combustible storage, and the classification, storage, dispensing and use of hazardous materials. For this reason, the IFC includes a provision authorizing the fire code official to require the owner to provide a technical opinion and report at no cost to the jurisdiction.

The person or firm providing the technical opinion or report must be approved by the fire code official. The section states that the fire code official can require the stamp of a registered design professional on the plans. There are many situations where the stamp of a design professional is warranted, such as the specific design criteria of a fire sprinkler system. However, when classifying hazardous materials into the fourteen categories in the IFC, the stamp of a design professional may not be necessary. It is most important that the person providing the report is qualified to perform the review. This person may, or may not, be a registered design professional.

Once the report is developed and submitted to the fire code official, it is the responsibility of the fire code official to review the report. Final approval rests with the fire code official and he or she could approve, conditionally approve or disapprove the technical report and opinion.

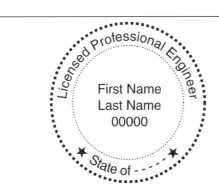

Technical assistance is an analysis of the documents submitted in a permit application. It can be a third party or a peer review, prepared at the applicant's expense. The fire code official has the authority to require that the materials be prepared and sealed by a registered design professional, such as an architect or engineer.

Topic: Alternative Materials and Methods	Category: Administration
Reference: IFC 104.10	Subject: General Authority

Code Text: *The provisions of this code are not intended to prevent the installation of any material or to prohibit any design or method of construction not specifically prescribed by this code, provided that any such alternative has been approved. An alternative material, design or method of construction shall be approved where the fire code official finds that the proposed design is satisfactory and complies with the intent of the provisions of this code, and that the material, method or work offered is, for the purpose intended, not less than the equivalent of that prescribed in this code in quality, strength, effectiveness, fire-resistance, durability and safety. Where the alternative material, design or method of construction is not approved, the fire code official shall respond in writing, stating the reasons why the alternative was not approved.*

Discussion and Commentary: The first sentence of this section emphasizes the facts that, (1) it is the intent of the code to allow for the use of new technologies, materials and methods, and (2) the IFC, similar to the other International Codes, is intended to be a performance-based code as well as a prescriptive code. The fire code official is given specific authorization to approve alternative materials and methods as long as they meet all of the criteria listed in the remainder of the section.

The fire code official reviews and evaluates the proposal for use of an alternative material or method. The fire code official can approve the proposal if he or she finds that the proposed design is satisfactory and complies with the intent of the provisions of the code and is at least equivalent in

- ✓ **Quality,**
- ✓ **Strength,**
- ✓ **Effectiveness,**
- ✓ **Fire resistance,**
- ✓ **Durability and**
- ✓ **Safety.**

Similar to the evaluation of modifications, it is important to carefully read the criteria in this section when evaluating proposals for alternate methods and materials. Note that, if the fire code official denies the proposal, the applicant may also appeal to the Board of Appeals. Performance based designs should be based on the criteria in the *ICC Performance Code® for Buildings and Facilities.*

Topic: Application for a Permit   **Category:** Administration

Reference: IFC 105.2   **Subject:** Permits

Code Text: *Application for a permit required by this code shall be made to the fire code official in such form and detail as prescribed by the fire code official. Applications for permits shall be accompanied by such plans as prescribed by the fire code official.*

Discussion and Commentary: The IFC specifies several permits that can be required before work can commence when such work is regulated by the code. When a permit is issued, it serves as the legal instrument allowing the construction or alteration to occur, or it allows a particular use such as dispensing of fuels, storage of hazardous materials or any of the other activities requiring a permit in IFC Sections 105.5 and 105.6. Information as to the nature of the work or operation along with plans must be submitted to the fire code official for review and approval.

Application for Permit
Request for Service
Kern County Fire Department
Fire Prevention
5642 Victor St. ~ Bakersfield, CA 93308
Telephone (661) 391-7080 ~ Fax (661) 391-7077

Date: _____   *To be completed by permit Applicant (PLEASE PRINT)*

Project Name: _____

Project Street Address: _____

City: _____

Mobile Equipment: VIN # _____   License # _____

☐ Fire Alarm   ☐ Hood Suppression   ☐ Automatic Sprinkler   ☐ Flammable Liquids
____ # of Devices   (Fire Protection Systems)   Remodel ☐ or New ☐   ____ # of tanks

☐ LPG Tank(s)   ☐ Spray Booth   ☐ Tents/Canopies   ☐ Other (describe)
____ # of tanks   (spraying & dipping)   (complete tent handout)   ____

☐ Special Effects   ☐ Plan Review   ☐ Knox Box   ☐ Flow Test
Description of project: _____

If additional space is needed please attach to this Application

Will any hazardous materials be stored: ☐ Yes ☐ No

If yes, include a list of containers and quantities: _____

Customer/Applicant Information

Applicant Name: _____   Phone # _____

Contractor/Company: _____   Phone # _____

Contractor Mailing Address: _____

City: _____   State: _____   Zip: _____

Contractor License # _____   Class: _____   Fax # _____

Contact Person: _____   Cell # _____

Email Address: _____

Permit applications may be submitted in person or mailed to:
Kern County Fire Department
Fire Prevention—Permits
5642 Victor St.   Visa and MasterCard Accepted
Bakersfield, CA 93308
Please include a check made payable to the **KERN COUNTY FIRE DEPARTMENT**

_____   A $45.00 *PROCESSING FEE WILL BE CHARGED FOR ANY*
Signature   *REFUNDS ISSUED BY KCFD.*

Also submit site plans, construction plans and specifications

KCFD 200 (0913)

(Application form courtesy of Kern County Fire Department, CA)

The application for a permit should provide adequate information to determine what work will be performed, where the work will be performed and who will be responsible. It is not uncommon for a jurisdiction to issue multiple permits for a single building, especially if the building is undergoing multiple tenant improvements, such as a new shell. In addition to the requirement for certain documentation to be included in permits, the permit is also required to be posted. See IFC Section 105.3.5.

Topic: Validity of Permit	Category: Administration
Reference: IFC 105.3.8	Subject: Permits

Code Text: *The issuance or granting of a permit shall not be construed to be a permit for, or an approval of, any violation of any of the provisions of this code or of any other ordinances of the jurisdiction. Permits presuming to give authority to violate or cancel the provisions of this code or other ordinances of the jurisdiction shall not be valid. The issuance of a permit based on construction documents, operational documents and other data shall not prevent the fire code official from requiring correction of errors in the documents or other data.*

Discussion and Commentary: The fire code official will review and approve various plans and permits. This section states that the fact that the plans and permit have been approved does not allow the owner or contractor to violate the code requirements. This means that even if the fire code official missed a violation on the plans, the designer and contractor are still obligated to comply with code and correct any deficiency.

Approval by the fire code official essentially means that construction can start. If during inspection the violation is found, it must be corrected even though the plans were approved.

This section can also be used in conjunction with Section 102.1 for application of construction requirements in existing buildings. Item 2 of that section states that the construction requirements in the current code apply when a situation is found that was "not legally in existence." The item never complied with the code and must be corrected.

If an error occurs during an inspection, or an item is missed, the owner is not relieved of the obligation to comply with the IFC and the adopted ordinances of the jurisdiction. When the item is discovered, if it did not comply with the code at the time of construction, it must be corrected. In this photograph, the sprinklers are installed too close together—they need to be separated by a minimum of six feet.

Code Text: *An operational permit is required to conduct additive manufacturing operations regulated by Section 320.3.*

Discussion and Commentary: An operational permit is issued after the application and associated documents have been reviewed and approved. Because the permit is a legal instrument, the scope and conditions of the permit are required to be documented. Any limitation or prohibition of certain activities or use of equipment should also be documented as part of the permit.

As part of the permit approval for an additive manufacturing process, Section 320 contains requirements specifying the process is only allowed in manufacturing facilities, the equipment must be listed, and gases and dusts must be handled appropriately. Where the quantities of hazardous materials exceed the maximum allowable quantities, then the occupancy would be classified as Group H.

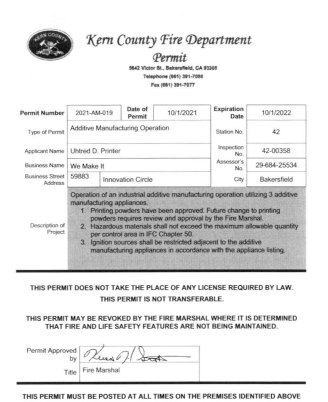

(*Permit courtesy of Kern County Fire Department, CA*)

This operational permit for a facility utilizing industrial additive manufacturing appliances provides criteria for operation to remain in compliance.

Code Text: *Work shall not be done beyond the point indicated in each successive inspection without first obtaining the approval of the fire code official. The fire code official, on notification, shall make the requested inspections and shall either indicate the portion of the construction that is satisfactory as completed, or notify the permit holder or his or her agent wherein the same fails to comply with this code. Any portions that do not comply shall be corrected and such portion shall not be covered or concealed until authorized by the fire code official.*

Discussion and Commentary: This section addresses construction that may involve progressive inspections, such as the installation of an automatic sprinkler system. In a new building, an automatic sprinkler system requires inspections of the underground fire protection water main, a rough inspection of the installed sprinklers and piping, witness of the flushing of the underground piping, a hydrostatic pressure test, an inspection to ensure complete installation of the fire sprinklers, and testing of the electronic supervision system for transmission of a water-flow alarm. These installations may be performed by one or more contractors, and multiple components of the building construction generally occur simultaneously. As with the systematic construction process (i.e., foundation, walls, roof, etc.), the inspections also need to be completed in a systematic process before the next phase conceals the materials and equipment that need to be inspected.

This section ensures that the appropriate inspections are requested and that the inspections are successful before work proceeds. Deficiencies found during inspections must remain uncovered until a subsequent inspection is performed and the corrections are approved.

Code Text: *Approval as the result of an inspection shall not be construed to be an approval of a violation of the provisions of this code or of other ordinances of the jurisdiction. Inspections presuming to give authority to violate or cancel provisions of this code or of other ordinances of the jurisdiction shall not be valid.*

Discussion and Commentary: In certain instances an inspector or plans examiner may issue a construction or operational permit in error. When errors occur, they cannot be construed as granting the authority to violate the IFC or any of the ordinances or regulations adopted by the jurisdiction. This section states that errors resulting from an inspection are not to be construed as an approval of a violation.

If an error occurs during an inspection, or an item is missed, it must be corrected for the building, facility or site to comply with the IFC and the adopted ordinances of the jurisdiction.

Code Text: *An application for appeal shall be based on a claim that the true intent of this code or the rules legally adopted thereunder have been incorrectly interpreted, the provisions of this code do not fully apply or an equivalent or better form of construction is proposed. The board shall not have authority to waive requirements of this code or interpret the administration of this code.*

Discussion and Commentary: This section clarifies the role of the Board of Appeals. Notice that the reasons for an application for appeal closely follow the duties of the fire code official that are listed in IFC Sections 104.1, 104.9 and 104.10. Unlike some appeals boards that may have the authority to grant waivers or variances from regulations, this Board of Appeals has no authority to waive the requirements of the IFC.

SUMMARY OF BOARD OF APPEALS DUTIES:

- Hear and decide appeals of
    - Orders,
    - Decisions, or
    - Determinations made by the fire code official regarding
        - Application of the *International Fire Code,*
        - Interpretation of the *International Fire Code* or
        - Policies or rules developed by the fire code official.

- Appeals must be based upon
    - Incorrect interpretation of intent of code or adopted rules,
    - Provisions of the code not fully applying, or
    - An equivalent proposed method of protection or safety.

The Board of Appeals is a useful tool for the fire code official. If he or she does not feel comfortable in approving a request for a modification or a proposal for the use of alternative materials or methods, the Board of Appeals provides another legitimate option for deciding the matter.

Topic: Intent and Notification	Category: Administration
Reference: IFC 1101.2, 1101.4	Subject: Construction Requirements for Existing Buildings

Code Text: *Intent. The intent of this chapter is to provide a minimum degree of fire and life safety to persons occupying existing buildings by providing minimum construction requirements where such existing buildings do not comply with the minimum requirements of the International Building Code.*

Owner notification. When a building is found to be in noncompliance with this chapter, the fire code official shall duly notify the owner of the building. Upon receipt of such notice, the owner shall, subject to the following time limits, take necessary actions to comply with the provisions of this chapter.

Discussion and Commentary: IFC Chapter 11 contains retroactive construction requirements for existing buildings. Section 1101.2 states that these requirements provide for a minimum acceptable level of fire and life safety for existing buildings. These provisions apply even though the building met the construction codes at the time of construction of the building.

The intent of Chapter 11 is to address construction methods that were allowed by previous codes, but have been determined to be inadequate for protecting the occupants. The items addressed in Chapter 11 are building design methods that are no longer allowed in the codes because of injuries and fatalities occurring in buildings. For example, protection of open stairways in multistory buildings.

Chapter 11 does not require compliance with the current code. In most cases, the items in Chapter 11 offer options on how to mitigate the hazard to provide a minimum level of safety without full compliance with new construction.

Section 1101.4 indicates that the owner must be notified when his or her building does not comply, and the notice needs to establish a time frame for compliance.

Some of the possible retroactive requirements in IFC Chapter 11 for this existing hotel could include
- Protection of interior vertical openings connecting three or more stories – 1103.4.2
- Installation of a fire alarm system, if not currently provided – 1103.7.5.1
- Installation of smoke alarms in sleeping rooms, if not currently provided – 1103.8.1
- Secondary power for illumination of exit signs and egress pathway – 1104.5, #7

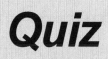

Quiz

Study Session 1 2021

IFC Chapters 1, 11 and Appendix A

1. Provisions in the appendices of the IFC shall not apply unless _____.

    a. they are specifically applicable to the individual situation

    b. the jurisdiction contains structures, facilities and conditions that are appropriate to the provisions of the appendices

    c. they are more restrictive than other provisions in the code

    d. the appendix is specifically adopted

    Reference _101.2.1_

2. The construction provisions of the IFC apply to _____.

    a. structures, facilities and conditions arising after the adoption of the code

    b. existing structures, facilities and conditions not legally in existence at the time of adoption of the code

    c. existing structures, facilities and conditions when specifically required in Chapter 11

    d. all of the above

    Reference _102.1_

3. What is the IFC prescribed frequency for inspection of buildings, facilities and properties?

    a. Annually

    b. The IFC does not establish an inspection frequency.

    c. The fire code official is authorized to perform inspections as needed to determine the extent of compliance with the provisions of the IFC.

    d. At the owner's request

    Reference _106.2_

4. Where there is a conflict between a general requirement and a specific requirement in the code, the _____ requirement shall apply.

    a. most restrictive   b. most general

    c. more specific   d. least restrictive

Reference 102.10

5. The fire code official is not authorized to _____ .

    a. waive requirements specifically provided for in the code

    b. render interpretations of the code

    c. adopt policies and procedures

    d. adopt rules and regulations

Reference 104.1

6. If the owner refuses to allow the fire code official to enter an occupied building or premises to conduct an inspection to enforce the code, the fire code official may _____.

    a. enter the building and conduct the inspection without permission

    b. shut down the business

    c. post an order to vacate

    d. obtain an inspection warrant

Reference 104.3.1

7. The fire code official shall retain official records for not less than _____ years or for as long as the structure or activity to which such records regulate remains in existence.

    a. three   b. five

    c. seven   d. ten

Reference 104.6

8. In order to determine the acceptability of technologies, processes, products or other features of a building subject to inspection by the fire code official, the fire code official is authorized to require the owner or agent to provide _____ at no cost to the jurisdiction.

   a. additional copies of the IFC and needed standards

   b. a technical opinion and report

   c. a cost estimate for the construction

   d. additional fire apparatus

   Reference 104.8.2

9. Construction documents and design submittals for a permit shall be prepared by a _____.

   a. professional consultant

   b. special expert

   c. licensed contractor, when required by local statutes

   d. registered design professional, when required by local statutes

   Reference 106.1

10. Whenever there are practical difficulties in carrying out the provisions of the IFC, the fire code official shall have the authority to grant modifications for _____.

   a. individual cases   b. identical situations

   c. all similar cases   d. individual persons

   Reference 104.9

11. Which of the following activities does not require an operational permit?

   a. An outdoor assembly event featuring a monster truck race with 2,500 attendees

   b. A fireworks display after the monster truck race

   c. The tire changing and repair area for the monster trucks

   d. The refueling operation for the monster truck vehicles

   Reference 105 , 106

12. Which one of the following is *not* included in a required operational permit regulated by the IFC?

   a. hot work   b. organic coatings

   c. floor finishing   d. compressed-gas-powered vehicles

   Reference 105.5

13. An operational permit is required to store, transport on site, dispense, use or handle a solid Class 2 oxidizer when the quantity exceeds _____.

    a. 10 pounds   b. 20 pounds

    c. 100 pounds   d. 500 pounds

Reference 105.5.22

14. An operational permit is required for a liquid Class 3 water-reactive material when the quantity exceeds _____.

    a. 5 gallons   b. 10 gallons

    c. 55 gallons   d. any amount

Reference 105.5.22

15. What amount of solid Class V organic peroxides requires an IFC operational permit?

    a. 10 pounds   b. 20 pounds

    c. any amount   d. a permit is not required

Reference 105.5.22

16. A construction permit for a 500 square foot, temporary tent that is open on all sides is not required if a minimum clearance of _____ feet to structures and other tents is maintained.

    a. 12   b. 15

    c. 20   d. 26

Reference 105.6.24

17. When the fire code official finds a structure that constitutes a clear threat to human life, safety or health, which of the following actions cannot be taken?

    a. Evacuate the building

    b. If the owner is not available on site, the fire code official shall order the immediate destruction of the building

    c. Serve notice on the owner identifying the unsafe conditions and required repairs

    d. Refer the building to the building code official for repair, alteration or remodeling

Reference 114

18. When the fire code official finds a building, premises, vehicle, storage facility or outdoor area that is in violation of the IFC, he or she is authorized to _____.

    a. order the building vacated   (b.) prepare a written notice of violation

    c. condemn the building   d. issue a stop work order

Reference 112.3

19. The referenced standards in IFC Chapter 80 are organized _____.

    a. alphabetically, by subject

    (b) alphabetically, by the issuing organization or agency

    c. by their publication date

    d. by chapters in the IFC

Reference Ch. 80

20. Referenced standards are to be applied _____.

    a. only if they are formally adopted

    b. only as guidelines

    (c) as if they are part of the IFC, and as specified in IFC Section 102.7

    d. only by the fire code official

Reference 102.7

21. Which of the following is not one of the agencies listed as promulgating referenced standards for the IFC?

    a. US Department of Treasury (DOTy)

    b. United States Code (USC)

    c. Builders Hardware Manufacturers Association (BHMA)

    (d) Building Owners and Managers Association (BOMA)

Reference Ch. 80

22. Which of the following is not considered part of the code's intent and purpose?

    a. provide a reasonable level of life safety

    b. establish a minimum set of requirements

    c. address dangerous conditions in new and existing buildings

    (d.) punish those who intentionally set fires

Reference 101.3

23. When does a construction permit issued under the authority of the IFC become invalid?

    a. after the construction commences

    (b.) after a period of 180 days when work is abandoned or suspended

    c. end of calendar year

    d. when the next edition of the code is adopted

Reference 103.1

24. The fire code official has the authority to authorize disconnection of utility services to a building under what conditions?

    a. To encourage compliance with a correction notice

    b. As part of emergency operations

    c. To eliminate an immediate hazard in the building

    (d.) Both B and C

Reference 110.1

25. Which of the following existing buildings or occupancies are required to be retrofit with a fire sprinkler system, if they are not already sprinklered?

    a. all buildings with a floor level greater than 120 feet above the lowest level of fire department vehicle access

    b. Group A-2 occupancies serving alcoholic beverages with an occupant load of 300 or more

    c. Group I-2, Condition 2 occupancies

    (d.) All of the above

Reference 1103.5

26. According to Appendix A, the Board of Appeals shall consist of _____ voting members.

    a. three   (b.) five

    c. six   d. seven

Reference App. A
101.3

27. The Board of Appeals, if Appendix A is adopted, is required to meet within _____ days after a notice of appeal has been received.

    a. five
    b. ten
    c. fourteen
    d. thirty

Reference _App. A 101.5_

28. According to Appendix A, members with a personal, professional or financial interest in a matter before the board shall _____.

    a. declare such interest before discussion or voting on such matters

    b. declare such interest and refrain from participating in discussions, deliberations and voting on such matters

    c. declare such interest, then lead the discussion, but not vote on such matters

    d. remain silent and refrain from stating a position one way or the other on such matters

Reference _App. A 101.3.6_

29. A construction permit has been issued for the installation of a fire alarm system in a new building. Which of the following is correct regarding inspections for work conducted under that construction permit?

    a. It is the permit holder's responsibility to call for inspection

    b. When an inspection is required, the work to be inspected shall not be concealed

    c. If a code violation is missed during inspection, the permit holder is still responsible to comply with the code

    d. All of the above

Reference _Ch. 1 106.2_

30. An operational permit is required to manufacture, store or handle an aggregate quantity of Level 2 or 3 aerosol products in excess of _____ pounds net weight.

    a. 55
    b. 100
    c. 500
    d. 1,000

Reference _Ch. 1 105.5.2_

31. Except for fuel oil used in connection with oil-burning equipment, an operational permit is required to store, handle or use Class II or Class IIIA liquids in excess of _____ gallons in a building.

    a.   5   b.   10

    c.   25   d.   any amount of

Reference _Ch. 1_
105.5.18 #3

32. Which of the following is not a requirement when tests are performed to demonstrate compliance with the IFC?

    a.   Tests are performed by an approved agency.

    b.   The fire code official shall personally witness the test.

    c.   The test method shall be as specified in the IFC or by other recognized test methods.

    d.   Test reports shall be retained as required for public records.

Reference _Ch. 1_
104.10.2

33. A historic building need not comply with the retroactive construction requirements in Chapter 11 provided it complies with a fire protection plan developed in accordance with _____.

    a.   the IEBC

    b.   NFPA 101

    c.   NFPA 914

    d.   requirements set forth by the fire code official

Reference _Ch. 11_
1103.1.1

34. What are the construction permit fees for the installation of an NFPA 13 automatic sprinkler system in a 16,000 square foot Group M occupancy?

    a.   As required by the fire code official.

    b.   Fees are not required.

    c.   Fees are based on the building's valuation in accordance with the IBC.

    d.   Fees shall be in accordance with the schedule established by the applicable governing authority.

Reference _Ch. 1_
107.2

35. What is required to protect an unenclosed, interior stairway in an existing 4-story hotel?

       a.   comply with requirements in the IBC for new construction

       b.   provide a 1-hour fire-resistance-rated enclosure

       c.   install a fire sprinkler system throughout the building

       (d.) either b or c

Reference _Ch. 11_

_1103.4.2_

2021 IFC Chapter 2 and IBC Chapters 3 and 5
Definitions and Occupancy Classification

OBJECTIVE: To understand how definitions apply, how uses associated with a building or premises are classified into occupancy groups and how occupancy classification is used in the administration of the *International Fire Code®* (IFC®).

REFERENCE: Chapter 2, 2021 IFC and Chapters 3 and 5, 2021 *International Building Code®* (IBC®).

KEY POINTS:
- How are definitions used in the IFC? What happens when a word or term is not defined in the code?
- Why are building uses divided into occupancy groups?
- How does an occupancy classification affect the treatment of a specific operation in the International Codes?
- What are the ten major occupancy categories?
- Why are some occupancy groups divided into subcategories?
- What are some of the qualifiers that change a use from a lower hazard occupancy to a higher-hazard occupancy?
- How can the occupancy groups be remembered and easily located in the IFC?
- Which types of activities are considered assembly uses? What is their general classification?
- How are small assembly uses classified when they are accessory to a different occupancy?
- What is the classification for restaurants and cafes? Night clubs and theaters? Places of religious worship, conference rooms and libraries? Arenas and grandstands?
- What is the use that is most typically classified as a B occupancy? What are some other uses classified as Group B?
- Which age range for occupants usually falls into the Group E category?
- Which types of day care may be classified as Group E occupancies?
- Is a Group E day care different than other Group E occupancies?

KEY POINTS:
(Cont'd)

- What occupancy group includes manufacturing operations? What are the characteristics that determine which subcategory is appropriate?
- How do the amounts of hazardous materials affect the occupancy classification? Where can the qualifying amounts of various types of materials be found in the IFC?
- Which occupancies have requirements to address physical hazards? Health hazards? Semiconductor fabrication facilities?
- What are the characteristics of occupants typically found in Group I occupancies?
- How are uses classified when the liberties of the occupants are restrained? What other types of conditions are applied?
- Which types of institutional occupancies may be constructed under the *International Residential Code*® (IRC®)?
- What type of building is classified as Group M? What other types of code provisions may apply?
- How are residential occupancies classified? Why do some Group R occupancies have more stringent requirements than others?
- What characteristics are used to classify Group S occupancies into Groups S-1 and S-2? How may a motor vehicle repair garage be classified as a Group S occupancy?
- What is a utility occupancy? How does its classification differ from that of other occupancies?
- How does the IBC deal with more than one occupancy in the same building?
- What are incidental uses?
- What is the difference between a separated mixed occupancy and nonseparated mixed use occupancy?
- What options are available for separating multiple occupancies in the same building? How can a building house multiple occupancies with no fire separations required between occupancies?
- How does occupancy classification fit into the IBC's provisions for determining allowable height?

Code Text: *Scope. Unless otherwise expressly stated, the following words and terms shall, for the purposes of this code, have the meanings shown in this chapter.*

Interchangeability. Words used in the present tense include the future; words stated in the masculine gender include the feminine and neuter; the singular number includes the plural and the plural, the singular.

Terms defined in other codes. Where terms are not defined in this code and are defined in the International Building Code, International Fuel Gas Code, International Mechanical Code *or* International Plumbing Code, *such terms shall have the meanings ascribed to them as in those codes.*

Terms not defined. Where terms are not defined through the methods authorized by this section, such terms shall have ordinarily accepted meanings such as the context implies. Merriam Webster's Collegiate Dictionary, 11th Edition, *shall be considered as providing ordinarily accepted meanings.*

Discussion and Commentary: Codes, by their very nature, are technical documents. Every word, term and punctuation mark can add to or change the meaning of a technical requirement. It is necessary to maintain a consensus on the specific meaning of each term contained in the code. Chapter 2 performs this function by stating clearly what specific terms mean for the purpose of the code.

Additionally, this section specifies that when a word is in the plural form, it also is to be applied in the singular form. For example, Section 906.2 states "… fire extinguishers shall be selected, installed and maintained…" Even though "fire extinguishers" is plural, if a facility is only required to provide one fire extinguisher, this section still applies.

Another nuance to the definitions is that defined terms are *italicized* in the code text. Where a word is not italicized, the general meaning of the term applies rather than the specific Chapter 2 definition. This information is not found in the code text; it is found in the Preface.

Examples of the importance of definitions

1. Container
   a. Defined in Chapter 2 as a maximum of 60 gallons.
   b. Container used in the term "LP-gas container" is not limited to 60 gallons.
2. Flammable
   a. "Flammable Liquid" is defined as a liquid with a flash point below 100°F.
   b. "Flammable Finishes" applies to finishes applied to products, and the finish material will burn, including combustible liquids and powder coating which are not flammable liquids.
3. Exit
   a. A specific term that in the code applies to only seven components of a means of egress that is actually considered an "exit".
   b. The term is used to identify the exit path for occupants when the code requires "EXIT" signs.

Code Text: *For the purposes of this code, certain occupancies are defined as follows:*

(See IFC Section 202 for full definition.)

Occupancy classification is the formal designation of the primary purpose of the building, structure or portion thereof. Structures shall be classified into one or more of the occupancy groups listed in this section based on the nature of the hazards and risks to building occupants generally associated with the intended purpose of the building or structure. An area, room or space that is intended to be occupied at different times for different purposes shall comply with all applicable requirements associated with such potential multipurpose. Structures containing multiple occupancy groups shall comply with Section 508. Where a structure is proposed for a purpose that is not specifically listed in this section, such structure shall be classified in the occupancy it most nearly resembles based on the fire safety and relative hazard. Occupied roofs shall be classified in the group that the occupancy most nearly resembles, according to the fire safety and relative hazard, and shall comply with Section 503.1.4. [IBC]

Discussion and Commentary: Uses are categorized into occupancies according to risk factors including the vulnerability of the occupants, such as infant care facilities, homes for the elderly or hospitals; or the hazards that might be present because of the uses or type and amount of materials housed in the occupancy, such as compressed gas facilities, flammable liquids storage facilities or businesses that handle highly toxic materials. The occupancy group classifications provide an overall system that is established in the IBC to determine the allowable area and height of buildings and other requirements based upon the use and character of the building or space (Occupancy), the degree of passive fire resistance built into the building (Type of Construction) and special construction requirements. The IFC uses those same occupancy classifications to determine requirements such as automatic sprinkler systems, fire alarm systems and emergency evacuation plans.

A	Assembly
B	Business
E	Educational
F	Factory
H	High-hazard
I	Institutional
M	Mercantile
R	Residential
S	Storage
U	Utility

The classification of the occupancy is an important skill in applying the requirements of the *International Fire Code.*

Code Text: *Assembly Group A. Assembly Group A occupancy includes, among others, the use of a building or structure, or a portion thereof, for the gathering of persons for purposes such as civic, social or religious functions; recreation, food or drink consumption; or awaiting transportation.*

Small buildings and tenant spaces. A building or tenant space used for assembly purposes with an occupant load of less than 50 persons shall be classified as a Group B occupancy.

Small assembly spaces. The following rooms and spaces shall not be classified as assembly occupancies: (1) A room or space used for assembly purposes with an occupant load of less than 50 persons and accessory to another occupancy shall be classified as a Group B occupancy or as part of that occupancy, (2) A room or space used for assembly purposes that is less than 750 square feet (70 m²) in area and accessory to another occupancy shall be classified as a Group B occupancy or as part of that occupancy.

Associated with Group E occupancies. A room or space used for assembly purposes that is associated with a Group E occupancy is not considered a separate occupancy.

Accessory to places of religious worship. Accessory religious educational rooms and religious auditoriums with occupant loads of less than 100 per room or space are not considered separate occupancies.

Special amusement areas. Special amusement areas shall comply with Section 411 of the International Building Code.

Discussion and Commentary: Group A occupancies can range from a conference room with an occupant load of 50 or more persons to a sports stadium with a capacity of several thousand occupants. The primary concern with assembly occupancies is that large numbers of people, often assembled together in high densities, might not be able to exit the facility safely in the event of a fire, explosion or other emergency situation. In many cases, the occupants are not entirely familiar with the building. They are aware of the path they took to get into the facility, but are often not aware of other paths to exit the building. An additional concern is that the occupants may be consuming alcohol, which can impair their ability to safely egress a building.

The code requirements for assembly occupancies place emphasis on crowd managers, adequate means of egress, early detection and notification of a fire, fire protection based on construction, fire and life safety with fire sprinkler systems, limiting the spread of smoke and other concerns related to moving a large number of people out of a structure safely.

Group A-1	**Group A-3**	Gymnasiums (without spectator seating)	**Group A-4**
Motion picture theaters	Amusement arcades		Arenas
Symphony and concert halls	Art galleries	Indoor swimming pools (without spectator seating)	Skating rinks
TV and radio studios with audience	Bowling alleys		Swimming pools
	Community halls	Indoor tennis courts (without spectator seating)	Tennis courts
Theaters	Courtrooms		
	Dance halls	Lecture halls	**Group A-5**
Group A-2	Exhibition halls	Libraries	Amusement park structures
Banquet halls	Funeral parlors	Museums	Bleachers
Casinos	Greenhouses for the conservation and exhibition of plants that provide public access	Places of religious worship	Grandstands
Nightclubs		Pool and billiards parlors	Stadiums
Restaurants		Waiting areas, transportation	
Taverns and bars			

Subcategories of Group A divide the occupancies into similar uses based on the density of occupants, awareness of surroundings and ability to egress. Note that a Group A-3 occupancy has a variety of uses that can include large fuel packages. Refer to the applicable provisions in the IBC and IFC for proper occupancy classification.

Code Text: *Business Group B occupancy includes, among others, the use of a building or structure, or a portion thereof, for office, professional or service-type transactions, including storage of records and accounts. Business occupancies shall include, but not be limited to, the following:* (See below for a list of uses.)

Discussion and Commentary: Group B occupancies can range in size from a one- or two-person office to a high-rise office building. The number of occupants is not restricted, so a Group B occupancy can house anywhere from one person to tens of thousands of people. Most occupants are of working age, and the occupants are generally able to exit without assistance. Fuel packages can vary based on the building's use.

Group B Occupancies

Airport traffic control towers
Ambulatory care facilities
Animal hospitals, kennels and pounds
Banks
Barber and beauty shops
Car wash
Civic administration
Clinic, outpatient
Dry cleaning and laundries (pick-up and delivery service)
Educational occupancies for students above the twelfth grade, including higher education laboratories
Electronic data processing
Food processing establishments and commercial kitchens not associated with restaurants, cafeterias and similar dining facilities not more than 2,500 sq. ft.
Laboratories, testing and research
Motor vehicle showrooms
Post offices
Print shops
Professional services (architects, attorneys, dentists, physicians, engineers, etc.)
Radio and television stations
Telephone exchanges
Training and skill development not within a school or academic program (This shall include, but not be limited to, tutoring centers, martial arts studios, gymnastics and similar uses regardless of the ages served, and where not classified as a Group A occupancy)

Group B occupancies do not require protection with an automatic sprinkler system unless they house an ambulatory care facility or have at least one floor with an occupant load of 30 or more that is 55 feet or more above the lowest level of fire department access.

Topic: Educational Occupancies—Group E   **Category:** Occupancy Classification
Reference: IFC 202, IBC 305.1, IBC 305.2   **Subject:** Classification and Use

Code Text: *Educational Group E. Educational Group E occupancy includes, among others, the use of a building or structure, or a portion thereof, by six or more persons at any one time for educational purposes through the 12th grade.*

Accessory to places of religious worship. Religious educational rooms and religious auditoriums, which are accessory to places of religious worship in accordance with Section 303.1.4 of the International Building Code *and have occupant loads of less than 100 per room or space, shall be classified as Group A-3 occupancies.*

Group E, Day care facilities. This group includes buildings and structures or portions thereof occupied by more than five children older than 2$^1/_2$ years of age who receive educational, supervision or personal care services for fewer than 24 hours per day.

Discussion and Commentary: Group E occupancies can range in size from a day care facility accommodating six occupants to a large high school with hundreds of students. By definition, colleges and universities are not assigned the Group E occupancy classification, because the students are beyond the twelfth grade. Life safety issues for educational occupancies are the safe egress of infants or early-age children who may not be capable of affecting self-preservation and who would require adult supervision.

Unlike other occupancies, the description of the Group E occupancy in the codes does not include a list of uses. Examples of Group E occupancies include:

- Day care centers (meeting Group E criteria)
- Public and private elementary schools
- Public and private high schools
- Public and private junior high or middle schools
- Public and private preschools (with children over 2$^1/_2$ years of age)

There are also allowances for day care operations that are not classified as Group E. At a place of religious worship, if the only day care functions occur during religious functions, then the day care areas are to be classified as part of the main occupancy. The day care function is considered accessory to the use of the main facility. However, as soon as those same day care rooms are used daily without being associated with any religious function, that use would be classified as Group E.

A Group E occupancy could be a school, day care facility or an infant care facility, which is normally classified as a Group I-4 institutional occupancy, but may be classified as a Group E occupancy if there are no more than 100 children, all 2$^1/_2$ years of age or less and each room is on the level of exit discharge with a direct exit to the exterior.

Code Text: *Factory Industrial Group F. Factory Industrial Group F occupancy includes, among others, the use of a building or structure, or a portion thereof, for assembling, disassembling, fabricating, finishing, manufacturing, packaging, repair or processing operations that are not classified as a Group H high-hazard or Group S storage occupancy.*

Factory Industrial F-1 Moderate-hazard occupancy. Factory industrial uses which are not classified as Factory Industrial F-2 Low Hazard shall be classified as F-1 Moderate Hazard and shall include, but not be limited to, the following:

(See IFC Section 202 or IBC Section 306.2 for a list of uses.)

Factory Industrial F-2 Low-hazard occupancy. Factory industrial uses that involve the fabrication or manufacturing of noncombustible materials which during finishing, packing or processing do not involve a significant fire hazard shall be classified as F-2 occupancies and shall include, but not be limited to, the following:

(See IFC Section 202 or IBC Section 306.3 for a list of uses.)

Discussion and Commentary: Group F occupancies house manufacturing, equipment reconditioning, packaging and processing activities. Hazardous materials are allowed in Group F occupancies, but the quantity in storage and use must be less than the maximum allowable quantities specified in IFC Chapter 50. Because the building is designed to shelter equipment used for manufacturing or similar activities, the density of the occupants is relatively low. Plant employees are alert and oriented to their surroundings, so they are typically capable of self-preservation. Although life safety of the occupants is the highest priority, the codes also emphasize property protection and the safety of emergency responders.

The description for Group F-2 occupancies include the phrase "...the fabrication or manufacturing of *noncombustible* materials..." (emphasis added). This greatly limits the manufacturing operations that may qualify for classification as Group F-2 occupancies and requires facilities that do not meet this criteria to be classified as Group F-1. The Group F definition also states that these operations are not classified as Group H or S occupancies. Semiconductor fabrication facilities are a *factory*, but when the amount of Hazardous Production Materials exceeds the maximum allowable quantity, then it is appropriate to assign a Group H-5 occupancy classification and the applicable engineering and administrative controls prescribed by the IFC.

Code Text: ***High-hazard Group H.*** *High-hazard Group H occupancy includes, among others, the use of a building or structure, or a portion thereof, that involves the manufacturing, processing, generation or storage of materials that constitute a physical or health hazard in quantities in excess of those allowed in control areas complying with Section 5003.8.3, based on the maximum allowable quantity limits for control areas set forth in Tables 5003.1.1(1) and 5003.1.1(2). Hazardous uses are classified in Groups H-1, H-2, H-3, H-4 and H-5 and shall be in accordance with this code and the requirements of Section 415 of the* International Building Code. *Hazardous materials stored or used on top of roofs or canopies shall be classified as outdoor storage or use and shall comply with this code.*

Uses other than Group H. *The storage, use or handling of hazardous materials as described in one or more of the following items shall not cause the occupancy to be classified as Group H, but it shall be classified as the occupancy that it most nearly resembles . . .*

(See IFC Section 202 and IBC Section 307.1.1 for the nineteen items.)

Discussion and Commentary: Group H is arguably the most complex occupancy classification. The reason is that the occupancy classification is based on the hazard classification of the hazardous materials and on whether the material is in storage or is used in an open or closed condition. Because of the hazards involved, all Group H occupancies are required to be protected by automatic sprinkler systems. Additional requirements also apply, and these are based on the hazardous materials being either a physical hazard (burns, accelerates burning, detonates or deflagrates) or a health hazard (a single exposure can incapacitate a person). The degree of required controls varies and can include storage in detached buildings, fire barriers in mixed occupancy buildings, and increased number of exits, reduction in exit travel distances, limitations for certain hazard classes, spill control or standby power.

An occupancy is a Group H if the amount of hazardous materials stored or used exceed the Maximum Allowable Quantities (MAQs) in IFC Tables 5003.1.1(1) and 5003.1.1(2). If the amount of hazardous materials is less than the MAQs, the building's use may be classified "...in the occupancy that it most nearly resembles."

Code Text: ***Uses other than Group H.*** *Display and storage of nonflammable solid and nonflammable or noncombustible liquid hazardous materials in quantities not exceeding the maximum allowable quantity per control area in Group M or S occupancies complying with Section 5003.8.3.5.1.*

Discussion and Commentary: The storage and display of hazardous materials in Group M and S occupancies have different requirements because of the use and character of the occupancies. Group M occupancies generally have some of the lowest fire loss history because they are protected by automatic sprinkler systems, and customers desire a clean, organized place to shop. Accordingly, the IFC allows an increased amount of nonflammable and noncombustible hazardous materials in these occupancies. The storage and display of hazardous materials in these occupancies must comply with IFC Section 5003.11.

IFC Section 5003.11 specifies container volume limits, storage and display heights as well as a maximum density per square foot of floor area for the products stored and displayed. These are important provisions because they can directly affect the performance of automatic sprinkler systems.

Code Text: *CONTROL AREA: Spaces within a building where quantities of hazardous materials not exceeding the maximum allowable quantities per control area are stored, dispensed, used or handled. See also the definition "Outdoor control area."*

Discussion and Commentary: If the maximum allowable quantities per control area (MAQs) of hazardous materials are less than or equal to the amounts allowed in IFC Tables 5003.1.1(1) and 5003.1.1(2), a building or facility is not required to be classified as a Group H occupancy. If the MAQs are exceeded, three choices are available: (1) the building or facility may be classified and constructed as a Group H occupancy, (2) the storage and use may be distributed into control areas, with each control area separated by fire-resistant construction and containing no more than the MAQ of hazardous materials without being classified as an H occupancy, or (3) the hazardous material may be moved outside of the building into an outdoor control area. IFC Chapter 50 and IBC Sections 414 and 415 contain additional and material-specific requirements for hazardous materials. As with most tables in the codes, the footnotes to these tables contain important provisions, such as allowing quantities to be increased in buildings that are sprinklered throughout or when materials are stored in approved storage cabinets, gas cabinets, listed safety cans or exhausted enclosures.

(Photograph courtesy of Getty Images.)

IFC Tables 5003.1.1(1) and 5003.1.1(2) establish maximum allowable quantities for storage, use-closed systems and use-open systems. These terms refer to materials that are being stored; are being used, mixed or dispensed in a closed system; or are being used, mixed or dispensed in a system in which the materials are open to the atmosphere, respectively. There is no difference for the MAQ between storage and use-closed systems. However, once the system is classified as a use-open system, the MAQs are significantly reduced because these processes can liberate vapors to the atmosphere.

Code Text: *Buildings and structures containing materials that pose a detonation hazard, shall be classified as Group H-1. Such materials shall include, but not be limited to, the following . . .*

(See IFC Section 202 and IBC Section 307.3 for requirements.)

Discussion and Commentary: A Group H-1 occupancy classification is assigned to buildings or structures that present a detonation hazard. IFC Section 202 defines a detonation as "an exothermic reaction characterized by the presence of a shock wave in the material which establishes and maintains the reaction. The reaction zone progresses through the material at a rate greater than the velocity of sound. The principal heating mechanism is one of shock compression. Detonations have an explosive effect." Because of this hazard, Group H-1 occupancies must be located in detached buildings.

The photograph illustrates a IFC-compliant Type 1 explosives magazine.

Topic: High-Hazard Group H-5

Reference: IFC 202, IBC 307.7

Category: Occupancy Classification

Subject: Classification and Use

Code Text: *Semiconductor fabrication facilities and comparable research and development areas in which hazardous production materials (HPM) are used and the aggregate quantity of materials is in excess of those listed in Tables 5003.1.1(1) and 5003.1.1(2) shall be classified as Group H-5. Such facilities and areas shall be designed and constructed in accordance with Section 415.11 of the International Building Code.*

Discussion and Commentary: Semiconductor fabrication facilities and comparable research and development areas in which hazardous production materials (HPM) are used and the aggregate quantity of materials is in excess of those listed in IFC Tables 5003.1.1(1) and 5003.1.1(2) shall be classified as Group H-5. Such facilities and areas shall be designed and constructed in accordance with Section 415.11 of the IBC. These facilities utilize a number of hazardous materials in equipment that is designed to handle the mixed associated hazards.

In most cases the quantity of hazardous materials within the Group H-5 are unlimited, but IFC Table 2704.2.2.1 limits the amount of hazardous production material allowed within a single fabrication area in the Group H-5 occupancy based on the material's physical state and hazard classification.

Code Text: *Institutional Group I occupancy includes, among others, the use of a building or structure, or a portion thereof, in which care or supervision is provided to persons who are not capable of self-preservation without physical assistance or in which persons are detained for penal or correctional purposes or in which the liberty of the occupants is restricted. Institutional occupancies shall be classified as Group I-1, I-2, I-3 or I-4.*

Discussion and Commentary: Group I is the occupancy group with the most vulnerable occupants, including young children, the elderly, unconscious patients in operating rooms, and inmates whose liberties may be restrained. The common characteristic for all institutional occupants is that, in the event of an emergency, they may not be able to exit a building safely without assistance. Important considerations include the presence and training of the staff, fire alarm systems, fire-resistant construction, automatic sprinkler systems, one or more areas of refuge and the means of egress systems. The capability of the occupants to self evacuate is considered in several of the Group I occupancies. Group I-1 and I-2 have two subcategories of Condition 1 and Condition 2. Essentially, the Condition 1 category contains occupants capable of self-preservation, while the Condition 2 category contains occupants needing either physical assistance or verbal guidance to evacuate. Group I-3 has five subcategories which are classified based on the amount of free movement provided to the occupants.

Group I-1:

Alcohol and drug centers

Assisted living facilities

Congregate care facilities

Group homes

Halfway houses

Residential board and custodial care facilities

Social rehabilitation facilities

Group I-2:

Foster care facilities

Detoxification facilities

Hospitals

Nursing homes

Psychiatric hospitals

Group I-3:

Correctional centers

Detention centers

Jails

Prerelease centers

Prisons

Reformatories

Group I-4:

Adult day care facilities

Child day care facilities

These occupancies have very specific criteria, including numbers of persons, hours of care, and age, for classifying them as Institutional occupancies or as Group E or R-3 occupancies.

Code Text: *Mercantile Group M occupancy includes, among others, the use of a building or structure or a portion thereof, for the display and sale of merchandise and involves stocks of goods, wares or merchandise incidental to such purposes and accessible to the public. Mercantile occupancies shall include, but not be limited to, the following:*

Department stores
Drug stores
Markets
Greenhouses for display and sale of plants that provide public access
Motor fuel-dispensing facilities
Retail or wholesale stores
Sales rooms

Discussion and Commentary: Group M occupancies can range from a small convenience store to a department store, a large furniture store or a warehouse-style store. A combination of code concerns exist, including the presence of relatively high densities of people such as customers and staff (life safety), the value of stored goods (property protection) and the protection of emergency responders. Combustible fuel loads can be high, and high-piled combustible storage may be an issue (see IFC Chapter 32). Group M occupancies may be adjacent to Group S storage occupancies or, in the case of a manufacturing facility with an adjacent sales room, Group F occupancies.

IFC Section 5003.8.3.5 permits the amounts of nonflammable solid and nonflammable or noncombustible liquid hazardous materials to exceed the quantities in IFC Tables 5003.1.1(1) and 5003.1.1(2) without classifying the building or use as a Group H occupancy. Storage of these materials must also comply with additional restrictions in IFC Section 5003.11.

IFC Section 5704.3.4.1 permits the amounts of flammable and combustible liquid hazardous materials to exceed the quantities in IFC Tables 5003.1.1(1) and 5003.1.1(2) without classifying the building or use as a Group H occupancy. Storage of these materials must also comply with the requirements in IFC Section 5704.3.6.

Code Text: *Residential Group R includes, among others, the use of a building or structure, or a portion thereof, for sleeping purposes when not classified as an Institutional Group I or when not regulated by the* International Residential Code *in accordance with Section 101.2 of the* International Building Code. *Group R occupancies not constructed in accordance with the* International Residential Code *as permitted by Sections 310.4.1 and 310.4.2 of the* International Building Code *shall comply with Section 420 of the* International Building Code.

(See IFC Section 202 and IBC Section 310 for a list of occupancies.)

Discussion and Commentary: The primary risk for Group R occupants is sleeping inside the structure. In multiple-family structures, another risk factor is that the occupants have no control over what their neighbors in the building might be doing. Therefore, the provisions of IFC and IBC Chapter 9 require that automatic sprinkler systems be installed throughout buildings with Group R fire areas. For residential occupancies, the IFC and IBC require early detection and warning (smoke alarms in sleeping areas), fire containment and extinguishment (fire-resistant separation and automatic sprinkler protection), and a means of escape and rescue (means of egress). The general classification of Group R has four subdivisions. Classification into each subdivision is based on the familiarity of the occupants with the facility (Group R-1 hotel/motel compared to Group R-2 apartment/condominium), the ability to egress (Group R-3 dwelling compared to Group R-4 assisted living facility). Certain Group R-3 and R-4 occupancies can be constructed under the IRC. When the IRC is utilized, the IFC has limited application as stated in Section 102.5. When the IRC is not used for construction of Group R occupancies, they must comply with IBC and IFC requirements.

Group R-3 occupancies, which include one- and two-family dwellings and townhouses, and adult and child care facilities accommodating five or fewer persons of any age for less than 24 hours, are regulated by the IRC.

Code Text: ***Storage Group S.*** *Storage Group S occupancy includes, among others, the use of a building or structure, or a portion thereof, for storage that is not classified as a hazardous occupancy.*

Accessory storage spaces. A room or space used for storage purposes that is accessory to another occupancy shall be classified as part of that occupancy.

Moderate-hazard storage, Group S-1. *Storage Group S-1 buildings occupied for storage uses which are not classified as Group S-2 including, but not limited to, storage of the following...*

(See IFC Section 202 and IBC Section 311.2 for a list of Group S-1 uses.)

Low-hazard storage, Group S-2. *Storage Group S-2 includes, among others, buildings used for the storage of noncombustible materials such as products on wood pallets or in paper cartons with or without single thickness divisions; or in paper wrappings. Such products are permitted to have a negligible amount of plastic trim, such as knobs, handles or film wrapping. Storage uses shall include, but not be limited to, storage of the following...*

(See IFC Section 202 and IBC Section 311.3 for a list of Group S-2 uses.)

Discussion and Commentary: Because of the high fuel loads associated with Group S-1 occupancies, these buildings are required to be equipped with automatic sprinkler systems if a fire area exceeds 12,000 square feet, if they are more than three stories above grade or if the combined Group S-1 fire areas in a building exceed 24,000 square feet.

Similar to Groups F-1 and F-2 where the lower hazard category specifies that the products are noncombustible, the distinction between Groups S-1 and S-2 is also based on noncombustible products, but they are packaged in combustible materials. For example, the storage of ceramic mugs packaged in single-thickness cardboard boxes on wooden pallets is considered a Group S-2.

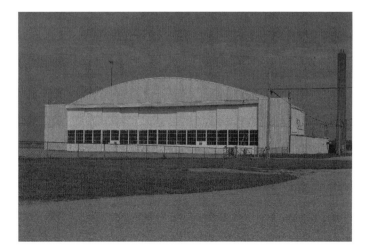

The difference between the storage occupancies is that the materials stored in S-2 occupancies must be noncombustible, with the exception of combustible pallets and packaging materials, which are allowed. This Group S-1 aircraft hangar contains a significant amount of fuel in the fueled aircraft.

Code Text: *Buildings and structures of an accessory character and miscellaneous structures not classified in any specific occupancy shall be constructed, equipped and maintained to conform to the requirements of this code commensurate with the fire and life hazard incidental to their occupancy. Group U shall include, but not be limited to, the following . . .*

(See IFC Section 202 and IBC Section 312.1 for a list of uses.)

Discussion and Commentary: Group U occupancies can range in size from a small shed or livestock shelter to a large barn or greenhouse, and also include other miscellaneous structures such as tanks or towers. These utility and miscellaneous uses are characterized by a relatively low risk to life or property, which is primarily due to either small size, none or very few occupants, occupancy only during limited time periods, locations that are usually removed from other buildings or uses, or a combination of some or all of these factors.

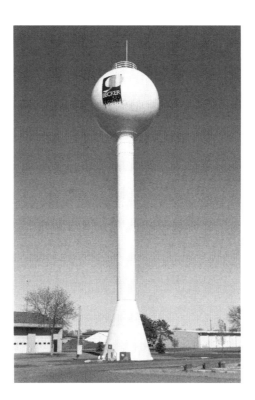

Group U occupancies can generally be divided into two types:
  (1) Buildings that are accessory to other more major uses or structures, such as private garages or carports.
  (2) Miscellaneous structures that cannot be classified as any other occupancy group, such as water tanks or towers.
Appendix C of the IBC, if it is specifically adopted by a jurisdiction, may be used to regulate Group U agricultural buildings.

Code Text: *General. Each portion of a building shall be individually classified in accordance with Section 302.1. Where a building contains more than one occupancy group, the building or portion thereof shall comply with the applicable provisions of Section 508.2, 508.3, 508.4 or 508.5, or a combination of these sections.*

Nonseparated occupancies. Buildings or portions of buildings that comply with the provisions of this section shall be considered as nonseparated occupancies.

Separated occupancies. Buildings or portions of buildings that comply with the provisions of this section shall be considered as separated occupancies.

Discussion and Commentary: Buildings and uses must be classified into occupancy classifications to determine the appropriate code requirements. Often, multiple uses or occupancies occur in a single building or business. Each different use is assigned an occupancy classification and the designer has the option to either separate the occupancies with fire-resistance-rated construction (referred to separated mixed occupancies); or construct the entire facility to comply with the requirements for all of the occupancies contained within (referred to nonseparated mixed occupancies). When the facility is constructed as a nonseparated mixed occupancy, the fire sprinkler and alarm requirements for one occupancy must be extended throughout all occupancies.

TABLE 508.4
REQUIRED SEPARATION OF OCCUPANCIES (HOURS)[f]

OCCUPANCY	A, E		I-1[a], I-3, I-4		I-2		R[a]		F-2, S-2[b], U		B[e], F-1, M, S-1		H-1		H-2		H-3, H-4		H-5	
	S	NS	S	NS	S	NS	S	NS	S	NS	S	NS	S	NS	S	NS	S	NS	S	NS
A, E	N	N	1	2	2	NP	1	2	N	1	1	2	NP	NP	3	4	2	3	2	NP
I-1[a], I-3, I-4	1	2	N	N	2	NP	1	NP	1	2	1	2	NP	NP	3	NP	2	NP	2	NP
I-2	2	NP	2	NP	N	N	2	NP	2	NP	2	NP	NP	NP	3	NP	2	NP	2	NP
R[a]	1	2	1	NP	2	NP	N	N	1[c]	2[c]	1	2	NP	NP	3	NP	2	NP	2	NP
F-2, S-2[b], U	N	1	1	2	2	NP	1[c]	2[c]	N	N	1	2	NP	NP	3	4	2	3	2	NP
B[e], F-1, M, S-1	1	2	1	2	2	NP	1	2	1	2	N	N	NP	NP	2	3	1	2	1	NP
H-1	NP	NP	NP	NP	NP	NP	NP	NP	NP	NP	NP	NP	N	NP	NP	NP	NP	NP	NP	NP
H-2	3	4	3	NP	3	NP	3	NP	3	4	2	3	NP	NP	N	NP	1	NP	1	NP
H-3, H-4	2	3	2	NP	2	NP	2	NP	2	3	1	2	NP	NP	1	NP	1[d]	NP	1	NP
H-5	2	NP	2	NP	2	NP	2	NP	2	NP	1	NP	NP	NP	1	NP	1	NP	N	NP

S = Buildings equipped throughout with an automatic sprinkler system installed in accordance with Section 903.3.1.1.

NS = Buildings not equipped throughout with an automatic sprinkler system installed in accordance with Section 903.3.1.1.

N = No separation requirement.

NP = Not Permitted.

a. See Section 420.

b. The required separation from areas used only for private or pleasure vehicles shall be reduced by 1 hour but not to less than 1 hour.

c. See Sections 406.3.2 and 406.6.4.

d. Separation is not required between occupancies of the same classification.

e. See Section 422.2 for *ambulatory care facilities*.

f. Occupancy separations that serve to define fire area limits established in Chapter 9 for requiring fire protection systems shall also comply with Section 707.3.10 and Table 707.3.10 in accordance with Section 901.7.

IBC Table 508.4 is used to determine the minimum fire-resistance rating for walls or floor/ceiling assemblies separating different occupancies when constructing a separated mixed occupancy building.

Code Text: *The incidental uses listed in Table 509.1 shall be separated from the remainder of the building or equipped with an automatic sprinkler system, or both, in accordance with the provisions of that table.*

Discussion and Commentary: Incidental uses are ancillary or associated uses within an occupancy. Incidental uses represent a greater hazard, but it is localized to a room inside a building. The hazards presented by the incidental uses need to be mitigated in all occupancies and require either separation, protection by an automatic sprinkler system or a combination of both. Separation is not required between a main occupancy and accessory occupancies unless it's prescribed by the IBC.

TABLE 509.1
INCIDENTAL USES

ROOM OR AREA	SEPARATION AND/OR PROTECTION
Furnace room where any piece of equipment is over 400,000 Btu per hour input	1 hour or provide automatic sprinkler system
Rooms with boilers where the largest piece of equipment is over 15 psi and 10 horsepower	1 hour or provide automatic sprinkler system
Refrigerant machinery room	1 hour or provide automatic sprinkler system
Hydrogen fuel gas rooms, not classified as Group H	1 hour in Group B, F, M, S and U occupancies; 2 hours in Group A, E, I and R occupancies.
Incinerator rooms	2 hours and provide automatic sprinkler system
Paint shops, not classified as Group H, located in occupancies other than Group F	2 hours; or 1 hour and provide automatic sprinkler system
In Group E occupancies, laboratories and vocational shops not classified as Group H	1 hour or provide automatic sprinkler system
In Group I-2 occupancies, laboratories not classified as Group H	1 hour and provide automatic sprinkler system
In ambulatory care facilities, laboratories not classified as Group H	1 hour or provide automatic sprinkler system
Laundry rooms over 100 square feet	1 hour or provide automatic sprinkler system
In Group I-2, laundry rooms over 100 square feet	1 hour
Group I-3 cells and Group I-2 patient rooms equipped with padded surfaces	1 hour
In Group I-2, physical plant maintenance shops	1 hour
In ambulatory care facilities or Group I-2 occupancies, waste and linen collection rooms with containers that have an aggregate volume of 10 cubic feet or greater	1 hour
In other than ambulatory care facilities and Group I-2 occupancies, waste and linen collection rooms over 100 square feet	1 hour or provide automatic sprinkler system
In ambulatory care facilities or Group I-2 occupancies, storage rooms greater than 100 square feet	1 hour
Electrical installations and transformers	See [IBC] Sections 110.26 through 110.34 and Sections 450.8 through 450.48 of NFPA 70 for protection and separation requirements.

For SI: 1 square foot = 0.0929 m², 1 pound per square inch (psi) = 6.9 kPa, 1 British thermal unit (Btu) per hour = 0.293 watts,
     1 horsepower = 746 watts, 1 gallon = 3.785 L, 1 cubic foot = 0.0283 m³

When automatic sprinkler protection is required by Table 509.1, it is required only in the incidental use room, unless protection is required throughout the fire area or building.

Quiz

Study Session 2
IFC Chapter 2 and IBC Chapters 3 and 5

1. Definitions in the IFC are found _____.

    a. in Chapter 2

    b. in the "02" sections of each chapter

    c. in both Chapter 2 and the "02" sections of each chapter

    d. in Chapter 80, Referenced Standards

    Reference 201.1

2. Terms not defined in the IFC or other International Codes are to have meanings, for the purposes of the code, that are _____.

    a. ordinarily accepted meanings

    b. defined by case law

    c. common sense meanings

    d. ordered by the chief

    Reference 201.4

3. A listing of occupancy classifications is found in _____.

    a. Chapter 10 of the IFC

    b. Chapter 2 of the IFC and Chapter 3 of the IBC

    c. Chapter 2 of the IBC

    d. Chapter 3 of the IFC

    Reference 202
    IBC Ch.3

4. A general-purpose meeting room in an office building with an occupant load of 45 persons is classified as Group _____.

    a. A-1   b. A-2

    c. A-3   (d.) B

    Reference IBC 303.1.2 #1

5. Which of the following uses are not classified as a Group A-2 occupancy?

    a. taverns and bars   (b.) bowling alleys

    c. night clubs   d. restaurants

    Reference IBC 303.3

6. A motor vehicle showroom is classified as a Group _____ occupancy.

    a. A-3   (b.) B

    c. H-3   d. S-1

    Reference IBC 304.1

7. A child day care facility that provides supervision and personal care for ten children under the age of $2^1/_2$ years is classified as a Group _____ occupancy.

    (a.) E   b. I-1

    c. I-4   d. R-3

    Reference 305.2

8. An example of a Group I-2 occupancy is a(n) _____.

    a. adult day care facility   b. alcohol and drug center

    c. detention center   (d.) hospital

    Reference 308.3

9. Group _____ is the occupancy classification that includes motor fuel-dispensing facilities.

    a. B   b. H-3

    (c.) M   d. S-1

    Reference 309.1

10. Group R-1 occupancies do not include _____.

    (a.) apartment houses   b. boarding houses (transient)

    c. hotels (transient)   d. motels (transient)

Reference 310.3

11. Group _____, among other uses, includes aircraft hangars that are accessory to one- or two-family residences.

    a. B   b. H-3

    c. S-2   (d.) U

Reference 312.1

12. A warehouse that is used to store electric coils on wooden pallets is classified as occupancy group _____.

    a. B   b. H-4

    c. S-1   (d.) S-2

Reference 311.3

13. A 749-sq. ft. training room that is accessory to an F-1 occupancy in a manufacturing plant is classified as a Group B or a Group _____.

    a. E   (b.) F-1

    c. F-2   d. A-3

Reference 303.1.2 #2

14. An outdoor sports stadium with grandstands is classified as an _____ occupancy.

    a. A-2   b. A-3

    c. A-4   (d.) A-5

Reference 303.6

15. High-hazard Group H-1 occupancies contain materials that pose a _____ hazard.

    a. conflagration   b. deflagration

    (c.) detonation   d. health

Reference 307.3

16. An occupancy that houses 17 people on a 24-hour basis as a halfway house is classified as a Group _____ occupancy.

    a. I-1   b. I-2

    c. R-3   d. R-4

Reference _308.2_

17. A Group _____ occupancy includes the display and sale of merchandise that also involves stocks of goods, wares or merchandise incidental to such purposes and accessible to the public.

    a. B   b. M

    c. S-1   d. S-2

Reference _309.1_

18. A building or tenant space used for assembly purposes by less than 50 persons shall be considered a Group _____ occupancy.

    a. A-3   b. B

    c. E   d. U

Reference _3031.2 #1_

19. A building that is used to manufacture, process, generate or store materials that constitute a physical hazard in quantities equal to or less than the quantities found in IFC Tables 5003.1.1(1) and 5003.1.1(2) is classified as a(n) _____.

    a. high-hazard Group H occupancy according to the type of materials present

    b. occupancy that it most nearly resembles

    c. high-hazard Group H-5 occupancy because hazardous production materials (HPM) are used

    d. H-3 due to the physical hazard

Reference _307.1.1_

20. Group U occupancies are to be _____.

    a. constructed commensurate with the fire and life hazard incidental to their occupancy

    b. exempted from regulation by the IFC

    c. constructed entirely of noncombustible materials in accordance with the IBC

    d. constructed as approved one-hour fire-resistance-rated construction in accordance with the IBC

Reference 312.1

21. The definition of BOARDING HOUSE is found in _____.

    a. Chapter 2 of the IRC

    b. Chapter 2 of the IFC

    c. Section 310.2 of the IBC and Chapter 2 of the IFC

    d. Chapter 3 of the IBC

Reference 202

22. Which of the following materials are not listed in the IFC as materials associated with High-hazard Group H-4 occupancies?

    a. corrosives   b. highly toxic materials

    c. organic peroxides   d. toxic materials

Reference 307.6

23. Which of the following uses is not classified as a Group E occupancy?

    a. day care facility for 25 1st graders

    b. elementary school

    c. high school

    d. university classroom

Reference 305

24. The use of a building for storage that is not classified as a hazardous occupancy is classified as _____.

    a. Moderate-hazard storage, Group S-1

    b. Low-hazard storage, Group S-2

    (c.) Group S-1 or S-2, depending on the types of materials being stored

    d. Utility and miscellaneous Group U

Reference _311.1_

25. Which of the following is *not* one of the uses or manufactured products listed in the codes that are classified as a Factory Industrial Group F-1 Moderate-hazard occupancy?

    (a.) beverages, up to and including 16 percent alcohol content

    b. electronics

    c. millwork (sash and door)

    d. motion pictures and television filming (without spectators)

Reference _306.2_

26. Religious educational rooms and religious auditoriums, which are accessory to a Group A-3 place of worship and have occupant loads of less than 100, shall be classified as Group _____ occupancies.

    (a.) A-3   b. B

    c. E   d. I-4

Reference _303.1,4_
_305.1.1_

27. Group F-2 low-hazard occupancies are factory or industrial uses that involve the fabrication or manufacturing of materials _____.

    a. that are not classified as Factory Industrial Group F-1

    b. that involve less than sixteen persons in the manufacturing process

    (c.) that are noncombustible and do not involve a significant fire hazard

    d. that involve less than 5,000 pounds in a single control area

Reference _306.3_

28. _____ occupancies are further divided into five different use conditions.

    a. Group A   b. Group H

    (c.) Group I-3   d. Group R

Reference _308.4_

29. Open public parking garages are classified as _____ occupancies.

    a. Group B   b. Group H-3

    c. Group S-1   (d.) Group S-2

Reference ___311.3___

30. In a separated mixed use occupancy, the minimum fire-resistance-rated construction for a wall separating a Group A-2 restaurant from a Group M mercantile business is _____.

    a. 1 hour, if the Group A-2 occupancy is sprinklered

    b. 1 hour, if the entire building is sprinklered

    c. 2 hour, if the entire building is sprinklered

    (d.) No rating required

Reference ___508.4___

31. According to the IBC, different occupancies located in the same building _____.

    a. must be separated by fire barriers

    b. may be nonseparated

    (c.) may be accessory, separated, nonseparated or a combination of these occupancies

    d. are not permitted

Reference ___508.1___

32. Where IBC Table 509.1 permits an automatic sprinkler system without a fire barrier to separate incidental uses from the rest of the building, the incidental use area shall also be separated by _____.

    a. a fire barrier or horizontal barrier complying with IBC Chapter 7

    (b.) construction capable of resisting the passage of smoke

    c. a fire wall

    d. not less than $\frac{1}{2}$-inch gypsum board applied to the incidental use area side

Reference ___509.4.2___

33. A multiple tenant building contains a Group I-4 day care and Group B office spaces. The building is sprinklered and constructed as a separated mixed occupancy. What is the minimum fire-resistance rating for the wall separating the day care use?

      a. 1 hour   b. 2 hour

      c. 3 hour   d. No rating required

Reference _506.4_

34. An ambulatory care facility is classified as a Group _____ occupancy.

      a. I-1   b. I-2

      c. I-4   d. B

Reference _304.1_

35. A refrigeration machinery room in a Group S-2 occupancy is considered an incidental use and the minimum level of protection can be _____.

      a. 1-hour construction

      b. Walls constructed to resist the passage of smoke and fire sprinklers in the incidental use area

      c. 2-hour construction and fire sprinklers throughout the building

      d. Either a or b

Reference _509.1_
_509.4.2_

Study Session

3

2021 IFC Chapters 3 and 4
General Requirements, Emergency Planning and Preparedness

OBJECTIVE: To gain an understanding of the issues, requirements and procedures related to general precautions against fire, emergency planning and preparedness.

REFERENCE: Chapters 3 and 4, 2021 *International Fire Code*® (IFC®)

KEY POINTS:
- What is the scope of Chapter 3 of the IFC, and how is its purpose best summarized?
- What are some of the key definitions related to general precautions against fire?
- How does the IFC deal with what might commonly be called trash? What are some of the specific requirements regarding types and amounts of materials?
- Where can additional information and details be found about the regulation of motion picture projection and the use and storage of cellulose nitrate film?
- How are bonfires and other types of open burning regulated in the IFC?
- What are some of the uses of open flame that are regulated, and where can details be found?
- What are the provisions regarding the storage, use and repair of forklifts?
- In what areas is smoking prohibited, and how is this enforced?
- Are there regulations for the maintenance of abandoned or vacant premises?
- How are indoor displays of highly combustible materials and vehicles or boats regulated?
- What are the requirements for indoor storage of combustible materials? Outdoor storage?
- Can idle wooden pallets be stored adjacent to the outside wall of a building?
- Are plastic pallets regulated the same as wooden pallets?
- What is the difference between industrial additive manufacturing and nonindustrial additive manufacturing?
- What are the requirements for a 3D printing operation?
- How does the code regulate landscaped roofs?

- How are fire protection appliances protected from vehicle impact?
- Can gasoline-fueled equipment be used inside a building?
- Can liquid-fueled or gaseous-fueled vehicles be displayed inside a building?
- What is the maximum height of stored products inside a building? Outside buildings?
- What portions of a mobile food preparation vehicle (catering truck) are regulated by the IFC?
- Which types of activities are regulated by Chapter 4 of the IFC?
- Under what circumstances is the fire code official authorized to require a fire watch?
- Which occupancy groups are required to develop a fire safety and evacuation plan?
- Which facilities are required to provide employees with training in fire emergency procedures?
- What are some of the more specific emergency planning requirements for certain uses and occupancies?
- Which facilities are required to make an announcement regarding the location of exits?
- How often are emergency evacuation drills to be conducted in an assisted living facility?
- In an assisted living facility, who must participate in the evacuation drill?
- When emergency evacuation drills are practiced at a restaurant, who needs to participate?
- What is a lockdown plan, and how is it prepared and implemented?
- Which types of buildings require the preparation and maintenance of a lease plan?
- Which IFC provision prohibits the installation of booby traps in buildings?
- What are the training requirements for employees and staff at facilities that handle hazardous materials?
- When are crowd managers required and what are their responsibilities?

Topic: Scope	**Category:** General Precautions
Reference: IFC 301.1	**Subject:** General

Code Text: *The provisions of this chapter shall govern the occupancy and maintenance of all structures and premises for precautions against fire and the spread of fire and general requirements of fire safety.*

Discussion and Commentary: There are a number of situations or activities that are widely known to either cause fires or exacerbate the spread of fires. As an example, the use of charcoal grills on balconies of apartment buildings constructed either partially or entirely of combustible materials has been the cause of countless fires that typically spread to the remainder of the building and threaten the occupants. The purpose of Chapter 3 is to identify common causes for the ignition and spread of fire, and to provide regulations to guard against this occurrence.

GENERAL REQUIREMENTS:

- PERMITS (required operational permits as listed in IFC Sec. 105.5)
- ASPHALT KETTLES (transport, fuel containers, attendant, etc.)
- COMBUSTIBLE WASTE MATERIAL (trash, weeds, under bleachers, oily rags, containers, dumpsters, etc.)
- IGNITION SOURCES (clearances to combustibles, hot ashes, flares, etc.)
- MOTION PICTURE PROJECTION ROOMS (See IFC Sec. 306, NFPA 40, IBC Sec. 409)
- OPEN BURNING, RECREATIONAL FIRES AND PORTABLE OUTDOOR FIREPLACES (permits, prohibitions, clearances, attendance)
- OPEN FLAMES (cooking, candles, lanterns, heaters, candelabra, etc.)
- POWERED INDUSTRIAL TRUCKS AND EQUIPMENT (forklifts, etc.)
- SMOKING ("No Smoking" areas, signs, ash trays, discarding materials)
- VACANT PREMISES (abandoned, vacant, empty tenant spaces, fire protection systems, removal of combustibles and hazardous materials, etc.)
- VEHICLE IMPACT PROTECTION
- FUELED EQUIPMENT (motorcycles, lawn care, portable cooking)
- INDOOR DISPLAYS (unobstructed exits, fueled vehicle requirements)
- GENERAL STORAGE (clearance to ceiling, stability, equipment rooms, outdoor storage, etc.)
- HAZARDS TO FIRE FIGHTERS (shafts, pits, rooftop obstructions, etc.)
- LANDSCAPED ROOFS (vegetation management, fire fighting, etc.)
- LAUNDRY CARTS (combustibility, sprinkler protection, etc.)
- MOBILE FOOD PREPARATION VEHICLES (fuel, cooking oil, safety devices, fire protection appliances, etc.)
- ADDITIVE MANUFACTURING (listing, combustible dusts, occupancy classification, etc.)
- ARTIFICIAL COMBUSTIBLE VEGETATION (combustibility, on rooftop, etc.)

NFPA Standard 550, *Guide to the Fire Safety Concepts Tree* published by the National Fire Protection Association, is a good source for additional information regarding the prevention of fire ignition and the management of fire impacts.

Topic: Trash Containers	Category: General Precautions
Reference: IFC 304.3.2	Subject: Combustible Waste Material

Code Text: *Capacity exceeding 5.33 cubic feet. Containers with a capacity exceeding 5.33 cubic feet (40 gallons) (0.15 m³) shall be provided with lids. Containers and lids shall be constructed of noncombustible materials or of combustible materials with a peak rate of heat release not exceeding 300 kW/m² where tested in accordance with ASTM E1354 at an incident heat flux of 50 kW/m² in the horizontal orientation.* **Exceptions:** *Wastebaskets complying with Section 808.*

Discussion and Commentary: Fires often occur in waste containers. The vast majority of contents in a waste container is combustible materials. Where trash containers are used inside buildings and the capacity of the container exceeds 40 gallons, the container must be provided with a lid. The container and the lid must be either noncombustible or manufactured from materials having a limited heat-release rate to ensure that the rate of fire development is controlled. Trash containers meeting the combustibility requirement will be stamped, typically on the bottom of the container.

The trash container on the right passed the ASTM E1354 fire test and did not contribute to the fire.

Code Text: *Clearance between ignition sources, such as luminaires, heaters, flame-producing devices and combustible materials, shall be maintained in an approved manner.*

Discussion and Commentary: This section can be applied to any number of situations where there are combustible materials near a source of ignition. If an open flame is present, an ignition source is available. A source of heat, such as a light fixture or luminaire, can also provide ignition. The section does not specify the minimum separation distance between the combustible materials and the source of heat. The separation required is based on the level of heat and the susceptibility of the exposed materials to ignite.

Various sources of heat are used in different environments, but they must all be separated from combustible materials.

Code Text: ***Portable outdoor fireplaces.*** *Portable outdoor fireplaces shall be used in accordance with the manufacturer's instructions and shall not be operated within 15 feet (3048 mm) of a structure or combustible material.* ***Exception:*** *Portable outdoor fireplaces used at one- and two-family dwellings.*

Discussion and Commentary: Outdoor fireplaces create a cozy gathering area. However, they still do create a hazard. As such, the IFC regulates the location of the portable outdoor fireplace at all facilities other than one- or two-family dwellings. The regulations are limited to portable appliances; permanent appliances are regulated by the IBC and *International Fuel Gas Code*® (IFGC®).

(Photograph courtesy of Getty Images.)

The fire hazard presented by outdoor fireplaces cannot be ignored. Portable outdoor fireplaces create a higher hazard because of the ease of relocating the appliance.

Code Text: *A person shall not take or utilize an open flame or light in a structure, vessel, boat or other place where highly flammable, combustible or explosive material is utilized or stored. Lighting appliances shall be well-secured in a glass globe and wire mesh cage or a similar approved device.*

Discussion and Commentary: This section prohibits several different uses of open flames. Where an open flame is present, an ignition source is available. All that is necessary to create a dangerous situation is to provide the fire with more fuel. Thus, the provisions of IFC Section 308 limit the amount of fuel that is available and keep the flames separated from the fuel sources.

This provision is intended to regulate a readily available ignition source.

Code Text: *Powered industrial trucks using liquid fuel, LP-gas or hydrogen shall be refueled outside of buildings or in areas specifically approved for that purpose. Fixed fuel-dispensing equipment and associated fueling operations shall be in accordance with Chapter 23. Other fuel-dispensing equipment and operations, including cylinder exchange for LP-gas-fueled vehicles, shall be in accordance with Chapter 57 for flammable and combustible liquids or Chapter 61 for LP-gas.*

Discussion and Commentary: Refueling of industrial trucks using LP-gas, compressed natural gas or conventional fuels such as gasoline or diesel fuel must comply with the requirements of Chapter 23. This is an important provision because of the hazards associated with the dispensing of fuels. IFC Section 309.6 requires fueling of industrial trucks and equipment be performed outside of the building to minimize the hazards to the occupants, or in an area that has been approved for a refueling by the fire code official.

Forklifts operated inside this building are driven outside to replace the empty LP-gas cylinder with a full cylinder.

Code Text: *Temporarily unoccupied buildings, structures, premises or portions thereof, including tenant spaces, shall be safeguarded and maintained in accordance with Sections 311.1.1 through 311.6.*

(See IFC Section 311 and subsections.)

Discussion and Commentary: Vacant premises can create potential hazards for a number of reasons. Typically, no one is present on a regular basis to watch over the facilities or maintain them in a safe condition. Abandoned buildings can be a nuisance to the community, subject to trespassing and use by neighborhood children, people seeking shelter or persons engaging in criminal activities. This combination of lack of oversight and unauthorized uses may lead to careless acts that can result in fires, accidents or other incidents that might endanger users, emergency responders and adjacent properties. IFC Section 311 provides tools to safeguard against these eventualities and to restore abandoned premises to a safe condition.

Section 311.1.1 includes references to the *International Property Maintenance Code*® (IPMC®), in which Sections 108–110 provide requirements that deal with unsafe structures, and to the IBC, in which Section 116 contains provisions to deal with unsafe structures and the maintenance of existing structures.

Code Text: *Vehicle impact protection required by this code shall be provided by posts that comply with Section 312.2 or by other approved physical barriers that comply with Section 312.3.*

Discussion and Commentary: Vehicle impact protection is commonly provided to protect equipment from impact by a vehicle. This can include automobiles, as well as industrial vehicles such as trucks and forklifts. The requirements in the IFC are based on prescriptive requirements in IFC Section 312.2 or performance based requirements found in IFC Section 312.3. Impact protection is commonly specified for sprinkler risers when located in warehouses using motorized material handling equipment and for above-ground storage tanks or pressure vessels that contain hazardous materials.

Vehicle impact protection is required by other sections of the IFC:

- Fire department connections, IFC Sec. 912.4.3
- Stationary fuel cell power systems, IFC Sec. 1206.7
- Energy storage systems, IFC Sec. 1207.4.5
- Motor fuel dispensing, above-ground tanks, IFC Sec. 2306.4
- Fuel-dispensing systems, IFC Sec. 2306.7.3
- LP-gas motor fuel-dispensing, above-ground tanks, IFC Sec. 2307.6.4, 6109.13
- Compressed gas vaults, IFC Sec. 5303.16.6
- Flammable & combustible liquid vaults, IFC Sec. 5704.2.8.6
- Flammable & combustible liquids, protected above-ground tanks, Sec. 5704.2.9.7.4

The photograph illustrates vehicle impact protection consisting of guard posts and a 6-inch curb for an LP-gas tank and dispensing location. The code only requires one method of vehicle impact protection.

Code Text: *Liquid-fueled or gaseous-fueled vehicles, aircraft, boats or other motorcraft shall not be located indoors except as follows: (1) The engine starting system is made inoperable or batteries are disconnected except where the fire code official requires that the batteries remain connected to maintain safety features, (2) Fuel in fuel tanks does not exceed one-quarter tank or 5 gallons (19 L) (whichever is least), (3) Fuel tanks and fill openings are closed and sealed to prevent tampering, (4) Vehicles, aircraft, boats or other motorcraft equipment are not fueled or defueled within the building.*

Discussion and Commentary: The display of gaseous-fueled or liquid-fueled vehicles in public spaces indoors, including covered malls, casinos, retail stores, exhibits, displays and conferences is quite common. Following the requirements of IFC Section 314.4 assures that the vehicles are not operable and that large amounts of flammable or combustible liquids or gases are not present.

With the advent of electric, hybrid and alternative-fuel vehicles, the requirement to disconnect the batteries is not mandated in all cases. Many alternative-fuel vehicles are equipped with sensors and detectors which are disabled when the battery is disconnected. Therefore, leaving the battery connected may be the safest choice as long as the starting system is disabled.

Note the links between Sections 313 and 314 regarding the conditions for, or prohibitions against, the storage, use or repair of fueled equipment inside of buildings, including the living space of Group R buildings.

Code Text: ***Outdoor pallet storage.*** *Pallets stored outdoors shall comply with Sections 315.7 through 315.7.7. Pallets stored within a building shall be protected in accordance with Chapter 32.*

Distance to lot line. *Pallet storage shall not be located within 10 feet (3048 mm) of a lot line.*

Storage height. *Pallet storage shall not exceed 20 feet (6096 mm) in height.*

Pallet pile stability and size. *Pallet stacks shall be arranged to form stable piles. Individual pallet piles shall cover an area not greater than 400 square feet (37 m²).*

Discussion and Commentary: Pallets create a tremendous fire hazard. The construction of a pallet allows all six sides of each piece of wood to be exposed and involved in fire at the same time. These fires create a significant amount of radiant heat. The IFC requires that pallets are either stored outside, or when stored inside a building are treated as high-piled combustible storage in accordance with Chapter 32. Section 315 contains requirements to limit pile sizes, separate from buildings and property lines and limit the storage height.

Plastic pallets are considered an equivalent fire hazard to wood pallets when they are listed and labeled to UL 2335 or FM 4996. Separations for plastic pallets that do not meet either standard are more restrictive than for wood pallets since the plastic pallets create a higher fire hazard.

Outdoor pallet storage must be separated from buildings and property lines to assist in the control of a fire and mitigate the spread of fire.

Topic: Obstructions on Roof	**Category:** General Requirements
Reference: IFC 316.4	**Subject:** Hazards to Fire Fighters

Code Text: *Wires, cables, ropes, antennas, or other suspended obstructions installed on the roof of a building having a roof slope of less than 30 degrees (0.52 rad) shall not create an obstruction that is less than 7 feet (2133 mm) high above the surface of the roof.* **Exceptions:** *(1) Such obstruction shall be permitted where the wire, cable, rope, antennae or suspended obstruction is encased in a white, 2-inch (51 mm) minimum diameter plastic pipe or an approved equivalent, (2) Such obstruction shall be permitted where there is a solid obstruction below such that accidentally walking into the wire, cable, rope, antennae or suspended obstruction is not possible.*

Discussion and Commentary: Obstructions on roofs can present entanglement or injury hazards to fire fighters. To limit the potential for injury, the IFC requires the guarding of wires or cables that enter within a 7-foot vertical plane measured from the roof surface. The requirements are limited to roofs with a slope less than 30 degrees. To prevent serious injury to fire fighters coming into contact with cables or guy wires, guards can be in the form of plastic pipe, which create a larger surface area which reduces the impact hazard and avoids being "clotheslined" by the hazard.

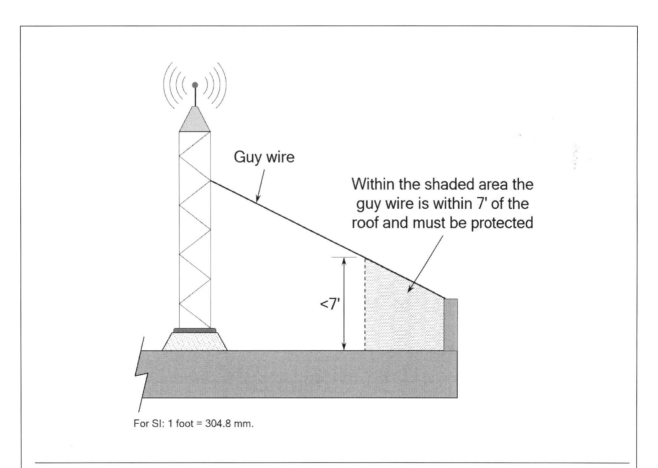

Guy wire

Within the shaded area the guy wire is within 7' of the roof and must be protected

<7'

For SI: 1 foot = 304.8 mm.

IFC Section 316.4, Exception 2 does not require protection when a person's ability to walk under the cable, rope or similar suspended objects is prohibited, such as by a screen wall.

Topic: Landscaped Roof Size	**Category:** General Requirements
Reference: IFC 317.2	**Subject:** Landscaped Roofs

Code Text: *Landscaped roof areas shall not exceed 15,625 square feet (1450 m²) in size for any single area with a maximum dimension of 125 feet (39 m) in length or width. A minimum 6-foot-wide (1.8 m) clearance consisting of a listed Class A roof assembly tested in accordance with ASTM E108 or UL 790 shall be provided between adjacent landscaped roof areas.*

Discussion and Commentary: Landscaped roofs are becoming more common. The rooftop provides an area for gathering, recreation or relaxation, and landscaping creates a soothing atmosphere. The landscaping creates several issues that the IFC addresses. Ventilation through the rooftop is now limited because of the soil added on top of the roof, and the vegetation can be combustible, especially when it dries out or dies. The area of the landscaping provided on a roof is limited to a maximum of 125 feet by 125 feet. Multiple landscaped areas can be provided on a rooftop if they are separated by 6 feet. The separation of 6 feet provides for a fuel break so the vegetation is not continuous across the roof, and it also provides access to the roof surface for ventilation if needed during a fire. IFC Section 905.3.8 also requires that when a landscaped roof is provided on a building equipped with a standpipe system, that fire hose connections are provided to reach all the landscaped areas.

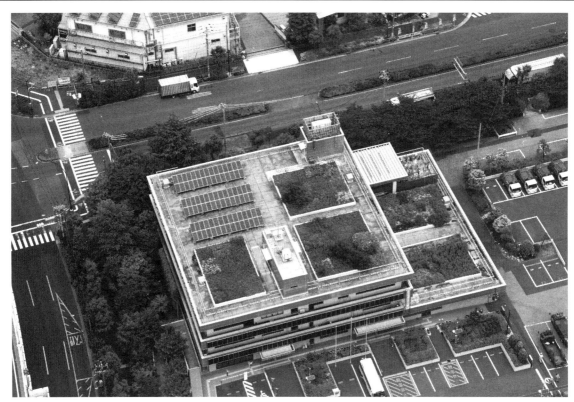

(Photograph courtesy of Getty Images.)

The fire code official can require a maintenance plan for the vegetation on the rooftop.

Code Text: ***General.*** *Mobile food preparation vehicles that are equipped with appliances that produce smoke or grease-laden vapors shall comply with this section.*

Exhaust hood. *Cooking equipment that produces grease-laden vapors shall be provided with a kitchen exhaust hood in accordance with Section 606.*

Fire protection for cooking equipment. *Cooking equipment shall be protected by automatic fire extinguishing systems in accordance with Section 904.13.*

Cooking oil storage containers. *Cooking oil storage containers within mobile food preparation vehicles shall have a maximum aggregate volume not more than 120 gallons (454 L), and shall be stored in such a way as to not be toppled or damaged during transport.*

Discussion and Commentary: Mobile food preparation vehicles are defined as "vehicles that contain cooking equipment that produce smoke or grease-laden vapors for the purpose of preparing and serving food to the public." They are regulated with regard to the hazards created by the cooking process, on-board fuels, cooking oils and combustibles. The IFC requires a permit to operate the vehicle and the vehicle must be equipped with fire extinguishers, fire-extinguishing system if creating grease-laden vapors, approved storage containers for cooking oils, LP-gas and other cooking fuels and exhaust ventilation systems.

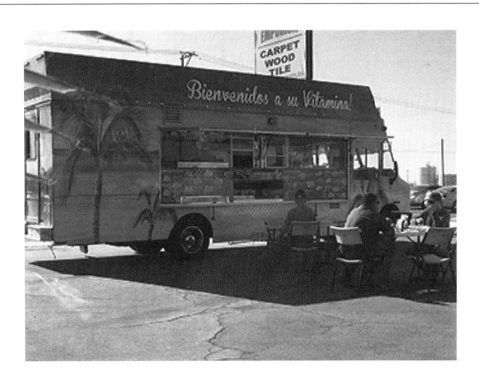

Mobile food preparation vehicles are regulated by the IFC with regard to fire and life safety requirements to protect the occupants and the customers.

| Topic: Industrial Additive Manufacturing | Category: General Requirements |
| Reference: IFC 320.3.1, 320.3.3, 320.3.4, 320.3.5, 320.3.6, 320.3.9 | Subject: Additive Manufacturing (3D Printing) |

Code Text: *Permits required. Permits shall be obtained from the fire code official in accordance with Section 105.5 prior to engaging in industrial additive manufacturing operations.*

Combustible dusts and metals. Industrial additive manufacturing operations that store, use or produce combustible dust, combustible particulate solids or combustible metals shall comply with Chapter 22 and this section.

Powder evaluation. Printing powders used in industrial additive manufacturing operations shall be tested for combustibility in accordance with NFPA 484 or NFPA 652 as applicable. A copy of test reports shall be provided to the fire code official upon request.

Combustible (nonmetallic) dusts. Industrial additive manufacturing operations that store, use or produce combustible (nonmetallic) dusts shall comply with NFPA 654.

Combustible metals. Industrial additive manufacturing operations that store or use combustible metals shall comply with NFPA 484.

Inert gas. Additive manufacturing processes that utilize inert gases shall comply with Chapter 53. Ventilation or gas detection shall be provided in accordance with Section 5307.

Discussion and Commentary: Industrial additive manufacturing is defined as 3D printing operations that typically utilize combustible powders or metals, an inert gas supply, a combustible dust collection system, or that create a hazardous (classified) location area or zone outside of the equipment. In other words, these are the 3D printers that have the potential to create a hazard. As such, these are 3D printers that are regulated. All other 3D printers fall under the group of non-industrial additive manufacturing.

Industrial additive manufacturing equipment is typically larger than nonindustrial additive manufacturing equipment and can include external powder feed supplies, dust collection systems or inert gases.

Some of the requirements for industrial operations include:

- Industrial 3D printers must be listed to UL 2011, but nonlisted equipment can be approved based on a field evaluation.
- Section 320.3.10 authorizes the code official to obtain technical assistance and require a report from an approved source evaluating the industrial additive manufacturing operation.
- Several NFPA standards are referenced to address the hazards associated with powders utilized in the 3D printing process.
- Industrial additive manufacturing is only allowed in manufacturing facilities.
- If the quantities of hazardous materials exceed the maximum allowable quantity per control area, the room or building will become a Group H occupancy.

(Photograph courtesy of Getty Images.)

This 3D printer is classified as an industrial additive manufacturing process and is producing a steel part.

Code Text: *Reporting of emergencies, coordination with emergency response forces, emergency plans, and procedures for managing or responding to emergencies shall comply with the provisions of this section.* **Exception:** *Firms that have approved on-premises fire-fighting organizations and that are in compliance with approved procedures for fire reporting.*

Discussion and Commentary: Two of the most important, and most difficult, tasks in fire prevention are (1) educating the occupants and staff of buildings and facilities regarding the fact that fires and other emergencies occur, and (2) making sure that they are trained to respond to such emergencies. Chapter 4 focuses on these issues, beginning with general requirements, such as the reporting of fires, and concluding with specific training requirements that are related to different occupancies and uses.

EMERGENCY PLANNING AND PREPAREDNESS SUMMARY

GENERAL (reporting, false alarms, interference)

EMERGENCY PREPAREDNESS REQUIREMENTS:

- GROUP A (seating plans, announcement of exit locations, crowd managers)
- GROUP B (plan, training, drills)
- GROUP E (plan, drills, assembly points)
- GROUP F (plan, training, drills)
- GROUP H-5 (plans and diagrams, emergency response team, drills)
- GROUP I-1 (fire safety and evacuation plans, training, drills, resident participation)
- GROUP I-2 (fire safety and evacuation plans, coded alarm signal may be used)
- GROUP I-3 (plan, training, keys to be readily available)
- GROUP M (plan, training, drills)
- GROUP R-1 (evacuation diagrams at doors, staff duties, guest evacuation options)
- GROUP R-2 (fire emergency guide, diagrams in dormitories, drills)
- GROUP R-4 (fire safety and evacuation plans, training, drills, resident participation)
- COVERED and OPEN MALLS (lease plans, identification of tenant and vacant spaces)
- HIGH-RISE BUILDINGS (plans, drills)
- UNDERGROUND BUILDINGS (plan, drills)
- BUILDINGS with HIGH-PILED STORAGE (plans, drills)
- PUBLIC SAFETY REQUIREMENTS (fire watches, public safety plans, crowd managers)

FIRE SAFETY, EVACUATION AND LOCKDOWN PLANS (where required, contents of fire evacuation, fire safety and lockdown plans)

EMERGENCY EVACUATION DRILLS (frequency of drills, who must participate)

EMPLOYEE TRAINING AND RESPONSE PROCEDURES (training, types, frequency)

HAZARD COMMUNICATION (SDS, training, inventory, closure)

Code Text: *In addition to the requirements of Section 404.2.2, a lease plan that includes the following information shall be prepared for each covered and open mall building. . .*

(See IFC Section 403.10.1.2 Items 1 through 3.9.)

Discussion and Commentary: The hazards and the potential for incidents in covered malls is compounded by the presence of multiple tenants, including many different types and sizes of retail stores and other uses, all contained within the same building. Much like the residents of multiple-family dwellings, the actions or inactions of one tenant can impact the entire facility, including relatively large numbers of occupants. Thus, it is important that emergency responders are fully aware of the current situation and all of the necessary details during a fire or other emergency. Lease plans are to include the information summarized below in addition to the fire safety and evacuation plans required under IFC Section 404.

LEASE PLAN CONTENTS

- Occupancies and tenants

- Exits from each tenant space

- Fire department connections (FDCs)

- Fire command center

- Smoke management system controls

- Elevators and elevator controls

- Hose valve outlets

- Sprinkler and standpipe control valves

- Automatic fire-extinguishing system zones

- Automatic fire detector zones

- Location of fire barriers

Vacant tenant spaces in a covered mall can present many of the same hazards as any vacant property (see IFC Section 311), except that, in a mall, many other tenant spaces and occupants can be adversely impacted by a fire or other incident arising from careless use. Section 403.10.1.6 addresses the maintenance of vacant tenant spaces, including the prohibition of storage, maintaining separations from other spaces and keeping vacant spaces secure and clean. Section 311.6 requires unoccupied tenant spaces to be separated by $^1/_2$-inch gypsum board, or equivalent from the remainder of the covered or open mall.

Code Text: *Crowd managers. Where facilities or events involve a gathering of more than 500 people, crowd managers shall be provided in accordance with Sections 403.11.3.1 through 403.11.3.3.*

Number of crowd managers. Not fewer than two trained crowd managers, and not fewer than one trained crowd manager for each 250 persons or portion thereof, shall be provided for the gathering. ***Exceptions:*** *(1) Outdoor events with fewer than 1,000 persons in attendance shall not require crowd managers, (2) Assembly occupancies used exclusively for religious worship with an occupant load not exceeding 1,000 shall not require crowd managers, (3) The number of crowd managers shall be reduced where, in the opinion of the fire code official, the fire protection provided by the facility and the nature of the event warrant a reduction.*

Discussion and Commentary: Crowd managers are required for Group A occupancies with occupant loads greater than 500. For outdoor public events or gatherings, Section 3106 requires crowd managers where the occupant load exceeds 1,000. When crowd managers are required, at least one crowd manager is to be provided for each 250 individuals. Crowd managers are typically employees of the facility and have designated functions during normal operations. When an emergency occurs, the employees who are crowd managers switch roles and provide for the safety and evacuation of the occupants.

Crowd managers need to be trained to fulfill their function. Crowd manager training can be provided through Fire Marshal Support Services available from www.crowdmanagers.com.

Community events such as the one in the photograph are an opportunity for cooperation between the fire department, law enforcement agencies, event organizers, local businesses and other community organizations. The common goal is to have a safe and successful event.

Code Text: *Fire safety plans shall include the following. . . (see below for details)*

Discussion and Commentary: Fire safety and evacuation plans, which are required by IFC Section 404.2 for certain occupancies and uses, are simply good planning, or preplanning, for emergency situations that can occur.

REQUIRED CONTENTS OF FIRE SAFETY PLANS

1. Fire or emergency reporting procedure
2. Life safety strategy
   - Occupant notification
   - Procedures for defend-in-place
   - Procedures for evacuation of persons in need of assistance
3. Site plans
   - Occupant assembly point
   - Fire hydrant locations
   - Fire department vehicle access routes
4. Floor plans
   - Exits
   - Primary evacuation routes
   - Secondary evacuation routes
   - Accessible egress routes
   - Areas of refuge
   - Manual fire alarm boxes
   - Portable fire extinguishers
   - Occupant-use hose stations
   - Fire alarm control and annunciation panel locations
5. Major fire hazards, maintenance and housekeeping procedures
6. Personnel responsible for maintenance of life safety systems
7. Personnel responsible for fuel hazard source

A fire safety plan should be requested at the time of construction or tenant renovations. Construction drawings commonly contain floor plans or fire safety plans that can be modified to meet the requirements of IFC 404.2.2 for fire safety plans.

Code Text: *Lockdown plans shall only be permitted where such plans are approved by the fire code official and are in compliance with Sections 404.2.3.1 and 404.2.3.2.*

Discussion and Commentary: Section 404.2.3 establishes requirements for the development and implementation of lockdown plans. These requirements were developed so that in the event of a lockdown, the level of life safety inside of the building is not reduced or compromised. The requirements in Section 404.2.3 establish requirements that ensure that when a lockdown is implemented, the event is done in accordance with an approved plan and so that a building's fire protection and life safety systems are not disabled.

LOCKDOWN PLAN CONTENTS

1. Individuals authorized to issue a lockdown order
2. Security measures that could affect egress or fire department operations
3. Description of emergency and security threats addressed by the plan
4. Methods of initiating lockdown
5. Procedures for reporting to the fire department
6. Method for emergency responder to determine the presence or absence of occupants
7. Two-way communication to all secured areas
8. Signal for terminating the lockdown
9. Individuals authorized to terminate a lockdown
10. Procedures for unlocking doors and verifying a "normal" status for the means of egress
11. Training procedures and frequency

MAINTENANCE OF THE LOCKDOWN PLAN

1. Reviewed annually
2. Updated as necessary

AVAILABILITY OF LOCKDOWN PLAN

1. Available to employees
2. Available to tenants, tenants provide to their employees
3. Copy available to fire code official

Lockdown plans, which originally started at schools, can now be found at all types of facilities. The IFC does not require a lockdown plan, but if such a plan exists at a facility, it must be approved by the fire code official.

Code Text: *The provisions of Sections 407.2 through 407.7 shall be applicable where hazardous materials subject to permits under Section 5001.5 are located on the premises or where required by the fire code official.*

Discussion and Commentary: The requirements of this section are important, both for fire prevention, in assuring that materials are stored and used in accordance with applicable requirements, and for emergency response, in knowing the types, quantities and locations of materials on the premises. These requirements typically apply only when the amount of hazardous materials that are present exceed the permit amounts listed in Table 105.5.22, but may also be applied at the direction of the fire code official.

OSHA has required safety data sheets as part of its Hazard Communication requirements for over 20 years. Many larger companies use online resources for storing and disseminating SDS sheets. These electronic resources meet the requirements of IFC Section 407.2.

Study Session 3

IFC Chapters 3 and 4

1. Smoking is prohibited in which of the following locations?

    a. Rooms storing or handling combustible liquids

    b. Patient care areas in Group I-2 occupancies

    c. Areas where smoking creates a fire hazard

    d. All of the above

    Reference _____

2. A _____ is not included within the definition of "POWERED INDUSTRIAL TRUCK."

    a. cotton harvesting machine   b. forklift

    c. platform lift truck   d. motorized hand truck

    Reference _____

3. An employee knowledgeable of the operations and hazards of an asphalt kettle shall be within _____ feet of an operating kettle and have the kettle within sight.

    a. 10   b. 20

    c. 25   d. 100

    Reference _____

4. Containers used to store combustible rubbish and waste materials within a structure must be provided with lids if their capacity exceeds _____ gallons.

    a. 5   b. 32

    c. 40   d. 55

    Reference _____

5. Where a combustible waste receptacle is used for the deposit of hot ashes and smoldering coals, the receptacle shall be located a minimum of _____ feet from combustible construction.

    a. 5   b. 10

    c. 25   d. 50

Reference _____

6. A recreational fire shall be located at least _____ feet from a structure or combustible material.

    a. 25   b. 50

    c. 75   d. 100

Reference _____

7. In Group A occupancies, all of the following devices can be used, within specified limitations, except _____.

    a. Hand-held candles in religious ceremonies

    b. Props in theatrical performances

    c. Ambiance lighting on tables, when the base is noncombustible and the flame is protected

    d. Hand-held torch to remove wallpaper

Reference _____

8. A fire extinguisher with a minimum 4-A:20-B:C rating shall be provided within _____ of the battery charger in a battery-charging area for forklifts.

    a. 10 feet   b. 20 feet

    c. 50 feet   d. 75 feet

Reference _____

9. Where posts are installed as required for vehicle impact protection, what is the minimum height of such posts?

    a. 30 inches   b. 33 inches

    c. 36 inches   d. 42 inches

Reference _____

10. Which of the following is not a requirement for the indoor display of gaseous-fueled vehicles?

    a. The starting system is made inoperable or the batteries are disconnected.

    b. Fuel in fuel tanks does not exceed one-quarter tank or 5 gallons, whichever is less.

    c. Ignition keys are not anywhere within the vehicle.

    d. Vehicles are not fueled or defueled within the building.

Reference _____

11. Except for storage along walls, the top of storage shall be maintained a minimum of _____ below sprinkler head deflectors in sprinklered areas of buildings.

    a. 12 inches   b. 18 inches

    c. 2 feet   d. 3 feet

Reference _____

12. What is the minimum roof classification required for a roofing system used to separate two or more landscaped roof areas, each with an area of 15,000 square feet?

    a. Type A   b. Class A

    c. Type B   d. Class B

Reference _____

13. Which of the following uses or occupancies does *not* require the preparation of an approved fire safety and evacuation plan?

    a. a Group M building with an occupant load of 1,000 persons

    b. a covered mall with 60,000 square feet in aggregate floor area

    c. a Group A-3 church with an occupant load of 1,500 persons

    d. a Group M department store with an atrium

Reference _____

14. Which of the following is not required to be shown on the site plan that is a required part of a fire safety plan?

    a. the occupant assembly point

    b. the locations of fire hydrants

    c. the location of the nearest fire station

    d. the normal routes of fire department vehicle access

Reference _____

15. Fire and evacuation drills in Group A occupancies are required to be conducted _____.

     a.   quarterly by staff

     b.   monthly by all occupants

     c.   annually on each shift by staff

     d.   prior to each type of event by staff

Reference _____

16. In Group E occupancies, the first emergency evacuation drill of each school year shall be conducted _____.

     a.   on the first day of classes

     b.   during the first week of school

     c.   prior to the first school holiday

     d.   within 10 days of the beginning of classes

Reference _____

17. In facilities that utilize hazardous production materials, the emergency response team shall conduct emergency drills _____.

     a.   at least twice per year

     b.   three times per year

     c.   not less than once every three months

     d.   at least six times per year

Reference _____

18. During emergency evacuation drills in Group I-2 occupancies, the movement of patients to safe areas or to the exterior of the building is not required _____.

     a.   when the weather is poor

     b.   at any time

     c.   if the patients are capable of self-preservation

     d.   in operating rooms when flammable anesthetic is used

Reference _____

19. Each tenant in a Group R-2 occupancy shall be given _____ prior to initial occupancy.

    a. a fire extinguisher   b. a copy of the emergency guide

    c. a map of the complex   d. a fire prevention seminar

    Reference _____

20. In Group R-4 occupancies, emergency evacuation drills shall be conducted _____ in the first year of operation.

    a. at least six times   b. two times for each shift

    c. twelve times   d. twice per month

    Reference _____

21. Unoccupied tenant spaces in a covered mall must be separated from the remainder of the building by at least _____ .

    a. partitions of $^1/_2$-inch gypsum board

    b. 1-hour fire barriers

    c. smoke barriers

    d. fire walls

    Reference _____

22. Outside storage of general combustible material shall be a maximum of_____ feet in height.

    a. 10   b. 12

    c. 20   d. 25

    Reference _____

23. Guard posts to protect fire equipment from vehicular impact must meet which of the following?

    a. at least 6 inches in diameter

    b. at least 4 feet from the item they protect

    c. set not less than 3 feet deep in a concrete footing

    d. spaced no more than 5 feet apart

    Reference _____

24. Wooden pallets stored outside must be a minimum of _____ feet from a lot line.

    a. 5   b. 10

    c. 15   d. 20

    Reference _____

25. A pile of 250 plastic pallets stored outside can be located no closer than _____ feet to a building with exterior walls of wood construction, no openings and no open sprinklers.

    a. 20   b. 50

    c. 100   d. 150

    Reference _____

26. Pallets stored outside cannot be stored underneath which of the following?

    a. high-voltage transmission lines

    b. elevated roadways

    c. elevated railways

    d. all of the above

    Reference _____

27. Trapdoors and scuttle covers, other than those within a dwelling unit or automatically operated, shall be _____.

    a. marked in red letters at least 6 inches high on a white background

    b. kept locked and secured at all times

    c. kept closed at all times except when in use

    d. marked with warning signs placed so as to be readily discernible

    Reference _____

28. Which of the following mobile food preparation vehicles requires a permit from the IFC?

    a. the vehicle uses appliances that create smoke or grease-laden vapors

    b. the vehicle has an LP-gas container greater than 5 gallons

    c. the vehicle only steams vegetables and hot dogs

    d. the vehicle has two espresso machines and makes cold sandwiches

    Reference _____

29. What is the maximum aggregate capacity of LP-gas containers used for cooking on a mobile food preparation vehicle?

    a. 100 pounds   b. 200 pounds

    c. 250 pounds   d. 500 pounds

    Reference _____

30. Landscaped roofs are limited by which of the following?

    a. maximum single area of 15,625 square feet

    b. maximum total area of 150,000 square feet

    c. maximum dimensions in any direction of 300 feet

    d. there is no limit on size provided the roof structure can support the load

    Reference _____

31. Storage in the attic of a Group B occupancy is prohibited unless _____.

    a. the attic is protected with an automatic sprinkler system

    b. the storage side of the ceiling is protected with 1-hour fire-resistance-rated construction with openings provided with noncombustible, self-closing assemblies

    c. Either A or B

    d. Both A and B are required

    Reference _____

32. When are laundry carts with an individual capacity of 1 cubic yard (200 gallons) or more, used in laundries within Group B, E, F-1, I, M and R-1 occupancies permitted to be of combustible materials?

    a. If tested to ASTM E1354

    b. When used in areas protected by an automatic sprinkler system

    c. If used in coin-operated laundries

    d. All of the above

    Reference _____

33. Industrial additive manufacturing can be conducted in which occupancies?

    a.   Offices in Group B

    b.   Manufacturing in Groups F or H

    c.   Office spaces in Group M, if protected with an automatic sprinkler system

    d.   Any of the above

Reference _____

34. Artificial vegetation located on a rooftop must meet flammability requirements of NFPA 701 when _____.

    a.   more than 6 feet in height and permanent in nature

    b.   within 10 feet of a doorway

    c.   of any size or location

    d.   the rooftop is used as a Group A-2

Reference _____

35. In a Group F-1 occupancy that is required to develop a fire safety and evacuation plan, when are evacuation drills required?

    a.   with one month of hiring any new employee

    b.   quarterly for all employees

    c.   only required when new equipment is installed or the process is changed

    d.   annually with all employees

Reference _____

2021 IFC Chapter 5 and Appendices B, C, D and L

Fire Service Features

OBJECTIVE: To gain an understanding of the issues, requirements and procedures related to general precautions against fire, emergency planning and preparedness and fire service features.

REFERENCE: Chapter 5 and Appendices B, C, D and L 2021 *International Fire Code*® (IFC®)

KEY POINTS:
- What is the scope of Chapter 5 of the IFC and what types of issues does it regulate?
- When do required fire apparatus roads and water supplies need to be installed when a new building or development is being constructed?
- What are the requirements for access roads?
- Under what circumstance is a dead-end fire apparatus access road allowed to exceed 150 feet in length?
- What are the minimum design criteria for a fire apparatus access road turnaround?
- When are two entrances onto a piece of property required for fire department access?
- When are two entrances into a residential development required for fire department access?
- Which code section requires that rooms containing fire protection equipment be identified by readily visible signs?
- When do the fire apparatus access roads need to be designed for the operation of aerial fire apparatus at a building?
- What is the minimum width and maximum slope of roadways for fire apparatus?
- Where does the code provide minimum design and construction provisions for fire apparatus access roads?
- When are fire lane signs required?
- What is the maximum size of a building before a stairway, or access, is required to reach the roof?
- When is the fire code official authorized to require the installation of a key box?

KEY POINTS:
(Cont'd)

- How are fire-flow requirements determined for buildings and facilities?
- Can the volume of required fire-flow be modified?
- What type of water sources are acceptable when providing the water supply for fire-fighting?
- How many fire hydrants are required to protect a building?
- What is the required clear space around a fire hydrant?
- Which buildings are required to provide a Fire Command Center?
- What components are required in a Fire Command Center?
- What is two-way emergency responder communication coverage, and when is it required in buildings?
- In a new building, what does the owner need to provide to comply with emergency responder communication coverage?
- When fire hydrants are required, where are they located?
- What is the maximum spacing between fire hydrants?
- How far from a building can a fire hydrant be located?
- What is the minimum size of address numbers/letters on a building?
- Does the type of construction affect the required fire flow?
- What are the components of a fire fighter air replenishment system?
- Where are air bottle fill stations required?
- What is required to ensure air quality in the fire fighter air replenishment station?

Topic: Scope	Category: Fire Service Features
Reference: IFC 501.1	Subject: General

Code Text: *Fire service features for buildings, structures and premises shall comply with this chapter (IFC Chapter 5).*

Discussion and Commentary: The intent of Chapter 5 is to ensure that fire departments have access to the building, that a reliable water supply is available and that fire protection systems are accessible. Chapter 5 provides requirements that apply to all buildings and occupancies and pertain to access roads, access to building openings and roofs, premises identification, key boxes, fire protection water supplies, fire command centers, fire department access to equipment and emergency responder communication coverage in buildings. Although many safety features are part of the building design, features such as proper fire department access roads, fire command centers and communication coverage are necessary in case of emergency and are important tools for emergency responders for public safety and their own safety.

Both a performance-based code and a prescriptive code, the IFC does not always specify requirements in detail, but often contains design parameters or references to nationally recognized standards. Chapter 5 references the AASHTO standard for bridges and NFPA standards for the design of the water supply and fire protection systems.

Code Text: *Approved fire apparatus access roads shall be provided for every facility, building or portion of a building hereafter constructed or moved into or within the jurisdiction. The fire apparatus access road shall comply with the requirements of this section and shall extend to within 150 feet (45 720 mm) of all portions of the facility and all portions of the exterior walls of the first story of the building as measured by an approved route around the exterior of the building or facility.*

Exceptions to IFC Section 503.1.1 authorize the fire code official to increase the 150-foot distance if (1) the building is equipped with the appropriate NFPA 13, 13R or 13D sprinkler system, (2) an access road is not feasible and approved alternative protection is provided, or (3) there are not more than two Group R-3 or U occupancies.

Discussion and Commentary: The intent of this section is to ensure that fire fighters are able to lay a hose line to reach any portion of the exterior walls of a building or facility. Note that the requirement specifically addresses "facility." Based on the definition in Chapter 2, this would include the building, structures, and any use in a fixed location which would include exterior storage. If any portion of a building is greater than 150 feet from an access road, an access road or roads constructed to fulfill fire apparatus access road standards must be extended so that the 150-foot requirement is met. The approved route language provides for unobstructed foot traffic around the exterior of the building for hose line operations.

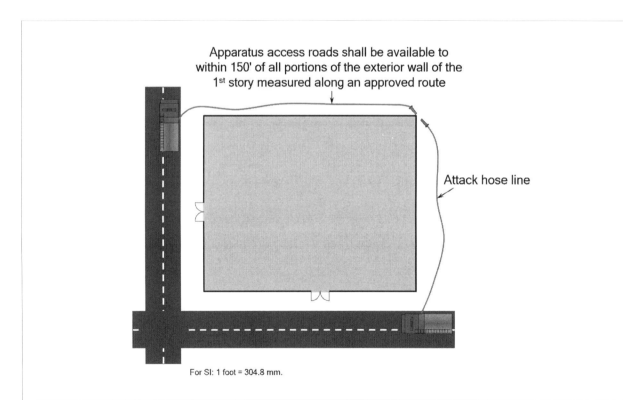

Apparatus access roads shall be available to within 150' of all portions of the exterior wall of the 1st story measured along an approved route

Attack hose line

For SI: 1 foot = 304.8 mm.

Appendix D of the IFC provides additional guidance on the design and layout of fire apparatus access roads and, if specifically adopted in the adopting ordinance, provides additional requirements for enforcement.

Topic: Fire Lane marking

Reference: IFC 503.3

Category: Fire Service Features

Subject: Fire Apparatus Access Roads

Code Text: *Where required by the fire code official, approved signs or other approved notices or markings that include the words "NO PARKING—FIRE LANE" shall be provided for fire apparatus access roads to identify such roads or prohibit the obstruction thereof. The means by which fire lanes are designated shall be maintained in a clean and legible condition at all times and be replaced or repaired when necessary to provide adequate visibility.*

Discussion and Commentary: Access roads can be generally broken down into two categories: (1) public access roads or common-use roads, and (2) on-site vehicular access such as driveways or drivable routes through a parking lot. "Fire lane" typically refers to the private, or on-site, driving routes. When fire lanes are specified on a piece of property, a shopping center for example, the fire lanes can and should be identified to eliminate parking or obstruction of the fire lanes. Fire lanes can be striped, or the curb can be painted, or signs can be posted to identify fire lanes. The specific type of marking is subject to approval by the fire code official and a local interpretation could be written to identify the acceptable marking criteria. Appendix D, if adopted, contains specific marking criteria for fire lane signs.

Fire lanes must be identified so that drivers are aware they cannot park or obstruct the fire lane.

Topic: Stairway Access to Roof	**Category:** Fire Service Features
Reference: IFC 504.3	**Subject:** Access to Building Openings and Roofs

Code Text: *New buildings four or more stories above grade plane, except those with a roof slope greater than four units vertical in 12 units horizontal (33.3-percent slope), shall be provided with a stairway to the roof. Stairway access to the roof shall be in accordance with Section 1011.12. Such stairway shall be marked at street and floor levels with a sign indicating that the stairway continues to the roof. Where roofs are used for landscaped roofs or for other purposes, stairways shall be provided as required for such occupancy classification.*

Discussion and Commentary: This requirement applies only to new buildings four or more stories in height. The purpose is to provide fire fighters with protected interior access to all floors and the roof for taller buildings, where exterior access may be difficult or not possible. This requirement correlates with IFC and *International Building Code*® (IBC®) Section 1023, which requires that stair enclosures connecting four stories or more have a 2-hour fire-resistance rating and that stairway floors be identified with signs, including the story number and whether or not roof accessibility is available.

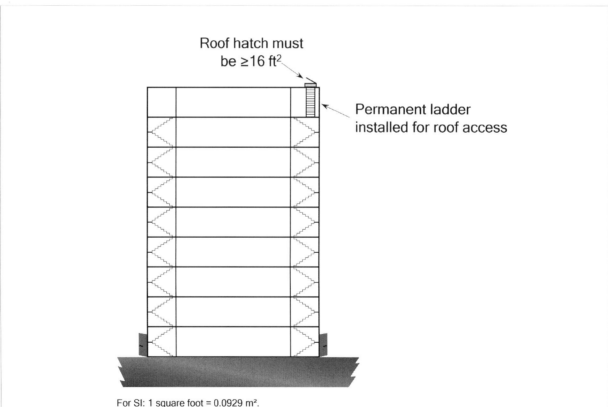

For SI: 1 square foot = 0.0929 m².

IFC Section 1011.12 and the exception to Section 1011.12.2 provide that, for buildings with roofs that are not otherwise occupied, the stairs from the top story to the roof may be an alternating tread device, a ship's ladder or a permanent ladder and access to the roof may be by a roof hatch or trap door.

Code Text: *New and existing buildings shall be provided with approved address identification. The address identification shall be legible and placed in a position that is visible from the street or road fronting the property. Address identification characters shall contrast with their background. Address numbers shall be Arabic numbers or alphabetical letters. Numbers shall not be spelled out. Each character shall be not less than 4 inches (102 mm) high with a minimum stroke width of $^1/_2$ inch (12.7 mm). Where required by the fire code official, address identification shall be provided in additional approved locations to facilitate emergency response. Where access is by means of a private road and the building cannot be viewed from the public way, a monument, pole or other sign or means shall be used to identify the structure. Address identification shall be maintained.*

Discussion and Commentary: Addresses provide the fire department with the ability to quickly locate the proper facility or building. In addition to the fire department, ambulance crews and law enforcement need the address to perform their function in a timely manner.

Several criteria in this section enhance the visibility of the address. First, this section applies to both new and existing buildings. Second, the address must be visible from the street. The address numbers or characters must be a minimum of 4 inches in height, but to be visible from the street they often must be larger. Third, they must have a contrasting background. This improves their visibility especially from a distance.

This address is larger than the minimum of 4 inches in height, because it must be visible from the street.

Code Text: *Where access to or within a structure or an area is restricted because of secured openings or where immediate access is necessary for life-saving or fire-fighting purposes, the fire code official is authorized to require a key box to be installed in an approved location. The key box shall be of an approved type listed in accordance with UL 1037, and shall contain keys to gain necessary access as required by the fire code official.*

Discussion and Commentary: The fire code official is granted the authority to require key boxes. The key box is a secure location to store keys into the building. All of the key boxes within a single jurisdiction are openable with the same key which is carried on the fire apparatus or in the vehicle of a chief officer.

Security can be enhanced in several ways:

- The key box can be mounted in a location that is accessible only with a ladder.
- The access key on the fire department vehicle can sound an alarm when it is removed from its holder.
- The key box can be fitted with a contact which is supervised by the fire alarm system and a supervisory signal is sent to the monitoring company.

The building owner does not have a key to the key box. In order for the owner to insert or replace keys in the key box, the fire department must open the box with their key.

Code Text: ***Required water supply.*** *An approved water supply capable of supplying the required fire flow for fire protection shall be provided to premises on which facilities, buildings or portions of buildings are hereafter constructed or moved into or within the jurisdiction.*

Type of water supply. *A water supply shall consist of reservoirs, pressure tanks, elevated tanks, water mains or other fixed systems capable of providing the required fire flow.*

Discussion and Commentary: The IFC requires that a water supply for fire-fighting purposes be provided for all new buildings, new additions to buildings and new facilities. The code specifies new facilities because there are occasions where the facilities, or operations, at an existing property may change without any change to the building.

Consider an existing grocery store that is converted to a hardware store. The building is not new, the occupancy is still Group M, but they have added outdoor lumber storage areas. This would be considered new facilities and water for fire fighting is required for this increased hazard.

The IFC does not stipulate that the water supply must be a fire hydrant. Section 507.2 states that reservoirs, tanks or other fixed systems can provide the water supply. Combining these two sections, the required water supply could be provided in various manners, but it must be approved by the fire code official.

A clear space with a radius of 3 feet is required around fire hydrants for access during fire-fighting operations and for general maintenance (IFC Section 507.5.5).

Code Text: *Where a portion of the facility or building hereafter constructed or moved into or within the jurisdiction is more than 400 feet (122 m) from a hydrant on a fire apparatus access road, as measured by an approved route around the exterior of the facility or building, on-site fire hydrants and mains shall be provided where required by the fire code official.* ***Exceptions:*** *(1) For Group R-3 and Group U occupancies, the distance requirement shall be 600 feet (183 m), (2) For buildings equipped throughout with an approved automatic sprinkler system installed in accordance with Section 903.3.1.1 or 903.3.1.2, the distance requirement shall be 600 feet (183 m).*

Discussion and Commentary: The premise of this requirement is that every portion of the building at grade should be within reach of 400 feet of hose. Exception 1 is based on the fact that one- and two-family dwellings and their smaller accessory buildings do not present as great a hazard or fuel load as commercial buildings. Exception 2 recognizes the value of automatic fire sprinkler systems in applying water to the point of origin, almost immediately limiting the growth and spread of the fire. Both Exceptions 1 and 2 allow the distance to the fire hydrant, or water supply, to be increased to 600 feet.

This fire hydrant has been installed at the rear of a building to meet the distance requirements in Section 507.5.1.

Code Text: *Where required by other sections of this code and in all buildings classified as high-rise buildings by the* International Building Code *and in all F-1 and S-1 occupancies with a building footprint greater than 500,000 square feet (46 452 m²), a fire command center for fire department operations shall be provided and shall comply with Sections 508.1.1 through 508.1.7.*

(See the IFC for additional requirements.)

Discussion and Commentary: Fire command centers are required in high-rise buildings and in large warehouses and factories, and may be present in other complex types of buildings where various combinations of life safety and fire protection systems exist, such as covered malls. The fire command center houses controls or annunciation panels for elevators, emergency voice/alarm communications systems, fire alarm systems, fire sprinkler systems, smoke control systems, standpipes and other complex systems. Because of the height of high-rise buildings, the fire department cannot attack a fire from the exterior. An interior fire attack is required. The fire command center is a protected space that contains all of the monitoring, communication and systems control devices necessary to coordinate and conduct fire-fighting operations in a single location.

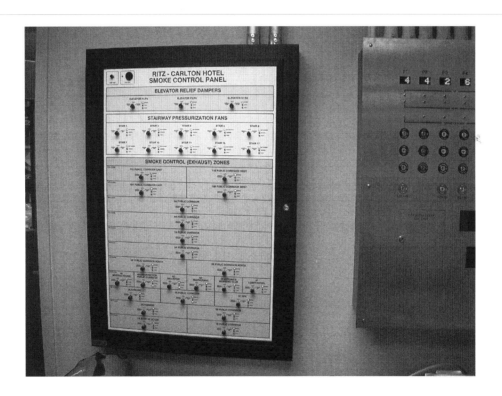

The fire command center is required to be separated from the rest of the building by at least a 1-hour fire-resistance-rated fire barrier. In buildings other than Group F-1 or S-1, the minimum size of the fire command center is 200 square feet; when the building area exceeds 1,333,3334 square feet the fire command center must be 0.015 percent times the total building area. A fire command center in Group F-1 or S-1 must be a minimum of 96 square feet. Fire command center requirements are duplicated in IBC Section 911.

Topic: Emergency Responder Communication Coverage	**Category:** Fire Service Features
Reference: IFC 510.1	**Subject:** Emergency Responder Communication Coverage

Code Text: *Approved in-building, two-way emergency responder communication coverage for emergency responders shall be provided in all new buildings. In-building, two-way emergency responder communication coverage within the building shall be based on the existing coverage levels of the public safety communication systems utilized by the jurisdiction, measured at the exterior of the building. This section shall not require improvement of the existing public safety communication systems.* ***Exceptions:*** *(1) Where approved by the building official and the fire code official, a wired communication system in accordance with Section 907.2.13.2 shall be permitted to be installed or maintained instead of an approved radio coverage system; (2) Where it is determined by the fire code official that the radio coverage system is not needed; (3) In facilities where emergency responder radio coverage is required and such systems, components or equipment required could have a negative impact on the normal operations of that facility, the fire code official shall have the authority to accept an automatically activated emergency responder radio coverage system.*

Discussion and Commentary: The goal of emergency responder radio coverage is to provide adequate fire department communications inside a building to facilitate the fire-fighting operations and provide for fire fighter safety. Many building construction methods impact radio frequencies as they pass through the building walls. Additionally, many interior appliances and equipment, such as metal storage racks and conveyor systems, disrupt the radio frequencies even further. This requirement is designed to allow radio frequencies to be enhanced to mitigate the negative impact the building creates.

This requirement is not used to upgrade the jurisdiction radio infrastructure. It applies to the building itself, and the impact that the building has on communications. The building must have a minimum signal strength of -95 dBm and delivered audio quality of 3.0 in 95 percent of the floor area, and in critical areas the signal criteria must be met in 99 percent of the floor area.

Wood frame construction has little impact on radio communications and normally does not require that any devices or equipment are required within the building to meet the emergency responder communication criteria.

Code Text: *The procedure for determining fire-flow requirements for buildings or portions of buildings hereafter constructed shall be in accordance with this appendix. This appendix does not apply to structures other than buildings.*

Discussion and Commentary: Appendix B provides a method for the fire code official to determine the required fire-flow. Table B105.1(2) contains the water flow requirements and the building size and type of construction is used to determine the minimum required fire-flow.

Tables B105.1(1) and B105.2 describe how to apply the criteria in Table B105.1(2). In all cases, whether or not the building is equipped with an automatic sprinkler system affects the application of the fire-flow table. Reductions in fire-flow apply when the building is sprinklered, but there is a difference between the type of fire sprinkler system based on the design standard.

Keep in mind that Appendix B only applies when the appendix is specifically adopted.

TABLE B105.2
REQUIRED FIRE FLOW FOR BUILDINGS OTHER THAN ONE- AND TWO-FAMILY DWELLINGS,
GROUP R-3 AND R-4 BUILDINGS AND TOWNHOUSES

AUTOMATIC SPRINKLER SYSTEM (Design Standard)	MINIMUM FIRE FLOW (gallons per minute)	FLOW DURATION (hours)
No automatic sprinkler system	Value in Table B105.1(2)	Duration in Table B105.1(2)
Section 903.3.1.1 of the *International Fire Code*	25% of the value in Table B105.1(2) [a]	Duration in Table B105.1(2) at the reduced flow rate
Section 903.3.1.2 of the *International Fire Code*	25% of the value in Table B105.1(2) [b]	Duration in Table B105.1(2) at the reduced flow rate

For SI: 1 gallon per minute = 3.785 L/m.

a. The reduced fire flow shall be not less than 1,000 gallons per minute.
b. The reduced fire flow shall be not less than 1,500 gallons per minute.

Table B105.2 describes how to apply Table B105.1(2). Note the difference in requirements when the sprinkler system is designed to NFPA 13R versus NPFA 13. Differences occur in the table and in the footnotes.

Code Text: *For buildings equipped with an approved automatic sprinkler system, the water supply shall be capable of providing the greater of: (1) The automatic sprinkler system demand, including hose stream allowance, (2) The required fire flow.*

Discussion and Commentary: There is often a question of how to determine fire-flow requirements when the building is sprinklered. For a given building, Table B105.2 might specify a fire-flow of 1,500 gallons per minute (gpm) when the building is sprinklered with NFPA 13. The definition of "fire-flow" in Section B102.1 states that the fire flow is available at 20 pounds per square inch (psi) residual pressure. However, the fire sprinkler system typically needs a higher pressure with a lower flow, such as 405 gpm at 50 psi. It has been a subject of much discussion whether to combine these two flows, and if so, how to combine them. Since the two flows specify different pressures, there is no simple way to combine the flows into a single requirement.

This section specifies that the water system must be capable of supplying both criteria, but not at the same time. Item 1 specifies that when considering the water demand for the fire sprinkler system, the hose stream allowance is included in the calculation. The section states that the requirement is based on the "...greater of..." the two requirements. One has a greater demand in pressure, while the other is a larger volume at a lower pressure. The available water supply at the site must be capable of providing each required flow.

Keep in mind that Appendix B only applies when the appendix is specifically adopted.

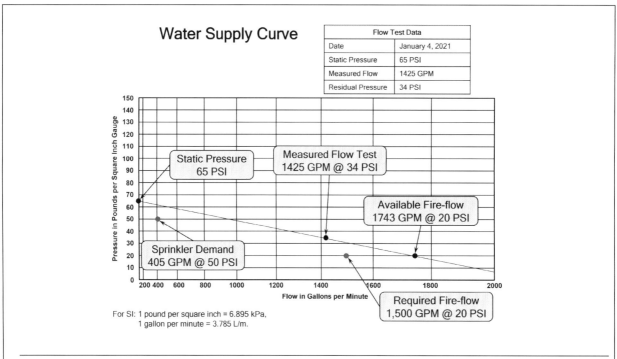

The water system capacity, depicted by the diagonal line, can provide any flow/pressure combination below the line. Both the fire sprinkler demand and the fire-flow requirement are below the line. Therefore, the water system is capable of meeting both requirements.

Code Text: *The number of fire hydrants available to a building shall be not less than the minimum specified in Table C102.1.*

Discussion and Commentary: Once the fire-flow requirements are established, the number of fire hydrants is based on the required fire-flow. Essentially, the more water needed for fire-fighting results in more fire hydrants needed to deliver that fire-flow.

Table C102.1 identifies the minimum number of fire hydrants and also specifies the spacing between the fire hydrants. Note that both criteria must be met.

Keep in mind that Appendix C only applies when the appendix is specifically adopted.

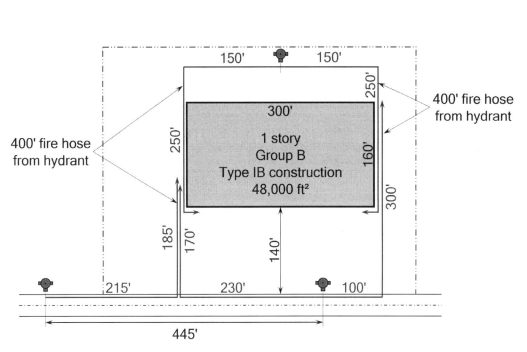

For SI: 1 foot = 304.8 mm, 1 square foot = 0.0929 m².

Only two fire hydrants are required by Table C102.1 based on a required fire-flow of 2,250 gallons per minute. However, a third hydrant is required to meet spacing requirements in Table C102.1 and distance to exterior wall requirements in Section 507.5.1.

Code Text: *Gates securing the fire apparatus access roads shall comply with all of the following criteria: (1) Where a single gate is provided, the gate width shall be not less than 20 feet (6096 mm). Where a fire apparatus road consists of a divided roadway, the gate width shall be not less than 12 feet (3658 mm); (2) Gates shall be of the horizontal swing, horizontal slide, vertical lift or vertical pivot type; (3) Construction of gates shall be of materials that allow manual operation by one person; (4) Gate components shall be maintained in an operative condition at all times and replaced or repaired when defective; (5) Electric gates shall be equipped with a means of opening the gate by fire department personnel for emergency access. Emergency opening devices shall be approved by the fire code official; (6) Methods of locking shall be submitted for approval by the fire code official; (7) Electric gate operators, where provided, shall be listed in accordance with UL 325; (8) Gates intended for automatic operation shall be designed, constructed and installed to comply with the requirements of ASTM F2200.*

Discussion and Commentary: Security gates are quite common, and typically installed across the fire apparatus access road or fire lane. The fire department must be able to open and pass through these gates. This section specifies the design and operation of the gates.

Keep in mind that Appendix D only applies when the appendix is specifically adopted.

This gate is closed at night and obstructs the vehicular access to the rear of the building. The access gate must be openable and meet the size requirements.

Topic: Buildings over Three Stories, 30 Feet
in Height or 62,000 Square Feet in Area
Reference: IFC D104.1, D104.2

Category: Fire Apparatus Access Roads

Subject: Commercial and Industrial Developments

Code Text: ***Buildings exceeding three stories or 30 feet in height.*** *Buildings or facilities exceeding 30 feet (9144 mm) or three stories in height shall have not fewer than two means of fire apparatus access for each structure.*

Buildings exceeding 62,000 square feet in area. *Buildings or facilities having a gross building area of more than 62,000 square feet (5760 m²) shall be provided with two separate and approved fire apparatus access roads.* ***Exception:*** *Projects having a gross building area of up to 124,000 square feet (11 520 m²) that have a single approved fire apparatus access road where all buildings are equipped throughout with approved automatic sprinkler systems.*

Discussion and Commentary: These sections require that means of access to the structure is required whenever it exceeds three stories or 30 feet in height, or 62,000 square feet in area. The exception to Section D104.2 allows sprinklered buildings up to 124,000 square feet to have only a single means of access.

The additional access point allows for flexibility when fighting a fire in the facility. In these larger fires, additional fire apparatus may be needed, or an approach from another wind direction is desired. The second point of access allows for these options.

Keep in mind that Appendix D only applies when the appendix is specifically adopted.

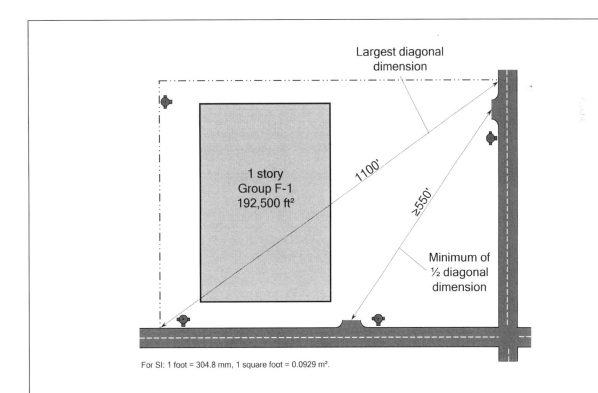

1 story
Group F-1
192,500 ft²

Largest diagonal dimension

1100'

≥550'

Minimum of ½ diagonal dimension

For SI: 1 foot = 304.8 mm, 1 square foot = 0.0929 m².

When a second access point is required, at least two access points must be separated by one-half of the maximum overall diagonal of the lot served (IFC Section D104.3).

Code Text: *Where the vertical distance between the grade plane and the highest roof surface exceeds 30 feet (9144 mm), approved aerial fire apparatus access roads shall be provided. For purposes of this section, the highest roof surface shall be determined by measurement to the eave of a pitched roof, the intersection of the roof to the exterior wall, or the top of parapet walls, whichever is greater. **Exception:** Where approved by the fire code official, buildings of Type IA, Type IB or Type IIA construction equipped throughout with an automatic sprinkler system in accordance with Section 903.3.1.1 and having fire fighter access through an enclosed stairway with a Class I standpipe from the lowest level of fire department vehicle access to all roof surfaces.*

Discussion and Commentary: Ladders extended from the ground are limited in the height they can reach. Aerial apparatus carry ladders up to 125 feet in length thus enabling exterior fire-fighting operations far above the height attainable by ground ladders. Appendix D requires taller buildings to provide an access road that is usable for aerial apparatus. This access road is required along one entire side of the building and must be at least 26 feet in width. The additional width allows the outriggers of the aerial to be deployed and still provide enough roadway for other apparatus to pass.

The exception allows for an alternative method of providing access to upper floors. The exception eliminates the access road requirement where the building is of Type IA, IB or IIA construction and has stairway access to all roof surfaces with a Class I standpipe in the stairway. This exception can only be used in situations approved by the code official.

Keep in mind that Appendix D only applies when the appendix is specifically adopted.

Section D105.4 states that overhead power and utility lines shall not be located over the aerial apparatus access roads. Power lines are not just an obstruction, but they present a life safety hazard for the fire fighters.

Topic: Roadway Access	**Category:** Fire Apparatus Access Roads
Reference: IFC D107.1	**Subject:** One- or Two-Family Residential Developments

Code Text: *Developments of one- or two-family dwellings where the number of dwelling units exceeds 30 shall be provided with two separate and approved fire apparatus access roads.* **Exceptions**: *(1) Where there are more than 30 dwelling units accessed from a single public or private fire apparatus access road and all dwelling units are equipped throughout with an approved automatic sprinkler system in accordance with Section 903.3.1.1, 903.3.1.2 or 903.3.1.3, access from two directions shall not be required; (2) The number of dwelling units accessed from a single fire apparatus access road shall not be increased unless fire apparatus access roads will connect with future development, as determined by the fire code official.*

Discussion and Commentary: Many residential developments can contain dwellings numbering up into the hundreds. When there are more than 30 dwelling units in a development, a second access route is required. This will allow for movement of vehicles and provide an alternative route when one direction is blocked. Developments where all of the dwellings are protected with fire sprinkler systems are not required to have a second access point.

Keep in mind that Appendix D only applies when the appendix is specifically adopted.

(Photograph courtesy of Jeffrey M. Shapiro, P.E., F.S.F.P.E., International Code Consultants, Austin, Texas.)

Each access route must comply with the access road requirements for grade, width, turning radius and load carrying capacity.

Study Session 4
IFC Chapter 5 and Appendices B, C, D and L

1. When Appendix B is adopted, what is the minimum required fire-flow for a 110,000 square foot Group M of Type IIB construction equipped with fire sprinklers?

    a. 1,000 gallons per minute
    b. 1,500 gallons per minute
    c. 1,750 gallons per minute
    d. 7,000 gallons per minute

    Reference B105.1(2)

2. When Appendix C is adopted, what is the minimum number of fire hydrants required for the building in Question 1?

    a. 1
    b. 2
    c. 3
    d. 4

    Reference C102.1

3. A water source or fire hydrant must be within _____ of all portions of the exterior wall of a nonsprinklered building.

    a. 200 feet
    b. 250 feet
    c. 300 feet
    d. 400 feet

    Reference 507.5.1

4. A fire hydrant is required within _____ feet of fire department connection for a standpipe system.

    a. 50
    b. 100
    c. 200
    d. 400

    Reference 507.5.1.1

5. Fire apparatus access roads are required to within _____ feet of all portions of the exterior wall of the first story of a nonsprinklered building.

    (a) 150

    b. 200

    c. 300

    d. same distance as exit access travel distance in the building

Reference 503.1.1

6. Electronic security gates installed across a fire apparatus access road must comply with which of the following?

    a. the gate can only be locked if the fire department has a key

    (b.) a construction permit is required for the installation of the security gate

    c. the gate must be at least 22 feet in width

    d. the gate must be no higher than 4'-8" so fire fighters can get over with fire hose

Reference 105.6.11

7. Which of the following buildings require access to the roof?

    a. all buildings over one story

    (b.) buildings four stories or more in height with a roof slope 4:12 or less

    c. buildings exceeding 30 feet in height with a roof slope 4:12 or less

    d. buildings with a landscaped roof

Reference 504.3

8. Which of the following would not be an acceptable source of water for fire fighting?

    a. elevated tank

    b. at grade reservoir

    c. cistern

    (d) seasonal stream

Reference 507.2

9. Which of the following are not required to be located within a fire command center?

    a.   fire pump, if a fire pump is provided

    b.   fire alarm annunciator, if a fire alarm is provided

    (c.) control panel for smoke control system, if a smoke control system is provided

    d.   building schematics and plans

Reference 508.1.6

10. A fire command center shall be protected from the remainder of the building by _____.

    a.   minimum 2-hour fire barriers and horizontal assemblies

    (b.) minimum 1-hour fire barriers and horizontal assemblies

    c.   fire partitions

    d.   smoke barriers

Reference 508.1.2

11. The inbound signal level for emergency responder communication coverage systems shall be a minimum of -95 dBm and sufficient to provide a minimum of a Delivered Audio Quality (DAQ) of _____ or an equivalent Signal-to-Interference-Plus-Noise Ratio (SINR) applicable to the technology for either analog or digital signals.

    a.   1.5   b.   2.0

    (c.) 3.0   d.   3.5

Reference 510.4.1.1

12. When Appendix L is adopted, a fire fighter air replenishment system is required in which buildings or occupancies?

    a.   Group A-2 over 3 stories

    b.   All high-rise buildings

    (c.) All underground buildings

    d.   Only those buildings or occupancies specifically identified in the adopting ordinance

Reference L 101.1
Section L

13. When conducting an acceptance test for emergency responder communication coverage systems, the test fails when it cannot provide success tests in _____ percent of the coverage area in non-critical areas.

    a. 50

    b. 75

    c. 90

    d. 95

    Reference 510.4.1

14. When determining required fire-flow and Appendix B is adopted, the fire-flow calculation area includes the floor area of the entire building except for which of the following situations?

    a. areas of the building separated by 4-hour fire walls with 3-hour opening protectives can be considered separately

    b. only the largest two successive floors in buildings protected throughout with sprinklers designed to NFPA 13

    c. only the largest three successive floors in Type IA or IB construction

    d. only the largest single floor for buildings of noncombustible construction

    Reference B 104.3
    Section B

15. When Appendix B is adopted, the minimum required fire-flow for a 4,000-square foot, single family dwelling of Type VB construction and equipped with fire sprinklers designed in accordance with the *International Residential Code* is _____ .

    a. 500 gallons per minute for ½ hour

    b. 875 gallons per minute for 1 hour

    c. 1,000 gallons per minute for 1 hour

    d. 1,750 gallons per minute for 2 hours

    Reference Table B105.1 (1)

16. When Appendix B is adopted, the minimum required fire-flow for an 80,000-square foot, Group B office building of Type IIA construction and equipped with fire sprinklers designed in accordance with NFPA 13 is _____ .

    a. 1,000 gallons per minute for 1 hour

    b. 1,000 gallons per minute for 2 hours

    c. 2,000 gallons per minute for 4 hours

    d. 4,000 gallons per minute for 4 hours

    Reference B105.2 /105.1

17. When Appendix C is adopted, which of the following is incorrect about fire hydrant spacing?

    a. fire hydrants can exceed the spacing requirements in Table C102.1 provided that the average spacing for all the hydrants does not exceed the Table C102.1

    b. fire hydrant spacing can be increased by 50 percent where the building is equipped with fire sprinklers designed in accordance with NFPA 13

    c. fire hydrants are required on both sides of the street when the street has a traffic count of 25,000 vehicles per day

    d. existing fire hydrants can be considered when spacing fire hydrants for a new building

Reference 102.1
Section C

18. When Appendix D is adopted, the grade of any fire apparatus access road shall be a maximum of _____ percent unless approved by the fire code official.

    a. 8   b. 10

    c. 12   d. 15

Reference D103.2
Section D

19. When Appendix D is adopted, fire lane signs are required on both sides of a fire apparatus access road when _____.

    a. the road exceeds 26 feet in width

    b. the road is between 12 and 20 feet in width

    c. the road is between 20 and 26 feet in width

    d. the road is used by delivery trucks

Reference D103.6.1
Section D

20. When Appendix D is adopted, what is the threshold for requiring two separate fire apparatus access roads for an apartment complex?

    a. 40 units

    b. 100 units

    c. 200 units if all structures, including accessory buildings, are protected with fire sprinklers

    d. both b and c

Reference D106.1
Section D

21. For a new sprinklered building, fire apparatus access roads shall have a minimum unobstructed width of _____ feet.

    a. 10   b. 12

    c. 20   d. 26

Reference 503.2.1

22. Which one of the following is *not* an exception for which the fire code official is authorized to increase the maximum distance of 150 feet from the fire apparatus access road to all portions of a building or facility?

    a. The building is equipped throughout with an approved automatic sprinkler system.

    b. The building has less than 5,000 square feet of floor area and is not a Group H occupancy.

    c. Fire apparatus access roads cannot be installed, and an approved alternative means is provided.

    d. There are not more than two Group R-3 or Group U occupancies.

Reference 503.1.1

23. Fire apparatus access roads shall have a minimum unobstructed vertical clearance of _____ feet.

    a. 12   b. 13

    c. 13½   d. 15

Reference 503.2.1

24. A turn around is required on dead-end fire apparatus access roads that exceed _____ feet in length.

    a. 100   b. 150

    c. 300   d. 600

Reference 503.2.5

25. A fire command center is required in a Group S-1 occupancy exceeding _____ square feet.

    a. 500,000   b. 1,000,000

    c. 1,500,000   d. 2,000,000

Reference 508.1.3

26. _____ buildings shall have approved address numbers, building numbers or approved building identification that is plainly legible and visible from the street or road fronting the property.

    a. New   b. New and existing

    c. Existing   d. Difficult to locate

    Reference 505.1

27. Unless otherwise approved by the fire code official, the system designer and lead installer for emergency responder communication coverage systems must have a valid FCC-issued general operators license and certification of in-building system training or_____.

    a. a general contractor's license

    b. a certificate of training issued by the equipment manufacturer

    c. general liability insurance

    d. a degree in electrical engineering

    Reference 510.5.3

28. On-site fire hydrants and mains shall be provided for a nonsprinklered commercial facility where a portion of the building or facility is more than _____ from a hydrant on a fire apparatus access road.

    a. 150 feet   b. 400 feet

    c. 150 yards   d. 600 feet

    Reference 507.5.1

29. Fire hydrants shall have a minimum clear space around the circumference of the hydrant of at least _____.

    a. 1 foot   b. 2 feet

    c. 3 feet   d. 4 feet on the side with the largest outlet

    Reference 507.5.5

30. Approved signs identifying rooms that contain controls for air-conditioning systems or fire protection systems must be _____.

    a. permanently installed and readily visible

    b. constructed with letters a minimum of 6 inches high

    c. mounted 8 inches to the right of the door at eye level

    d. clearly written in at least two languages

    Reference 509.1

31. Which of the following is incorrect about key boxes for access into a building?

    (a) The fire code official is authorized to require key boxes.

    b. Key boxes must be red in color.

    c. Key boxes must be installed in an approved location.

    d. Key boxes shall be listed in accordance with UL 1037.

    Reference _506.1_

32. For new construction, fire apparatus access roads and fire-fighting water supply must be installed before _____.

    a. permit is issued

    b. the inspector shows up on site

    c. the first fire

    (d.) construction commences unless approved alternate methods are provided

    Reference _501.4_

33. When Appendix L is adopted, fire fighter air replenishment systems must meet all of the following maintenance requirements except _____.

    a. Must be continuously maintained in an operative condition

    b. Must be inspected not less than annually

    c. Must have an air sample taken from the system and tested in accordance with NFPA 1989

    (d.) Must have trapped air removed and replaced every 5 years

    Reference _L106.1_

34. Which of the following statements is incorrect about rooms or areas containing fire protection equipment?

    (a.) Storage of combustible materials is prohibited within the room.

    b. Storage of noncombustible materials is allowed in the room.

    c. Access is required for immediate operation of fire protection equipment.

    d Equipment shall be identified in an approved manner.

    Reference _509.7_

35. The water supply test for new fire hydrant installations must be _____.

    a. witnessed by the fire code official or documentation provided that is acceptable to the fire code official

    b. performed during peak traffic hours

    c. performed by the fire code official or authorized representative

    d. designed to flow a minimum 150% of the required fire-flow

Reference 507.4

2021 IFC Chapters 6, 7, 8 and 12
Building Services and Systems; Fire and Smoke Protection Features; Interior Finish, Decorative Materials and Furnishings; and Energy Systems

OBJECTIVE: To obtain an understanding of the issues, requirements and procedures associated with building services and systems, fire-resistance-rated construction, energy systems, interior finishes, decorative materials and furnishings.

REFERENCE: Chapters 6, 7, 8 and 12, 2021 *International Fire Code*® (IFC®)

KEY POINTS:
- What is the scope of Chapter 6? What types of equipment does it regulate?
- What are the different types of storage batteries, and how do these differences affect how they are stored, used and regulated?
- How do the provisions in Chapter 6 interrelate to the other International Codes and other code officials? Which other codes are referenced in Chapter 6 of the IFC?
- How much fuel oil may be stored inside of buildings or outside in above-ground tanks?
- What authority does the fire code official have over unsafe heating equipment?
- How does the IFC regulate portable outdoor gas-fired heating appliances?
- What types and sizes of buildings, and which occupancies or uses, are required to be equipped with emergency and standby power systems?
- What is the toxicity and flammability classification system used for refrigerants?
- What types of refrigerants are regulated in the IFC?
- Where can the requirement for "In fire emergency, do not use elevator. Use exit stairs." signage be found?
- What are the requirements for the emergency recall and emergency operation of elevators?
- What special requirements apply to VRLA battery systems?
- What special requirements apply to capacitor energy storage systems?
- What special requirements apply to fuel cells?
- What distinguishes a Type I commercial kitchen hood from other types of hoods?

KEY POINTS:
(Cont'd)

- What are the operations and maintenance requirements for commercial kitchen hoods?

- What is the scope and purpose of Chapter 7 of the IFC?

- Which chapter of the *International Building Code®* (IBC®) also relates to fire-resistance-rated construction?

- How is fire-resistance-rated construction to be maintained? What is required if new penetrations or holes are created in fire-resistance-rated construction?

- What is fireblocking and draftstopping? What are smoke barriers and opening protectives?

- What role does signage play in the maintenance of opening protectives?

- What are the requirements for the use of acoustical ceiling systems that are part of a fire-resistance-rated floor/ceiling or roof/ceiling assembly?

- How often are sliding and rolling fire doors required to be inspected and tested?

- What are shafts, and how are they to be protected?

- Why are interior finishes important? How are they tested and classified?

- Which sections of Chapter 8 are applicable to both new and existing buildings? Existing buildings only?

- What general requirements for interior finishes apply to all of the occupancies?

- How are mattresses and upholstered furniture regulated in the IFC?

- In which occupancy group are natural cut trees prohibited under any circumstances?

- What requirements apply to interior decorations and trim?

- What are some of the referenced standards used to regulate interior wall and ceiling finishes?

- What flame spread classification is required for textile wall coverings?

- Where are the interior wall and ceiling finish requirements for different occupancies located?

- What types of energy systems are regulated in Chapter 12?

- Where are the requirements for solar photovoltaic power systems?

- What is rapid shutdown and what is required when it is provided in a building?

- Are there other types of electrical power sources regulated by the IFC other than generators, batteries and solar photovoltaic systems?

- What is the fire hazard associated with clothes dryers, and what are the requirements?

Code Text: *The provisions of this chapter shall apply to the installation, operation and maintenance of the following building services and systems: (1) Electrical systems, equipment and wiring, (2) Information technology server rooms, (3) Elevator systems, emergency operation and recall, (4) Fuel-fired appliances, heating systems, chimneys and fuel oil storage, (5) Commercial cooking equipment and systems, (6) Commercial cooking oil storage, (7) Mechanical refrigeration systems, (8) Hyperbaric facilities, (9) Clothes dryer exhaust systems.*

Discussion and Commentary: Chapter 6 specifies the requirements for building services and systems. This chapter references other chapters in the IFC or other International Codes. For example, most of the general fire-prevention-related provisions about mechanical refrigeration are contained in Chapter 6, but references are made to requirements in other chapters in the IFC, as well as other codes and standards, including the *International Mechanical Code*® (IMC®) and the *International Fuel Gas Code*® (IFGC®). As computerization of building systems continues, operating and maintaining building services and systems in a safe and appropriate manner is an increasingly important part of fire prevention and emergency response.

Similar to other specific requirements in the IFC, the subjects regulated in Chapter 6 provide additional reliability to systems and equipment and improve life safety to building occupants and emergency responders. Properly maintained building systems are less likely to be the cause of fires or other incidents that may hinder or endanger emergency responders. Building systems like the Phase 1 elevator recall and Phase 2 fire service operation of this elevator are important in a fire situation.

Code Text: *An approved pictorial sign of a standardized design shall be posted adjacent to each elevator call station on all floors instructing occupants to use the exit stairways and not to use the elevators in case of fire. The sign shall read: "IN FIRE EMERGENCY, DO NOT USE ELEVATOR. USE EXIT STAIRS." **Exceptions:** (1) The emergency sign shall not be required for elevators that are part of an accessible means of egress complying with Section 1009.4, (2) The emergency sign shall not be required for elevators that are used for occupant self-evacuation in accordance with Section 3008 of the* International Building Code.

Discussion and Commentary: Elevators can be used by emergency responders as part of their operations during fires or other emergencies. Use of the elevators by occupants could place them at risk in the event of elevator failure and could also impede fire department operations. All new elevators, regardless of travel distance, are required to be equipped with the recall function as described above plus emergency fire fighter operation from inside the elevator car. See ASME A17.3 for existing elevators and ASME A17.1 for new elevators.

Existing elevators in nonsprinklered buildings that have a travel distance of 25 feet or more are required to either provide recall operation or install fire doors over the hoistway openings to protect the hoistway and limit smoke spread. Elevators in existing high-rise buildings must be provided with elevator recall and emergency operation features.

The "USE EXIT STAIRS" signage required by IFC Section 604.4 is not required if the elevator is part of an accessible means of egress as specified in IFC (and IBC) Section 1009.4 or an occupant evacuation elevator complying with IBC Section 3008. This means that the elevator is equipped for emergency operation and signaling, has standby power and is either accessed from an area of refuge or a horizontal exit or is located in a fully sprinklered building.

Code Text: *Where fire service access elevators are required by Section 3007 of the* International Building Code, *fire service access elevator fire protection and safety features and lobbies required by Section 3007 of the* International Building Code *shall be maintained free of storage and furniture.*

Discussion and Commentary: Fire service access elevators serve a dual purpose: (1) the elevators are used during normal, daily building operation, and (2) these elevators are specifically designed for use by the fire department during an emergency situation. The elevator lobbies will be used for staging of equipment and personnel for assignment and use on the fire floor. Fire operations can be hindered by storage or furniture within the lobby.

When corridors are fire-resistance-rated and an elevator lobby is provided as opening protection for the hoistway doors, storage is prohibited in the elevator lobby. This requirement, in Section 604.5.3, applies to all types of elevators, but only restricts storage. Section 604.5.1 goes beyond this requirement and restricts furniture also in elevator lobbies serving fire service access elevators.

(Photograph courtesy of Getty Images.)

Storage and furniture is prohibited in elevator lobbies serving fire service access elevators.

Code Text: *The fire code official is authorized to order that measures be taken to prevent the operation of any existing stove, oven, furnace, incinerator, boiler or any other heat-producing device or appliance found to be defective or in violation of code requirements for existing appliances after giving notice to this effect to any person, owner, firm or agent or operator in charge of the same. The fire code official is authorized to take measures to prevent the operation of any device or appliance without notice when inspection shows the existence of an immediate fire hazard or when imperiling human life. The defective device shall remain withdrawn from service until all necessary repairs or alterations have been made or replaced in accordance with Section 605.1.*

Discussion and Commentary: This section authorizes a fire code official to order that the use of an unsafe appliance be stopped until safe and proper operating conditions are restored. Note that, because of legal due process concerns, the fire code official is normally required to give notice prior to taking action. However, if there is an imminent fire hazard or threat to human life, the code states that no prior notice is necessary. In other words, there may be situations where the threat is obvious, and the owner or person responsible may not be available. The fire code official then needs to take action immediately.

IFC Section 605.6.2 emphasizes the importance of manufacturer's instructions. Previously prescriptive requirements may have applied to most appliances. It is important that the manufacturer's instructions, which are provided as part of the appliance's listing and approval, be available so the fire code official can determine the safe installation, operation and maintenance requirements.

Topic: Portable Outdoor Gas-Fired Heating Appliances

Category: Building Services and Systems

Reference: IFC 605.5.2

Subject: Fuel-Fired Appliances

Code Text: *Portable gas-fired heating appliances located outdoors shall be in accordance with Sections 605.5.2.1 through 605.5.2.3.4.*

Discussion and Commentary: These requirements apply to patio heaters, which are commonly used to heat outdoor seating areas at restaurants and similar establishments. The requirements stipulate permissible and prohibited locations, listing and maintenance of the appliances and the fuel-gas containers. Section 605.5.2.1.1 prohibits the use of portable outdoor gas-fired heating appliances inside buildings, tents, canopies and membrane structures. These heaters are also prohibited on exterior balconies of apartment buildings and similar multi-family residential uses as prescribed in NFPA 58, *Liquefied Petroleum Gas Code*. NFPA 58 prohibits the use or storage of LP-gas containers on exterior balconies of apartments when the container volume is greater than 1.08 pounds of propane.

Portable outdoor gas-fired heating appliances are required by Section 605.5.2.2.1 to be listed. For patio heaters, the applicable standard is ANSI Z83.26/CSA 2.37, *Gas-Fired Outdoor Infrared Patio Heaters.*

Topic: Where Required	Category: Building Services and Systems
Reference: IFC 606.2	Subject: Commercial Kitchen Hoods

Code Text: *A Type I hood shall be installed at or above all commercial cooking appliances and domestic cooking appliances used for commercial purposes that produce grease vapors.* **Exceptions:** *(1) Factory-built commercial exhaust hoods that are listed and labeled in accordance with UL 710, and installed in accordance with Section 304.1 of the* International Mechanical Code, *shall not be required to comply with Sections 507.1.5, 507.2.3, 507.2.5, 507.2.8, 507.3.1, 507.3.3, 507.4 and 507.5 of the* International Mechanical Code, *(2) Factory-built commercial cooking recirculating systems that are listed and labeled in accordance with UL 710B, and installed in accordance with Section 304.1 of the* International Mechanical Code, *shall not be required to comply with Sections 507.1.5, 507.2.3, 507.2.5, 507.2.8, 507.3.1, 507.3.3, 507.4 and 507.5 of the* International Mechanical Code. *Spaces in which such systems are located shall be considered to be kitchens and shall be ventilated in accordance with Table 403.3.1.1 of the* International Mechanical Code. *For the purpose of determining the floor area required to be ventilated, each individual appliance shall be considered as occupying not less than 100 square feet (9.3 m²), (3) Where cooking appliances are equipped with integral down-draft exhaust systems and such appliances and exhaust systems are listed and labeled for the application in accordance with NFPA 96, a hood shall not be required at or above them, (4) A Type I hood shall not be required for an electric cooking appliance where an approved testing agency provides documentation that the appliance effluent contains 5 mg/m³ or less of grease when tested at an exhaust flow rate of 500 cfm (0.236 m³/s) in accordance with UL 710B.*

Discussion and Commentary: IMC Sections 506 through 509 contain detailed requirements for commercial kitchen hoods and duct systems. Type I hoods are required where grease-laden vapors are likely to exist, such as over commercial kitchen grills, deep fat fryers and other grease producing appliances. Where only heat, steam and moisture exist, a Type II hood is sufficient. Exceptions 1 and 2 eliminate the requirement for a Type I hood over cooking appliances listed to UL 710 and UL 710B, respectively. Exception 4 does not require an appliance listed to UL 710B, only that the cooking appliance has been evaluated using the Emissions Test in UL 710B. Essentially, samples are selected, prepared, tested, and the effluent is captured. Then the effluent is analyzed to determine how much grease was contained in the effluent. If the effluent contained 5 mg/m³ or less of grease, then the exception would apply.

(Photograph courtesy of Target Corporation, Minneapolis, MN.)

This pizza oven has passed the Emissions Test in UL 710B and qualifies under the exception. A fire-extinguishing system is not required since IFC Section 904.2.2 requires the fire-extinguishing system in situations where the Type I hood is required.

Code Text: *Hoods, grease-removal devices, fans, ducts and other appurtenances shall be inspected at intervals specified in Table 606.3.3.1 or as approved by the fire code official. Inspections shall be completed by qualified individuals.*

TABLE 606.3.3.1
COMMERCIAL COOKING SYSTEM INSPECTION FREQUENCY

TYPE OF COOKING OPERATION	FREQUENCY OF INSPECTION
High-volume cooking operations such as 24-hour cooking, charbroiling or wok cooking	3 months
Low-volume cooking operations such as places of religious worship, seasonal businesses and senior centers	12 months
Cooking operations utilizing solid-fuel burning cooking appliances	1 month
All other cooking operations	6 months

Discussion and Commentary: Requirements for the operation and maintenance of commercial cooking equipment include inspection frequencies based on the type of cooking operations as well as requiring qualified individuals to inspect and clean Type I hoods. The removal of byproducts produced by rendered animal fats, vegetable oils or solid fuels such as charcoal or wood limits the amount of available fuel in the event of a fire. Table 606.3.3.1 specifies the minimum inspection frequency for commercial cooking operations based on the amount of cooking performed or the type of fuel used.

If the inspection results in the need to clean the hood and duct system, Section 606.3.3.2 requires the cleaning to be in accordance with ANSI/IKECA C 10, *Standard for the Methodology for Cleaning of Commercial Kitchen Exhaust Systems.* This standard provides that a grease residue no thicker than 0.002 inch be present after completion of the cleaning process.

Routine cleaning of commercial cooking equipment exhaust hoods, filters, plenums, ductwork and exhaust fans removes the accumulated grease residue and reduces the fire hazard.

Code Text: *Refrigerants shall be classified in accordance with the* International Mechanical Code.

Discussion and Commentary: The IMC references ASHRAE 34, *Designation and Safety Classification of Refrigerants* for the classification of refrigerants. Refrigerants are classified as to their toxicity and flammability using an alphanumeric classification system. The letter in the ASHRAE 34 classification system is the toxicity classification for the refrigerant. The toxicity classifications are:

- Class A signifies refrigerants for which toxicity has not been identified at concentrations less than or equal to 400 PPM (parts per million).
- Class B signifies refrigerants for which there is evidence of toxicity at concentrations below 400 PPM.

The number in the ASHRAE 34 classification system is the refrigerant's flammability rating. The flammability classifications are:

- Class 1 indicates refrigerants that do not show flame propagation when tested in air at 14.7 psia (101 kPa) at 140°F (60°C).
- Class 2L indicates refrigerants having a lower flammability limit of more than 0.0062 pounds per cubic foot (0.10 kg/m³) at 140°F (60°C) at 14.7 psia (101 kPa), with a heat of combustion of less than 8169 Btu/lb (19 000 kJ/kg) and a maximum burning velocity of not more than 3.9 inches per second (10 cm/s) at 14.7 psia (101 kPa).
- Class 2 indicates refrigerants having a lower flammability limit of more than 0.0062 pounds per cubic foot (0.10 kg/m³) at 140°F (60°C) at 14.7 psia (101 kPa) and a heat of combustion of less than 8169 Btu/lb (19 000 kJ/kg).
- Class 3 indicates refrigerants that are highly flammable as defined by having a lower flammability limit of less than or equal to 0.0062 pounds per cubic foot (0.10 kg/m³) at 140°F (60°C) at 14.7 psia (101 kPa) and a heat of combustion equal to or greater than 8169 Btu/lb (19 000 kJ/kg).

IMC Table 1103.1 contains the classification of refrigerants used in mechanical refrigeration systems. Consider the refrigerants methyl formate R-611 and water R-718. Note that water is assigned a classification of A1 because it is not toxic or flammable. Conversely, methyl formate is assigned a B2 classification because it has toxic effects at concentrations below 400 PPM and is flammable.

REFRIGERANT CLASSIFICATION

- **IMC Section 1103.1 requires refrigerants to be classified in accordance with ASHRAE 34.**
- **Refrigerants are classified based on their toxicity and flammability.**
- **ASHRAE 34 uses an alphanumeric rating system.**
- **Class B refrigerants pose a greater health hazard than Class A.**
- **The higher the class number, the greater the flammability hazard of the refrigerant.**

IMC Table 1103.1 also contains the classification of refrigerants based on the criteria in Chapter 50 as well as the NFPA 704 hazard classification of refrigerants.

Code Text: *Where flammable refrigerants are used and compliance with Section 1106 of the* International Mechanical Code *is required, remote control of the mechanical equipment and appliances located in the machinery room as required by Sections 608.10.1 and 608.10.2 shall be provided at an approved location immediately outside the machinery room and adjacent to its principal entrance.*

Discussion and Commentary: A refrigeration machinery room is required by the IMC to provide controls directly outside of the room. The purpose of the controls is to provide emergency responders with a method of stopping the refrigeration compressors and ensuring that the mechanical ventilation system is operating. When the refrigerant is flammable, activation of the emergency shutdown control must deactivate power to the refrigeration machinery room, with the exception of the refrigerant vapor detector and the mechanical ventilation system.

IFC Section 608.10.2 requires that the emergency ventilation start switch be of a break-glass design as illustrated in this photograph or be fitted with a tamper-resistant cover.

Code Text: *Permanently installed refrigeration systems in machinery rooms containing more than 6.6 pounds (3 kg) of flammable, toxic or highly toxic refrigerant or ammonia shall be provided with an emergency pressure control system in accordance with Sections 608.11.1 and 608.11.2.*

Discussion and Commentary: The IFC requires larger refrigeration systems to have an emergency pressure control system installed that is designed to prevent the accidental release of anhydrous ammonia or other refrigerants classified as flammable, toxic or highly toxic. Note that anhydrous ammonia is classified as a corrosive liquefied compressed gas and is not classified as a flammable or toxic based on the definitions in the IFC.

An emergency pressure control system uses pressure sensors and automatic crossover valves so that in the event a refrigeration system has an overpressure condition, refrigerant is safely transferred from the high pressure to the low pressure side of the system until the pressures are balanced in the two systems. Activation of the pressure sensors causes the automatic crossover valves to open and shut down the compressors serving the affected portion of the refrigeration system. Shutting down the compressors stops any continued pressurization and movement of refrigerant in the system.

An important consideration for fire code officials is the system's design pressure. It is not uncommon for refrigeration systems to be designed to operate in the 250–300 PSIG range. The pressure relief devices generally are set to operate at or below the system design pressure. Code officials should ensure that the set points for the pressure-sensing devices are set to within 10 percent of the pressure relief devices of the system, that the sensors are compatible with the refrigerant, and that the crossover valves are also compatible with the refrigerant and designed for the pressure rating of the system.

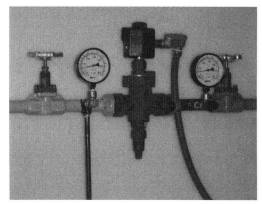

(Photograph courtesy of Jeffrey M. Shapiro, P.E., F.S.F.P.E., International Code Consultants, Austin, Texas.)

The emergency pressure control system offers improved safety for refrigeration systems using anhydrous ammonia or systems using flammable, toxic or highly toxic refrigerants. The system is designed to limit the threat of system overpressurization and subsequent operation of the pressure relief devices. The code requires that pressure relief devices for mechanical refrigeration systems be terminated outdoors and, with some exceptions, discharge through a treatment system, flare or diffusion system. This system, when properly maintained, limits the likelihood of an atmospheric discharge that is due to system overpressurization.

Code Text: *The owner shall maintain an inventory of all required fire-resistance-rated construction, construction installed to resist the passage of smoke and the construction included in Sections 703 through 707 and Sections 602.4.1 and 602.4.2 of the* International Building Code. *Such construction shall be visually inspected by the owner annually and properly repaired, restored or replaced where damaged, altered, breached or penetrated. Records of inspections and repairs shall be maintained. Where concealed, such elements shall not be required to be visually inspected by the owner unless the concealed space is accessible by the removal or movement of a panel, access door, ceiling tile or similar movable entry to the space.*

Discussion and Commentary: Fire-resistance-rated construction is designed to prevent the spread of fire. Unprotected openings in assemblies can significantly impact the ability of the assembly to perform properly. Therefore, these components need to be inspected regularly. Openings or penetrations made in required fire-resistance-rated or smoke-resistant construction must be properly protected with an opening protective or repaired and sealed to maintain the integrity of the building. Required fire protection of assemblies and structural elements with noncombustible protection such as gypsum or sprayed fire-resistant materials also needs to be maintained.

IBC Section 703.5 requires marking on concealed portions of fire-resistance-rated construction and smoke barriers and smoke partitions to alert future maintenance or construction crews that the integrity of the assembly needs to be maintained.

Code Text: *Opening protectives in fire-resistance-rated assemblies shall be inspected and maintained in accordance with NFPA 80. Opening protectives in smoke barriers shall be inspected and maintained in accordance with NFPA 80 and NFPA 105. Openings in smoke partitions shall be inspected and maintained in accordance with NFPA 105. Fire doors and smoke and draft control doors shall not be blocked, obstructed, or otherwise made inoperable. Fusible links shall be replaced promptly whenever fused or damaged. Opening protectives and smoke and draft control doors shall not be modified.*

Discussion and Commentary: The term *opening protectives* refers to fire doors, fire shutters, fire dampers or fire-rated glazing. Listed fire door assemblies include the door frames and are to be either self-closing or automatic-closing. Automatic-closing doors are normally held in the open position by electromagnetic hold-open devices that release the doors to close in case of power failure, fire alarm activation, sprinkler activation or smoke detector activation. Other opening protectives may also be designed to operate in a similar manner such as a temperature-sensitive fusible link installed on a fire damper. Maintenance of opening protectives can require installation of field-applied labels when required by the fire code official.

IBC Section 716 and 717 specify the required fire-resistance rating for fire doors, fire shutters, fire dampers and fire windows based on the fire-resistance rating of the wall or horizontal assembly in which they are installed. This motorized fire damper must meet the specified fire-resistance rating based on the fire-resistance rating of the wall assembly.

Code Text: *The provisions of this section shall limit the allowable fire performance and smoke development of interior wall and ceiling finishes and interior wall and ceiling trim in existing buildings based on location and occupancy classification. Interior wall and ceiling finishes shall be classified in accordance with Section 803 of the* International Building Code. *Such materials shall be classified in accordance with NFPA 286, as indicated in Section 803.1.1, or in accordance with ASTM E84 or UL 723, as indicated in Section 803.1.2.*

Materials tested in accordance with Section 803.1.1 shall not be required to be tested in accordance with Section 803.1.2.

Discussion and Commentary: The IFC recognizes ASTM E84, *Standard Test Method for Surface Burning Characteristics of Building Materials*, UL 723, *Standard for Test Method for Surface Burning Characteristics of Building Materials*, or NFPA 286, *Standard Methods of Fire Tests for Evaluating Contributions of Wall and Ceiling Interior Finish to Room Fire Growth*, as the evaluating criteria for interior wall and ceiling finishes and trim. ASTM E84 and UL 723 are commonly known as the Steiner Tunnel test. The Steiner Tunnel test was developed by Underwriters Laboratories in 1944 for evaluating interior finish materials. The horizontal furnace is used to measure the rate of horizontal fire spread and the optical density of the smoke. The flame spread index (FSI) and smoke development index (SDI) are calculated based on their performance when compared to two control materials: cementitious board (FSI and SDI of 0) and red oak flooring (FSI and SDI of 100).

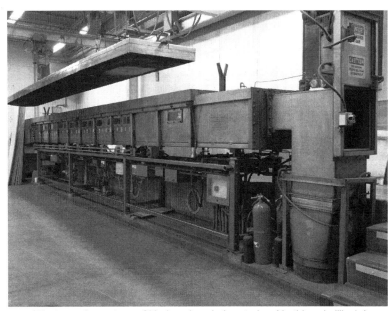

(Photograph courtesy of Underwriters Laboratories, Northbrook, Illinois.)

The UL 723 fire test apparatus, commonly referred to as the Steiner Tunnel Test.

Topic: Acceptance Criteria for NFPA 286	**Category:** Interior Finish, Decorative Materials and Furnishings
Reference: IFC 803.1.1.1	**Subject:** Interior Wall and Ceiling Finish in Existing Buildings

Code Text: *The interior finish shall comply with the following: (1) During the 40 kW exposure, flames shall not spread to the ceiling, (2) The flame shall not spread to the outer extremity of the sample on any wall or ceiling, (3) Flashover, as defined in NFPA 286, shall not occur, (4) The peak heat release rate throughout the test shall not exceed 800 kW, (5) The total smoke released throughout the test shall not exceed 1,000 m^2.*

Discussion and Commentary: The IFC references NFPA 286, *Standard Method of Fire Tests for Evaluating Contribution of Wall and Ceiling Interior Finish to Room Fire Growth.* In this test, three walls and the ceiling (or ceiling only for interior ceiling finishes) are covered with the material to be tested. The material is then heated by a gas burner to 40 kilowatts (kW) for five minutes and then to 160 kW for 10 minutes. For a successful test the flame cannot spread to the extremities of the test sample, and flashover cannot occur. Additionally, the total area of smoke released by the fire cannot exceed 1,000 m^2 over the 15-minute test period.

This photograph shows an NFPA 286 room corner fire test being performed to evaluate a wall covering.

Topic: Interior Finish Requirements Based on Occupancy

Reference: IFC 803.3

Category: Interior Finish, Decorative Materials and Furnishings

Subject: Interior Wall and Ceiling Finish in Existing Buildings

Code Text: *Interior wall and ceiling finish shall have a flame spread index not greater than that specified in Table 803.3 for the group and location designated. Interior wall and ceiling finish materials tested in accordance with NFPA 286, and meeting the acceptance criteria of Section 803.1.1.1, shall be used where a Class A classification in accordance with ASTM E84 or UL 723 is required.*

Discussion and Commentary: Fire statistics show that the rapid spread of fire across noncompliant interior finish materials poses a significant safety issue. Table 803.3 establishes the minimum flame spread index allowed, based on the classification of the occupancy and whether the occupancy is protected throughout by an automatic sprinkler system.

TABLE 803.3
INTERIOR WALL AND CEILING FINISH REQUIREMENTS BY OCCUPANCY [k]

GROUP	SPRINKLERED[l]			NONSPRINKLERED		
	Interior exit stairways and ramps and exit passageways[a, b]	Corridors and enclosure for exit access stairways and ramps	Rooms and enclosed spaces[c]	Interior exit stairways and ramps and exit passageways[a, b]	Corridors and enclosure for exit access stairways and ramps	Rooms and enclosed spaces[c]
A-1 and A-2	B	B	C	A	A[d]	B[e]
A-3[f], A-4, A-5	B	B	C	A	A[d]	C
B, E, M, R-1, R-4	B	C[m]	C	A	B[m]	C
F	C	C	C	B	C	C
H	B	B	C[g]	A	A	B
I-1	B	C	C	A	B	B
I-2	B	B	B[h, i]	A	A	B
I-3	A	A[j]	C	A	A	B
I-4	B	B	B[h, i]	A	A	B
R-2	C	C	C	B	B	C
R-3	C	C	C	C	C	C
S	C	C	C	B	B	C
U	No Restrictions			No Restrictions		

For SI: 1 inch = 25.4 mm, 1 square foot = 0.0929 m²

Footnote "l" permits interior finish materials to be reduced by one class level in vertical exits, exit passageways, corridors, spaces or rooms in buildings sprinklered in accordance with NFPA 13 or, for Group R occupancies up to and including four (4) stories in height, NFPA 13R.

Like the footnotes in most tables in the International Codes, Footnotes "a" through "m" (see the text of the footnotes in the *International Fire Code*) contain requirements or exceptions.

Sections 803.14 and 803.15 permit the use of very thin wall coverings (thickness less than 0.036 inch) and Type IV construction, respectively, neither of which are required to meet flame spread and smoke-development limitations.

Code Text: *The provisions of this chapter shall apply to the installation, operation maintenance, repair, retrofitting, testing, commissioning and decommissioning of energy systems used for generating or storing energy. It shall not apply to equipment associated with the generation, control, transformation, transmission, or distribution of energy installations that is under the exclusive control of an electric utility or lawfully designated agency.*

Discussion and Commentary: Chapter 12 addresses the current technologies for energy systems. It includes requirements for generation and storage of energy, and the design and use of energy systems inside and outside of buildings. The expansion of energy systems is related to meeting today's energy, environmental and economic challenges. Ensuring appropriate criteria to address the safety of such systems in building and fire codes is an important part of protecting the public at large, building occupants and emergency responders. More specifically, this chapter addresses standby and emergency power, portable generators, photovoltaic systems, fuel cell energy systems, battery storage systems and capacitor energy storage.

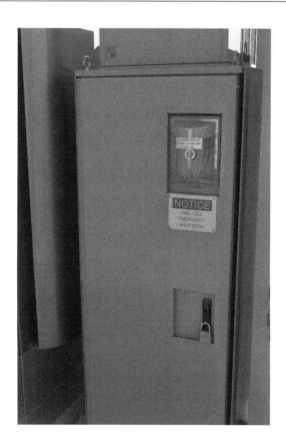

Each of the energy storage and energy generation systems require specific safety features like this manual shutoff for an outdoor fuel cell.

Code Text: *Emergency and standby power systems shall be maintained in accordance with NFPA 110 and NFPA 111 such that the system is capable of supplying service within the time specified for the type and duration required.*

Discussion and Commentary: Emergency power generators and standby power generators provide electricity to certain fire/life safety systems or building functions during a power interruption. They can power items such as fire pumps, fire alarm systems, elevator operation, smoke removal equipment, or ventilation and treatment systems for toxic gas. These generators will be relied upon during an emergency and must be ready to operate at any time.

This section specifies that the power source must be maintained properly to ensure reliability. The two standards referenced, NFPA 110, *Standard for Emergency and Standby Power Systems* and NFPA 111, *Standard on Stored Electrical Energy Emergency and Standby Power Systems*, address different types of secondary power systems and include specific testing and maintenance criteria.

In addition to inspecting the maintenance log for an emergency generator, the fill level of the fuel tank should be checked. This generator sits atop the fuel tank.

Code Text: *Panels and modules installed on Group R-3 buildings shall not be placed on the portion of a roof that is below an emergency escape and rescue opening. A pathway of not less than 36 inches (914 mm) wide shall be provided to the emergency escape and rescue opening.*

Discussion and Commentary: Solar installations are occurring on new buildings and also existing buildings. Where solar photovoltaic systems are installed on Group R-3 occupancies care must be taken not to obstruct or hinder the use of emergency escape and rescue openings.

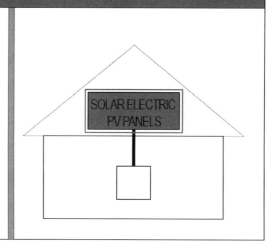

SOLAR PV SYSTEM EQUIPPED WITH RAPID SHUTDOWN

TURN RAPID SHUTDOWN
SWITCH TO THE
"OFF" POSITION TO
SHUT DOWN PV SYSTEM
AND REDUCE
SHOCK HAZARD
IN ARRAY

SOLAR ELECTRIC
PV PANELS

Solar photovoltaic systems mounted on buildings and equipped with a rapid shutdown switch shall be identified with a sign indicating which portions of the solar system are shut down when the switch is thrown (IFC Section 1205.4).

Code Text: ***General.*** *The provisions in this section are applicable to stationary and mobile electrical energy storage systems (ESS).* ***Exception:*** *ESS in Group R-3 and R-4 occupancies shall comply with Section 1207.11.*

Scope. *ESS having capacities exceeding the values shown in Table 1207.1.1 shall comply with this section.*

TABLE 1207.1.1
BATTERY STORAGE SYSTEM THRESHOLD QUANTITIES

TECHNOLOGY	CAPACITY[a]
Capacitor ESS	3 kWh
Flow batteries[b]	20 kWh
Lead acid, all types	70 kWh[c]
Lithium-ion batteries	20 kWh
Nickel metal hydride (Ni-MH)	70 kWh
Nickel cadmium (Ni-Cd)	70 kWh
Other battery technologies	10 kWh
Other electrochemical ESS technologies	3 kWh

a. Energy capacity is the total energy capable of being stored (nameplate rating), not the usable energy rating. For units rated in amp-hours, kWh shall equal rated voltage times amp-hour rating divided by 1,000.

b. Shall include vanadium, zinc-bromine, polysulfide-bromide, and other flowing electrolyte-type technologies.

c. Fifty gallons of lead-acid battery electrolyte shall be considered equivalent to 70 kWh.

Discussion and Commentary: Energy storage systems include a number of different designs, and new technologies are constantly being tested and developed. Table 1207.1.1 identifies the energy storage capacity of the system to determine whether the system needs to comply with the requirements in the code. Note that different technologies have different thresholds since the hazard changes with the technology.

As energy research continues, other types of battery technologies may emerge. Therefore, the last two entries in Table 1207.1.1 are designed to address future designs not currently listed in the code.

While battery storage systems (shown above) are still the most common type of electrical storage method, the IFC also regulates capacitor energy storage systems.

Code Text: *An approved automatic smoke detection system or radiant energy-sensing fire detection system complying with Section 907.2 shall be installed in rooms, indoor areas and walk-in units containing electrochemical ESS. An approved radiant energy-sensing fire detection system shall be installed to protect open parking garage and rooftop installations. Alarm signals from detection systems shall be transmitted to a central station, proprietary or remote station service in accordance with NFPA 72, or where approved to a constantly attended location.*

Discussion and Commentary: All rooms containing an electrochemical energy storage system must be protected with a smoke detection system or a radiant energy-sensing fire detection system, regardless of the type of energy storage technology. Note that energy storage systems are also required to be protected by an automatic fire-extinguishing system in Section 1207.5.5, unless the energy storage system is used exclusively for telecommunication equipment and consists of lead-acid batteries or nickel-cadmium batteries. The smoke detection system is required to provide early notification in the event of an incipient fire. Typically, the radiant energy-sensing detector or smoke detector activates long before the sprinklers when a battery goes into thermal runaway.

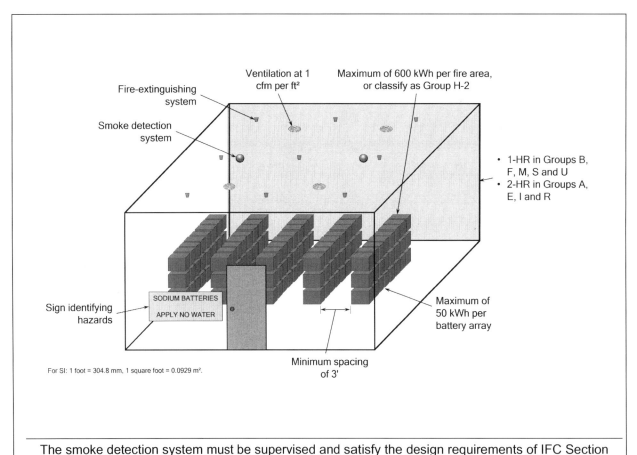

The smoke detection system must be supervised and satisfy the design requirements of IFC Section 907.2.

Quiz

Study Session 5
IFC Chapters 6, 7, 8 and 12

1. A Type I hood is a kitchen hood for collecting and removing _____.

    a. grease vapors and smoke

    b. hazardous production materials

    c. carbon monoxide

    d. toxic fumes

    Reference 202
    Hood

2. In a fuel-fired appliance, a fuel oil containing _____ shall not be used.

    a. diesel fuel   b. gasoline

    c. No. 2 fuel oil   d. waste crankcase oil

    Reference 605.1.3

3. The maximum amount of fuel oil that may be stored outdoors above ground without additional protection is _____ gallons.

    a. 55   b. 100

    c. 660   d. 1,000

    Reference 605.4.1

4. Where Class II or III combustible liquids are stored in complying storage tanks, the maximum amount of fuel oil storage allowed inside an unsprinklered building shall be _____ gallons.

    a. 5   b. 55

    c. 660   d. 3,000

    Reference 605.4.2.2

5. Listed and approved unvented fuel-fired heaters are permitted in _____ .

    a. apartments   b. boarding houses

    c. hotel guest rooms   (d.) one- and two-family dwellings

Reference 605.5
EXC.1

6. Which of the following elevators are required to be provided with a method to prevent sprinkler water from infiltrating the elevator shaft?

    a. fire service access elevator   b. occupant evacuation elevator

    c. all elevators   (d.) both a and b

Reference 604.5.4

7. Emergency and standby power systems are not required for _____ .

    a. 150-ft-high office buildings

    (b) 55-ft-high airport traffic control towers

    c. smoke control systems

    d. emergency responder communication coverage systems

Reference 1203.2

8. The standby power system required for the smoke control system shall pick up its connected loads _____ after failure of the normal power supply.

    a. immediately   b. within 10 seconds

    (c) within 60 seconds   d. within 5 minutes

Reference 1203.1.4
1203.2.18

9. Relocatable power taps and current taps must be directly connected to a permanent receptacle, except

    a In a Group A occupancy, no more than five relocatable power taps can be connected together or connected to an extension cord for temporary use to supply power to electronic equipment when approved by the fire code official.

    b. In a Group B meeting room, no more than five relocatable power taps can be connected together or connected to an extension cord for temporary use to supply power to electronic equipment when approved by the fire code official.

    c. Where used for 90 days or less for the purpose of testing the performance of such power taps or current taps.

    (d.) All of the above

Reference 603.5.2

10. Temporary wiring for electrical power and lighting installations is allowed for a maximum period of _____.

    a. two weeks

    b. 30 days

    c. 90 days

    d. six months

Reference 603.8

11. Mechanical refrigeration systems containing 20 pounds or more of ammonia refrigerant shall discharge vapor to the atmosphere only _____.

    a. through an approved treatment system, flaring system, or ammonia diffusion system

    b. if the point of discharge is located not less than 15 feet above the adjoining grade level

    c. if the point of discharge is at least 20 feet from any window, ventilation opening or exit

    d. when allowed by the *International Mechanical Code*

Reference 608.13.4

12. Refrigeration systems having a refrigerant circuit containing more than 220 pounds of Group A1 or 30 pounds of any other group refrigerant are *not* required to _____.

    a. have a minimum of three paths of egress

    b. periodically test emergency devices

    c. provide a NFPA 704 hazard sign

    d. be provided with access for the fire department

Reference 608.6
608.7
608.8

13. Keys for the elevator car doors and fire-fighter service keys shall be kept _____.

    a. inside the elevator car

    b. in an approved location for immediate use

    c. in the building engineer's office

    d. in an approved key box

Reference 604.6.1

14. Rooms containing energy storage systems shall have a minimum separation from other portions of the building by _____.

    a.   Full height partitions

    b.   1-hour fire-resistance-rated construction

    c.   2-hour fire-resistance-rated construction

    d.   4-hour fire-resistance-rated construction

    Reference 1207.4.3
    1207.7 A

15. Where calculations are not provided, rooms containing lead-acid battery systems with a capacity of more than 70 kWh are to be ventilated at a rate of _____.

    a.   2 air changes per hour

    b.   12 air changes per hour

    c.   0.5 cfm per square foot

    d.   1.0 cfm per square foot

    Reference 1207.6.1
    1207.6

16. Which of the following are required for an energy storage system composed of lithium-ion batteries with a capacity of 200 kWh?

    a.   Exhaust ventilation

    b.   Safety caps

    c.   Spill control and neutralization

    d.   Thermal runaway protection

    Reference 1207.6

17. The hanging and displaying of salable goods and other decorative materials from acoustical ceiling systems that are part of a fire-resistance-rated floor/ceiling or roof/ceiling assembly, is _____.

    a.   limited to noncombustible materials

    b.   limited to a material with a flame spread rating of 25 or less

    c.   limited to 20 percent of the ceiling area

    d.   prohibited

    Reference 701.2.1

18. Solar panels installed on the roof of a Group M building must _____.

    a.   be 4 feet from the edge of the roof when the smallest dimension of the building is 250 feet or less

    b.   be provided with pathways with a clear width of 4 feet

    c.   have the solar panel arrays limited to 150 feet measured along either axis

    d.   meet all of the above requirements

    Reference 1205.3.1
                 1205.3.2

19. When are the access requirements for solar photovoltaic panels installed on roofs of Group R-3 waived by the IFC?

    a.   These requirements are always applicable, regardless of roof construction design.

    b.   The IFC waives the requirements when the roof slope is two units vertical in twelve units horizontal (2:12) or less.

    c.   The IFC waives the requirements when the roof slope is two units vertical in twelve units horizontal (2:12) or more.

    d.   The IFC has no requirements for access to building roofs.

    Reference 1205.2.1
              Exec. 2

20. When is a standardized fire service elevator key required for elevators?

    a.   When the elevator has Phase I emergency recall features.

    b.   When the elevator has Phase II emergency in-car operation.

    c.   When the elevator is designed as a fire service access elevator.

    d.   All of the above.

    Reference 604.6.2

21. Existing fusible-link-type automatic door-closing devices are permitted if the fusible link rating is a maximum of _____.

    a.   100°C   b.   135°F

    c.   165°F   d.   212°F

    Reference 704.3

22. IFC Section 806 applies to _____ .

    a. new buildings

    b. existing buildings

    (c) both new and existing buildings

    d. certain types of new and existing buildings

    Reference _806.1_

23. In Group E occupancies, the amount of artwork and teaching materials on corridor walls is limited to a maximum of _____ percent of the wall area.

    a. 10   b. 15

    (c.) 20   d. 25

    Reference _807.5.2.2_

24. Upholstered furniture belonging to the patient in a sleeping room of a Group I-2 Condition 1 nursing home does not need to resist ignition by cigarettes if _____ .

    a. both c and d are correct

    b. limited to one chair per sleeping room

    c. the room or space is protected by an approved automatic sprinkler system

    (d) a smoke detector is installed in the room

    Reference _805.2.1.1_

25. In Group B ambulatory care facilities, metal waste containers with a capacity of more than 20 gallons shall be _____ .

    a. Listed to UL 1315

    b. Provided with noncombustible lids

    c. Limited to an aggregate density of 0.5 gallons per square foot in an individual room

    (d) All of the above

    Reference _808.1_

26. In which of the following occupancies is a natural cut tree not permitted even if the tree is located in an area protected by an approved automatic sprinkler system?

    a. A   b. E

    (c) I-4   d. R-2

    Reference _806.1.1_
                 Exc.1

27. In Group I-3, combustible decorations _____.

    (a) are prohibited

    b. are allowed in limited quantities

    c. shall not exceed 50 percent of the aggregate wall area

    d. shall be flame resistant

    Reference 807.5.4

28. A Class A interior finish material has a flame spread index of _____.

    (a) 0–25   b. 26–75

    c. 76–200   d. >200

    Reference 803.1.2

29. Chapter 8 of the IFC does not regulate wallpaper in existing buildings, as long as it is applied directly to the surface of walls and ceilings and is not more than _____ inch thick.

    a. 0.01   (b.) 0.036

    c. 0.05   d. 0.125

    Reference 803.1.4

30. What minimum class of interior finish material is allowed in the administrative spaces of a sprinklered Group I-2 hospital?

    a. Class A   b. Class B

    (c.) Class C   d. Class D

    Reference 803.3
                 Footnote b

31. What type of storage tank does the IFC prescribe when storing more than 1,320 gallons of fuel oil inside of a building?

    a. field erected storage tank

    b. shop fabricated storage tank

    c. fire-resistant storage tank

    (d) protected above-ground storage tank

    Reference 605.4.2.2
                 #3

32. Where may portable outdoor gas-fired heating appliances be used?

    a. outdoor locations   b. inside of buildings

    c. inside of tents   d. on exterior balconies

    Reference 605, 5.2.1.1

33. What is the required inspection frequency for a Type I hood in a commercial kitchen over a barbeque smoker using hard pecan wood as a solid fuel?

    a. 3 months   b. 12 months

    c. 1 month   d. 6 months

    Reference Table 606.3.3.1

34. Capacitor energy storage systems are not regulated by the IFC when the system capacity is _____ kWh or less.

    a. 3   b. 20

    c. 50   d. 70

    Reference 1207.1.1

35. Which of the following are required for a vented nickel-cadmium (Ni-Cd) energy storage system?

    a. ventilation   b. spill control and neutralization

    c. thermal runaway protection   d. all of the above

    Reference Table 1207.6

2021 IFC Chapter 9
Fire Protection and Life Safety Systems—Part I

OBJECTIVE: To gain an understanding of the fundamental requirements of the *International Fire Code®* (IFC®) for required fire protection systems, the various types of systems that are required or may be approved by the fire code official, and the IFC requirements for specific occupancies or hazards. Part I covers general requirements for all fire protection systems and specific requirements for automatic sprinkler systems, fire pumps standpipes and smoke management systems.

REFERENCE: Chapter 9, 2021 IFC

KEY POINTS:
- What is the minimum required project documentation for fire protection systems?
- What are the requirements for recalled fire protection system components?
- What are the requirements for acceptance and maintenance inspections of fire protection systems?
- What differentiates the requirements for required versus nonrequired fire protection systems?
- If a fire protection system is impaired or removed from service, what are the requirements during these events?
- Which occupancies require an automatic sprinkler system?
- In what occupancies are NFPA 13, 13R and 13D automatic sprinkler systems required?
- What revisions to the NFPA sprinkler standards are contained in the code?
- When are automatic sprinkler systems required to be monitored, and what are the requirements for alarms and supervisory signals?
- Can there be areas in a building that are not protected with fire sprinklers when the building is considered "sprinklered throughout"?
- How is a "fire area" different from the "floor area" and when does it apply?
- What are the fire protection system requirements for special occupancies and building uses?

KEY POINTS:
(Cont'd)

- Which fire sprinkler systems require a fire department connection and where does it need to be located?

- When is a Class I, II or III standpipe system required in new and existing buildings?

- When can an alternative automatic fire-extinguishing system be used in lieu of an automatic sprinkler system?

- What are the requirements for fire department connections?

- What are the inspection, testing and maintenance requirements for fire pumps?

- How is the fire pump room designed to protect the fire pump and provide for service during a fire? What are the requirements for protecting the electrical circuits serving the fire pump?

- What are the three different methods of mechanical smoke control?

- What are the three different methods of smoke control?

- What are the required elements for acceptance of a smoke control system?

- What are the areas of focus for an existing smoke control system?

- How is the total required vent area determined for smoke and heat vents in a building?

- What are the design and installation requirements for smoke and heat vents and mechanical smoke removal systems?

- What are the inspection, testing and maintenance requirements for fire pumps?

- What are the fire protection system requirements for special occupancies and building uses?

- What are the design and installation requirements for smoke and heat vents?

- What is a "limited area sprinkler system" and how can one be utilized?

- When a building contains multiple fire protection or life safety systems which are interconnected, how are the systems tested?

- Who is the impairment coordinator, and what are their duties?

Code Text: *Fire protection and life safety systems required by this code or the* International Building Code *shall be installed, repaired, operated, tested and maintained in accordance with this code. A fire protection or life safety system for which a design option, exception or reduction to the provisions of this code or the* International Building Code *has been granted shall be considered to be a required system.*

Discussion and Commentary: The IFC requires the installation of fire protection systems and life safety systems in a number of occupancies and uses. Additionally, fire protection or life safety systems may be installed at the desire of the owner, designer or insurance carrier. The IFC and *International Building Code®* (IBC®) both allow modification of a significant number of requirements based on the installation of an automatic sprinkler system. Even though the code does not require the installation of an automatic sprinkler system, if such a system is installed and the building design or operations are modified because of the sprinkler system, then the automatic sprinkler system becomes a required system.

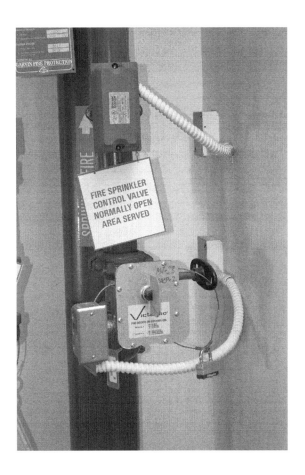

The installation of an automatic sprinkler system allows modifications to many code requirements in the IFC and IBC.

Code Text: *Fire protection and life safety systems or portion thereof not required by this code or the* International Building Code *shall be allowed to be furnished for partial or complete protection provided that such installed systems meet the applicable requirements of this code and the* International Building Code.

Discussion and Commentary: Design professionals may choose to add additional fire protection or life safety systems that are not required by the IFC. This may result from a hazard analysis that shows the risk of fire to the business is greater than the risk accepted by the IFC. For example, many firms with computer networks chose to install clean agent fire suppression systems in computer rooms that are normally not required. Even if the fire protection or life safety system is not required, it must comply with the requirements of the IFC and the IBC.

Nonrequired fire protection and life safety systems are subject to inspection, maintenance and testing in accordance with IFC Section 901.6. If the owner elects to remove a nonrequired fire protection system, this is allowed by IFC Section 901.6. Note that a permit is required to remove a nonrequired automatic fire-extinguishing or fire alarm and detection system.

Code Text: ***Inspection, testing and maintenance.*** *Fire protection and life safety systems shall be maintained in an operative condition at all times, and shall be replaced or repaired where defective. Nonrequired fire protection and life safety systems and equipment shall be inspected, tested and maintained or removed in accordance with Section 901.8.*

Standards. *Fire protection systems shall be inspected, tested and maintained in accordance with the referenced standards listed in Table 901.6.1.*

TABLE 901.6.1
FIRE PROTECTION SYSTEM MAINTENANCE STANDARDS

SYSTEM	STANDARD
Portable fire extinguishers	NFPA 10
Carbon dioxide fire-extinguishing systems	NFPA 12
Halon 1301 fire-extinguishing systems	NFPA 12A
Dry-chemical extinguishing systems	NFPA 17
Wet-chemical extinguishing systems	NFPA 17A
Water-based fire protection systems	NFPA 25
Fire alarm systems	NFPA 72
Smoke and heat vents	NFPA 204
Water-mist systems	NFPA 750
Clean-agent extinguishing systems	NFPA 2001
Aerosol fire-extinguishing systems	NFPA 2010

Discussion and Commentary: The installation of fire protection and life safety systems must meet the design criteria at the time of installation and acceptance testing, and must continually be maintained to ensure reliability and operability throughout the life of the project. For example, fire alarm systems require recalibration of smoke detectors one year after installation, and fire pumps must be tested to determine that minimum flows and pressures continue to be provided.

Required fire protection systems must be maintained so that they are available in the event of ignition and a subsequent fire. Section 901.6 specifies that nonrequired systems must also be maintained and inspected, or removed from the building if they are not maintained.

The frequency for inspections and the specific testing criteria varies from system to system. However, all standards require that the fire protection system be inspected, tested and maintained.

(Photograph courtesy of Professional Development Inc.)

The types of tests are dictated by the applicable codes and standards governing each system. It is common to use one or more standards for a single building. For example, the automatic sprinkler system in a six-story office building is regulated by NFPA 13, the standpipe system is under NFPA 14, and the fire pump is under NFPA 20.

Code Text: *Where two or more fire protection or life safety systems are interconnected, the intended response of subordinate fire protection and life safety systems shall be verified when required testing of the initiating system is conducted. In addition, integrated testing shall be performed in accordance with Sections 901.6.2.1 and 901.6.2.2.*

Discussion and Commentary: The IFC requires proper operation of all fire protection and life safety systems within a building, even nonrequired systems (see Section 901.6). In many cases, such as monitoring the fire sprinkler system with the fire alarm system and notifying a monitoring service when a fire sprinkler operates, the integration is relatively simple. However in some cases, such as a fire alarm system initiating a complex combination of door closures, damper operations, elevator captures and fan activations in a high-rise building, the integration can be highly complex, and in most cases it involves the coordination of many different trades, control units and systems. This section requires integrated testing of these interconnected systems.

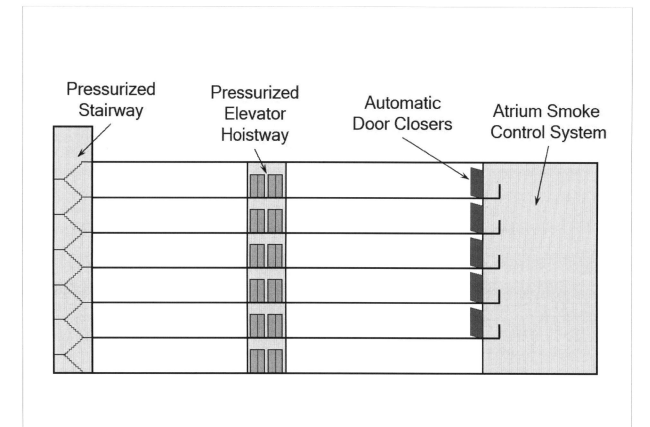

Multiple systems must be inspected and tested to work both independently and simultaneously, and in the correct operating sequence.

Code Text: *Any fire protection system component regulated by this code that is the subject of a voluntary or mandatory recall under federal law shall be replaced with approved, listed components in compliance with the referenced standards of this code. The fire code official shall be notified in writing by the building owner when the recalled component parts have been replaced.*

Discussion and Commentary: This provision requires that fire protection components recalled by the manufacturer or the Consumer Products Safety Commission are replaced with listed components that comply with the applicable standard and that the fire code official is notified when the replacement process is completed. This section specifically states that the items must be replaced regardless of whether it is a 'mandatory' recall or a 'voluntary' recall.

Gems Sensors Recalls Pressure Transducers Used in Fire Pump Controllers Due to Risk of Failure in a Fire

FOR IMMEDIATE RELEASE
April 24, 2012
Release #12-156

Firm's Recall Hotline: (855) 877-9666
CPSC Recall Hotline: (800) 638-2772
CPSC Media Contact: (301) 504-7908

Gems Sensors Recalls Pressure Transducers Used in Fire Pump Controllers Due to Risk of Failure in a Fire

WASHINGTON, D.C. - The U.S. Consumer Product Safety Commission, in cooperation with the firm named below, today announced a voluntary recall of the following consumer product. Consumers should stop using recalled products immediately unless otherwise instructed. It is illegal to resell or attempt to resell a recalled consumer product.

Name of Product: Gems 3100 Pressure Detectors/Transducers

Units: About 25,000

Importer: Gems Sensors Inc., of Plainville, Conn.

Hazard: The transducer can fail to accurately detect water pressure in a fire suppression sprinkler system. This could cause the sprinkler system to fail to activate and pump water to the sprinklers in the event of a fire.

Incidents/Injuries: None.

Description: The Gems 3100 Pressure Transducer is used to detect pressure in a range of applications, including the detection of water pressure as part of a fire pump controller in a fire suppression sprinkler system. The transducer has "Gems Sensors & Controls," as well as the 18- digit part number, printed on a label affixed to the center of the transducer. Part numbers beginning with "3100" are included in this recall.

Sold by: Gems sold the recalled 3100 Pressure Transducers directly to end-users and through distributors from January 2006 through February 2012 for about $250.

Manufactured in: England

Remedy: Contact Gems to receive enhanced twice monthly inspection instructions and information about a free replacement transducer, when warranted. End-users who use the 3100 Pressure Transducer in other applications in which water pressure is measured should contact Gems to determine if their units are affected.

Consumer Contact: For additional information, call the company toll-free at (855) 877-9666, between 8 a.m. and 4:30 p.m. ET, Monday through Friday, or visit the firm's website at http://www.gemssensors.com

Gems 3100 Pressure Transducer

The U.S. Consumer Product Safety Commission is charged with protecting the public from unreasonable risks of injury or death associated with the use of thousands of types of consumer products under the agency's jurisdiction. Deaths, injuries, and property damage from consumer product incidents cost the nation more than $1 trillion annually. CPSC is committed to protecting consumers and families from products that pose a fire, electrical, chemical or mechanical hazard. CPSC's work to help ensure the safety of consumer products - such as toys, cribs, power tools, cigarette lighters and household chemicals — contributed to a decline in the rate of deaths and injuries associated with consumer products over the past 40 years.

Federal law bars any person from selling products subject to a publicly-announced voluntary recall by a manufacturer or a mandatory recall ordered by the Commission.

To report a dangerous product or a product-related injury go online to www.SaferProducts.gov or call CPSC's Hotline at (800) 638-2772 or teletypewriter at (301) 595-7054 for the hearing impaired. Consumers can obtain news release and recall information at www.cpsc.gov, on Twitter @USCPSC or by subscribing to CPSC's free e-mail newsletters.

The recall above is a "voluntary" recall. The Consumer Products Safety Commission maintains an internet-accessible database of all recalls initiated by the agency at www.cpsc.gov.

Code Text: *An automatic sprinkler system shall be provided throughout stories containing Group A-3 occupancies and throughout all stories from the Group A-3 occupancy to and including the levels of exit discharge serving that occupancy where one of the following conditions exists: (1) The fire area exceeds 12,000 square feet (1115 m²), (2) The fire area has an occupant load of 300 or more, (3) The fire area is located on a floor other than a level of exit discharge serving such occupancies.*

Discussion and Commentary: With the exception of Group A-5 occupancies, the threshold at which an automatic sprinkler system is required in Group A occupancies depends on three independent variables: (1) The fire area of the assembly use; (2) The occupant load, and; (3) The location of the assembly occupancy in relation to the level of exit discharge. In the case of Group A-1 occupancies that are constructed as a multiple-theater complex, an automatic sprinkler system is required regardless of the fire area. Once the threshold requiring an automatic sprinkler system is crossed, the sprinkler system must be installed on the entire story, the stories between that story and the levels of exit discharge serving that story and the level of exit discharge.

Compared to other assembly occupancies, IFC Section 903.2.1.2 lowers the occupant load threshold from 300 to 100 for assembly occupancies intended for food or drink consumption because of the increased hazard in such occupancies.

Code Text: *An automatic sprinkler system shall be installed throughout the entire floor containing an ambulatory care facility where either of the following conditions exist at any time: (1) Four or more care recipients are incapable of self-preservation, (2) One or more care recipients that are incapable of self-preservation are located at other than the level of exit discharge serving such a facility.*

*In buildings where ambulatory care is provided on levels other than the level of exit discharge, an automatic sprinkler system shall be installed throughout the entire floor as well as all floors below where such care is provided, and all floors between the level of ambulatory care and the nearest level of exit discharge, the level of exit discharge, and all floors below the level of exit discharge. **Exception:** Floors classified as an open parking garage are not required to be sprinklered.*

Discussion and Commentary: This section establishes minimum code requirements for ambulatory care facilities, which are classified by the IBC as Group B occupancies. However, because individuals are not capable of self-preservation, these requirements provide fire and life safety provisions beyond those typically found in Group B occupancies. The IFC requires the installation of automatic sprinkler systems and automatic fire detection and signaling systems to provide early notification and control of fires in these occupancies.

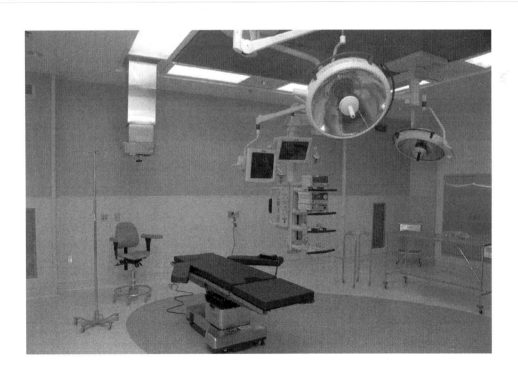

The definition for the term "Incapable of Self-preservation" is "persons who, because of age, physical limitations, mental limitations, chemical dependency or medical treatment, cannot respond as an individual to an emergency situation" (IFC Section 202).

Code Text: *An automatic sprinkler system shall be provided throughout a Group F-1 fire area used for the manufacture of distilled spirits.*

Discussion and Commentary: The manufacturing of distilled spirits can be a hazardous situation. Many new facilities are constructed with a restaurant, or other Group A occupancy, accessory to the distillery. The manufacturing of distilled spirits is specifically classified as Group F-1. Even though some of the process may handle flammable liquids above the maximum allowable quantity per control area, as long as the process complies with the IFC it is not classified as Group H—it is a Group F-1 occupancy.

Since these facilities are now classified as Group F-1, all new distilleries are required to be sprinklered. This section does not provide for a minimum threshold; it requires all distilleries to be sprinklered. The requirement in this section is different than the general requirement for Group F-1 occupancies in that Section 903.2.4 requires the entire building to be sprinklered, this section only requires the fire area to be sprinklered.

All new distilleries must be equipped with an automatic sprinkler system. Additionally, new requirements in Chapter 40 address the storage of distilled spirits.

Code Text: *An automatic sprinkler system shall be installed in Group H occupancies.*

Discussion and Commentary: Group H occupancies present the most significant challenge to emergency responders. Accordingly, these occupancies require automatic sprinkler protection. Though the storage and manufacturing of explosives is relatively rare, code officials who must deal with explosive hazards (Group H-1 occupancies) will be questioned on the requirements for sprinklers. Fire code officials should recognize that hazards such as mass detonation, mass deflagration or mass fire explosives cannot, or are difficult at best to, be controlled with automatic sprinklers. Accordingly, the code official should require a technical opinion and report in these instances in accordance with Section 104.8.2. When requiring sprinklers in Group H occupancies, only the occupancy is required to be sprinklered.

If a building is classified a Group H-4 occupancy because it contains corrosive solids or liquids, corrosion-resistant sprinklers and piping should be considered. Certain chlorine-based compounds can liberate a very weak form of chlorine that can attack and corrode brass sprinkler frames and carbon steel pipe and pipe hangers.

Code Text: *Group M. An automatic sprinkler system shall be provided throughout buildings containing a Group M occupancy where one of the following conditions exists: (1) A Group M fire area exceeds 12,000 square feet (1115 m²), (2) A Group M fire area is located more than three stories above grade plane, (3) The combined area of all Group M fire areas on all floors, including any mezzanines, exceeds 24,000 square feet (2230 m²).*

Group M upholstered furniture or mattresses. An automatic sprinkler system shall be provided throughout a Group M fire area where the area used for the display and sale of upholstered furniture or mattresses exceeds 5,000 square feet (464 m²).

Discussion and Commentary: The sprinkler threshold for Group M occupancy buildings is nearly identical to the thresholds for Group F-1 and S-1 occupancies. This is owing to similar size and types of fuel packages in these occupancies. It is notable that the amount of flammable and combustible liquids inside of these occupancies can be increased significantly in IFC Chapter 57 when compared to the maximum allowable quantities in Chapter 50. However, the amounts in IFC Table 5704.3.4.1 are based on the low loss fire history in these occupancies, the use of metal packaging and the container volumes being less than 55 gallons.

Section 903.2.7.2 addresses retail occupancies with upholstered furniture or mattresses. Once the display and sale area for upholstered furniture exceeds 5,000 square feet, the fire area must be sprinklered. This is different than the requirement in Section 903.2.7, which requires the entire building to be sprinklered.

When Group M occupancies are equipped with an automatic sprinkler system, NFPA 13 requires them to be designed using a minimum Ordinary Hazard Group II discharge density and design area.

Code Text: *An automatic sprinkler system installed in accordance with Section 903.3 shall be provided throughout all buildings with a Group R fire area.*

Discussion and Commentary: This provision applies to hotels, motels, apartments and group homes because these are regulated by the IBC. The provision does not apply to one- and two-family dwellings and townhomes which are regulated by the *International Residential Code*® (IRC®).

Depending on the building's height and occupancy classification, residential buildings can be protected with a sprinkler system designed to NFPA 13, 13R or 13D.

Topic: Mechanical-access Enclosed Parking Garages	**Category:** Fire Protection and Life Safety Systems
Reference: IFC 903.2.10.2	**Subject:** Automatic Sprinkler Systems

Code Text: *An approved automatic sprinkler system shall be provided throughout buildings used for the storage of motor vehicles in a mechanical-access enclosed parking garage. The portion of the building that contains the mechanical-access enclosed parking garage shall be protected with a specially engineered automatic sprinkler system.*

Discussion and Commentary: Enclosed mechanical-access parking facilities are being constructed on an increasing basis because storage of vehicles is denser, allowing a smaller building footprint. Mechanical-access parking garages are defined in the IBC as "An enclosed parking garage that employs parking machines, lifts, elevators or other mechanical devices for vehicle moving from and to street level and in which public occupancy in the garage is prohibited in all areas except the vehicle access bay." This definition specifically excludes parking facilities where the vehicle owner drives to the parking space and the vehicle is hoisted 6 feet, so another vehicle can park beneath. Mechanical-access parking facilities pick up the vehicle and move it to the parking space for storage and then retrieve it when the customer is ready to use the vehicle.

The facilities typically have multiple tiers and very limited access for interior fire-fighting operations. Therefore, they are required to be provided with an automatic sprinkler system.

(Photograph courtesy of Paul Armstrong, Paul Armstrong Code Consulting Services.)

This relatively small mechanical-access parking garage it must still meet all the requirements in the IFC and IBC which include sprinklers, 2-hour separation from attached occupancies, mechanical smoke removal, and emergency shut down of the automated operation.

Code Text: *An automatic sprinkler system shall be installed throughout buildings that have one or more stories with an occupant load of 30 or more located 55 feet (16 764 mm) or more above the lowest level of fire department vehicle access, measured to the finished floor.* **Exception:** *Occupancies in Group F-2.*

Discussion and Commentary: This provision requires automatic sprinklers in most buildings where the finished floor level of the upper story is 55 feet or more above the level of fire department vehicle access, and has an occupant load of 30 or more. The requirement is based on the difficulties of manual fire-fighting operations at multiple levels above grade. A building between 55 and 75 feet above a fire department access roadway is not classified as a high-rise building in accordance with IBC Section 403; accordingly, it does not require all of the other fire protection and life safety features prescribed for a high-rise building.

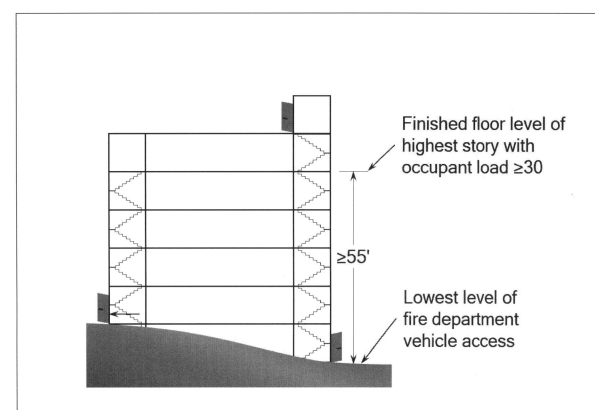

Finished floor level of highest story with occupant load ≥30

≥55'

Lowest level of fire department vehicle access

For SI: 1 foot = 304.8 mm.

This provision is based on finished floor level height and occupant load and applies to all occupancies except Groups F-2 and U (IFC Sections 902.3.11 and 902.11.3).

Code Text: *Automatic sprinklers shall not be required in the following rooms or areas where such rooms or areas are protected with an approved automatic fire detection system in accordance with Section 907.2 that will respond to visible or invisible particles of combustion. Sprinklers shall not be omitted from a room merely because it is damp, of fire-resistance-rated construction or contains electrical equipment.*

(See IFC Section 903.3.1.1.1 Items 1 through 6).

Discussion and Commentary: This section allows the omission of automatic sprinklers in certain areas of buildings when the area is provided with an automatic fire detection system. Consider an acetylene charging plant. NFPA 51A specifically prohibits the installation of automatic sprinklers in calcium carbide storage areas because water mixed with calcium carbide forms acetylene, a flammable gas that is also an unstable (reactive) material unless it is chemically stabilized. In such a case, the sprinklers can be omitted using Item 1 as the basis for approving the design.

Where sprinklers are omitted from the locations specified in Section 903.3.1.1.1, the room or area is required to be equipped with a fire detection system.

Topic: NFPA 13R Sprinkler Systems	**Category:** Fire Protection and Life Safety Systems
Reference: IFC 903.3.1.2	**Subject:** Automatic Sprinkler Systems

Code Text: *Automatic sprinkler systems in Group R occupancies shall be permitted to be installed throughout in accordance with NFPA 13R where the Group R occupancy meets all of the following conditions: (1) Four stories or less above grade plane, (2) The floor level of the highest story is 30 feet (9144 mm) or less above the lowest level of fire department vehicle access, (3) The floor level of the lowest story is 30 feet (9144 mm) or less below the lowest level of fire department vehicle access.*

The number of stories of Group R occupancies constructed in accordance with Sections 510.2 and 510.4 of the International Building Code *shall be measured from grade plane.*

Discussion and Commentary: Section 903.2.8 requires that all Group R occupancies be sprinklered. In a Group R occupancy, the sprinkler design could be based on NFPA 13 or NFPA 13R, depending on the building design. This section specifies when NFPA 13R can be utilized as the design standard.

The sprinkler system can be designed to NFPA 13R if all of the following criteria are met:

- The upper floor of the Group R occupancy is no more than four stories above grade plane.
- The upper floor level is no more than 30 feet above the lowest level of fire department vehicle access.
- The lowest floor level is no more than 30 below the lowest level of fire department vehicle access.

Typically, other sections of the code will measure stories below grade to the highest level of fire department vehicle access. This section measures both the 30 feet above, and the 30 feet below, from the lowest level of fire department vehicle access.

The NFPA 13R standard is scoped to be applicable to this building, but the IFC specifically limits the use of NFPA 13R and under the IFC this building must be sprinklered with NFPA 13. IFC Section 102.7.1 states that when a conflict occurs between the code and the standard, the language in the code prevails.

Code Text: *Valves controlling the water supply for automatic sprinkler systems, pumps, tanks, water levels and temperatures, critical air pressures, and waterflow switches on all sprinkler systems shall be electrically supervised by a listed fire alarm control unit.*

(See IFC Section 903.4 for Exceptions 1 through 8.)

Discussion and Commentary: Fire loss data confirms that the primary reason for automatic sprinkler system failure is the water supply being shut off. Although NFPA 13 requires all control valves to be the indicating type, closed valves, or partially closed valves, still occur. Accordingly, the IFC requires that system control valves be electrically supervised. Supervision is commonly in the form of valve tamper switches, which are listed devices designed to send an electrical signal to a fire alarm control unit indicating that a valve is closed.

IFC Section 903.4 contains eight exceptions that address water supply valves for NFPA 13R and 13D systems, control valves for local hazards such as commercial cooking kitchen hoods and spray booths, and trim valves on sprinkler risers or fire pump pressure maintenance pumps.

Topic: Required Installations Based on Height   **Category:** Fire Protection and Life Safety Systems
Reference: IFC 905.3.1   **Subject:** Standpipe Systems

Code Text: *Class III standpipe systems shall be installed throughout buildings where any of the following conditions exist: (1) Four or more stories are above or below grade plane, (2) The floor level of the highest story is located more than 30 feet (9144 mm) above the lowest level of the fire department vehicle access, (3) The floor level of the lowest story is located more than 30 feet (9144 mm) below the highest level of fire department vehicle access.*

(See IFC Section 905.3.1 Exceptions 1 through 6.2.)

Discussion and Commentary: Fire attack handline deployment is dependent on the staffing level of the fire department and the location of the fire. Once beyond the third floor, handline deployment using conventional methods such as deployment of ladders becomes more challenging. Accordingly, the IFC requires a Class III standpipe when the building is more than 30 feet above or below the level of fire department vehicle access, or when the building is four or more stories above or below the level of fire department vehicle access.

Hose connections need to be accessible for use by the fire department.

Code Text: *Smoke and heat vents or a mechanical smoke removal system shall be installed as required by Sections 910.2.1 and 910.2.2. **Exceptions:** (1) Frozen food warehouses used solely for storage of Class I and II commodities where protected by an approved automatic sprinkler system, (2) Smoke and heat removal shall not be required in areas of buildings equipped with early suppression fast-response (ESFR) sprinklers, (3) Smoke and heat removal shall not be required in areas of buildings equipped with control mode special application sprinklers with a response time index of 50 $(m \times s)^{1/2}$ or less that are listed to control a fire in stored commodities with 12 or fewer sprinklers.*

Discussion and Commentary: The IFC requires smoke and heat vents or a mechanical smoke removal system in certain Group F-1 and S-1 occupancies and in most buildings with high-piled combustible storage. Smoke and heat vents are designed to automatically open and vent smoke and fire gases from the building. Smoke and heat removal is not required in frozen food warehouses storing Class I and II commodities that are sprinklered. Smoke and heat removal is also not required in buildings protected with control mode special application sprinklers with an RTI of 50 or less or ESFR sprinklers since the sprinkler design is tested to control the fire in an unvented building.

IFC Section 910.3.1 requires smoke and heat vents to be listed and labeled in accordance with UL 793 or FM 4430.

Code Text: *The mechanical smoke removal system shall be sized to exhaust the building at a minimum rate of two air changes per hour based upon the volume of the building or portion thereof without contents. The capacity of each exhaust fan shall not exceed 30,000 cubic feet per minute (14.2 m³/s).*

Discussion and Commentary: Mechanical smoke removal systems are a design alternative to smoke and heat vents. The mechanical smoke removal system is to provide a minimum of two air changes per hour calculated on the volume of the empty building. Once product is moved into the building, this ventilation rate may be closer to four air changes per hour as a result of the volume occupied by the product. IFC Section 910.4.5 requires that the controls for the smoke removal fans be located in a room protected by one-hour fire-resistance-rated construction that is accessible from the exterior. This control room allows the fire department to ventilate the building without placing fire fighters on the roof.

The maximum size of each smoke removal fan cannot exceed 30,000 cfm. This increases the number of fans and provides for an even distribution throughout the roof area.

Code Text: *Fire department connections shall be located on the street side of buildings or facing approved fire apparatus access roads, fully visible and recognizable from the street, fire apparatus access road or nearest point of fire department vehicle access or as otherwise approved by the fire code official.*

Discussion and Commentary: Use of the fire department connection (FDC) is an important step during fire-fighting operations. This section requires that the FDC be located along the street or access road and visible to the responding apparatus. This allows for the establishment of quick connection to allow the fire equipment to increase the effectiveness of the fire sprinkler system.

IFC Section 912.2.2 requires signs identifying the location of the FDC where it is not visible to approaching fire apparatus.

Quiz

Study Session 6

IFC Chapter 9—Part I

1. What is the requirement for an automatic sprinkler system in a mechanical-access enclosed parking garage classified as a Group S-2 occupancy?

    a. Sprinklers only throughout the fire area containing the mechanical-access parking garage.

    b. Sprinklers throughout the building containing the mechanical-access parking garage.

    c. Sprinklers only throughout the fire area when the fire area exceeds 12,000 ft².

    d. Sprinklers throughout the building when the fire area exceeds 48,000 ft²

    Reference 903.2.10.

2. Which of the following organizations is required to be notified in the event of a planned or emergency impairment of a fire protection system?

    a. Notifications are not required.   b. Fire Department

    c. Police Department   d. Building Department

    Reference 901.7

3. Given: A nightclub of 3,500 square feet with fixed seating. The club is located in a one-story building. The occupant load for the building is 117. Does the building require an automatic sprinkler system?

    a. yes

    b. no, because its occupant load is < 300

    c. no, because its area is < 5,000 ft²

    d. no, because the level of exit discharge is at the grade level of the building

    Reference 903.2.1.2

4. Given: A fire area of 27,000 square feet housing a plastics manufacturing plant classified as a Group F-1 occupancy. The one-story building will not contain high-piled combustible storage. Does the building require an automatic sprinkler system?

    a. yes, because it exceeds the fire area limitation

    b. yes, because it is manufacturing a hazardous material

    c. yes, because it contains plastics

    d. no, because the level of exit discharge is on the first floor of the building

Reference 903.2.4

5. Given: A Group M grocery store of 18,200 square feet is divided into two equal fire areas by a two-hour fire barrier. The building height is one story. The architect wants to know if the building requires an automatic sprinkler system based on IFC requirements.

    a. yes, because it exceeds the fire area limitation

    b. yes, because they installed a fire barrier and not a fire wall

    c. no, unless the store will have high-piled storage

    d. yes, because it has an occupant load of > 300

Reference 903.2.7

6. Given: A one story 8,000 square foot vehicle repair shop. The building has a basement of 5,400 square feet used for the repair of electric hybrid cars. Does the building require an automatic sprinkler system if the building is a single fire area?

    a. yes, because the total area exceeds 10,000 ft^2

    b. yes, because repairs occur in the basement

    c. no, because of the building area

    d. both a and b are correct

Reference 903.2.9.1

7. An automatic sprinkler system is required in a fire area of a Group M occupancy when upholstered furniture or mattresses are displayed _____.

    a. and the area of upholstered furniture exceeds 12,000 ft^2

    b. and the area of upholstered furniture exceeds 5,000 ft^2

    c. and the occupancy has an area over 5,000 ft^2

    d. and the occupancy has an area over 2,500 ft^2

Reference 903.2.7.2

8. What is the requirement for an automatic sprinkler system in Group F-1 occupancies manufacturing distilled spirits?

    a. Sprinklers throughout the fire area regardless of size.

    b. Sprinklers throughout the fire area if the fire area exceeds 2,500 ft².

    c. Sprinklers throughout the building when the fire area exceeds 12,000 ft².

    d. Both a and c are correct.

    Reference 903.2.4.2 / 903.2.4

9. Which of the following sprinkler system components requires electronic monitoring?

    a. jockey pump control valves locked in the open position

    b. sealed control valves to commercial cooking hoods

    c. a sprinkler control valve for a paint spray booth that is locked in the open position

    d. sprinkler control valve for the second floor in a 3-story building

    Reference 903.4

10. Which of the following existing buildings require an automatic sprinkler system to be retroactively installed?

    a. it is a Group A-2 occupancy with an occupant load of 425

    b. it is a Group I-2 occupancy

    c. it is a high-rise building with an occupied floor 145 feet above the lowest level of fire department vehicle access

    d. all of the above

    Reference 903.6, 1103.5.1, 1103.5.4, 1105.9

11. Which of the following is a required condition to allow the fire code official to approve the removal of occupant-use hose lines in an existing building?

    a. the occupant-use hose lines are not being maintained as required

    b. the hose lines would not be utilized by fire department personnel or on-site trained employees

    c. the outlets must be capped or sealed

    d. the building is protected with an automatic fire sprinkler system throughout

    Reference 901.8.2

12. When is a Class III standpipe required in a Group M occupancy

    a. when the highest floor level is over 30 feet above the lowest level of FD vehicle access

    b. a standpipe is not required

    c. when the building has 4 or more stories

    d. both a and c are correct

Reference 905.3.1

13. Is a standpipe required in an existing building?

    a. the code has no retroactive provisions

    b. yes, where there is an occupied floor more than 50 feet below the highest level of fire department vehicle access

    c. yes, where the highest occupied floor level is more than 50 feet above the lowest level of fire department vehicle access

    d. both b and c are correct

Reference 905.17 / 1103.6.1

14. Given: A building has multiple risers for the Class I standpipe hose connections. Which of the following buildings require the standpipes to be interconnected?

    a. Building containing either a Group A-1 or A-2 occupancy

    b. High-rise Group B occupancy

    c. Covered mall

    d. Interconnection is required in all buildings

Reference 905.4.2

15. What type of automatic sprinkler eliminates the requirement for smoke and heat removal?

    a. ordinary response

    b. quick response

    c. early suppression fast response

    d. control mode special application with RTI of 65

Reference 910.2

16. Given: A one-story building with a floor area of 3,000 square feet that will be used as a nightclub. The building has an occupant load of 189 persons and will serve food and alcoholic beverages. What is the occupancy classification of the building, and is an automatic sprinkler system required?

    a. A-1, A-2; no   b. A-2; yes

    c. A-3; no   d. A-3; yes

    Reference 903.7.1.2

17. Given: A one-story building with a floor area of 11,200 square feet that is used for woodworking operations. The manufacturing process will produce finely divided combustible waste. What is the occupancy classification of the building, and is an automatic sprinkler system required?

    a. Group F-1; yes   b. Group F-1; no

    c. Group B; yes   d. Group B; no

    Reference 903.2.4.1

18. Given: A new multistory building is planned which will have an electric fire pump to supply the fire sprinkler system and standpipe system, and the fire pump will be located within the building. Which of the following is not required for the fire pump room?

    a. Construction of the room in accordance with the IBC

    b. Maintain the temperature in the fire pump room above 40°F

    c. The electric cables outside of the fire pump room must be protected for a 1-hour fire exposure

    d. The fire pump must located in the fire command center

    Reference 913

19. What is the minimum automatic sprinkler system design criterion for the exit corridors in a semiconductor fabrication facility storing and handling hazardous product materials in excess of the maximum allowable quantities?

    a. Light Hazard   b. Ordinary Hazard Group 1

    c. Ordinary Hazard Group 2   d. Extra Hazard Group 2

    Reference 903.2.5.2

20. Given: A 100,000-square-foot Group S-1 occupancy used for the storage of Class IV commodities. The ceiling height is 27 feet. The design professional designed a mechanical smoke removal system, and each fan is rated at an exhaust capacity of 30,000 CFM. How many fans are required?

    a. 2   b. 3

    c. 10   d. 12

    Reference 910.4.3

21. Based on the commodity classification, which of the following does *not* require smoke and heat removal?

    a. Class I commodities

    b. Class II commodities

    c. Group C plastics

    d. Class I and II commodities that are frozen foods

    Reference 910.2

22. Group F-1 and S-1 occupancies do not require a smoke and heat removal system when the undivided area of the building is a maximum of _____.

    a. 25,000 ft²   b. 50,000 ft²

    c. 75,000 ft²   d. 100,000 ft²

    Reference 910.2.1

23. Smoke and heat vents shall be a minimum of _____ feet from fire walls.

    a. 4   b. 8

    c. 10   d. 20

    Reference 910.3.2

24. The required aggregate vent area in square feet for a sprinklered 60,000-square-foot Group F-1 occupancy with a ceiling height of 24 feet is _____ square feet.

    a. 100   b. 160

    c. 200   d. 1,600

    Reference 910.3.3

25. An unsprinklered Group B occupancy utilizes a natural gas-fired furnace with a rating of 460,000 Btu per hour input. The building is of Type VB construction, so the designer decides to utilize a limited area sprinkler system to protect the furnace room. Which of the following is incorrect about protection of this incidental use?

    a. hydraulic calculations shall demonstrate that available water flow and pressure are adequate to supply all sprinklers installed in the furnace room

    b. the limited area sprinkler system in the furnace room is allowed to have a maximum of six sprinklers in the fire area

    c. since the supply is the domestic plumbing system, there is no limitation or requirements on the valves in the system

    d. the piping for the sprinklers can be supplied by the domestic water system in the building provided it is capable of supplying the domestic and sprinkler demands

    Reference 903.3.8.4

26. What is the required temperature resistance for conductors supplying power to mechanical smoke removal systems?

    a. 500°F for 10 minutes   b. 500°F for 15 minutes

    c. 1,000°F for 10 minutes   d. 1,000°F for 15 minutes

    Reference 910.4.6

27. Given: Mechanical exhaust fans are being installed for smoke removal in a sprinklered Group S-1 occupancy with high-piled combustible storage. Which of the following is incorrect about the operation of the mechanical smoke removal system?

    a. The exhaust fans can be used as part of the normal building ventilation system, provided they shut down in accordance with the *International Mechanical Code*® (IMC®).

    b. Manual controls for fire department operation of the exhaust fans shall be provided in a room separated from the storage area by 1-hour fire-resistance-rated construction.

    c. The exhaust fans shall activate automatically upon smoke detector activation.

    d. The exhaust fans shall be rated for operation at a minimum of 221°F.

    Reference 910.4.4

28. Given: A 36,000-square-foot aircraft hangar of Type IIIB construction. For fire suppression purposes, what is the hangar's group designation?

    a. Group I   (b.) Group II

    c   Group III   d. Group IV

Reference 914.8.3

29. A secondary water supply for the sprinkler system is required on the property when the building is _____.

    a. a high-rise building

    b. an underground building

    c. a covered mall building

    (d.) a high-rise building in Seismic Design Category C, D, E or F

Reference 914.3.2

30. When exceeding what minimum building height are the automatic sprinkler systems required to be supplied from two separate risers?

    a. 75 feet   b. 120 feet

    c. 420 feet   d. No such requirement exists.

Reference 914.3.1.1

31. Which of the following is not a method for designing a smoke control system?

    a. pressurization method   b. airflow design method

    (c.) smoke barrier method   d. exhaust method

Reference 909.5

32. Given: A stage with an area of 2,800 square feet in a Group A-1 occupancy. Is a standpipe required, and if so, what class of standpipe is required?

    a. no; standpipe is not required.

    b. yes; Class I standpipe

    (c.) yes; Class II standpipe

    d. yes; Class III standpipe

Reference 905.3.4

33. Which of the following is a method to protect the riser and laterals for a Class I stand-pipe in a seven-story sprinklered building?

    a. Locate the risers in exit access stairways

    b. Locate the risers in a 1-hour fire-resistance-rated shaft

    (c.) No protection is required for the laterals if the risers are located in interior exit stairways

    d. No protection is required for risers or laterals since the building is sprinklered

Reference _905.4.1_

34. Given: A 17-story Group B high-rise building. The high-rise building is constructed on top of a 4-story Group S-2 open parking garage. Does the parking garage require an automatic sprinkler system?

    a. no

    b. yes, because it is over three stories

    (c.) yes, because it is part of the high-rise building

    d. yes, because all parking garages are required to be sprinklered

Reference _914.3.1_

35. Given: An existing sprinklered building with the fire department connection located on the rear side of building. Which of the following is correct regarding this FDC?

    a. The FDC must be relocated to the street side of the building.

    b. A sign shall be provided indicating the location of the FDC.

    c. Lighting, with standby power, must be provided in the area of the FDC.

    d. The FDC must be painted neon orange.

Reference _912.2.2_

Study Session

7

2021 IFC Chapter 9

Fire Protection and Life Safety Systems—Part II

OBJECTIVE: To gain an understanding of the fundamental requirements of the *International Fire Code®* (IFC®) for required fire protection and life safety systems, the various types of systems that are required or may be approved by the fire code official, and the IFC requirements for specific occupancies or hazards. Part II covers alternative fire-extinguishing systems, portable fire extinguishers, alarm systems, explosion control, carbon monoxide detection and gas detection systems.

REFERENCE: Chapter 9, 2021 IFC

KEY POINTS:
- When is a fire protection system required to protect cooking appliances?
- What is a Type I commercial kitchen hood, and what are the requirements for an automatic fire-extinguishing system?
- How often is a fire-extinguishing system in the exhaust hood over a commercial appliance inspected and maintained?
- Are domestic cooking appliances treated differently than commercial cooking appliances?
- When can an alternative automatic fire-extinguishing system be used in lieu of an automatic sprinkler system?
- What are the different types of alternative automatic fire-extinguishing systems and what determines which system is appropriate for a hazard?
- What are the inspection requirements for fire-extinguishing systems?
- In which occupancies are portable fire extinguishers required? What are the requirements for inspections and proper installation?
- How often are portable fire extinguishers inspected and maintained?
- In which occupancies is a fire alarm and detection system required?
- Which existing occupancies require the retroactive installation of a fire alarm system?

KEY POINTS:
(Cont'd)

- What are the inspection frequencies and requirements for acceptance testing, maintenance and inspection of fire alarm and detection systems?

- What is the purpose of emergency voice/alarm communication systems, and where are they required?

- What is the difference between an emergency voice/alarm communication system and an emergency alarm system?

- Which occupancies or uses require an emergency alarm system?

- What is the scope and purpose of explosion control?

- What is a detonation or deflagration? When is explosion control required for buildings that store hazardous materials that present these hazards?

- When are both audible and visual alarms required on a fire alarm system, and how are spacing and location determined?

- Which occupancies and situations require the installation of carbon monoxide alarms?

- What hazards require the installation of a gas detection system?

- What are the components of a gas detection system?

- What are the inspection, testing and maintenance requirements for a gas detection system?

- When an automatic sprinkler system is installed in a building, are portable fire extinguishers still required?

- What is the difference between a fire alarm system and a mass notification system?

- When is mass notification required?

Code Text: *Monitoring. Alarm, supervisory and trouble signals shall be distinctly different and shall be automatically transmitted to an approved supervising station or, where approved by the fire code official, shall sound an audible signal at a constantly attended location.* ***Exception:*** *Backflow prevention device test valves located in limited area sprinkler system supply piping shall be locked in the open position. In occupancies required to be equipped with a fire alarm system, the backflow preventer valves shall be electrically supervised by a tamper switch installed in accordance with NFPA 72 and separately annunciated.*

Monitoring. Where a building fire alarm system is installed, automatic fire-extinguishing systems shall be monitored by the building fire alarm system in accordance with NFPA 72.

Monitoring. Fire alarm systems required by this chapter or by the International Building Code *shall be monitored by an approved supervising station in accordance with NFPA 72.* ***Exception:*** *Monitoring by a supervising station is not required for: (1) Single- and multiple-station smoke alarms required by Section 907.2.11, (2) Smoke detectors in Group I-3 occupancies, (3) Automatic sprinkler systems in one- and two-family dwellings.*

Discussion and Commentary: Automatic sprinkler systems and fire alarm systems are required to be monitored. The monitoring for sprinkler systems includes control valves and water flow detection. The fire alarm system is monitored for alarm, trouble and supervisory alarms. When a fire alarm system is installed in a building, Section 904.3.5 requires that all fire-extinguishing systems be monitored by the fire alarm system.

The monitoring provides for early notification to the fire department when an incident occurs. There are some exceptions in Section 907.6.6 that eliminate the monitoring requirements, but generally all fire alarm systems are monitored.

Monitored systems shall send a signal off-site to a proprietary station or central station monitoring service, or an on-site signal can be sent to a constantly attended location. The constantly attended location must be staffed at all times, even when the business is closed.

Code Text: ***Where permitted.*** *Automatic fire-extinguishing systems installed as an alternative to the required automatic sprinkler systems of Section 903 shall be approved by the fire code official.*

Restriction on using automatic sprinkler system exceptions or reductions. *Automatic fire-extinguishing systems shall not be considered alternatives for the purposes of exceptions or reductions allowed for automatic sprinkler systems or by other requirements of this code.*

Discussion and Commentary: In certain instances water may not serve as the best fire extinguishing agent. Accordingly, this section allows the fire code official to permit alternative agents such as clean agents, dry chemical, dry powder for Class D hazards or wet chemicals for commercial kitchen cooking hazards.

Although alternative agent systems may be a good choice for a given hazard, when they replace sprinklers, the building is no longer considered sprinklered throughout. The IFC and *International Building Code®* (IBC®) only recognize an automatic sprinkler system provided throughout the building for the purpose of code modifications, such as allowable area or height increases, reductions in the required fire-resistance-rated assemblies, increase in travel distance, or the increase in maximum allowable quantity of hazardous materials.

The fire-extinguishing system in the exhausted enclosure is required to be monitored by the fire alarm system in the building.

Code Text: *Each required commercial kitchen exhaust hood and duct system required by Section 606 to have a Type I hood shall be protected with an approved automatic fire-extinguishing system installed in accordance with this code.*

Discussion and Commentary: A Type I exhaust hood conveys grease-laden vapors or smoke in a commercial cooking operation. Because of the increased fire hazard in these areas of commercial cooking operations, the IFC requires an approved automatic fire-extinguishing system in these areas.

Either automatic sprinkler protection or an alternative automatic fire-extinguishing system can be used to protect Type I hoods and plenums.

Code Text: *High-pressure cylinders shall be weighed and the date of the last hydrostatic test shall be verified at six-month intervals. Where a container shows a loss in original content of more than 10 percent, the cylinder shall be refilled or replaced.*

Discussion and   High-pressure carbon dioxide (CO_2) cylinders are subject to the inspection requirements
Commentary: of the US Department of Transportation. These cylinders require a hydrostatic examination every 12 years. Because the design of CO_2 systems is based on a minimum discharge concentration in an enclosure, the amount of agent must be verified every six months. This is accomplished by weighing the cylinders and comparing the total weight to the tare weight of stored CO_2. If the cylinder loses more than ten percent of its product weight it must be recharged to the minimum required weight.

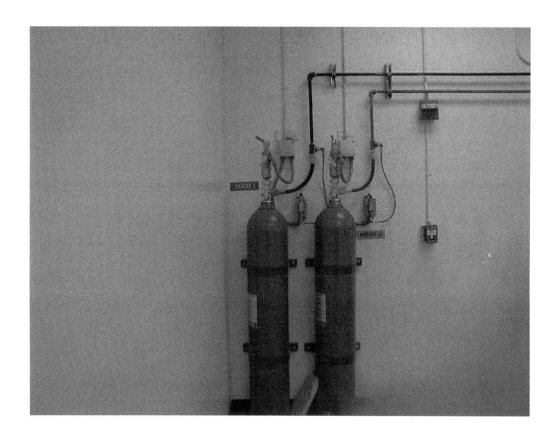

In addition to being subject to the requirements of NFPA 12, CO_2 cylinders are subject to the requirements of IFC Chapter 53 for compressed gases.

Topic: Commercial Cooking Systems

Reference: IFC 904.13

Category: Fire Protection and Life Safety Systems

Subject: Alternative Automatic Fire-Extinguishing Systems

Code Text: *The automatic fire-extinguishing system for commercial cooking systems shall be of a type recognized for protection of commercial cooking equipment and exhaust systems of the type and arrangement protected. Preengineered automatic dry- and wet-chemical extinguishing systems shall be tested in accordance with UL 300 and listed and labeled for the intended application. Other types of automatic fire-extinguishing systems shall be listed and labeled for specific use as protection for commercial cooking operations. The system shall be installed in accordance with this code, NFPA 96, its listing and the manufacturer's installation instructions. Automatic fire-extinguishing systems of the following types shall be installed in accordance with the referenced standard indicated, as follows:*

(See IFC Section 904.13 Items 1 through 6 and the exception.)

Discussion and Commentary: The most common method of protecting commercial kitchen cooking operations located under a Type I hood is the use of a pre-engineered dry- or wet-chemical fire-extinguishing system meeting UL 300. New kitchen hoods are generally protected with wet chemical fire-extinguishing agents. Other methods include carbon dioxide, automatic sprinkler, automatic water mist and foam-water sprinklers or foam-water spray systems.

This photograph shows part of the UL 300 testing process for a fire-extinguishing system. IFC Section 904.13.5.1 requires the fire-extinguishing system to meet current code requirements when the cooking media is changed or cooking appliances are replaced or repositioned. This can result in existing dry-chemical fire-extinguishing systems to be replaced with a system meeting the current UL 300 requirements.

Code Text: *A manual actuation device shall be located at or near a means of egress from the cooking area not less than 10 feet (3048 mm) and not more than 20 feet (6096 mm) from the kitchen exhaust system. The manual actuation device shall be installed not more than 48 inches (1200 mm) nor less than 42 inches (1067 mm) above the floor and shall clearly identify the hazard protected. The manual actuation shall require a maximum force of 40 pounds (178 N) and a maximum movement of 14 inches (356 mm) to actuate the fire suppression system. **Exception:** Automatic sprinkler systems shall not be required to be equipped with manual actuation means.*

Discussion and Commentary: NFPA 96 states that the fire-extinguishing system for a Type I hood is the primary level of protection. Therefore, if the detection system or certain operating components fail, the IFC requires a manual means of activating the alternative fire-extinguishing system.

The manual release device must be identified and located in the path of egress from the cooking appliance.

Topic: Domestic Cooking Facilities	Category: Fire Protection and Life Safety Systems
Reference: IFC 904.14	Subject: Alternative Automatic Fire-Extinguishing Systems

Code Text: *Cooktops and ranges installed in the following occupancies shall be protected in accordance with Section 904.14.1: (1) In Group I-1 occupancies where domestic cooking facilities are installed in accordance with Section 420.9 of the* International Building Code, *(2) In Group I-2, occupancies where domestic cooking facilities are installed in accordance with Section 407.2.7 of the* International Building Code, *(3) In Group R-2 college dormitories where domestic cooking facilities are installed in accordance with Section 420.11 of the* International Building Code.

Discussion and Commentary: Domestic cooking appliances are allowed to be installed in Group I-1, I-2, and R-2 college dormitories. These appliances are typically installed in the common areas for resident use. When these cooking appliances are installed, they need to be protected with a fire-extinguishing system listed to UL 300A, or the cooking appliance can be listed to provide ignition prevention.

The fire-extinguishing system would be listed to UL 300A *Outline of Investigation for Extinguishing System Units for Residential Range Top Cooking Surfaces*, These systems are not equivalent to systems listed to UL 300, because they are designed for lower hazard domestic-type cooking appliances.

Ignition prevention is designed so that if the cooking appliance is set on high, a pot of cooking oil will not ignite within 30 minutes. Additionally, if the cooking appliance is not manipulated or used during a 30-minute period, the appliance will automatically shut off.

(Photograph courtesy of Denlar Fire Protection, Chester, CT.)

The exhaust hood over this domestic cooking appliance is equipped with a fire-extinguishing system listed to UL 300A.

Code Text: *Portable fire extinguishers shall be installed in all of the following locations: (1) In new and existing Group A, B, E, F, H, I, M, R-1, R-2, R-4 and S occupancies. **Exceptions:** (1) In Group R-2 occupancies, portable fire extinguishers shall be required only in locations specified in Items 2 through 6 where each dwelling unit is provided with a portable fire extinguisher having a minimum rating of 1-A:10-B:C, (2) In Group E occupancies, portable fire extinguishers shall be required only in locations specified in Items 2 through 6 where each classroom is provided with a portable fire extinguisher having a minimum rating of 2-A:20-B:C.*

(See IFC Section 906.1 Exception 3 and Items 2 through 6.)

Discussion and Commentary: The IFC prescribes the occupancies and locations inside of buildings that require portable fire extinguishers. This includes areas where flammable and combustible liquids are stored, used and dispensed, and special hazard areas. The IFC requires portable fire extinguishers in all occupancies protected throughout by an automatic sprinkler system. In Group R-2 and E occupancies, portable fire extinguishers are only required in areas specified in Items 2 through 6.

Group S storage areas, where the primary occupants are forklift or powered industrial truck operators, can eliminate fire extinguishers placement throughout the facility by mounting extinguishers on each vehicle. Each portable fire extinguisher must be rated at 40A:80B:C and operators must be trained in their use (IFC Section 906.1, Exception 3).

	Topic: Class A Fire Hazards	**Category:** Fire Protection and Life Safety Systems

Topic: Class A Fire Hazards

Reference: IFC 906.3.1, Table 906.3(1)

Category: Fire Protection and Life Safety Systems

Subject: Portable Fire Extinguishers

Code Text: *The minimum sizes and distribution of portable fire extinguishers for occupancies that involve primarily Class A fire hazards shall comply with Table 906.3(1).*

TABLE 906.3(1)
FIRE EXTINGUISHERS FOR CLASS A FIRE HAZARDS

	LIGHT (Low) HAZARD OCCUPANCY	ORDINARY (Moderate) HAZARD OCCUPANCY	EXTRA (High) HAZARD OCCUPANCY
Minimum-rated single extinguisher	2-A[c]	2-A	4-A[a]
Maximum floor area per unit of A	3,000 square feet	1,500 square feet	1,000 square feet
Maximum floor area for extinguisher[b]	11,250 square feet	11,250 square feet	11,250 square feet
Maximum distance of travel to extinguisher	75 feet	75 feet	75 feet

For SI: 1 foot = 304.8 mm, 1 square foot = 0.0929 m^2, 1 gallon = 3.785 L.

a. Two 2^1/$_2$-gallon water-type extinguishers shall be deemed the equivalent of one 4-A rated extinguisher.

b. Annex E.3.3 of NFPA 10 provides more details concerning application of the maximum floor area criteria.

c. Two water-type extinguishers each with a 1-A rating shall be deemed the equivalent of one 2-A rated extinguisher for Light (Low) Hazard Occupancies.

Discussion and Commentary: Class A fire hazards are found in all buildings and consist of paper, cloth, wood and other ordinary combustibles. The IFC requires portable fire extinguishers to meet the spacing requirements for Class A fire hazards. Where other hazards exist, such as flammable liquids, portable fire extinguishers must also have a Class B rating and must be spaced within the maximum distance to that particular hazard.

Class K portable fire extinguishers are required for commercial cooking operations. One Class K extinguisher is to be provided for every group of four deep fat fryers. If individual deep fat fryers exceed 80 gallons of cooking medium or 6 square feet, the manufacturer's instructions for the number of extinguishers must be followed (IFC Section 906.4.2).

Code Text: *An approved fire alarm system installed in accordance with the provisions of this code and NFPA 72 shall be provided in new buildings and structures in accordance with Sections 907.2.1 through 907.2.23 and provide occupant notification in accordance with Section 907.5, unless other requirements are provided by another section of this code.*

Not fewer than one manual fire alarm box shall be provided in an approved location to initiate a fire alarm signal for fire alarm systems employing automatic fire detectors or waterflow detection devices. Where other sections of this code allow elimination of fire alarm boxes due to sprinklers, a single fire alarm box shall be installed.

(See IFC Section 907.2 for exceptions.)

Discussion and Commentary: This IFC section stipulates when either a manual fire alarm system or an automatic fire detection system is required in new buildings or structures. In many occupancies where a fire sprinkler system and a manual fire alarm system are installed, the IFC allows the elimination of all but one of the manual fire alarm boxes as long as it is installed in an approved location.

Exception 2 allows the elimination of all the manual fire alarm boxes in Group R-2, unless the fire code official requires a single manual fire alarm box. If required, that single manual fire alarm box is not to be located in an area available to the public.

Topic: Emergency Voice/Alarm Communications
in Group A Occupancies

Category: Fire Protection and Life
Safety Systems

Reference: IFC 907.2.1.1

Subject: Fire Alarm and Detection Systems

Code Text: *Activation of the fire alarm in Group A occupancies with an occupant load of 1,000 or more shall initiate a signal using an emergency voice/alarm communications system in accordance with Section 907.5.2.2.* ***Exception:*** *Where approved, the prerecorded announcement is allowed to be manually deactivated for a period of time, not to exceed 3 minutes, for the sole purpose of allowing a live voice announcement from an approved, constantly attended location.*

Discussion and Commentary: An emergency voice/alarm communication system is designed to annunciate a verbal signal that informs the building occupants of a required evacuation or shelter-in-place. The system is designed so that emergency responders can also direct building occupants based on the nature of the emergency. These systems are required in Group A occupancies with an occupant load of 1,000 or more.

Grandstands and stadiums with 15,000 seats or more and capable of providing audible and captioned announcements are required to provide the prerecorded and live messages via captions (IFC Section 907.2.1.2).

Code Text: *A manual fire alarm system, which activates the occupant notification system in accordance with Section 907.5, shall be installed in Group B occupancies where one of the following conditions exists: (1) The combined Group B occupant load of all floors is 500 or more, (2) The Group B occupant load is more than 100 persons above or below the lowest level of exit discharge, (3) The fire area contains an ambulatory care facility.* **Exception:** *Manual fire alarm boxes are not required where the building is equipped throughout with an automatic sprinkler system installed in accordance with Section 903.3.1.1 and the occupant notification appliances will activate throughout the notification zones upon sprinkler water flow.*

Discussion and Commentary: Occupants in Group B occupancies are generally aware of their surroundings and can be directed to egress a building. To facilitate the safe evacuation of the building occupants, IFC Section 907.2.2 requires a manual fire alarm system in Group B occupancies when the total occupant load is 500 persons or greater, or when more than 100 persons are above or below the lowest level of exit discharge. If the building is protected throughout by an automatic sprinkler system, only one manual fire alarm box is required in an approved location. Occupant notification devices that are activated by a sprinkler system are required.

NFPA 72 contains installation requirements and criteria for location of alarm notification appliances.

Code Text: *A manual fire alarm system that activates the occupant notification system in accordance with Section 907.5 shall be installed in Group S public- and self-storage occupancies three stories or greater in height for interior corridors and interior common areas. Visible notification appliances are not required within storage units. **Exception:** Manual fire alarm boxes are not required where the building is equipped throughout with an automatic sprinkler system installed in accordance with Section 903.3.1.1, and the occupant notification appliances will activate throughout the notification zones upon sprinkler water flow.*

Discussion and Commentary: Public-storage and self-storage facilities containing three or more stories must be provided with a manual fire alarm system. This system is intended to alert occupants of an emergency in another part of the facility and allow time to escape. The manual fire alarm system is required to provide audible notification throughout the entire facility, but visible notification is not required within the individual storage units. Visible notification appliances are provided in the common areas. If the building is sprinklered, which is required in IFC Section 903.2.9, then only one manual fire alarm box is required in an approved location.

This self-storage facility is required to be provided with an automatic sprinkler system and a manual fire alarm system. The IFC will also require the sprinkler system and alarm system to be monitored by a supervising station in accordance with NFPA 72.

Code Text: *Upon completion of the installation, the fire alarm system and all fire alarm components shall be tested in accordance with NFPA 72.*

Discussion and Commentary: A functional test of all alarm initiating and signaling devices, the fire alarm control panel, power supply and conductors must be performed to verify that the system complies with NFPA 72. This includes supplemental functions such as operation of motorized fire and smoke dampers and verification of device addresses. NFPA 72 establishes clear criteria for inspections of new or modified fire alarm and detection systems.

IFC Section 907.7.2 also requires a record of completion in accordance with NFPA 72 to the fire code official that documents the system was installed and tested in accordance the approved plans and specifications.

Code Text: *Emergency alarms for the detection and notification of an emergency condition in Group H occupancies shall be provided as required in Chapter 50.*

Discussion and Commentary: An emergency alarm system is required for all semiconductor fabrication facilities (Group H-5 occupancies) and, for other Group H occupancies, when specified by IFC Sections 5004.9 and 5005.4.4. Emergency alarm initiating devices are required outside of interior exit or exit access doors, and activation of the system initiates a local alarm. Alarm signals for semiconductor fabrication facilities are required to be transmitted to the Emergency Control Station in accordance with IFC Section 2703.12.3.

Where hazardous materials exceeding maximum allowable quantities are stored, the emergency alarm system requires supervision and monitoring in accordance with IFC Section 5004.10.

Code Text: *Cables used for survivability of circuits supplying fire pumps shall be protected using one of the following methods: (1) Cables used for survivability of required critical circuits shall be listed in accordance with UL 2196 and shall have a fire-resistance rating of not less than 1 hour, (2) Electrical circuit protective systems shall have a fire-resistance rating of not less than 1 hour. Electrical circuit protective systems shall be installed in accordance with their listing requirements, (3) Construction having a fire-resistance rating of not less than 1 hour; (4) The cable or raceway is encased in a minimum of 2 inches (51 mm) of concrete. **Exception:** This section shall not apply to cables, or portions of cables, located within a fire pump room or generator room that is separated from the remainder of the occupancy with fire-resistance-rated construction.*

Discussion and Commentary: Electrical wiring to fire pumps is expected to survive during a fire incident and therefore must be protected. This section specifies several options for protecting the cables. The cables could be encased in 2-inches of concrete, listed to UL 2196 *Standard for Fire Test for Circuit Integrity of Fire-resistive Power, Instrumentation, Control and Data Cables,* or protected with 1-hour construction. Installations complying with UL 2196 are likely to include a combination of fire resistive cables, support and mounting details, and a description of the building assembly to which they are to be attached, such as a concrete or masonry wall or concrete floor. Note that this requirement does not apply within the fire pump room—this protection is for the electrical cables from the power supply to the fire pump room.

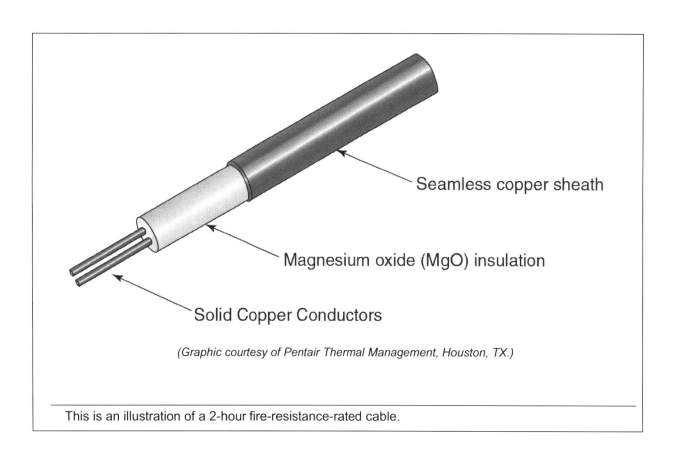

Seamless copper sheath

Magnesium oxide (MgO) insulation

Solid Copper Conductors

(Graphic courtesy of Pentair Thermal Management, Houston, TX.)

This is an illustration of a 2-hour fire-resistance-rated cable.

Code Text: *Carbon monoxide detection shall be provided in Group I-1, I-2, I-4 and R occupancies and in classrooms in Group E occupancies in the locations specified in Section 915.2 where any of the conditions in Sections 915.1.2 through 915.1.6 exist.*

Discussion and Commentary: Annually over 400 lives are lost and approximately 50,000 people visit the emergency room as a result of carbon monoxide poisoning according to the Centers for Disease Control and Prevention. Carbon monoxide (CO) is created anytime materials containing carbon are burned. When the combustion of the material is less complete, more carbon monoxide is formed. Many buildings are tight enough that the CO is retained inside the building unless outdoor ventilation is provided. The IFC requires CO detection in occupancies with a high life hazard. If a building with any of these occupancies contains fuel-burning appliances, or the HVAC utilizes fuel-burning appliances, or there is an attached garage, CO detection is required.

Per IFC 915.4.4, combination carbon monoxide/smoke alarms shall be an acceptable alternative to carbon monoxide alarms. Combination carbon monoxide/smoke alarms shall be listed in accordance with UL 217 and UL 2034. Per IFC 915.5.3, combination carbon monoxide/smoke detectors installed in carbon monoxide detection systems shall be an acceptable alternative to carbon monoxide detectors, provided that they are listed in accordance with UL 268 and UL 2075.

Code Text: *Inspection and testing of gas detection systems shall be conducted not less than annually. Sensor calibration shall be confirmed at the time of sensor installation and calibration shall be performed at the frequency specified by the sensor manufacturer.*

Discussion and Commentary: Many manufacturing or processing facilities use or generate gases. The IFC requires gas detection systems in rooms or areas where highly flammable, toxic or highly toxic gases can be released. Those requirements are located throughout the code, and refer to Section 916 for the design and installation of the gas detection system.

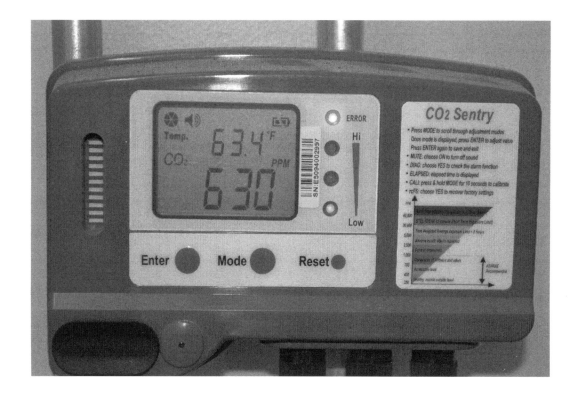

Carbon dioxide (CO_2) gas detectors are required for CO_2 enrichment systems. The CO_2 detector is required to provided a low-level alarm at 5,000 ppm and a high-level alarm at 30,000 ppm (IFC Section 5307.4.3).

Quiz

Study Session 7

IFC Chapter 9—Part II

1. What is the maximum internal pressure allowed for a deflagration relief panel or venting device?

    a. 10 lb/ft²   b. 15 lb/ft²

    c. 20 lb/ft²   d. 25 lb/ft²

    Reference 911.2

2. Which of the following is incorrect about gas detection systems?

    a. Where flammable gas concentrations exceed 25 percent of the lower flammability limit, the gas detection alarm shall be activated.

    b. Where nonflammable gas concentrations exceed 25 percent of the IDLH, the gas detection alarm shall be activated.

    c. Gas sampling intervals for toxic gas shall not exceed 5 minutes, unless that gas is HPM.

    d. Audible and visible alarms for a gas detection system shall be distinct from fire alarm signals and carbon monoxide signals.

    Reference 916.8

3. Given: A 30,000-square-foot, two-story Group B occupancy. The building is sprinklered in all areas, except in the computer room on the first story. The computer room is protected with a clean agent fire-extinguishing system. Which of the following is correct when referring to the sprinkler protection in the building?

    a. the building is considered sprinklered throughout, and all code modifications based on sprinklers are applicable

    b. the building is considered sprinklered throughout, and all code modifications based on sprinklers are applicable, except in the computer room

    c. the building is not considered sprinklered throughout since there are no sprinklers in the computer room; therefore, no code modifications based on sprinklers are allowed

    d. the building is considered sprinklered throughout, but the code modifications based on sprinklers are only applicable on the second story

    Reference 904.2.1

4. The minimum sound pressure level for audible notification appliances is _____.

    a. 60 dBA

    b. 75 dBA

    c. 90 dBA

    d. 15 dBA above the ambient sound level or 5 dBA above the maximum sound level

    Reference 907.5.2.1.1

5. Which of the following require a mass notification system?

    a. a university building with an occupant load of 1,000 or more

    b. a university with multiple buildings

    c. a university with multiple buildings and an aggregate occupant load of 1,000 or more

    d. a university with multiple buildings and an aggregate occupant load of 1,000 or more and a risk analysis in accordance with NFP 72 determines that mass notification is needed

    Reference 917.1.1

6. Which components must be interlocked with a fire-extinguishing system in a commercial kitchen hood?

    a. fuel supply to the cooking equipment

    b. ventilation system

    c. electric power to the cooking equipment

    (d.) both a and c

Reference 904.13.2

7. Which of the following are required for a CO_2 automatic fire-extinguishing system predischarge alarm?

    a. a warning sign

    b. an audible and visual signal

    c. notification when a door does not shut properly

    (d.) both a and b

Reference 904.3.4

8. What is the minimum internal pressure requirement for the walls and ceiling of a room that houses a deflagration hazard?

    a. 100 pounds per square inch

    b. 20 pounds per square foot

    (c.) 100 pounds per square foot

    d. 20 pounds per square inch

Reference 911.2#1

9. When is an emergency voice/alarm communication system required in Group A occupancies?

    a. when the occupant load exceeds 300

    b. when the fire area is greater than 5,000 ft²

    (c.) when the occupant load is 1,000 or more

    d. when the fire area is greater than 12,000 ft²

Reference 907.2.1.1

10. What is the system air flow rate that requires the installation of duct smoke detectors in air conditioning systems in a high-rise building?

    a. 500 CFM   b. 1,200 CFM

    c. 1,500 CFM   d. 2,000 CFM

    Reference 907.2.13.1.2, #1

11. Activation of a duct smoke detector initiates a _____ signal at a constantly attended location.

    a. trouble

    b. audible occupant notification

    c. supervisory

    d. visual occupant notification

    Reference 907.3.1

12. When are carbon monoxide alarms required in Group I-1 buildings?

    a. When the building contains a fuel-burning appliance.

    b. When the building has an attached garage.

    c. When the building contains a fuel-burning forced-air furnace.

    d. all of the above

    Reference 915.1.1

13. What is the minimum number of sleeping units in a 180 unit R-1 occupancy that require visible alarms?

    a. 12   b. 14

    c. 17   d. 5 percent of the total number of units

    Reference 907.5.2.3.2

14. A fire alarm system is retroactively required in all existing two-story Group R-1 hotels and motels with a minimum of ____ sleeping units.

    a. 11   b. 21

    c. 25   d. 50

    Reference 907.9, 1103.7.5.1

15. In a Group R occupancy, which of the following is incorrect about the placement of smoke alarms?

    a.   Smoke alarms must be at least 3 feet from the door into a bathroom with a tub or shower.

    (b.) Ionization smoke alarms can only be installed in bedrooms.

    c.   Photoelectric smoke alarms must be at least 6 feet from permanently installed cooking appliances.

    d.   A smoke alarm must be installed in each room used for sleeping purposes.

Reference 907.2.11.2   907.2.11.3   907.2.11.4

16. Given: A five-story building with an atrium. Which of the following occupancies does *not* require an emergency voice/alarm communications system?

    (a.) Group B   b.   Group A

    c.   Group E   d.   Group M

Reference 907.2.14

17. What UL standard governs the listing of a fire-extinguishing system installed to protect the domestic cooking facilities in a Group R-2 college dormitory?

    a.   UL 142   b.   UL 300

    (c.) UL 300A   d.   UL 2085

Reference 904.14.1.1, #1

18. Given: A 19,000-square-foot one-story Group B office building. The building is not equipped with an automatic sprinkler system. At what occupant load is a manual fire alarm system required?

    a.   300   (b.) 500

    c.   750   d.   1,000

Reference 907.2.2, #1

19. What is the minimum rating required for a portable fire extinguisher designed for use against Class A fire hazards in an Extra Hazard Occupancy?

    a.   1-A   b.   2-A

    c.   3-A   (d.) 4-A

Reference 906.3(1)

20. What is the maximum travel distance to a portable fire extinguisher used to protect flammable liquids with an estimated spill depth of 0.25 inches inside of a light hazard occupancy? The extinguisher has a rating of 10-B.

    a.   20 feet   b.   30 feet

    c.   50 feet   d.   75 feet

Reference _906.3(3)_

21. What is the maximum installed height above a finished floor to the top of a portable fire extinguisher with a weight of 25 pounds?

    a.   2 feet   b.   3 feet

    c.   4 feet   d.   5 feet

Reference _906.9.1_

22. For commercial kitchen cooking systems equipped with an automatic fire-extinguishing system, a manual means of activation shall be located _____ feet from the kitchen exhaust system.

    a.   not less than 5 and not more than 15

    b.   not less than 10 and not more than 15

    c.   it is not required

    d.   not less than 10 and not more than 20

Reference _904.13.1_

23. What is the minimum size for a Class K portable fire extinguisher protecting two deep fat fryers with a cooking medium capacity of 75 pounds?

    a.   1 gallon   b.   1.5 gallons

    c.   2 gallons   d.   2.5 gallons

Reference _906.4.2#1_

24. Given: A nonsprinklered 23,000-square-foot Group F-1 occupancy divided in half by a fire wall. The building occupant load is 500. The building is one story in height. Is a fire alarm system required?

    a.   yes, because fire walls no longer create separate buildings and the occupant load is 500

    b.   no

    c.   yes, because the entire building is over 12,000 square feet

    d.   yes, all Group F-1 occupancies require a fire alarm system

Reference _907.2.4, #1_

25. Given: A Group H-5 occupancy with a fire alarm system and an emergency alarm system. Which of the following is correct about the interface between the two alarm systems?

    a. The emergency alarm system, where interfaced with the building's fire alarm system, shall produce a supervisory signal.

    b. The emergency alarm system shall be connected to the fire alarm system and shall activate the fire alarm notification appliances.

    c. The emergency alarm system shall be connected to the fire alarm system and shall produce a trouble signal.

    d. The emergency alarm system shall not be connected to the fire alarm system.

Reference 908.3

26. Open mall buildings exceeding _____ square feet in total floor area within the perimeter line shall be provided with an emergency voice/alarm communication system.

    a. 15,000   b. 35,000

    c. 45,000   d. 50,000

Reference 907.2.20

27. Given: A facility is provided with a manual fire alarm system, carbon monoxide alarms and a gas detection system. Which of the following is correct about the audible and visible alarm signals of these three systems?

    a. All three systems can share the same alarm signal because the goal is evacuation of the building.

    b. The gas detection system can share alarm signals with the fire alarm system because the released gas could result in fire.

    c. The gas detection system shall have a distinct alarm from the fire alarm signal and carbon monoxide signal.

    d. There is no restriction as long as the facility has a Fire Safety and Evacuation Plan and fire drills are practiced semi-annually.

Reference 916.8

28. What type of device or component originates transmission of a change of state condition, such as a smoke detector or water flow switch?

    a. fire detector, automatic   b. detector, heat

    c. initiating device   d. emergency alarm system

Reference 902.1, 202

29. What type of fire-extinguishing agent is formulated with water and a potassium-carbonate-based or potassium-acetate-based chemical?

    a.   dry-chemical extinguishing agent

    b.   wet-chemical extinguishing agent

    c.   clean agent

    d.   foam-extinguishing system

Reference 902.1.202

30. A rational analysis required to determine and justify the type of smoke control system installed in a building must include all of the following except:

    a.   stack effect

    b.   occupant movement

    c.   temperature effect of fire

    d.   wind effect

Reference 909.4

31. What is the required frequency for replacing fusible links utilized to activate a wet-chemical fire-extinguishing system in a commercial kitchen hood?

    a.   only when they operate

    b.   each required hood inspection

    c.   each time the hood and plenum is cleaned

    d.   annually

Reference 904.13.5.3

32. When are automatic water mist fire-extinguishing systems required to be provided with a secondary water supply?

    a.   all water mist systems require secondary water supply

    b.   system pressure is less than 900 pounds

    c.   when a secondary water supply is required for an automatic sprinkler system

    d.   when it is substituted for automatic fire sprinkler system

Reference 904.11.1.4

33. Automatic fire-extinguishing systems protecting commercial kitchen hoods are required to be capable of manual activation except for _____.

    a. automatic sprinkler systems

    b. dry-chemical extinguishing systems

    c. wet-chemical extinguishing systems

    d. carbon dioxide extinguishing systems

    Reference _904.13.1_

34. Which of the following areas do not require smoke alarms in a Group R-2 occupancy?

    a. sleeping rooms

    b. kitchen

    c. outside the sleeping rooms and in the immediate vicinity of bedrooms

    d. each story

    Reference _907.2.11.2_

35. In a hotel with residential suites containing a kitchen, ionization smoke alarms must be located a minimum of_____ feet from the permanently installed cooking appliances.

    a. 5   b. 6

    c. 10   d. 20

    Reference _907.2.11.3_

Study Session

8

2021 IFC Chapter 10
Means of Egress

OBJECTIVE: To obtain an understanding of the basic design requirements of a means of egress system, including the determination of occupant load, the required width of egress components, identification and illuminations of means of egress, accessibility in an egress path, and requirements for doors, ramps and other egress components.

REFERENCE: Chapter 10, 2021 *International Fire Code®* (IFC®)

KEY POINTS:
- What are the three distinct elements of a means of egress system?
- What is the minimum required ceiling height in a means of egress?
- What are the prescribed controls for projections that extend below the minimum ceiling height?
- In areas without fixed seats, what is the correct method of determining the occupant load?
- What method is used to calculate the occupant load for fixed seating such as booths, benches or chairs?
- When does a room or story need to have two exits? Three exits?
- When more than one exit door is required, does it matter how close they are together?
- How may the design occupant load be increased over what is calculated?
- In what rooms or spaces must the maximum occupant load be posted?
- What is the maximum travel distance to an exit door? How is it determined?
- What are the requirements for exits that serve more than one floor?
- How is the minimum width of different egress components determined?
- Does an occupied roof need to meet the same requirements as a story in the building?
- Can a door encroach in the required egress width?
- Can turnstiles be installed in the egress path? If they can, what are the requirements?
- When is illumination required for a means of egress?

KEY POINTS:
(Cont'd)

- When is emergency power required for illumination of the means of egress?
- What is considered an accessible means of egress?
- When is two-way communications required for an accessible means of egress?
- When are exit signs required? When must they be illuminated? What type of power sources are required?
- What is a guard, and when are they required?

- What is the minimum height and width of an egress door?
- What is the maximum width of an exit door or exit access door?
- When must doors swing in the direction of egress travel?
- What types of locks or latched are allowed on egress doors?
- What is the difference between locks and latches on egress doors?
- When is panic hardware required?
- What is the difference between panic hardware and fire exit hardware?
- How is the minimum required stairway width determined?
- What is the purpose of a stairway landing, and how are they regulated?
- When are handrails required, and what are the construction requirements?
- When is a stairway required to provide access to a roof?
- How does the desire for increased security impact the requirements to allow occupants to exit?
- Can exit doors be locked or secured at any time when the building is occupied?
- How is the path of means of egress protected from the impacts of fire?
- What is the maximum distance that occupants can travel to reach an exit, and how can it be increased?
- What are the maintenance requirements for the means of egress components?

Code Text: *Buildings or portions thereof shall be provided with a means of egress system as required by this chapter. The provisions of this chapter shall control the design, construction and arrangement of means of egress components required to provide an approved means of egress from structures and portions thereof. Sections 1003 through 1031 shall apply to new construction. Section 1032 shall apply to existing buildings. **Exception:** Detached one- and two-family dwellings and multiple single-family dwellings (townhouses) not more than three stories above grade plane in height with a separate means of egress and their accessory structures shall comply with the* International Residential Code.

Discussion and Commentary: The *International Building Code®* (IBC®) regulates the design and construction of the means of egress system, which comprises three elements: the exit access, the exit and the exit discharge. In the IFC, Sections 1003 through 1031 apply to any new construction, and the IFC requirements are consistent with the requirements in the IBC. IFC Sections 1032 and Chapter 11 apply to any existing buildings other than detached one- and two-family dwellings. Detached one- and two-family dwellings and townhouses up to three stories in height are regulated by the *International Residential Code®* (IRC®).

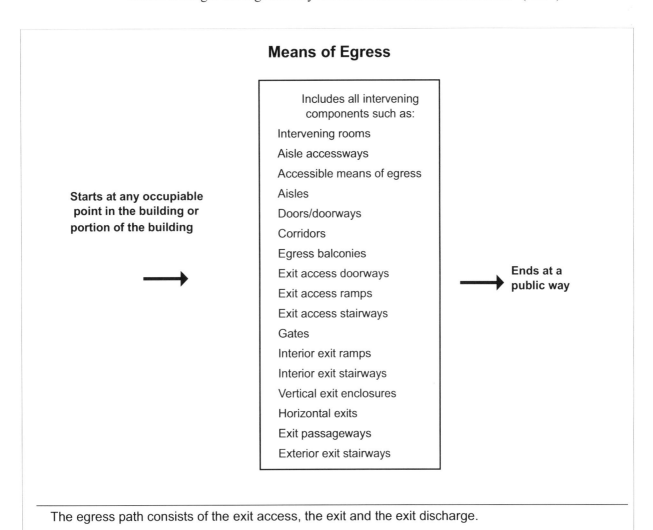

Means of Egress

Starts at any occupiable point in the building or portion of the building

Includes all intervening components such as:

Intervening rooms
Aisle accessways
Accessible means of egress
Aisles
Doors/doorways
Corridors
Egress balconies
Exit access doorways
Exit access ramps
Exit access stairways
Gates
Interior exit ramps
Interior exit stairways
Vertical exit enclosures
Horizontal exits
Exit passageways
Exterior exit stairways

Ends at a public way

The egress path consists of the exit access, the exit and the exit discharge.

Code Text: *A continuous and unobstructed path of vertical and horizontal egress travel from any occupied portion of a building or structure to a public way. A means of egress consists of three separate and distinct parts: the exit access, the exit and the exit discharge.*

Discussion and Commentary: The exit access begins at any occupied location within a building and does not end until it reaches the door to an exit passageway, an interior exit stairway or ramp, a horizontal exit, an exterior exit stairway or ramp, or an exterior door at ground level. Travel distance and egress width are regulated throughout the entire exit path. The path of travel may or may not be separated from other portions of the building by fire-resistance-rated construction. At the exit discharge, which begins where the exit ends, egress remains regulated until the public way is reached.

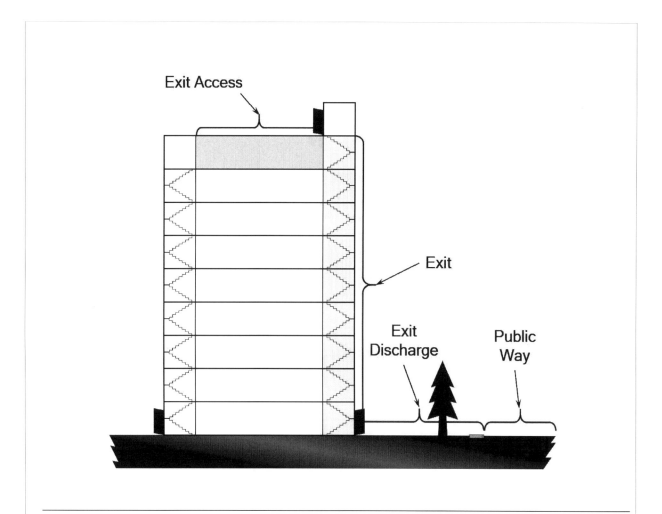

The distance of travel in the exit access is regulated. The exit component affords protection, and travel distance there is not limited. The travel distance in the exit discharge, from the exit to a public way, is unlimited.

Code Text: *The means of egress shall have a ceiling height of not less than 7 feet 6 inches (2286 mm) above the finished floor.*

(See IFC Section 1003.2 for exceptions.)

Discussion and Commentary: The IFC requires that the minimum clear height of a means of egress be maintained at least 7 feet 6 inches above the walking surface. There are eight exceptions to the general requirement that permit a limited reduction in the mandated height. Under most conditions, the vertical clearance at a stairway or doorway may be reduced to 80 inches. Protruding objects such as automatic sprinklers or light fixtures are also permitted to extend below the minimum required ceiling height for up to 50 percent of the ceiling area of the means of egress, provided that such objects maintain a minimum clearance of at least 80 inches. Special provisions are also cited for sloped ceilings.

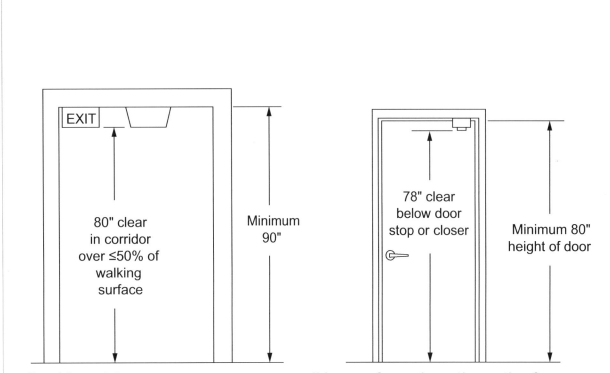

Corridor, aisle, passageway or any walking surface along the path of egress

For SI: 1 inch = 25.4 mm.

The clear height for ceilings and doorways is regulated for the entire path of egress (IFC Section 1003.3.1).

Code Text: *In determining means of egress requirements, the number of occupants for whom means of egress facilities shall be provided shall be determined in accordance with this section.*

Discussion and Commentary: When determining the occupant load of a space, it is assumed that under normal conditions all portions of the building are fully occupied at the same time. The density of individuals for given building or space uses is determined based on the identified functions in Table 1004.5. For most occupancies, the gross area is used to calculate the occupant load. However, several occupant load factors are based on the net floor area, which allows the deduction of areas such as toilet rooms, corridors, closets and equipment rooms.

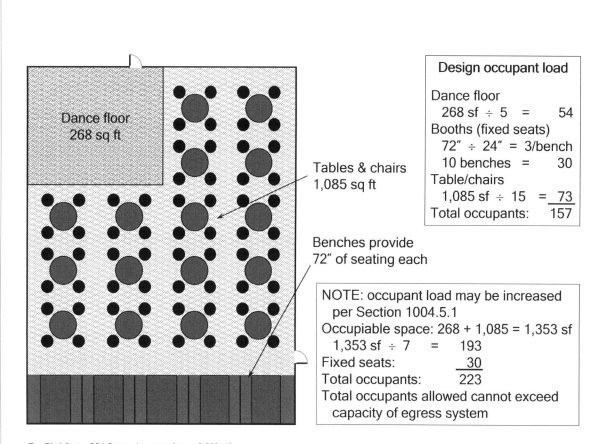

For SI: 1 foot = 304.8 mm, 1 square foot = 0.093 m².

When fixed seating is installed, IFC Section 1004.6 specifies that the occupant load is determined by counting the number of seats. For benches and pews, the factor is one occupant for each 18 inches of width. For seating booths with tables, the factor is 24 inches for each occupant.

Code Text: *Yards, patios, occupied roofs, courts and similar outdoor areas accessible to and usable by the building occupants shall be provided with means of egress as required by this chapter. The occupant load of such outdoor areas shall be assigned by the fire code official in accordance with the anticipated use. Where outdoor areas are to be used by persons in addition to the occupants of the building, and the path of egress travel from the outdoor areas passes through the building, means of egress requirements for the building shall be based on the sum of the occupant loads of the building plus the outdoor areas.* ***Exceptions:*** *(1) Outdoor areas used exclusively for service of the building need only have one means of egress, (2) Both outdoor areas associated with Group R-3 and individual dwelling units of Group R-2.*

Discussion and Commentary: This section addresses use of outdoor areas where the egress path travels through the building. This is a common scenario at restaurants, or outdoor lounges on upper floors of a multistory building. The code official establishes the occupant load in accordance with the anticipated use and all applicable egress requirements apply to the outdoor area. When the occupants travel through the building, the occupant load from the outdoor area must be added to the occupant load of the room or space where they enter the building. Egress requirements from that room are based on the accumulated occupant load.

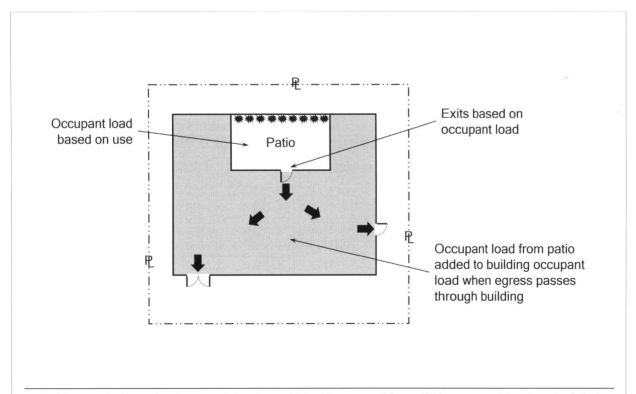

Outdoor reviewing stands, grandstands and bleachers must have their occupant loads calculated according to the specific type of seating arrangements such as chairbacks, benches or unsecured chairs.

Code Text: *The capacity, in inches, of means of egress components other than stairways shall be calculated by multiplying the occupant load served by such a component by a means of egress capacity factor of 0.2 inch (5.1 mm) per occupant. **Exceptions:** (1) For other than Group H and I-2 occupancies, the capacity, in inches, of means of egress components other than stairways shall be calculated multiplying the occupant load served by such component by a means of egress capacity factor of 0.15 inch (3.8 mm) per occupant in buildings equipped throughout by an automatic sprinkler system installed in accordance with Section 903.3.1.1 or 903.3.1.2 and an emergency voice/alarm communications system in accordance with Section 907.5.2.2.*

(See IFC Section 1005.3.2 for Exceptions 2 and 3.)

Discussion and Commentary: For a given means of egress, stairways will afford different exit discharge capacities when compared to corridors and other means of egress components. The most restrictive component will establish the capacity of the overall egress system. Doorways, corridors, aisles and ramps all have minimum widths that must be provided. The minimum width of 0.2 inch per occupant applies to all portions of the means of egress other than stairways.

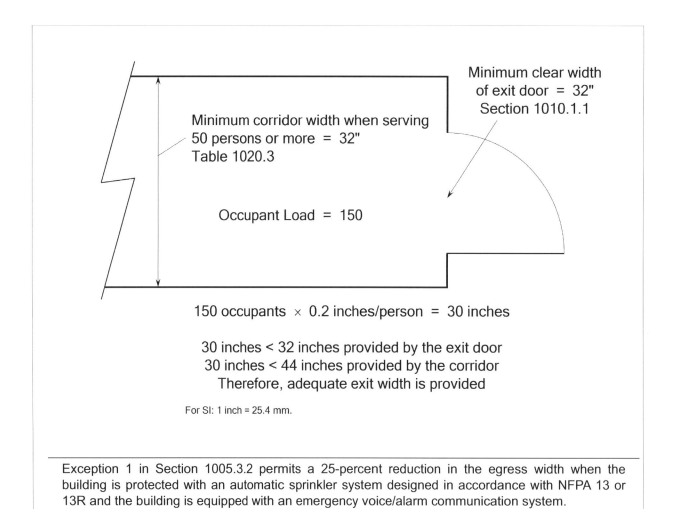

Minimum clear width of exit door = 32"
Section 1010.1.1

Minimum corridor width when serving 50 persons or more = 32"
Table 1020.3

Occupant Load = 150

150 occupants × 0.2 inches/person = 30 inches

30 inches < 32 inches provided by the exit door
30 inches < 44 inches provided by the corridor
Therefore, adequate exit width is provided

For SI: 1 inch = 25.4 mm.

Exception 1 in Section 1005.3.2 permits a 25-percent reduction in the egress width when the building is protected with an automatic sprinkler system designed in accordance with NFPA 13 or 13R and the building is equipped with an emergency voice/alarm communication system.

Code Text: *Where more than one exit, or access to more than one exit, is required, the means of egress shall be configured such that the loss of any one exit, or access to one exit, shall not reduce the available capacity to less than 50 percent of the required capacity or width.*

Discussion and Commentary: This section only applies when more than one exit is provided and stipulates that when one of the egress paths is blocked the other exit paths must provide at least one half of the required width. Where three or more means of egress are available, one of the egress points is considered unusable during an incident and the other egress routes must provide for 50 percent of the occupant load. Fire incidents have repeatedly proven that the majority of people will try to exit using the same path they entered a building. Consequently, where one of the exits is larger than the others, it logically should be the main entrance, because this will typically be used as the main exit.

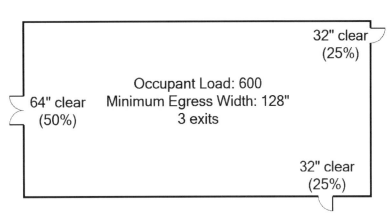

Given: Group M occupancy with 3 exits and a required egress width of 128".

Determine: The manner in which the egress width can be distributed.

Solution: Any manner is acceptable as long as when a single exit is blocked or unavailable, the remaining egress width provides at least 50% of the required egress width.

Egress Width Distribution

For SI: 1 inch = 25.4 mm.

A basic fundamental concept in the design of means of egress is that the capacity of the egress path shall not be diminished until the public way is reached. Regardless of the minimum required component width, the calculated width based on the occupant load served by the building or area must be maintained.

Code Text: *In the event of power supply failure, in buildings that require two or more exits or access to exits, an emergency electrical system shall automatically illuminate all of the following areas: (1) Interior exit access stairways and ramps, (2) Interior and exterior exit stairways and ramps, (3) Exit passageways, (4) Vestibules and areas on the level of discharge used for exit discharge in accordance with Section 1028.2, (5) Exterior landings as required by Section 1010.1.5 for exit doorways that lead directly to the exit discharge.*

Discussion and Commentary: Referred to as emergency lighting, a completely independent source of electrical power that is connected to certain portions of the building's lighting system is required when the life safety risk in a building reaches or exceeds a certain threshold. This threshold is recognized as the point at which the occupant load of the room, area or building is large enough to require two means of egress. In addition to the above locations, rooms or spaces requiring two or more exits must be provided with emergency lighting in the aisles, corridors and exit access stairways and ramps. This secondary source of power provides a minimal level of lighting to allow for egress when the main power supply is lost. See Section 1006 for determination of when two or more exits or exit access doorways are required.

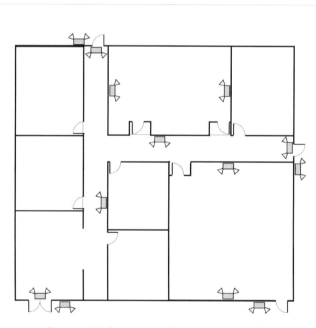

- Rooms with 2 or more exit or exit access doors
- Corridors where 2 or more exits are required
- Exterior landings at exit doors

So that the occupants are afforded the minimum level of safety required for a means of egress, the entire system must be illuminated any time the building is occupied. The emergency illumination must provide an intensity of a minimum one footcandle at the floor level (IFC Section 1008.2).

Topic: Two-Way Communications

Category: Means of Egress

Reference: IFC 1009.8

Subject: Accessible Means of Egress

Code Text: *A two-way communication system complying with Sections 1009.8.1 and 1009.8.2 shall be provided at the landing serving each elevator or bank of elevators on each accessible floor that is one or more stories above or below the level of exit discharge.*

(See IFC Section 1009.8 for exceptions.)

Discussion and Commentary: Section 1009.8 requires a two-way communication system at the accessible elevator landing of each floor of a building located above or below the story of exit discharge. This system is provided to offer a means of assistance to impaired individuals who need assistance. Such a system can be useful not only in the event of a fire but also in the case of a natural or technological disaster by providing emergency responders with the location of individuals who will require assistance in safely evacuating from a building.

(Photo Courtesy of Housing Devices Inc., Medford, MA.)

The two-way communication system provides communication between the required location and either the fire command center or a central control point approved by the fire department (IFC Section 1009.8.1).

Code Text: *Doors in the means of egress shall comply with the requirements of Sections 1010.1.1 through 1010.3.4. Exterior exit doors shall also comply with the requirements of Section 1022.2. Gates in the means of egress shall comply with the requirements of Sections 1010.4 and 1010.4.1. Turnstiles in the means of egress shall comply with the requirements of Sections 1010.5 through 1010.5.4.*

Doors, gates and turnstiles provided for egress purposes in numbers greater than required by this code shall comply with the requirements of this section.

Doors in the means of egress doors shall be readily distinguishable from the adjacent construction and finishes such that the doors are easily recognizable as doors. Mirrors or similar reflecting materials shall not be used on means of egress doors. Means of egress doors shall not be concealed by curtains, drapes, decorations or similar materials.

Discussion and Commentary: During a fire or an emergency, occupants will attempt to exit through those doors that they believe will eventually lead to the exterior. Accordingly, any doors, gates or turnstiles that suggest an egress path must meet specific requirements in Chapter 10. This includes door size, direction of swing, locking hardware and landings. Means of egress doors must be obvious and available for immediate use by the building occupants.

Gates and turnstiles installed in the means of egress present possible obstructions and must meet the requirements to be allowed in the egress path, or a clear and separate egress path must be provided.

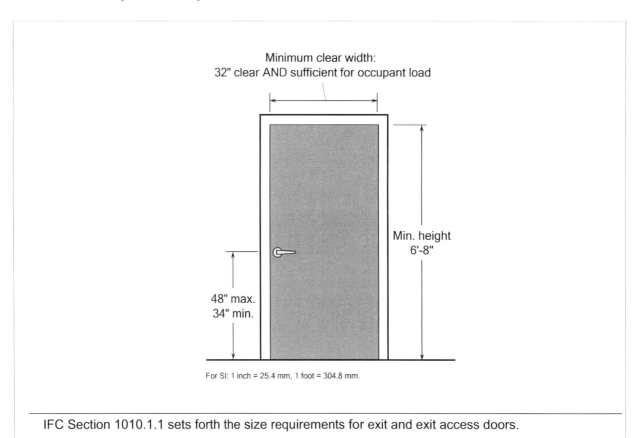

Minimum clear width:
32" clear AND sufficient for occupant load

Min. height
6'-8"

48" max.
34" min.

For SI: 1 inch = 25.4 mm, 1 foot = 304.8 mm.

IFC Section 1010.1.1 sets forth the size requirements for exit and exit access doors.

Code Text: *The required capacity of each door opening shall be sufficient for the occupant load thereof and shall provide a minimum clear opening width of 32 inches (813 mm). The clear opening width of doorways with swinging doors shall be measured between the face of the door and the stop, with the door open 90 degrees (1.57 rad). Where this section requires a minimum clear opening width of 32 inches (813 mm) and a door opening includes two door leaves without a mullion, one leaf shall provide a minimum clear opening width of 32 inches (813 mm). In Group I-2, doors serving as means of egress doors where used for the movement of beds shall provide a minimum clear opening width not less than 41½ inches (1054 mm). The minimum clear opening height of doors shall be not less than 80 inches (2032 mm).*

(See IFC Section 1010.1.1 for exceptions.)

Discussion and Commentary: Per IFC Section 1010.1.1.1, a clear width of 32 inches is required only to a height of 34 inches above the floor or ground. Beyond this point, projections up to 4 inches into the required width are permitted. Door latches and locks are required to be installed between 34 and 48 inches above the floor (IFC Section 1010.2.3). Although a single doorway is expected to be used for the egress of one individual at a time, it must also be adequate for wheelchair users.

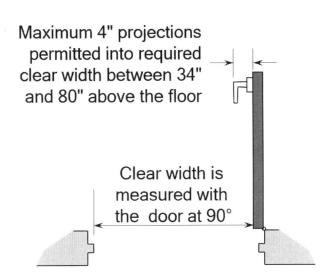

Maximum 4" projections permitted into required clear width between 34" and 80" above the floor

Clear width is measured with the door at 90°

Egress width at doors is net dimension

For SI: 1 degree = 0.01745 rad, 1 inch = 25.4 mm.

The width of a door leaf is no longer limited to 48 inches. The limitation on width is based on the effort needed in opening the door. Section 1010.1.3 limits the opening force to 15 pounds for fire-rated swinging doors and 5 pounds for all other swinging doors.

Code Text: ***Egress Door Types.*** *Egress doors shall be of the side-hinged swinging door, pivoted door or balanced door types.*

(See IFC Section 1010.1.2 for exceptions.)

Direction of swing. *Side-hinged swinging doors, pivoted doors and balanced doors shall swing in the direction of egress travel where serving a room or area containing an occupant load of 50 or more persons or a Group H occupancy.*

Forces to unlatch and open doors*. The forces to unlatch doors shall comply with the following: (1) Where door hardware operates by push or pull, the operational force to unlatch the door shall not exceed 15 pounds (66.7 N), (2) Where door hardware operates by rotation, the operational force to unlatch the door shall not exceed 28 inch-pounds (315 N-cm).*

The force to open doors shall comply with the following: (1) For interior swinging egress doors that are manually operated, other than doors required to be fire rated, the force for pushing or pulling open the door shall not exceed 5 pounds (22 N), (2) For other swinging doors, sliding doors or folding doors, and doors required to be fire rated, the door shall require not more than a 30-pound (133 N) force to be set in motion and shall move to a full-open position when subjected to not more than a 15-pound (67 N) force.

Discussion and Commentary: Doors serving a room or area with an occupant load of 50 persons or more or a Group H occupancy must swing in the direction of exit travel.

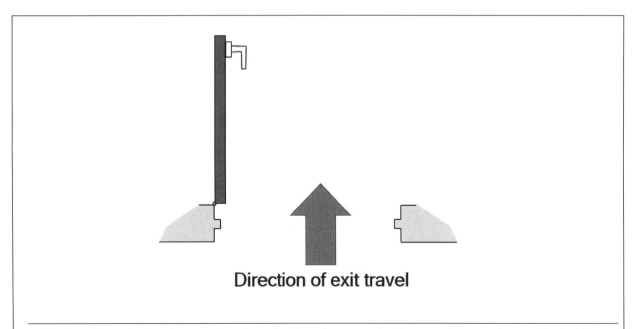

Direction of exit travel

Interior side swinging doors not equipped with a closer mechanism must open when subjected to a force not exceeding 5 pounds. Where a closer mechanism is provided such as for opening protective doors (fire doors) or exterior doors, the opening force is increased to 15 pounds so that the closure device can function properly.

Code Text: *Except as specifically permitted by this section, egress doors shall be readily openable from the egress side without the use of a key or special knowledge or effort.*

Discussion and Commentary: Every element along or within the path of exit travel in a means of egress system, including doors, must be under the control of, and operable by, the person seeking egress. The intent of this section is that the hardware that is installed be of a type familiar to most building occupants, readily recognizable and useable in an emergency. IFC Section 1010.2.5 specifically prohibits the use of manual flush or surface bolts because they require special knowledge to operate.

IFC Section 1010.2.4, Item 3 allows key operated locking devices in Group B, F, M and S occupancies, as well as religious facilities and assembly uses with an occupant load of 300 or less.

Code Text: *Locks and latches shall be permitted to prevent operation of doors where any of the following exist:*

(See IFC Section 1010.2.4 for Items 1 through 7)

8. Other than egress courts, where occupants must egress from an exterior space through the building for means of egress, exit access doors shall be permitted to be equipped with an approved locking device where installed and operated in accordance with all of the following:

8.1. The maximum occupant load shall be posted where required by Section 1004.9. Such sign shall be permanently affixed inside the building and shall be posted in a conspicuous space near all the exit access doorways.

8.2. A weatherproof telephone or two-way communication system installed in accordance with Sections 1009.8.1 and 1009.8.2 shall be located adjacent to not less than one required exit access door on the exterior side.

8.3. The egress door locking device is readily distinguishable as locked and shall be a key-operated locking device.

8.4. A clear window or glazed door opening, not less than 5 square feet (0.46 m²) in area, shall be provided at each exit access door to determine if there are occupants using the outdoor area.

8.5. A readily visible durable sign shall be posted on the interior side on or adjacent to each locked required exit access door serving the exterior area stating: "THIS DOOR TO REMAIN UNLOCKED WHEN THE OUTDOOR AREA IS OCCUPIED." The letters on the sign shall be not less than 1 inch (25.4 mm) high on a contrasting background.

8.6. The occupant load of the occupied exterior area shall not exceed 300 occupants in accordance with Section 1004.

Discussion and Commentary: These provisions are designed to meet the egress requirements and still provide security for outdoor areas and patios where the exits from the outdoor area must pass through the building. Outdoor dining areas having an occupant load of 50 or more must provide two exit paths, exit doors and exit access doors must swing in the direction of egress, and panic hardware is required on those doors (IFC Section 1006). When the door leads back into the building, installing panic hardware on the exterior side of the door does not provide any level of security.

These provisions allow for the doors to swing into the building, but don't require panic hardware. The doors can be locked with a key-operated deadbolt which remains locked until the patio or outdoor area is occupied. This allowance is limited to an area that accommodates no more than 300 occupants and there must be a phone or method of communication on the patio side of the doors in case someone does get trapped. This provides an acceptable means of egress while providing a way to secure the building.

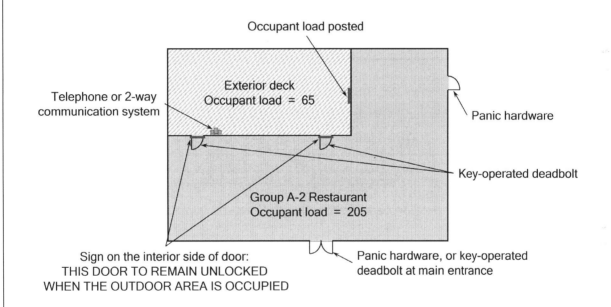

Occupant load posted

Telephone or 2-way
communication system

Exterior deck
Occupant load = 65

Panic hardware

Key-operated deadbolt

Group A-2 Restaurant
Occupant load = 205

Sign on the interior side of door:
THIS DOOR TO REMAIN UNLOCKED
WHEN THE OUTDOOR AREA IS OCCUPIED

Panic hardware, or key-operated
deadbolt at main entrance

Adjacent to the doors to the patio or outdoor area, a glazed opening of at least five square feet is required so an employee on the interior side can determine if the outdoor area is occupied prior to locking the door.

Code Text: *Swinging doors serving a Group H occupancy and swinging doors serving rooms or spaces with an occupant load of 50 or more in a Group A or E occupancy shall not be provided with a latch or lock other than panic hardware or fire exit hardware.* ***Exceptions:*** *(1) A main exit of a Group A occupancy shall be permitted to have locking devices in accordance with Section 1010.2.4, Item 3, (2) Doors provided with panic hardware or fire exit hardware and serving a Group A or E occupancy shall be permitted to be electrically locked in accordance with Section 1010.2.12 or 1010.2.11, (3) Exit access doors serving occupied exterior areas shall be permitted to be locked in accordance with Section 1010.2.4, Item 8, (4) Courtrooms shall be permitted to be locked in accordance with Section 1010.2.13, Item 3.*

Discussion and Commentary: Panic hardware is a door-latching assembly incorporating a device that releases the latch when force is applied in the direction of exit travel. It is utilized in assembly occupancies because of the hazard that occurs when a large number of occupants reach an exit door at the same instance. In Group H occupancies, the concern is rapid egress that is due to the potential for exposure to toxic or highly toxic materials or the rapid fire spread these materials can exhibit. Fire exit hardware is panic hardware listed for use on a fire-rated door assembly.

To ensure that contact with the door actuates the release mechanism, the code requires that the actuating portion extend for at least one-half the door width. Where balanced doors are used, the device width is again limited to one half of the door width for leverage purposes. (IFC Section 1010.2.9.3 and 1010.2.9.4)

Code Text: *Delayed egress locking systems shall be permitted to be installed on doors serving the following occupancies in buildings that are equipped throughout with an automatic sprinkler system in accordance with Section 903.3.1.1 or an approved automatic smoke or heat detection system installed in accordance with Section 907: (1) Group B, F, I, M, R, S and U occupancies, (2) Group E classrooms with an occupant load of less than 50, (3) In courtrooms in Group A-3 and B occupancies, delayed egress locking systems shall be permitted to be installed on exit or exit access doors, other than the main exit or exit access door, in buildings that are equipped throughout with an automatic sprinkler system in accordance with Section 903.3.1.1.*

Discussion and Commentary: Delayed egress is one method of meshing the need for safe and quick egress with the need for building and property security. The delayed-egress latch is designed to release when the fire sprinkler system or fire alarm system activates, or when the building experiences a loss of power. In other than Group I occupancies, the egress path from any point in the building cannot be required to pass through more than one delayed-egress door. (IFC Section 1010.2.13.1, Item 5)

Delayed egress normally delays the unlatching of the door for 15 seconds. When approved, the delay can be extended up to a maximum of 30 seconds (IFC Section 1010.2.13.1, Item 4).

Code Text: *In Groups B, F, M and S, horizontal sliding or vertical security grilles are permitted at the main exit and shall be openable from the inside without the use of a key or special knowledge or effort during periods that the space is occupied. The grilles shall remain secured in the full-open position during the period of occupancy by the general public. Where two or more exits or access to exits are required, not more than one-half of the exits or exit access doorways shall be equipped with horizontal sliding or vertical security grilles.*

Discussion and Commentary: Desires for security and the need for egress can result in conflicting requirements. It is common for businesses to use security grilles to provide security. The grilles are allowed provided the requirements are met for operation of the grilles and the provision exits other than through the security grille.

Horizontal or vertical security grilles are allowed at the main entrance provide they are secured in the full-open position during business hours.

Code Text: *Flights of stairways shall have handrails on each side and shall comply with Section 1014. Where glass is used to provide the handrail, the handrail shall also comply with Section 2407 of the* International Building Code.

(See IFC Section 1011.11 for exceptions.)

Discussion and Commentary: Handrails are a very important safety element of any stairway and must be located within relatively easy reach of every stair user. In most applications, a handrail must be provided on both sides of the stairway. In the case of extremely wide stairways, such as a monumental stair, the requirements for additional rails located throughout the width of the stairway is based on the required egress width, not the actual width.

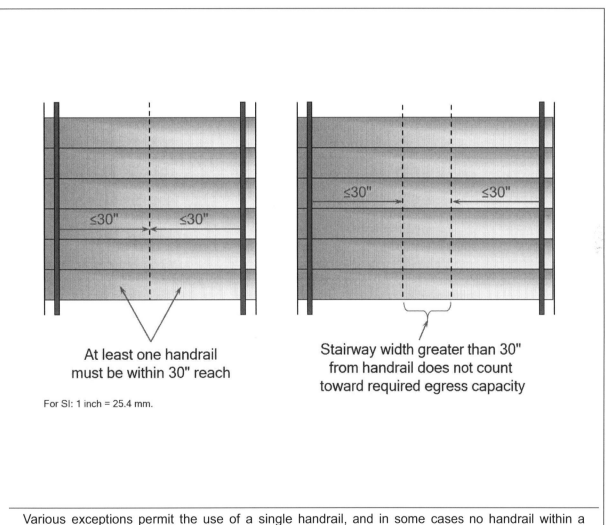

At least one handrail
must be within 30" reach

For SI: 1 inch = 25.4 mm.

Stairway width greater than 30"
from handrail does not count
toward required egress capacity

Various exceptions permit the use of a single handrail, and in some cases no handrail within a dwelling unit. In addition, aisle stairs with a center handrail, or those serving seating on only one side, are permitted to use a single handrail. When measuring egress width on a stairway, only the stair tread within 30 inches of a handrail is considered (IFC Section 1014.9).

Code Text: *Exits and exit access doors shall be marked by an approved exit sign readily visible from any direction of egress travel. The path of egress travel to exits and within exits shall be marked by readily visible exit signs to clearly indicate the direction of egress travel in cases where the exit or the path of egress travel is not immediately visible to the occupants. Intervening means of egress doors within exits shall be marked by exit signs. Exit sign placement shall be such that no point in an exit access corridor or exit passageway is more than 100 feet (30 480 mm) or the listed viewing distance for the sign, whichever is less, from the nearest visible exit sign.*

(See IFC Section 1013.1 for exceptions.)

Discussion and Commentary: Exit signs are only required when the room or area under consideration is required to have two or more exits or exit access doors. Other locations are also specified where the presence of an exit sign is deemed unnecessary, such as clearly identifiable main exit doors. Although the appropriate locations for exit signs should be identified during plan review, a true evaluation of their effectiveness should be done prior to occupancy so that the correct location and orientation of the signs can be inspected.

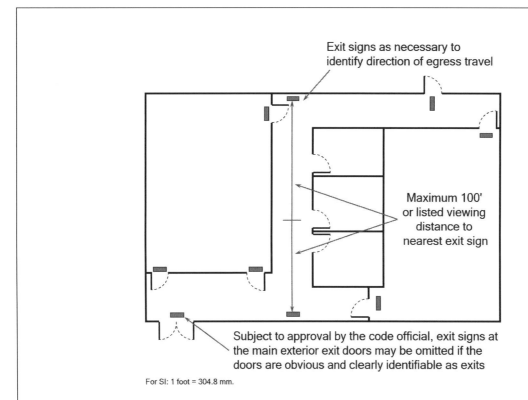

Exit signs as necessary to identify direction of egress travel

Maximum 100' or listed viewing distance to nearest exit sign

Subject to approval by the code official, exit signs at the main exterior exit doors may be omitted if the doors are obvious and clearly identifiable as exits

For SI: 1 foot = 304.8 mm.

Additional exit signs may be necessary in lengthy exit access corridors to reinforce the direction of egress travel. It is possible that individuals subjected to extended travel would question the availability of an exit and attempt to locate an alternative egress path.

Code Text: *Exit signs shall be illuminated at all times. To ensure continued illumination for a duration of not less than 90 minutes in case of primary power loss, the sign illumination means shall be connected to an emergency power system provided from storage batteries, unit equipment or an on-site generator. The installation of the emergency power system shall be in accordance with Section 1203. Group I-2, Condition 2 exit sign illumination shall not be provided by unit equipment battery only.* **Exception:** *Approved exit sign illumination types that provide continuous illumination independent of external power sources for a duration of not less than 90 minutes, in case of primary power loss, are not required to be connected to an emergency electrical system.*

Discussion and Commentary: To ensure visibility during an emergency, required exit signs must always be illuminated. The code official can approve alternative types of signs or lighting systems to those specified, provided that equivalent lighting levels can be achieved. A separate source of power is required for all required exit signs, regardless of the occupant load served, much in the same manner as is required for the path of travel illuminations.

Exit signs must be illuminated during normal operations and for 90 minutes after a power loss. Additionally, IFC Section 1013.2 requires low-level exit signs in Group R-1 occupancies.

Quiz

Study Session 8

IFC Chapter 10

1. A yard that provides access to a public way for one or more exits is considered a(n) _____.

    a. exit accessway   (b.) egress court

    c. public way   d. horizontal exit

    Reference 1002.1 202

2. Which of the following elements is not a distinct and separate part of the means of egress?

    a. exit discharge   b. exit access

    c. exit   (d.) exit conveyance

    Reference 1002.1 202

3. That portion of the exit access that occupants must traverse before two separate and distinct paths of egress travel to two exits are available is called a _____.

    a. means of egress

    b. single egress path

    (c.) common path of egress travel

    d. limited egress travel distance

    Reference 1002.1 202

4. In a dining room without fixed seating, the occupant load is determined by dividing the _____ floor area by a factor of one occupant per _____ square feet.

    a. net, 7   (b.) net, 15

    c. gross, 15   d. net, 20

    Reference 1004.5

5. A 1,500 square foot wood working shop classroom in a high school is considered to have a design occupant load of _____ persons.

    a. 20   b. 30
    c. 50   d. 100

    Reference 1004.5

6. For areas having fixed seating and aisles, the occupant load for bench seating without armrests is based on one occupant for each _____ inches of seating length.

    a. 15   b. 18
    c. 24   d. 30

    Reference 1004.6

7. In a completely sprinklered Group B office building having an occupant load of 3,200 persons that is not equipped with an emergency voice/alarm communication system, the minimum required means of egress width by egress other than stairways shall be _____ inches.

    a. 320   b. 480
    c. 640   d. 960

    Reference 1005.3.2

8. A stairway serving 200 occupants in a fully sprinklered Group I-2 hospital shall have a minimum width of _____ inches.

    a. 60   b. 80
    c. 120   d. 160

    Reference 1005.3.1

9. Given: A building with 3 required exits. The means of egress shall be sized so that the loss of any one means of egress shall not reduce the available capacity by more than _____ of the required capacity.

    a. 10%   b. 25%
    c. 33^1/$_3$%   d. 50%

    Reference 1005.5

10. When fully open, a door is permitted to project into the required width of the path of egress travel a maximum of _____ .

    a. $\frac{1}{2}$ the required width   b.   4 inches

    c. $4\frac{1}{2}$ inches   (d.)   7 inches

Reference 1005.7.1

11. Up to 50 percent of the ceiling area of a means of egress may have a minimum ceiling height of _____ where reduced by protruding objects.

    a.   78 inches   (b.)   80 inches

    c.   84 inches   d.   90 inches

Reference 1003.3.1

12. At doorways, the minimum headroom clearance below any door closer or stop shall be _____ .

    a.   76 inches   (b.)   78 inches

    c.   80 inches   d.   84 inches

Reference 1003.3.1

13. Given: A sprinklered, two-story Group B occupancy with an occupant load of 400 on each story. What is the maximum common path of egress travel distance on the 1st floor?

    a.   20 feet   b.   75 feet

    (c.)   100 feet   d.   There is no restriction on the 1st floor.

Reference 1006.2.1

14. In general, a door opening shall provide a minimum clear width of _____ inches.

    a.   30   (b.)   32

    c.   34   d.   36

Reference 1010.1.1

15. In a Group I-2 hospital, means of egress doors used for the movement of beds shall have a minimum width of _____ inches.

    a. 32   b. 36

    (c.) $41^1/_2$ d. 44

Reference 1010.1.1

16. The minimum required width for door openings does not apply to storage closets less than _____ square feet in floor area.

    (a.) 10   b. 25

    c. 50   d. 100

Reference 1010.1.1

17. At a door opening, the maximum permitted projection into the required clear width shall be _____ at any point below 34 inches above the floor.

    (a.) 0 inches, no projections are permitted

    b. $^1/_2$ inch

    c. 1 inch

    d. 4 inches

Reference 1010.1.1.1

18. A facility is required to provide three exits because the occupant load is 600 persons. The building has provided more exterior exit doors than are required by the code. Which of the following is not required for these additional doors?

    a. Must be same size and direction of swing as the required exit doors.

    (b.) Must be provided with exit signs as required for the exit doors.

    c. Must be provided with the same door hardware as required for the exit doors.

    d. Must meet the same opening force requirements as required for the exit doors.

Reference 1010.1

19. In a Group B occupancy, egress doors shall swing in the direction of egress travel when serving an occupant load of _____ persons or more.

    a. 3   b. 10

    c. 30   (d.) 50

Reference 1010.1.2.1

20. Which occupancy requires low-level exit signs?

    a. Group A   b. Group B

    c. Group E   (d) Group R-1

Reference 1013.2

21. Externally illuminated exit signs shall have a minimum intensity at the face of the sign of _____ footcandles.

    a. 1   (b) 5

    c. 10   d. 12

Reference 1013.6.2

22. What is the minimum required operating duration of the secondary power source for an electric exit sign in the event the primary building power is lost?

    a. 15 minutes   b. 30 minutes

    c. 60 minutes   (d.) 90 minutes

Reference 1013.6.3

23. In a Group B occupancy in a fully sprinklered building, the maximum permitted exit access travel distance is _____ feet.

    a. 200   b. 250

    (c.) 300   d. 350

Reference 1017.2

24. In a nonsprinklered Group F-1 manufacturing facility, the maximum permitted exit travel distance is _____ feet.

    (a.) 200   b. 250

    c. 300   d. 350

Reference 1017.2

25. What is the minimum corridor width required for a Group E occupancy serving a design occupant load of 100 or more persons?

    a. 24 inches   b. 36 inches

    c. 44 inches   (d.) 72 inches

Reference 1020.3

26. Given: A Group F-1 occupancy that is not equipped with an automatic sprinkler system. The design occupant load for the building is 180 persons. What is the required fire-resistance rating for an exit corridor that serves all of the occupants?

    a.   0 hours   b.   30 minutes

    c.   1 hour   d.   2 hours

Reference 1020.2

27. What is the maximum occupant load allowed for a single-story Group S occupancy equipped with one means of egress?

    a.   29   b.   49

    c.   50   d.   Two means of egress are required.

Reference 1006.3.4 (2)

28. Given: A boiler room housing a natural gas fired boiler with a heat exchange rate of 900,000 BTUs. The area of the boiler room is 1,400 square feet. How many exit access doorways are required?

    a.   one   b.   two

    c.   three   d.   four

Reference 1006.2.2.2

29. An anhydrous ammonia refrigeration machinery room larger than _____ square feet shall have not less than two exits or exit access doors.

    a.   300   b.   500

    c.   750   d.   1,000

Reference 1006.2.2.2

30. When a Group A occupancy has an occupancy load greater than _____ the main exit must be sized to accommodate one-half of the occupant load.

    a.   100   b.   300

    c.   500   d.   1,000

Reference 1030.2

31. The maximum length of a dead-end corridor allowed in a Group F occupancy protected by an NFPA 13 compliant automatic sprinkler system is _____.

    a.   20 feet   b.   30 feet

    c.   40 feet   d.   50 feet

Reference 1020.5

32. When is a luminous egress path marking system required in Group R-1 occupancies?

    a. When the occupant load exceeds 50.

    b. When the fire area is greater than 3,000 ft².

    c. When the Group R-1 occupancy is located in a high-rise building.

    d. Such a marking system is not required.

Reference 1025.1

33. What is the minimum required testing frequency for two-way communication systems serving an area of refuge?

    a. monthly   b. every 3 months

    c. every 6 months   d. yearly

Reference 1032.8

34. A room classified as a Group A-2 occupancy has dimensions of 60 feet by 80 feet and is in a sprinklered building. What is the minimum required separation distance between two of the exits?

    a. 33.3 feet   b. 50 feet

    c. 62.7 feet   d. 100 feet

Reference 1007.1.1

35. What are the testing requirements for emergency lighting for egress illumination?

    a. test each time bulbs are replaced

    b. test monthly for 30 seconds

    c. test annually for 90 minutes

    d. both b and c

Reference 1032.10.1
1032.10.2

2021 IFC Chapters 20 through 24

Special Occupancies and Operations, Part I: Aviation Facilities; Dry Cleaning; Combustible Dust-producing Operations; Motor Fuel-dispensing Facilities and Repair Garages; and Flammable Finishes

OBJECTIVE: To obtain an understanding of the *International Fire Code*® (IFC®) requirements for occupancies housing aviation facilities, dry cleaning and combustible dust-producing operations, and fire protection features for fuel-dispensing facilities and application of flammable finishes.

REFERENCE: Chapters 20 through 24, 2021 IFC

KEY POINTS:
- What are some of the specific hazards associated with aircraft-related occupancies, and how are they dealt with in the IFC?
- What are the basic general requirements that apply to all aircraft-related operations and facilities?
- How and where are flammable and combustible liquid finishes to be applied to aircraft?
- What requirements apply to aircraft repair work that requires the use of open flames or spark-producing devices?
- When and where are fire extinguishers required in aviation facilities, and what types are to be provided?
- What requirements apply to the refueling of aircraft motor vehicles?
- What are the electrical requirements for bonding of fueling equipment and aircraft?
- How often are emergency fuel shutoff devices required to be tested?
- How do the requirements differ for overwing and underwing fueling operations?
- How is the operation of radar equipment related to aircraft fuel-servicing operations?
- What is the difference between a heliport and a helistop, and which requirements apply to each?
- What are the characteristics of the different classes of solvents used in dry cleaning processes?

- Which class of dry cleaning plant is prohibited? What general requirements apply to all plants?

- What are the ventilation requirements for dry cleaning facilities?

- What construction requirements for dry cleaning plants are found in the IFC?

- What are the maximum quantities allowed for solvents, and how are they to be stored?

- When are automatic sprinkler systems and automatic fire-extinguishing systems required in dry cleaning plants? What may be substituted for an automatic fire-extinguishing system?

- What is the definition of combustible dust?

- Where can the permit requirements for combustible dust be found in the IFC?

- Are any permits required for combustible dust-producing operations?

- What general precautions are required for all activities where combustible dust is present?

- How can you determine when the accumulation of combustible dust creates a potential hazard?

- What are the allowed methods for cleaning fugitive combustible dust?

- When is a dust collection system required?

- Which motor vehicle fuels are regulated in the IFC?

- What are the requirements for attended and unattended self-service dispensing of motor vehicle fuels?

- What are the specific requirements for the inspection and repair of dispensers and dispensing equipment?

- What types of storage tanks can be used for the storage of motor vehicle fuels? Where can these tanks be located in relation to buildings, property lines, dispensers and other tanks?

- How is the potential for spills or releases from above-ground storage tanks storing Class I, III and III liquids controlled?

- What are the requirements for locating and installing dispensers for alternative fuels such as liquefied petroleum gas, compressed natural gas and either compressed or cryogenic hydrogen?

- How are the ventilation requirements for repair garages for alternative fuel vehicles different than those used for the repair of conventional fuel vehicles?

- What operations are regulated under application of flammable finishes?

- For flammable finish areas, what are the general requirements to protect against explosions and fires? How are potential sources of ignition controlled?

- How are spray rooms and spray booths constructed, and what are the size limitations?

- What are the ventilation requirements for areas where flammable liquids are sprayed?

- How are dip tanks constructed? What are the applicable fire protection and alarm requirements?

- What requirements apply to hardening and tempering tanks? Or flow-coating and roll-coating operations?

- What is electrostatic spraying? What is paint detearing? How are the additional hazards that are present during these operations addressed by the IFC?

Code Text: *Regulations not specifically contained herein pertaining to airports, aircraft mainte-*
nance, aircraft hangars and appurtenant operations shall be in accordance with nation-
ally recognized standards.

Discussion and
Commentary: Many of the subject areas in the IFC can become complex, and it may not be possible to
address all of the issues and technical details that may arise while performing a fire prevention inspection. Aviation facilities are no exception. Chapter 20 includes numerous
references to other chapters or sections in the IFC, the *International Building Code®*
(IBC®), NFPA 70 and other nationally recognized standards. IFC Section 2001.2 makes it
clear that the fire code official is authorized to enforce such related nationally recognized
standards for items not specifically addressed in Chapter 20.

SECTION	REFERENCE	SUBJECT
2001.3	IFC 105.5	Permits for aircraft-refueling vehicles, application of flammable or combustible finishes, hot work, etc.
2003.2	IFC 310	"No Smoking" signs
2003.4	IFC Chapter 5	Fire apparatus access roads
2003.5	IFC Chapter 57	Dispensing, transferring and storage of flammable and combustible liquids
2003.5	IFC Chapter 23	Aircraft motor vehicle fuel-dispensing stations
2003.7	IFC Chapter 50	Hazardous materials storage
2004.2	IFC Chapter 24	Application of flammable and combustible liquid finishes
2004.3	IFC 5705.3.6	Cleaning with flammable and combustible liquids
2004.4.3	IFC 5003.3	Mitigation of flammable and combustible liquid spills
2004.6	IBC, various	Repair of aircraft indoors using open flame, etc., to comply with IBC requirements for F-1 occupancies
2004.7	NFPA 410	Construction, modification, maintenance and repair of aircraft
2005	IFC 906	Portable fire extinguishers, multiple references
2006.1	IFC Chapter 23	Aircraft motor vehicle fuel-dispensing facilities
2006.2	NFPA 407	Design and construction of airport fuel systems
2006.3	NFPA 407	Design and construction of aircraft-fueling vehicles and accessories
2006.3.4	NFPA 70	Protection of electrical equipment, to be vapor-tight, etc.
2006.8	IFC 5706.5.1.12	Loading racks for aircraft-fueling vehicles
2006.17	IBC, various	Indoor fuel transfer areas to meet IBC F-1 occupancy requirements
2007.1	IBC, various	Helistops and heliports on buildings to be constructed in accordance with the IBC
2007.4	IBC 412.7	Exits and stairways
2007.6	IFC 903, 904, 905	Automatic sprinkler systems, standpipes and foam-extinguishing systems
2007.7	IFC 906	Fire extinguishers
2007.8	FAA (Federal Aviation Administration)	FAA approval required before operating helistops and heliports

The referenced standards are listed in IFC Chapter 80.

Code Text: *Open flames, flame-producing devices and other sources of ignition shall not be permitted in a hangar, except in approved locations or in any location within 50 feet (15 240 mm) of an aircraft-fueling operation.*

Discussion and Commentary: IFC Section 2003 contains provisions to regulate seven items that have been proven to cause fires at aviation facilities. The requirements for control of ignition sources, housekeeping and proper storage of combustible materials and hazardous materials, as well as maintaining fire department access, can reduce the risks of fire at aviation facilities.

NFPA 409 contains fire protection requirements for aircraft hangars (IFC Section 914.8). NFPA 410 contains requirements for aircraft maintenance and operations both in the hangar and at the aviation facility (IFC Section 2004.7).

Code Text: *Portable fire extinguishers suitable for flammable or combustible liquid and electrical-type fires shall be provided as specified in Sections 2005.2 through 2005.6 and Section 906. Extinguishers required by this section shall be inspected and maintained in accordance with Section 906.*

Discussion and Commentary: Portable fire extinguishers are designed for the occupants to attack a fire at its incipient stage. IFC Section 906 contains the requirements for extinguishers in buildings, including aviation facilities. IFC Section 2005.1 requires extinguishers in locations away from buildings, including on aircraft-servicing vehicles, where the combination of ignition sources and the presence of large amounts of fuel being dispensed at high flow rates creates a major fire risk. NFPA Standards 10 and 407 provide additional guidance.

PORTABLE FIRE EXTINGUISHERS FOR AVIATION FACILITIES

REQUIRED LOCATION	MINIMUM NUMBER AND TYPE
On aircraft towing vehicles	One (1) extinguisher 20-B:C
On welding apparatus	One (1) extinguisher 2-A:20-B:C
On aircraft fuel-servicing tank vehicles	Two (2) extinguishers* 20-B:C
On hydrant fuel-servicing vehicles	One (1) extinguisher 20-B:C
AT FUEL-DISPENSING STATIONS	
OPEN-HOSE DISCHARGE CAPACITY	MINIMUM NUMBER AND TYPE
Up to 200 gpm	Two (2) extinguishers 20-B:C
More than 200 gpm, not more than 350 gpm	One (1) wheeled extinguisher 80-B:C, 125 lb agent
More than 350 gpm	Two (2) wheeled extinguishers 80-B:C, 125 lb agent

* readily accessible from either side of vehicle

Section 2007.7 also requires at least one portable fire extinguisher with a minimum 80-B:C rating to be provided at each permanent takeoff and landing area for helicopters and at helicopter parking areas.

Code Text: *Airport fuel systems shall be designed and constructed in accordance with NFPA 407.*

Discussion and Commentary: NFPA 407 is a nationally recognized standard that provides additional useful and detailed information regarding airport fuel systems, including aircraft-fueling vehicles and accessories. One of the main focuses of IFC Section 2006 is the separation of ignition sources, such as heat, sparks, open flames and powerful radar beams, from aviation fuels.

CONTROLLING SOURCES OF IGNITION DURING AIRCRAFT FUELING

IGNITION SOURCE	IFC REQUIREMENT	CODE SECTION
Internal combustion engine for fuel pump on transfer apparatus	Separation distance, separate compartment, exhaust system shielding	2006.3.1.1
Gear- or chain-driven fuel pump on transfer apparatus	Approved design installed & maintained in an approved manner	2006.3.1.2
Dispensing hoses and nozzles	Bonding cable attached to aircraft	2006.3.3
Electrical equipment	Enclosed in vapor-tight housing, electrical motors approved for classified (hazardous) location use per *National Electrical Code*	2006.3.4
Aircraft-fueling vehicles	Fuel transfer apparatus metallically interconnected (bonded) with tanks, chassis, axles and springs	2006.3.7
Bonding cables	Electrical cable for bonding to be attached to vehicle, clamped to aircraft	2006.3.7.1
Bond cable protection	Bonding cable to be protected, stored to prevent kinks or breakage	2006.3.7.2
Smoking in vehicles	Smoking is prohibited and "No Smoking" signs are required in vehicles	2006.3.8
Smoking equipment	Prohibited in fueling vehicles	2006.3.9
Equipment maintenance	To be performed in approved areas	2006.4.1
Positioning at aircraft fuel system vent openings	Maintain 10 ft. between aircraft fuel system vent openings & aircraft-fueling vehicle	2006.5.1.2
Attachment of bond cables	Electrically bond fueling vehicle to aircraft prior to making fueling connections & removal the bond after fueling connections have been uncoupled	2006.5.2
Hoses	Shall be conductive	2006.5.2.1
Nozzles	Equipped with bonding conductors designed to attach to the aircraft	2006.5.2.2
Funnels	Metal, with direct contact between nozzle & aircraft	2006.5.2.3
Passengers	No smoking or open flame on or within 50 ft of aircraft	2006.9
Flame producing equipment	Fueling operations separated by 50 ft.	2006.10
Aircraft engines and heaters	Shut off during fueling operations unless permitted by the Exceptions	2006.12
Other vehicles	Vehicles and equipment not associated with fueling operation require a separation of 50 ft. with one exception	2006.13
Fueling equipment location	Not allowed beneath wing for overwing fueling when tank vents are on the upper wing	2006.13.1
Electrical equipment	Not to be connected or disconnected during fuel service operations	2006.14
Electrical or other spark-producing equipment	Not to be used within 10 ft. of fueling equipment, fill or vent points or spill areas unless intrinsically safe and approved for use in explosive atmosphere	2006.14.1
Open flames & open-flame devices	Prohibited within 50 ft. of fuel-servicing operations or fueling equipment	2006.15
Matches and lighters	Personnel not to carry; prohibited in, on or about fueling equipment	2006.15.2
Lightning	Fire code official may require written procedures for suspension of fueling	2006.16
Indoor aircraft fuel transfer	With two exceptions, indoor fuel transfer is prohibited	2006.17
Buildings or structures; boiler, heater or incinerator intake vents	A minimum separation of 25 feet from buildings and 50 feet. from intake vents for aircraft being fueled	2006.17.1
Radar equipment	Depending on the activity, a minimum 100 to 300 separation is required between weather-mapping radar & aircraft fuel servicing	2006.21
Radar beam direction	Not to be directed toward fuel storage or loading racks (see exceptions)	2006.21.1

Aircraft-fueling vehicles shall only be attended and operated by persons instructed in the proper use and operation of the vehicle, be trained as to the hazards of the fuel, and have received fire safety training (IFC Section 2006.5.3).

Code Text: *Aircraft-fueling vehicles shall comply with this section and shall be designed and constructed in accordance with NFPA 407.*

Discussion and Commentary: NFPA 407 also provides additional detailed recommendations on the design, construction and operation of aircraft-fueling vehicles. The fuel-related provisions of IFC Section 2006 are directed toward the "Fuel" side of the Fire Triangle in that they attempt to prevent leaks or spills that expose flammable or combustible liquids to the combination of oxygen and ignition sources that can and do result in fires.

AIRCRAFT FUELING VEHICLES – LEAK, SPILL AND IGNITION CONTROLAND PREVENTION FEATURES

COMPONENT OR OPERATION	IFC REQUIREMENT	CODE SECTION
Fuel pumps	Bypass relief valve, pressure gauge on discharge side	2006.3.2
Hoses and nozzles	Shortest efficient length, shutoff nozzle, self-closing, hand pressure only, no hold open devices	2006.3.3
Hose reels	Packing gland or other device to prevent fuel leakage between reels and fuel manifolds	2006.3.6
Vehicle Integrity	Shall be maintained leak free at all times	2006.4.2
Leaking fueling equipment	Defuel & remove from service immediately	2006.4.3
Movement of fueling vehicle during fueling	Set parking brake & deploy two chock blocks to prevent movement of fueling vehicle	2006.5.1.3
Transfer personnel	One at nozzle and one at pumping equipment (see exceptions)	2006.5.4
Fuel flow control	"Dead man" control of fuel flow valve at nozzle	2006.5.5
Emergency fuel shutoff	Procedures for mitigating, investigating and notifying the fire department of fuel spills are required	2006.6
Hose protection	Hoses properly stored before moving vehicle, no hose dragging	2006.7
Loading and unloading	Approved loading operations complying with Section 5706.5.1.12 (see exceptions)	2006.8
Equipment maintenance	Equipment shall be maintained and free from leaks	2006.11.1
Fuel nozzles	Fuel nozzles shall not dragged	2006.11.2
Fueling from containers	If the container volume is > 5 gallons an approved pump is required	2006.11.3
Fuel spill procedures	In the event of fuel spill the transfer operation shall be stopped and a supervisor notified	2006.11.4
Report of spill incidents	Fire department must be notified once the notification criteria is met	2006.11.5
Investigation	All spills requiring a fire department notification must be investigated	2006.11.6
Multiple fueling vehicles	Simultaneous dispensing into two or more aircraft is prohibited unless a means of backflow prevention is provided	2006.11.7
Inspection of hoses	Fuel dispensing hoses are subject to periodic daily and monthly inspections	2006.19.1
Repaired hoses	After hose repairs, inspection and pressure testing is required before use	2006.19.3
New hoses	New hoses require a visually inspection before being placed in service	2006.19.4
Parking fuel-servicing vehicles	The parking area allows for rapid removal of vehicles of one tank vehicle is found to have leaks. The location must limit the potential of leakage from impacting exposure buildings and storm drains	2006.20

Knowing the hazards of aviation fuel is an important element of applying IFC requirements. Kerosene formulations, such as commercial JET A, JET A-1 and military JP-8, are Class II combustible liquids with a flash point of 100°F or above. Aviation gasoline (AVGAS) and blends of kerosene and gasoline, such as JET B and JP-4, are Class IB flammable liquids with flash points below 73°F.

Code Text: *Hoses shall be designed for the transferring of hydrocarbon liquids and shall not be any longer than necessary to provide efficient fuel-transfer operations. Hoses shall be equipped with an approved shutoff nozzle. Fuel-transfer nozzles shall be self-closing and designed to be actuated by hand pressure only. Notches and other devices shall not be used for holding a nozzle valve handle in the open position. Nozzles shall be equipped with a bonding cable complete with proper attachment for aircraft to be serviced.*

Discussion and Commentary: This section deals with the safety and reliability of the fuel transfer hose. Hoses which are longer than needed result in extra wear and abuse. However, the length needed is most likely subject to the type of aircraft being fueled. Oftentimes the fuel vehicle must avoid baggage handling operations and personnel replenishing supplies on the aircraft.

The fueling vehicle operator must set the parking brake, position two chock blocks at the tires of the fueling vehicle and make the bonding and grounding connections prior to making the fuel connections to the aircraft (IFC Section 2006.5).

Kerosene and kerosene-gasoline blends in jet fuels can easily become ionized and discharge a static spark because of the high transfer rates during large aircraft fueling. Transfer rates of 100–200 gallons per minute are not uncommon. If the ionized electrical energy is not safely discharged to an electrical ground, an electrical arc can be produced that can ignite the fuel.

Code Text: *Dry cleaning solvents shall be classified according to their flash points as follows:*

Dry cleaning plants and systems shall be classified based on the solvents used as follows: (See table below.)

Discussion and Commentary: The classification system for dry cleaning solvents is a simplified version of the classification system for flammable and combustible liquids found in IFC Chapter 57. All three classes of flammable liquids are combined into Type I. This works well with the simplified treatment of flammable liquids in Chapter 21. Type I plants and systems are prohibited, and only limited amounts of Type I (flammable) solvents are permitted for spotting and pretreating. The three combustible liquids are classified according to their closed cup flash point temperature as Class II, IIIA or IIIB combustible solvents. The Type IV classification is added for nonflammable solvents.

CLASSIFICATION OF DRY CLEANING SOLVENTS

SOLVENT CLASS	FLASH POINT	EXAMPLE	FLAMMABLE AND COMBUSTIBLE LIQUID CLASSIFICATION (IFC SEC. 202)
I	<100°F	Petroleum Naptha	Class IB or IC, depending on formulation
II	≥100°F <140°F	Mineral Spirits, Stoddard Solvent	Class II
IIIA	≥140°F <200°F	Isoparaffins, Aliphatic hydrocarbon, Isoalkanes	Class IIIA
IIIB	≥200°F	Propylene Glycol Ether	Class IIIB
IV	Nonflammable	Perchloroetylene	Nonflammable

CLASSIFICATION OF DRY CLEANING PLANTS

SOLVENT CLASS	CAN DRY CLEANING BE PERFORMED BY THE PUBLIC (SELF-SERVICE)	CLASSIFICATION OF DRY CLEANING PLANT OR SYSTEM
I	No	Type I
II	No	Type II
IIIA	No	Type III-A
IIIB	No	Type III-B
IV	No	Type IV
IV	Yes	Type V

Perchlorethylene, or Perc, is a common solvent used in dry cleaning plants and shops. It is a nonflammable liquid and thus is a Class IV solvent used in Class IV and V plants, machines and systems. Perchloroethylene is nonflammable; however, during a fire, it can decompose into hydrogen chloride and phosgene, which can be toxic.

Code Text: *Building services and systems shall be designed, installed and maintained in accordance with this section and Chapter 6.*

Discussion and Commentary: Similar to many uses and their associated hazards that are addressed in the IFC, there are a number of precautions that, when properly taken, can prevent a high percentage of the fires or other incidents that might otherwise occur in dry cleaning plants. IFC Section 2104.2 requires mechanical ventilation in accordance with the *International Mechanical Code®* (IMC®), the use of approved heating and electrical equipment, and the proper bonding and grounding of electrical equipment when combustible liquids are used as a dry cleaning fluid.

New dry cleaning processes have been developed that use nontoxic substances such as carbon dioxide or other methods such as water-based cleaning systems that reduce flammability, health and air emissions concerns. Even if new processes see widespread use, Type I, II and III solvents are likely to continue to be used for spotting and pretreating.

Code Text: ***Class I solvents.*** *The maximum quantity of Class I solvents permitted at any work station shall be 1 gallon (4 L). Spotting or prespotting shall be permitted to be conducted with Class I solvents where they are stored in and dispensed from approved safety cans or in sealed DOT-approved metal shipping containers of not more than 1-gallon (4 L) capacity.*

      Spotting and prespotting. *Spotting and prespotting shall be permitted to be conducted with Class I solvents where dispensed from plastic containers of not more than 1 pint (0.5 L) capacity.*

Discussion and Commentary: Class I dry cleaning plants and Class I dry cleaning equipment is prohibited (IFC Section 2104.1); however, Class I flammable liquids can be stored and used in limited quantities. Class I liquids are often used for spotting garments or pretreating areas.

      The limitations for Class I flammable liquids are as follows:

- Largest container size of one gallon—this container must be a metal shipping container or a metal safety can
- Maximum of one gallon at a work station
- Containers at the work station can be plastic with a maximum size of 1 pint, or metal with a maximum size of 1 gallon
- The aggregate quantity cannot exceed the maximum allowable quantity per control area

(Photograph courtesy of Getty Images.)

Open-use of Class IB flammable liquids is limited to 30 gallons in storage per control area, which can be increased by 100 percent when the building is protected by an automatic sprinkler system. Storing the liquids in a flammable liquid storage cabinet can also increase the maximum allowable quantity by 100 percent (IFC Table 5003.1.1(1) Footnotes d and e).

Code Text: *An automatic sprinkler system shall be installed in accordance with Section 903.3.1.1 throughout dry cleaning plants containing Type II, Type III-A or Type III-B dry cleaning systems.*

(See IFC Section 2108.2 for exceptions.)

Discussion and Commentary: The IFC recognizes alternative engineering controls for an automatic sprinkler system for dry cleaning plants using Class III combustible liquids as an alternative to less environmentally friendly dry cleaning fluids.

The *International Building Code*® (IBC®) is referenced for the design and construction of buildings containing dry cleaning plants, which are classified as Group B and F-1 occupancies. IBC Section 415.9.3 refers to the IMC for ventilation and the *International Plumbing Code*® (IPC®) for sanitary sewers and drains, NFPA 32 for additional construction criteria and refers back to the IFC for the classification of dry cleaning solvents and systems.

Code Text: *The equipment, processes and operations involving dust explosion hazards and use or handling of combustible dust shall comply with the provisions of this chapter.* ***Exceptions:*** *(1) Storage and use of consumer materials in Group B or R occupancies, (2) Storage and use of commercially packaged materials in Group M occupancies, (3) Materials displayed in original packaging in Group M occupancies and intended as building materials or for personal or household use, (4) Storage of sealed containers of combustible dust at facilities not associated with an operation that uses, handles or generates combustible dust, (5) Materials stored or used in farm buildings or similar occupancies intended for on-premises agricultural purposes.*

Discussion and Commentary: Chapter 22 references NFPA 652, *The Fundamentals of Combustible Dust*, and various other NFPA standards that address the proper handling and removal of combustible dusts. These standards require the dust to be tested to evaluate its susceptibility to ignition and its potential energy if a deflagration occurs. The standards also require the establishment of a management of change program so that plant employees and contractors are aware of the dust deflagration hazard.

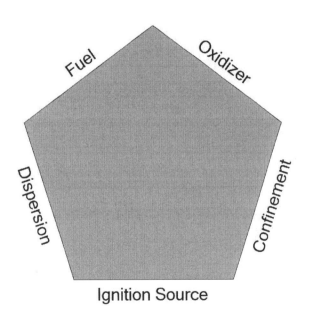

DEFLAGRATION PENTAGON

In past years, dating back to what may be the first recorded dust explosion in an Italian flour mill in 1785, coal dust and grain or flour dust explosions were common. Although agricultural combustible dust continues to present a dust deflagration hazard, more recent explosions have also involved dust from man-made substances, including polyethylene, phenolic resin powder and various types of metals.

Code Text: *The maximum dust layer on all surfaces, including but not limited to walls, ceilings, beams, equipment, furniture, pipes and ducts, shall not exceed the critical depth layer specified in Table 2203.1. The critical depth layer is permitted to be adjusted for explosion hazard where further evaluated in accordance with one of the following: (1) Section 7.2.1.3 of NFPA 654. (2) Section 4.1.3.3 of NFPA 664 for wood floor.*

Accumulated combustible dust shall be collected by one of the methods listed in Section 2203.5.

TABLE 2203.1
CRITICAL DEPTH LAYER

TYPE OF DUST	CRITICAL DEPTH LAYER (INCHES)
Wood flour	$\frac{1}{8}$
All other dusts	$\frac{1}{32}$

For SI: 1 inch = 25.4 mm.

Discussion and Commentary: The most important issue in combustible dust-producing facilities is handling the dust as it is generated and as it disperses into the atmosphere. Horizontal surfaces will accumulate this fugitive dust. When the accumulated dust layer exceeds the critical depth layer, there is adequate dust for a dust explosion. The fugitive dust must be removed from the building, typically by portable vacuum equipment. Any cleaning method that disperses the dust into the air are only allowed after several steps have been taken to reduce the quantity of dust. See IFC Section 2203.5 for further housekeeping details.

(Photograph courtesy of Getty Images.)

The most efficient method of handling dust is with a dust collection system. The dust collection system can collect dust at the point of generation and vastly reduce the amount of fugitive dust.

Topic: Scope	Category: Motor Fuel-Dispensing Facilities and Repair Garages
Reference: IFC 2301.1	Subject: General

Code Text: *Automotive motor fuel-dispensing facilities, marine motor fuel-dispensing facilities, fleet vehicle motor fuel-dispensing facilities, aircraft motor-vehicle fuel-dispensing facilities and repair garages shall be in accordance with this chapter and the* International Building Code, International Fuel Gas Code *and the* International Mechanical Code. *Such operations shall include both those that are open to the public and private operations.*

Discussion and Commentary: The dispensing of fuel from underground storage tanks (USTs), above-ground storage tanks (ASTs) or tanks in a vault are regulated by Chapter 23. Note that this chapter regulates where the tank or pressure vessel can be located and all associated engineering and administrative controls for the installation of pumps, piping and dispensers. The material specific chapters of the IFC also will apply. For example, if an UST is used for the storage of gasoline, its design and installation also must comply with Chapter 57.

Alternative fuels can include ethanol/gasoline, bio-diesel, compressed or cryogenic (refrigerated) natural gas, compressed or cryogenic hydrogen or liquefied petroleum gas.

Topic: Location	**Category:** Motor Fuel-Dispensing Facilities and Repair Garages
Reference: IFC 2303.1	**Subject:** Dispensing Devices

Code Text: *Dispensing devices shall be located as follows: (1) Ten feet (3048 mm) or more from lot lines, (2) Ten feet (3048 mm) or more from buildings having combustible exterior wall surfaces or buildings having noncombustible exterior wall surfaces that are not part of a 1-hour fire-resistance-rated assembly or buildings having combustible overhangs.* ***Exception:*** *Canopies constructed in accordance with the* International Building Code *providing weather protection for the fuel islands, (3) Such that all portions of the vehicle being fueled will be on the premises of the motor fuel-dispensing facility, (4) Such that the nozzle, where the hose is fully extended, will not reach within 5 feet (1524 mm) of building openings, (5) Twenty feet (6096 mm) or more from fixed sources of ignition, (6) Such that fuel dispensing is in view of the attendant at attended self-service motor fuel-dispensing facilities, as required by Section 2304.2.4.*

Discussion and Commentary: Fuel-dispensing devices must be located so that the dispenser itself creates a minimal hazard, and the fuel transfer operation creates as minimal a hazard as possible. All hazards cannot be eliminated because the fuels are Class I, II or III liquids and they are designed to burn.

The dispensers are located away from exposures and provided with vehicle impact protection. When the dispenser hose is fully extended, it cannot reach to within five feet of an opening in a building. Note that under the IBC, an opening would be a door, an operable window, or a nonoperable window. All of these items create an opening in the wall structure of the building.

This facility is an unattended self-service station. Unattended self-service stations are only allowed where approved by the fire code official in accordance with Section 2304.3.1. The separation requirements help maintain the safety of these facilities.

Topic: Supervision of Dispensing	**Category:** Motor Fuel-Dispensing Facilities and Repair Garages
Reference: IFC 2304.1	**Subject:** Dispensing Operations

Code Text: *The dispensing of fuel at motor fuel-dispensing facilities shall be conducted by a qualified attendant or shall be under the supervision of a qualified attendant at all times or shall be in accordance with Section 2304.3.*

Discussion and Commentary: The requirements for dispensing of fuels vary based on the method of dispensing and the fuel. For conventional hydrocarbons, the dispensing operation can be performed by either an attendant or by patrons, and the respective requirements of Section 2304 are applicable. For LP-gas, dispensing must be performed by a qualified attendant unless the dispenser is specifically designed for public fueling in accordance with Section 2307.7. Compressed natural gas dispensing is limited to those vehicles that are designed for this fuel, and the operator must ensure that users are trained (IFC Section 2308.4). Section 2309.4 has even more extensive requirements for hydrogen dispensing as does Section 2310 for marine dispensing. Therefore, the requirements based on the specific fuel in addition to the requirements in Section 2304 must be reviewed.

IFC Section 2304.2.4 indicates that the attendant shall have a direct line of sight to observe fuel-dispensing operations at all times. Even though this attendant is not actually fueling the vehicles in most cases, this is considered an attended self-service station.

Code Text: *The dispensing of flammable or combustible liquids into portable approved containers shall comply with Sections 2304.4.1 through 2304.4.3.*

Discussion and Commentary: Filling of portable containers is necessary because many consumer products are fueled by gasoline or diesel fuel. However, the activity must be performed in accordance with the requirements of this section. Section 2304.4.3 requires the container to be removed from the vehicle when it is being filled. Many containers are constructed of plastic, and fires have been reported when containers in the beds of pickup trucks equipped with plastic bedliners were being filled. The cause of these fires has been attributed to static discharges.

Section 202 defines a container as having a volume of 60 gallons or less. However, when dispensing Class I, II or IIIA fuels into portable containers, Section 2304.4.1 limits the container size to 6 gallons.

Code Text: *This chapter shall apply to locations or areas where any of the following activities are conducted: (1) The application of flammable finishes to articles or materials by means of spray apparatus, (2) The application of flammable finishes by dipping or immersing articles into the contents of tanks, vats or containers of flammable or combustible liquids, including coating, finishing, treatment or similar processes, (3) The application of flammable finishes by applying combustible powders to articles or materials utilizing powder spray guns, electrostatic powder spray guns, fluidized beds or electrostatic fluidized beds, (4) Floor surfacing or finishing operations using Class I or II liquids in areas exceeding 350 square feet (32.5 m²), (5) The application of flammable finishes consisting of dual-component coatings or Class I or II liquids where applied by brush or roller in quantities exceeding 1 gallon (4 L).*

Discussion and Commentary: Chapter 24 regulates the hazards of either atomizing a flammable or combustible liquid or the suspension of combustible dusts in air. Both activities are commonly performed to provide a durable finish on a variety of materials that improves the final product appearance or makes it resistant to wear or corrosion. The activities can include spray application of flammable finishes, powder coating with solid paint particles, finishing with polyester resins, dip tanks where parts are submerged in a solvent solution or the manufacturing of reinforced plastics.

Certain sections of this chapter also reference NFPA 33 for the construction of paint spray booths and NFPA 34 for the construction of dip tanks.

Code Text: *Electrical wiring and equipment in flammable vapor areas shall be of an explosionproof type approved for use in such hazardous locations. Such areas shall be considered to be Class I, Division 1, or Class II, Division 1, hazardous locations in accordance with NFPA 70.*

Discussion and Commentary: The IFC references the *National Electrical Code* (NEC or NFPA 70). The NEC establishes the hazardous location boundaries inside of spray booths and rooms. These classifications are based on the presence of flammable vapors or combustible dust being present as part of normal operations, such as a flammable spray area, or an area adjacent to a spray booth, such as a door opening. In these examples, the spray area is classified as a Division 1 location, whereas the space outside of booths or rooms but within 3 feet of the openings are classified as Division 2 locations. Based on the NEC requirements, the electrical equipment must be designed and installed so that it does not serve as an ignition source.

Spray booths are allowed in all occupancies except Group A, E, I or R. The aggregate area of spray booths cannot exceed 10 percent of the floor area of the building or the allowable area of a Group H-2 occupancy, and must meet the requirements in Section 2404.3.3.5 (IFC Section 2404).

Code Text: *Dip tanks shall be constructed in accordance with Sections 2405.3.1 through 2405.3.4.3 and NFPA 34. Dip tanks, including drain boards, shall be constructed of noncombustible material and their supports shall be of heavy metal, reinforced concrete or masonry.*

Discussion and Commentary: Dipping operations pose hazards because when the tanks are open, flammable liquid vapors are evaporated from the liquid surface and from dipped articles emerging from tanks. In some cases, detearing, quenching and drying operations are the next step in the process, and this creates additional hazards. Fire prevention requirements include ventilation, noncombustible construction, tank drains, interlocks, temperature controls and alarms, portable fire extinguishers and automatic fire-extinguishing systems.

This concrete dip tank, which is greater than 500 gallons, requires a trapped overflow pipe, bottom drain with automatic and manual operation, and a fire protection system (IFC Sections 2405.3 and 2405.4).

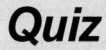

Quiz

Study Session 9
IFC Chapters 20 through 24

1. Dip tanks greater than _____ gallons in capacity or _____ square feet in liquid surface area shall be equipped with a trapped overflow pipe leading to an approved location outside the building.

    a. 10, 6   b. 55, 5
    c. 150, 10   d. 500, 10

    Reference 2405.3.1

2. Class _____ liquids shall not be used to clean aircraft, aircraft parts or aircraft engines.

    a. IA flammable   b. IB flammable
    c. IC flammable   d. IIIB combustible

    Reference 2004.3

3. The dispensing of flammable and combustible liquids from a fixed aircraft fueling facility is to be in accordance with _____.

    a. IFC Chapter 23   b. IBC Section 412
    c. IFC Chapter 57   d. NFPA 58

    Reference 2006.1

4. Tempering tanks require an automatic fire-extinguishing system when:

    a. The tank volume is greater than 500 gallons.

    b. The liquid surface area is greater than 25 square feet.

    c. Both a and b.

    d. Either a or b.

    Reference 2405.9.4

5. Repairing of aircraft requiring the use of open flames, spark-producing devices or the heating of parts above 500°F shall only be done outdoors or in an area complying with IBC requirements for a Group _____ occupancy.

    a. F-1   b. F-2

    c. H-3   d. S-1

Reference 2004.6

6. A minimum of two listed wheeled extinguishers complying with IFC Section 906 and having a minimum extinguishing rating of 80-B:C each, and a minimum agent capacity of 125 pounds, shall be provided where the open-hose discharge capacity of the fueling system is more than _____ gallons per minute.

    a. 100   b. 200

    c. 300   d. 350

Reference 2005.6 (3)

7. Floor surfacing and finishing operations exceeding _____ square feet and using Class I or Class II liquids shall comply with the requirements of Chapter 24.

    a. 100   b. 250

    c. 350   d. 500

Reference 2410.1

8. Aircraft-fueling vehicles that have accumulations of oil, grease or fuel or have leaking pipes, hoses or valves are to be _____ .

    a. repaired within 24 hours

    b. immediately scheduled for repairs

    c. used only in emergencies

    d. defueled and removed from service immediately

Reference 2006.4.3

9. Which of the following must be completed before connecting the fuel hose to an aircraft?

    a. Park the aircraft-fueling vehicle at least 10 feet from fuel-system vent openings on the aircraft.

    b. Place a minimum of two chock blocks at the aircraft-fueling vehicle tires.

    c. Secure the bonding connection to the aircraft.

    d. All of the above.

Reference 2006.5.1 / 2006.5.2

10. Open flames and open-flame devices are prohibited within _____ feet of any aircraft fuel-servicing operation or fueling equipment.

    a. 10   b. 25

    c. 40   (d.) 50

    Reference 2006.15

11. Aircraft being fueled shall be positioned such that any fuel system vents and other fuel tank openings are a minimum of _____ feet from buildings or structures other than jet bridges.

    a. 10   b. 15

    (c.) 25   d. 50

    Reference 2006.17.1

12. An automatic sprinkler system is required where indoor manufacturing processes involving spray or hand application of reinforced plastics using more than _____ gallons of resin in a 24-hour period occur.

    a. 1   b. 2

    c. 3   (d.) 5

    Reference 2409.1

13. Unless located in a Group H-2 occupancy, the maximum amount of Class II solvents allowed in a nonsprinklered Type III-A dry cleaning plant when the solvent is used for spotting?

    a. 0 gallons, Class II is prohibited

    (b.) 30 gallons

    c. 60 gallons

    d. 120 gallons

    Reference 2106.3/5003.1.1

14. Where a building with a rooftop helistop or heliport is equipped with a standpipe system, all portions of the helistop and heliport area shall be within _____ feet of a 2.5-inch outlet on a Class I or III standpipe.

    a. 100   (b.) 150

    c. 300   d. 600

    Reference 2007.5

15. What is the minimum design area for an automatic sprinkler system protecting a reinforced plastics manufacturing area?

    a. 1,500 square feet   b. 2,000 square feet

    c. 2,500 square feet   d. 3,000 square feet

Reference 2409.3

16. Type I dry cleaning plants _____ .

    a. shall be sprinklered

    b. are limited to 10 gallons of Type I solvent

    c. shall be prohibited

    d. shall not exceed 1,000 square feet in area

Reference 2104.1

17. Type IV and V dry cleaning systems without exhaust hoods shall be provided with an automatically activated exhaust ventilation system to maintain a minimum of _____ through the loading door when the door is opened.

    a. 100 feet per minute air velocity

    b. 100 cubic feet per minute

    c. 100 cfm per square inch of door area

    d. 100 inches of water column pressure

Reference 405.3

18. The maximum quantity of Type I solvents permitted at any work station for spotting and pretreating operations shall be _____ .

    a. 1 pint   b. 1 quart

    c. $1/2$ gallon   d. 1 gallon

Reference 2106.2

19. The maximum depth of the layer of combustible dust on horizontal surfaces in a pharmaceutical facility generating combustible dust is _____ .

    a. $1/32$-inch   b. $1/16$-inch

    c. $1/8$-inch   d. $1/4$-inch

Reference 2203.1

20. An automatic sprinkler system installed in accordance with Section 903.3.1.1 is required throughout a Type III-B dry cleaning plant when the aggregate quantity of Class III-B solvents exceeds _____ gallons.

    a. 330

    b. 660

    c. 3,300

    d. Sprinkler system is not required in Type III-B dry cleaning plants

    Reference _2108.2 Exc. 2_

21. The size of a combustible dust particle is defined as material that is _____ microns or less in diameter and will pass through a US No. _____ standard sieve.

    a. 350, 30   b. 420, 40

    c. 560, 50   d. 660, 60

    Reference _2202.1 / ch. 202_

22. _____ is permitted in areas where combustible dust is generated, stored, manufactured, processed or handled.

    a. Smoking

    b. The use of spark-producing equipment

    c. Maintenance with listed portable vacuum cleaners

    d. Welding

    Reference _2203.4 / 2203.5_

23. For a wood processing facility, the critical depth layer of combustible dust can be modified based on an evaluation in accordance with _____.

    a. NFPA 664   b. NFPA 482

    c. NFPA 654   d. NFPA 48

    Reference _2203.1_

24. At a motor vehicle fuel-dispensing facility, what is the minimum required separation distance between a dispensing device and a fixed source of ignition, such as a boiler?

    a. 5 feet   b. 10 feet

    c. 15 feet   d. 20 feet

    Reference _2303.1 (5)_

25. For electrostatic spraying operations, a space at least _____ the sparking distance shall be maintained between goods being painted or deteared and electrodes, electrostatic atomizing heads or conductors. A sign stating the sparking distance shall be conspicuously posted near the assembly.

   a.   equal to   b.   twice

   c.   four times   d.   10 times

   Reference _2407.2_

26. When repairs are performed to a motor vehicle fuel-dispenser for Class I liquids, what is the minimum separation distance for vehicle traffic and individuals not authorized to be in the work area?

   a.   12 feet   b.   15 feet

   c.   20 feet   d.   No separation is required.

   Reference _2305.2.3 (4)_

27. Given: An 8,000 gallon protected above-ground storage tank for the storage and dispensing of unleaded gasoline, which is classified as a Class IB flammable liquid. What is the minimum required separation distance between the tank and the nearest lot line that can be built upon?

   a.   3 feet   b.   5 feet

   c.   15 feet   d.   25 feet

   Reference _Table 2306.2.3_

28. What is the largest volume for a single above-ground tank storing a Class II combustible liquid for motor vehicle fuel-dispensing?

   a.   12,000 gallons   b.   15,000 gallons

   c.   20,000 gallons   d.   80,000 gallons

   Reference _2306.2.3 (3)_

29. What type of above-ground storage tank for liquid motor vehicle fuels does not require drainage control and diking?

   a.   uninsulated tank

   b.   fire-resistant tank

   c.   a listed secondary containment tank

   d.   all tanks require drainage control and diking

   Reference _2306.5_

30. What are the permitted locations for storage tanks storing Class II combustible liquids at dry cleaning plants?

    a. underground in accordance with Chapter 57

    b. outside in above-ground storage tanks in accordance with Chapter 57

    c. indoors in accordance with NFPA 32

    d. all of the above

    Reference 2107.3

31. Given: A woodworking facility generating combustible dust and equipped with a dust collection system. When can a flexible hose be used as part of the dust collection system?

    a. Never

    b. If no longer than 18 inches

    c. If properly grounded

    d. Both b and c

    Reference 2203.3.2

32. The aggregate surface area to be sprayed in limited spraying areas is limited to _____ square feet.

    a. 5   b. 9

    c. 15   d. 19

    Reference 2404.9.1

33. The termination point for the mechanical ventilation system in a spray booth using flammable and combustible liquids must be located a minimum of _____ feet from a lot line.

    a. 3

    b. 6

    c. 10

    d. 30

    Reference 2404.7.6

34. Electrical wiring and equipment located outside of but within _____ feet horizontally and _____ feet vertically of openings in a spray booth or a spray room shall be approved for Class I, Division 2, or Class II, Division 2, hazardous locations, whichever is applicable.

    a. 2, 2   b. 3, 3

    c. 3, 5   d. 5, 5

    Reference _2403.2.1.3_

35. Means of egress doors from premanufactured spray booths shall be a minimum of _____ inches in width.

    a. 30   b. 32

    c. 36   d. 48

    Reference _2404.3.3.4 EXC._

Study Session

10

2021 IFC Chapters 25 through 29
Special Occupancies and Operations, Part II: Fruit and Crop Ripening; Fumigation and Insecticidal Fogging; Semiconductor Fabrication Facilities; Lumber Yards and Agro-industrial, Solid Biomass and Woodworking Facilities; and Manufacture of Organic Coatings

OBJECTIVE: To obtain an understanding of the *International Fire Code*® (IFC®) requirements for crop ripening and fumigation processes, semiconductor fabrication, lumber yards, woodworking and manufacturing of organic coatings.

REFERENCE: Chapters 25 through 29, 2021 IFC

KEY POINTS:
- What are the hazards associated with fruit and crop ripening processes?
- What are the hazards of ethylene gas, and how can accidents associated with its use be prevented?
- Which fumigation methods are regulated in Chapter 26?
- What must occur in a building that was fumigated before it is safe to enter?
- How are limits placed upon the use of insecticidal fogging liquids?
- Which occupancy group applies to semiconductor fabrication facilities?
- What are some of the terms associated with semiconductor fabrication facilities?
- What is HPM?
- Which *International Building Code*® (IBC®) section contains additional requirements for semiconductor fabrication facilities?
- What other sections or chapters of the IFC apply to semiconductor fabrication facilities?
- What are the general safety provisions for semiconductor fabrication facilities? What types of additional precautions, systems or features are required?
- What are the requirements for storage of HPM, and where are these provisions in the IFC?
- What are the limits to quantities of HPM that are stored and used?
- What are fabrication areas and workstations? Which requirements apply to each of these areas?

KEY POINTS:
(Cont'd)

- How are workstations to be constructed? What precautions and clearances are required?

- What requirements apply to carts and trucks used to transport HPM?

- What are the general fire safety requirements for lumber yards and woodworking facilities?

- What are the fire protection and fire safety requirements for storage piles of wood chips or hogged material?

- What are the limitations for the size of piles containing wood chips, fines and woodworking waste? What is the minimum separation distance between each pile?

- When is a fire protection plan required at biomass and recycling facilities?

- When is a means of temperature measurement required for static piles of wood chips, woodworking waste or compost located in recycling yards?

- Concerning finished lumber storage, what are the pile volume limits and the minimum required fire protection systems?

- Are there limitations on the size of piles of pallets at a pallet recycling facility?

- Is fire department vehicle access required to or around an outdoor lumber storage area?

- What is the maximum size of a pile at a composting facility?

- In what areas of a building can organic coating manufacturing operations be located?

- What are the fire alarm and mechanical ventilation requirements for process structures that are used for manufacturing organic coatings?

- Where can process mills using nitrocellulose be located? What amount of nitrocellulose is allowed in areas housing process mills and kettles?

- What safety controls are required for process kettles used for manufacturing organic coatings?

- What are the requirements for storage of raw materials and finished organic coating products?

Code Text: *Ripening processes where ethylene gas is introduced into a room to promote the ripening of fruits, vegetables and other crops shall comply with this chapter.* ***Exception:*** *Mixtures of ethylene and one or more inert gases in concentrations which prevent the gas from reaching greater than 25 percent of the lower explosive limit (LEL) when released to the atmosphere.*

Discussion and Commentary: Ethylene is a naturally produced byproduct of fruit and vegetable ripening. Because it can ripen fruit, packagers and marketers of citrus fruits and vegetables may use ethylene to keep the appearance marketable to consumers. One hundred percent concentration of ethylene is not used. Instead, commercially available ethylene generators only produce concentrations of ethylene that are less than 25 percent of the lower explosive limit for this material and are listed for this use.

(Photograph courtesy of Catalytic Generators, LLC.)

Listed generators commonly use ethyl alcohol, a Class IB flammable liquid. These generators heat the ethyl alcohol to create ethylene.

Code Text: *During the period fumigation is in progress, except where fumigation is conducted in a gastight vault or tank, a responsible watchperson shall remain on duty at the entrance or entrances to the enclosed fumigated space until after the fumigation is completed and the building, structure or space is properly ventilated and safe for occupancy. Sufficient watchers shall be provided to prevent persons from entering the enclosed space under fumigation without being observed.*

Discussion and Commentary: Fumigation operations pose several distinct problems. Where gas is used, it is a poison, it is intended to kill the pests. Many of these gases are also flammable. Therefore, ignition sources in the building must be shut off and Section 2603.5 requires that the material used to tent, or cover, the building must have flame resistant properties. As an additional safety measure, watch personnel are required where a possibility exists for someone to enter the fumigated structure.

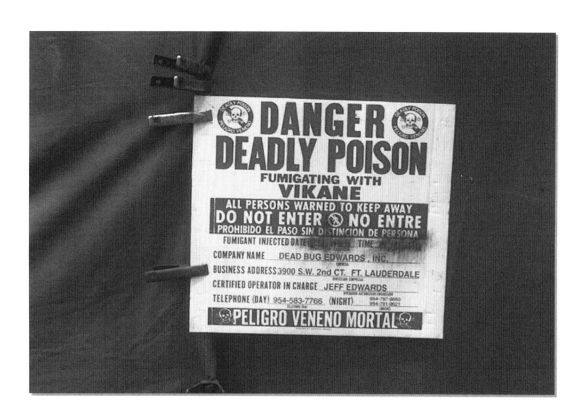

The IFC requires warning signs on building where fumigation operations are occurring (IFC Section 2603.3.1).

Code Text: *Semiconductor fabrication facilities and comparable research and development areas classified as Group H-5 shall comply with this chapter and the* International Building Code. *The use, storage and handling of hazardous materials in Group H-5 shall comply with this chapter, other applicable provisions of this code and the* International Building Code.

Discussion and Commentary: Terms such as semiconductor fabrication facilities and hazardous production material (HPM), along with other terms that are unique to the multiple step process, are defined in IFC Section 202. Materials used include flammable liquids (IFC Chapter 57), pyrophoric gases (IFC Chapter 64), flammable gases (IFC Chapter 58), toxic substances (IFC Chapter 60) and corrosives (IFC Chapter 54). Some operations occur in clean room environments where even a single dust particle can ruin the finished product. Code requirements include provisions regarding emergency control stations; numerous references to other areas of the IFC, the IBC and the *International Mechanical Code*® (IMC®); emergency plans; special egress and security requirements; automatic sprinkler systems; gas cabinets; special exhaust systems; multiple alarm systems; continuous gas detection systems; ventilation; emergency power; limitations on quantities of HPM; storage; drainage; containment; and transportation and handling for HPM.

Electrical equipment and devices within 5 feet of workstations in which flammable or pyrophoric gases or flammable liquids are used need to comply with NFPA 70 for Class I, Division 2 hazardous locations. Workstations cannot be energized without adequate exhaust ventilation (IFC Section 2703.7.2).

Code Text: *Supply piping and tubing for HPM gases and liquids having a health-hazard ranking of 3 or 4 shall be welded throughout, except for connections located within a ventilation enclosure if the material is a gas, or an approved method of drainage or containment provided for connections if the material is a liquid.*

Discussion and Commentary: Because of the health or flammability hazards associated with most conventional HPM gases, the IFC requires that the piping be assembled using welded fittings and joints. The IFC does permit the use of ventilated enclosures for housing of piping or an approved method of drainage and containment if the piping contains liquids.

Appendix F, Table F101.2 can be used to identify the materials with a health hazard ranking of 3 or 4. Excerpts from Table F101.2 shown below

TABLE F101.2 (excerpts)
FIRE FIGHTER WARNING PLACARD DESIGNATIONS BASED ON HAZARD CLASSIFICATION CATEGORIES

HAZARD CATEGORY	DESIGNATION
Cryogenic flammable	F4, H3
Cryogenic oxidizing	OX, H3
Corrosive	H3, COR
Toxic	H3
Highly toxic	H4

F-Flammable category
H-Health category
OX-Special hazard: oxidizing properties
COR-Corrosive

Emergency control stations shall receive signals from emergency equipment, alarm systems and detection systems, which includes, but is not limited to, the following:

- Automatic sprinkler system
- Manual fire alarm
- Emergency alarms
- Gas detection systems
- Smoke detection systems
- Emergency power systems
- Automatic detection and alarm systems for
  ° Pyrophoric liquids
  ° Class 3 water-reactive liquids
- Exhaust ventilation flow alarm devices for
  ° Pyrophoric liquids
  ° Class 3 water-reactive liquids
  ° Gas cabinet exhaust ventilation

An emergency control station is required in semiconductor fabrication facilities (IFC Section 2703.1).

Topic: Exhaust Ducts for HPM

Category: Semiconductor Fabrication Facilities

Reference: IFC 2703.10.4

Subject: Automatic Sprinkler Systems

Code Text: *An approved automatic sprinkler system shall be provided in exhaust ducts conveying gases, vapors, fumes, mists or dusts generated from HPM in accordance with this section and the* International Mechanical Code.

Discussion and Commentary: The requirements for automatic sprinkler protection in HPM exhaust systems is based on the duct diameter, the duct's material of construction and the makeup of the exhaust air stream. For a metallic or noncombustible nonmetallic duct system, such as is shown in the photograph, automatic sprinklers are required when the cross-sectional diameter of a duct is 10 inches or greater, the duct is located inside of the building, and the duct is conveying flammable gases or vapors. For nonmetallic combustible exhaust ducts, automatic sprinkler protection is required regardless of what is being conveyed in the air stream when the cross sectional diameter of the duct is 10 inches or greater.

Automatic sprinkler protection is specified by the IFC for duct work conveying hazardous production materials. IFC Section 2703.10.4.2 allows the elimination of automatic sprinklers from combustible nonmetallic ducts when it is listed or approved for applications without automatic sprinkler protection.

Code Text: *Automatic sprinklers installed in exhaust duct systems shall be hydraulically designed to provide 0.5 gallon per minute (gpm) (1.9 L/min) over an area derived by multiplying the distance between the sprinklers in a horizontal duct by the width of the duct. Minimum discharge shall be 20 gpm (76 L/min) per sprinkler from the five hydraulically most remote sprinklers.*

Discussion and Commentary: IFC Section 2703.10.4 requires automatic sprinkler protection in certain HPM ducts installed inside of or outdoors of semiconductor fabrication facilities. For combustible nonmetallic ducts, sprinklers are required in ducts regardless of what material is handled. The concern is that a fire involving a semiconductor tool constructed using plastic components and exhausted using ducts constructed of combustible materials can extend through the building if the duct is not sprinklered. This section requires that the five most hydraulically remote duct sprinklers be calculated at a minimum flow rate of 20 GPM. If the duct is conveying corrosive vapors, sprinklers must be listed for use in corrosive atmospheres.

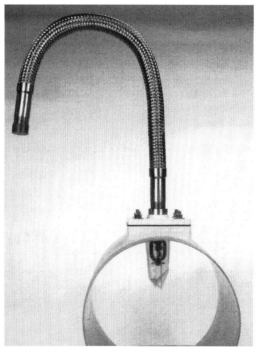

(Photograph courtesy of Flexhead Inc., Holliston, MA.)

Because the sprinkler tubing is flexible and can be purchased in different lengths, each type of flexible head installation as illustrated will have different discharge coefficient (k-factor). Accordingly, fire code officials should require that hydraulic calculations be submitted with the design of each sprinkler installation to ensure that the required hydraulic demand is satisfactory.

Code Text: *Where required. A gas detection system shall be provided in the areas identified in Sections 2703.13.1.1 through 2703.13.1.4.*

Fabrication areas. A gas detection system shall be provided in fabrication areas where HPM gas is used in the fabrication area.

HPM rooms. A gas detection system shall be provided in HPM rooms where HPM gas is used in the room.

Gas cabinets, exhausted enclosures and gas rooms. A gas detection system shall be provided in gas cabinets and exhausted enclosures for HPM gas. A gas detection system shall be provided in gas rooms where HPM gases are not located in gas cabinets or exhausted enclosures.

Corridors. Where HPM gases are transported in piping placed within the space defined by the walls of a corridor and the floor or roof above the corridor, a gas detection system shall be provided where piping is located and in the corridor. Exception: A gas detection system is not required for occasional transverse crossings of the corridors by supply piping that is enclosed in a ferrous pipe or tube for the width of the corridor.

Discussion and Commentary: Gas detection systems are required when HPM gases have a physiological warning threshold level (PWTL) that is greater than the permissible exposure limit (PEL) of the stored gas, and for all flammable gases. PTWL values are contained in the *Chemical Hazard Response Information System* (CHRIS) manual published by the United States Coast Guard and the American Industrial Hygiene Association. When the PWTL is less than the PEL for a given HPM gas, a gas detection system is not required, because the predominance of occupants of the building can detect a leak and will most likely not suffer from health effects, given that the amount inhaled will be less than the permissible exposure limit. Section 916.7 requires sample analysis to occur at intervals not exceeding 30 minutes for HPM gas detection systems.

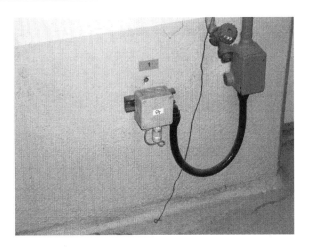

Activation of the gas detection system requires the transmission of an alarm signal to the emergency control station and a visual and audible alarm in the gas storage area where the leak has been detected (IFC Section 2703.13.2.1).

Code Text: *The gas detection system shall automatically close the shutoff valve at the source on gas supply piping and tubing related to the system being monitored for which gas is detected when a short-term hazard condition is detected. Automatic closure of shutoff valves shall comply with the following:*

(See IFC Section 2703.13.2.2 for Items 1 through 3 and an exception.)

Discussion and Commentary: Activation of the vapor or gas detection system in a semiconductor fabrication facility provides a means of notifying employees of a potential leak. HPM gases are stored in gas cabinets or exhausted enclosures and generally distributed via valve manifold boxes (piping distribution manifold enclosures) to the workstations. Because different gases can be supplied through valve manifold boxes, the IFC requires that activation of the gas detector in each cabinet, exhausted enclosure or valve manifold box stop the flow in the event of a leak. This is accomplished by using automatic shutoff valves in the system.

Because the compressed gas storage cylinders illustrated in this photograph are not stored in gas cabinets or exhausted enclosures, activation of the gas detection system for the specific HPM gas in this compressed gas room requires that the automatic shutoff valve for each cylinder of the specific HPM gas close upon detection of a leak (IFC Section 2703.13.2.2, Item 2).

Topic: Location of HPM Storage in Fabrication Areas	**Category:** Semiconductor Fabrication Facilities
Reference: IFC 2704.2.1	**Subject:** Storage

Code Text: *Storage of HPM in fabrication areas shall be within approved or listed storage cabinets, gas cabinets, exhausted enclosures or within a workstation as follows: (1) Flammable and combustible liquid storage cabinets shall comply with Section 5704.3.2, (2) Hazardous materials storage cabinets shall comply with Section 5003.8.7, (3) Gas cabinets shall comply with Section 5003.8.6. Gas cabinets for highly toxic or toxic gases shall also comply with Section 6004.1.2, (4) Exhausted enclosures shall comply with Section 5003.8.5. Exhausted enclosures for highly toxic or toxic gases shall also comply with Section 6004.1.3, (5) Workstations shall comply with Section 2705.2.3.*

Discussion and Commentary: HPM stored within a Group H-5 occupancy is required to be located in approved flammable or combustible liquid cabinets, hazardous materials storage cabinets, or gas cabinets or exhausted enclosures. Storage at workstations is required to be located such that the vessel is protected in accordance with IFC Section 2705.2.3. Additionally, if the HPM is a liquid, each workstation is required to be connected to a drainage system. Generally, all semiconductor fabrication facilities have a centralized waste collection system because of the amount and variety of chemical waste generated in these occupancies.

The photograph illustrates gas cabinets that are used for the storage of HPM gases.

Code Text: *The maximum quantities of hazardous materials stored or used in a single fabrication area shall not exceed the quantities set forth in Table 2704.2.2.1.*

Discussion and Commentary: Quantities are limited in Group H-5 occupancies based on the area of the semiconductor fabrication environment. The larger the area of the fabrication area, the greater the amount of certain hazardous materials permitted. The hazard classification also limits the amount of HPM. Note that for flammable liquids, a 90 percent reduction in quantity is required for Class IA flammable liquids when compared to Class IB flammable liquid. Concerning pyrophoric, toxic and highly toxic gases, Footnote d specifies a maximum quantity limit of 9,000 cubic feet, and Footnote e further limits the amount of pyrophoric gases to 2,000 cubic feet because of the requirements in IFC Table 5003.8.2.

TABLE 2704.2.2.1
QUANTITY LIMITS FOR HAZARDOUS MATERIALS IN A SINGLE FABRICATION AREA IN GROUP H-5[a]

HAZARD CATEGORY	SOLIDS (pounds/square foot)	LIQUIDS (gallons/square foot)	GAS (cubic feet @ NTP/square foot)
PHYSICAL-HAZARD MATERIALS			
Combustible dust	Note b	Not Applicable	Not Applicable
Combustible fiber Loose Baled	Note b Notes b and c	Not Applicable	Not Applicable
Combustible liquid Class II Class IIIA Class IIIB Combination Class I, II and IIIA	Not Applicable	0.01 0.02 Not Limited 0.04	Not Applicable
Cryogenic gas Flammable Oxidizing	Not Applicable	Not Applicable	Note d 1.25
Explosives	Note b	Note b	Note b
Flammable gas Gaseous Liquefied	Not Applicable	Not Applicable	Note d Note d
Flammable liquid Class IA Class IB Class IC Combination Class IA, IB and IC Combination Class I, II and IIIA	Not Applicable	0.0025 0.025 0.025 0.025 0.04	Not Applicable
Flammable solid	0.001	Not Applicable	Not Applicable
Organic peroxide Unclassified detonable Class I Class II Class III Class IV Class V	Note b Note b 0.025 0.1 Not Limited Not Limited	Not Applicable	Not Applicable
Oxidizing gas Gaseous Liquefied Combination of Gaseous and Liquefied	Not Applicable	Not Applicable	1.25 1.25 1.25
Oxidizer Class 4 Class 3 Class 2 Class 1 Combination oxidizer Class 1, 2, 3	Note b 0.003 0.003 0.003 0.003	Note b 0.03 0.03 0.03 0.03	Not Applicable
Pyrophoric	0.01	0.00125	Notes d and e
Unstable reactive Class 4 Class 3 Class 2 Class 1	Note b 0.025 0.1 Not Limited	Note b 0.0025 0.01 Not Limited	Note b Note b Note b Not Limited

(continued)

Example: if a Group H-5 occupancy has a single fabrication area of 67,000 square feet, the maximum amount of liquid Class 3 oxidizer permitted is (67,000 ft²) x (0.03 gallons/ft²) = 2010 gallons.

Code Text: *Equipment or machinery located inside buildings that generates or emits combustible dust shall be provided with an approved dust collection and exhaust system installed in accordance with Chapter 22 and the* International Mechanical Code. *Equipment or systems that are used to collect, process or convey combustible dusts shall be provided with an approved explosion control system.*

Discussion and Commentary: For manufacturing areas processing wood using mechanical equipment, the equipment can create chips, flakes, dust and flour. Chips and flakes can present a rapid burning fire hazard, while dust and wood flour can contribute to a dust deflagration. Accordingly, the IFC requires a means of dust collection to capture and remove these materials. Point of use dust collection systems are allowed in IMC Section 511.1.1 when installed in accordance with the IFC. The general requirement in the IMC and NFPA 664 is to locate the collector outdoors, however, there are exceptions in both documents which permit installation indoors.

NFPA 664 is referenced in IFC Table 2205.1 for control of combustible wood dust.

Code Text: *Protection from ignition sources shall be provided in accordance with Sections 2803.5.1 through 2803.5.3.*

Discussion and Commentary: Woodworking facilities, biomass, composting and lumber yards can contain a fairly large fuel load. Worse, the configuration of the individual pieces can present a large surface area with very little mass, such as chips, flakes or dust. In this configuration fuels are easily ignited and can rapidly spread to and involve larger finished and raw wood products. To minimize this risk, IFC Section 2803.5 specifies controls for ignition sources, including cutting and welding operations, the potential for a static electricity discharge or smoking.

IFC Section 2809.3 requires access roads to and around the exterior storage areas of finished lumber and solid biofuel products. Chapter 5 and Section 2809.5 provide the ability to require a water supply for fire-fighting purposes at the exterior storage areas.

Topic: Automatic Sprinkler Systems	**Category:** Lumber Yards and Agro-industrial, Solid Biomass and Woodworking Facilities
Reference: IFC 2804.4	**Subject:** Fire Protection

Code Text: *Automatic sprinkler systems shall be installed in accordance with Section 903.3.1.1.*

Discussion and Commentary: IFC Section 903.2 is the charging section for when automatic sprinkler systems are required. IFC Section 903.2.4.1 requires an automatic sprinkler system in all wood work-ing occupancies with an area of more than 2,500 square feet that produce finely divided combustible waste or uses finely divided combustible materials.

Section A.4.3.4 of NFPA 13 states that wood machining and wood products assembly requires a minimum Ordinary Hazard Group 2 discharge density and design area. Saw mills are classified as an Extra Hazard Group 1 occupancy by NFPA 13.

Code Text: *Piles or stackable products are permitted to be increased beyond the dimensions in Section 2808.3 provided that a written fire protection plan is approved by the fire code official. The fire protection plan shall include, but not be limited to, the following: (1) Contact information for after-hours response by facility personnel, (2) Storage yard areas and material-handling equipment selection, pile design and arrangement shall be based on sound safety and fire protection principles, (3) Fire apparatus access roads around the piles or stacks and access roads to the top of piles, if applicable, shall be established, identified and maintained, (4) The potential for spontaneous heating shall be evaluated and provisions made to control the temperature of the piles. Methods for monitoring the internal temperature of the pile shall be provided, (5) Routine yard inspections shall be conducted by trained personnel, (6) A means for early fire detection and reporting to the public fire department shall be provided, (7) Facilities and equipment needed by the fire department for fire extinguishment shall be provided, including a water supply in compliance with Section 507 and heavy equipment necessary to move material, (8) A de-inventory plan shall be utilized to remove alternating piles or stacked products in a manner to increase the separation distances between the remaining piles or stacks, (9) The increased pile size shall be based on the capabilities of the installed fire protection systems and features, (10) A controlled burn area shall be provided on-site for smoldering or damaged product.*

Discussion and Commentary: Storage and processing of wood chips, hogged materials, fines, compost, solid biomass feedstock and raw product produced from yard waste, debris and agro-industrial and recycling facilities requires careful planning to provide fire safety. Product is often stored in large piles which can be up to 2,000,000 cubic feet. The space between piles or stacks serves as access for maintenance and fire department equipment, and it also provides a fire break between the fuel. The pile size is generally limited, but it can be increased based on an approved fire protection plan. This plan needs to address the ability to handle a fire in the product and must include the above ten items at a minimum.

Pile sizes of wood-based materials can be increased beyond the limitations in Section 2808.3, but only when the code official approves a Fire Protection Plan which includes additional fire protection to address the increase in pile size.

Code Text: *Static piles shall be monitored by an approved means to measure temperatures within the static piles. Internal pile temperatures shall be monitored and recorded weekly. Such records shall be maintained. An operational plan indicating procedures and schedules for the inspection, monitoring and restricting of excessive internal temperatures in static piles shall be submitted to the fire code official for review and approval.*

Discussion and Commentary: Fires involving biomass products, mulch or composts can occur because the moisture content in the pile is reduced because of evaporation and the temperature increases as the material decomposes. Accordingly, the IFC requires that the temperature of static piles be monitored to ensure that when the pile temperature approaches a critical threshold, the pile is rotated and wetted with water or other fluid to control the temperature and prevent ignition.

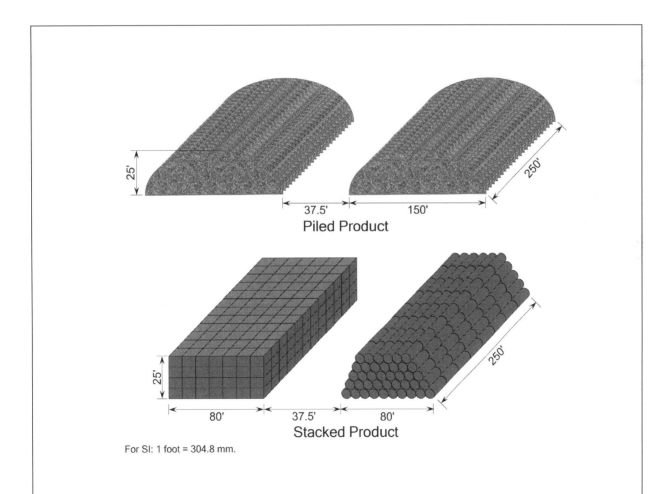

Piled Product

Stacked Product

For SI: 1 foot = 304.8 mm.

IFC Section 2808.3 allows piles and stacks up to 25 feet in height. The distance between the piles or stacks is 1.5 times the height of the pile or stack. Section 2808.3.1 allows the pile or stack size to increase based on an approved fire protection plan, which must include monitoring the piles for spontaneous heating.

Topic: Outdoor Storage of Pallets	**Category:** Lumber Yards and Agro-industrial, Solid Biomass and Woodworking Facilities
Reference: IFC 2810.6, 2810.7, 2810.8	**Subject:** Pallet Manufacturing and Recycling Facilities

Code Text: *Clearance to property line. Stacks of pallets shall not be stored within 0.75 times the stack height or 8 feet (2438 mm) of the property line, whichever is greater, or shall comply with Section 2810.11.*

Clearance to important buildings. Stacks of pallets shall not be stored within 0.75 times the stack height of any important building on site, or shall comply with Section 2810.11.

Height. Pallet stacks shall not exceed 20 feet (6096 mm) in height.

Discussion and Commentary: Ignition of piles of idle pallets results in significant fires with tremendous amounts of radiated heat. These provisions place restrictions on distances to property lines and important buildings. Note that the separation is to important buildings. Frequently, these facilities will have a small shed or roof structure within, or adjacent to, the pallet stacks. This small structure may house tools or equipment used in the yard. These are typically not considered important buildings as compared to the main structure where pallets are manufactured or repaired.

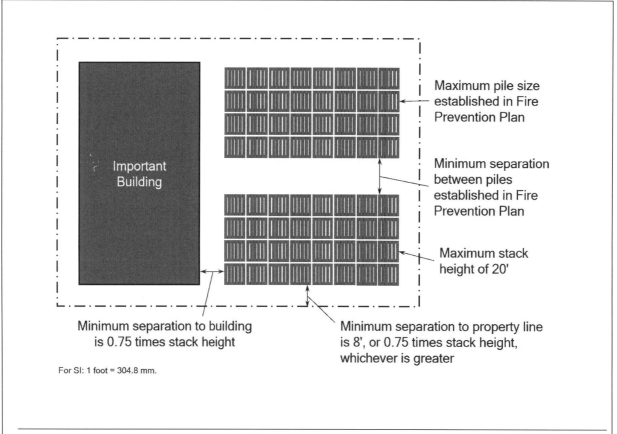

Minimum separation to building
is 0.75 times stack height

Minimum separation to property line
is 8', or 0.75 times stack height,
whichever is greater

For SI: 1 foot = 304.8 mm.

An alternative approach to pile sizing and separations is provided in Section 2810.11. This section authorizes the code official to allow larger stacks and reduced separations where additional fire protection features are provided.

Code Text: ***Building features.*** *Manufacturing of organic coatings shall be done only in buildings that do not have pits or basements.*

__Location.__ Organic coating manufacturing operations and operations incidental to or connected with organic coating manufacturing shall not be located in buildings having other occupancies.

__Fire-fighting access.__ The fire department shall be able to access the organic coating manufacturing operations from not less than one side for the purpose of fire control. Approved aisles shall be maintained for the unobstructed movement of personnel and fire suppression equipment.

Discussion and Commentary: Manufacturing organic coatings regulated by Chapter 29 typically involves the use of binders such as alkyd, nitrocellulose, acrylic or oil, mixed with flammable and combustible solvents such as hydrocarbon, ester, ketone or alcohol. Products are mixed, heated and packaged.

These sections contain criteria affecting the building location and design. The facility cannot be in a mixed occupancy building because of the hazard it presents. The building cannot have a basement or pits which could potentially trap flammable liquids or vapors. The portion of the facility where organic coatings are manufactured or processed must have at least one exterior wall that is accessible by the fire department.

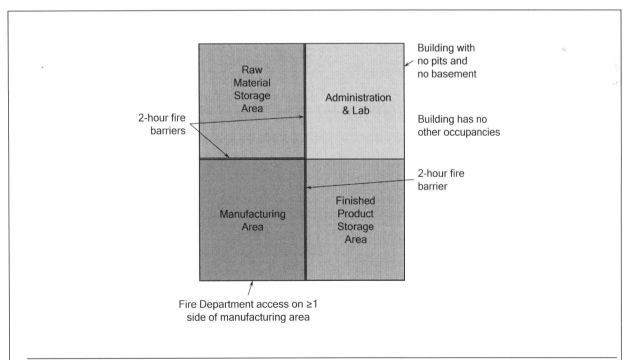

Construction requirements are contained in the IFC and NFPA 35 in addition to the requirements in the IBC. NFPA 35 requires a 2-hour fire-resistance-rated separation between manufacturing areas and raw product storage areas and finished product storage areas.

Code Text: *Where Class I liquids are exposed to the air, the design of equipment and ventilation of structures shall be such as to limit the Class I, Division 1, locations to the following: (1) Piping trenches, (2) The interior of equipment, (3) The immediate vicinity of pumps or equipment locations, such as dispensing stations, open centrifuges, plate and frame filters, opened vacuum filters, change cans and the surfaces of open equipment. The immediate vicinity shall include a zone extending from the vapor liberation point 5 feet (1524 mm) horizontally in all directions and vertically from the floor to a level 3 feet (914 mm) above the highest point of vapor liberation.*

Discussion and Commentary: When Class I flammable liquids are exposed to air, the IFC specifies the physical boundaries for the installation of electrical equipment that is listed for use in Class I, Division 1 locations. This type of electrical equipment can include intrinsically safe or hermetically sealed equipment or equipment that is designed to be explosion proof. The electrical equipment is designed so as to not serve as a source of ignition.

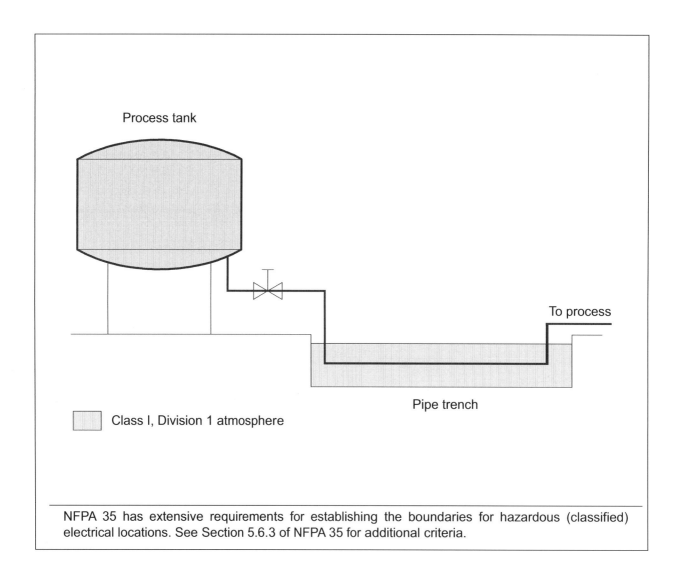

Process tank

To process

Pipe trench

Class I, Division 1 atmosphere

NFPA 35 has extensive requirements for establishing the boundaries for hazardous (classified) electrical locations. See Section 5.6.3 of NFPA 35 for additional criteria.

Topic: Ventilation	**Category:** Manufacture of Organic Coatings
Reference: IFC 2905.5	**Subject:** Process Structures

Code Text: *Enclosed structures in which Class I liquids are processed or handled shall be ventilated at a rate of not less than 1 cubic foot per minute per square foot [0.00508 m³/(s × m²)] of solid floor area. Ventilation shall be accomplished by exhaust fans that take suction at floor levels and discharge to a safe location outside the structure. Noncontaminated intake air shall be introduced in such a manner that all portions of solid floor areas are provided with continuous uniformly distributed air movement.*

Discussion and Commentary: Mechanical ventilation is an important safety element of any operation involving the storage and use of flammable or combustible liquids. IFC Section 2905.5 requires that the mechanical ventilation system be designed to exhaust at a minimum flow rate of 1 cfm per square foot of floor area. The air flow is required to be uniform so that no vapors can pocket, and adequate makeup air is also required.

The design of the mechanical ventilation system must also comply with the requirements of the *International Mechanical Code.*

Code Text: *Tank storage for flammable and combustible liquids located inside of structures shall be limited to storage areas at or above grade which are separated from the processing area in accordance with the* International Building Code. *Processing equipment containing flammable and combustible liquids and storage in quantities essential to the continuity of the operations shall not be prohibited in the processing area.*

Discussion and Commentary: This provision requires that indoor storage tanks be separated from the organic coating processing area in accordance with the IBC. IBC Section 415.9.1 specifies the requirements for separation of fire areas that contain storage tanks, and other engineering controls such as mechanical ventilation and leakage alarms in the event of a spill or leak.

The design and installation of storage tanks inside of a building must also comply with IFC Chapter 57.

Quiz

Study Session 10
IFC Chapters 25 through 29

1. An operational permit is required for a woodworking plant that processes more than _____ board feet of material.

    a. 50,000   b. 75,000

    c. 100,000   d. 125,000

    Reference _____

2. In a woodworking plant, portable fire extinguishers or standpipes and hose supplied from an approved water system shall be provided within a travel distance of _____ feet to any machine producing shavings or sawdust.

    a. 15   b. 50

    c. 75   d. 100

    Reference _____

3. Exterior lumber storage shall be arranged to form stable piles with a maximum height of _____ feet and piles shall not exceed _____ cubic feet in volume.

    a. 20; 100,000   b. 12; 150,000

    c. 20; 150,000   d. 25; 300,000

    Reference _____

4. Which of the following is not required for fire protection at a facility with outdoor storage piles of solid biofuel products?

    a. Piles at least 8 feet from the property line

    b. Fire apparatus access roads

    c. Security fence at least 6 feet in height

    d. Portable fire extinguishers or fire hydrants and hose

    Reference _____

5. What are the horizontal and vertical boundaries for Class I, Division 1 electrical equipment located near the surface of open equipment using Class I flammable liquids in an organic coating manufacturing facility?

    a. 5 feet horizontal; 3 feet vertical

    b. 10 feet horizontal; 3 feet vertical

    c. 10 feet horizontal; 5 feet vertical

    d. 15 feet horizontal; 5 feet vertical

Reference _____

6. A minimum mechanical ventilation exhaust rate of _____ per square foot is required for organic coating manufacturing areas in rooms where Class I flammable liquids are processed.

    a. 1 PSI   b. 1 CFM

    c. 1 ATM   d. 1 kPA

Reference _____

7. What is the minimum test duration and pressure for organic coating process piping?

    a. 15 minutes; 5 PSIG at the highest point in the system

    b. 30 minutes; 1.5 × the working pressure OR at least 5 PSIG at the highest point in the system

    c. 30 minutes; 1.5 × the working pressure OR 5 PSIG at the highest point in the system, whichever is less

    d. 5 minutes; 1.5 × the working pressure

Reference _____

8. In a fruit-ripening process, valves controlling discharge of ethylene shall provide positive and fail-closed control of flow and shall be set to limit the concentration of gas in air below _____ parts per million (ppm).

    a. 100   b. 500

    c. 1,000   d. 5,000

Reference _____

9. In a fruit-ripening process, ethylene generators shall be used in rooms having a volume of not less than _____.

    a. 100 square feet   b. 500 cubic feet

    c. 1,000 square feet   d. 1,000 cubic feet

Reference _____

10. Electrical wiring and equipment in rooms used for fruit-ripening using compressed ethylene gas shall be of _____ classification.

    a. Ordinary   b. Class I, Division 1

    c. Class I, Division 2   d. Class II, Division 1

Reference _____

11. Insecticidal fogging materials that are classified as Class _____ liquids are permitted to be used.

    a. IA flammable   b. IB flammable

    c. IC flammable   d. II combustible

Reference _____

12. Hazardous production material is a solid, liquid or gas associated with semiconductor manufacturing that has a degree-of-hazard rating in health, flammability or instability of Class _____ as ranked by NFPA 704 and which is used directly in research, laboratory or production processes that have as their end product materials that are not hazardous.

    a. 2   b. 3 or lower

    c. 3 or 4   d. 4 or higher

Reference _____

13. In Group H-5 occupancies, electrical equipment and devices within _____ feet of workstations in which flammable or pyrophoric gases or flammable liquids are used shall comply with the NEC for Class I, Division 2 hazardous locations.

    a. 3   b. 5

    c. 10   d. 15

Reference _____

14. Automatic sprinklers for HPM exhaust plenums of combustible workstations shall be installed at _____ -foot intervals in horizontal ducts and at changes in direction.

    a. 6   b. 10

    c. 12   d. 25

Reference _____

15. The monitoring detection threshold level for gas detection systems for flammable gases in an HPM room shall be vapor concentrations in excess of _____ percent of the lower flammable limit (LFL).

    a. 20   b. 25

    c. 30   d. 50

    Reference _____

16. Exhaust ventilation systems for HPM shall not penetrate _____.

    a. smoke partitions   b. fire partitions

    c. fire barriers   d. fire walls

    Reference _____

17. Exhaust ventilation systems in HPM rooms are allowed to be designed to operate at not less than _____ the normal fan speed on the emergency power system when it is demonstrated that the level of exhaust will maintain a safe atmosphere.

    a. one-quarter   b. one-third

    c. one-half   d. three-quarters

    Reference _____

18. The storage of HPM in fabrication areas is specifically permitted within _____.

    a. gas cabinets   b. hazardous material storage cabinets

    c. workstations   d. all of the above

    Reference _____

19. The storage of HPM in quantities greater than those listed in Sections 5003.1.1 and 5704.3.4 shall be in a room complying with the requirements of the IBC and the IFC for a _____.

    a. liquid storage room   b. HPM room

    c. gas room   d. a, b or c as appropriate

    Reference _____

20. The maximum allowable quantities of flammable HPM allowed at a workstation may be increased to _____ for closed system operations when the workstation is also protected internally with an approved automatic fire-extinguishing or suppression system complying with Chapter 9.

    a. 50 percent   b. 100 percent

    c. 200 percent   d. 400 percent

    Reference _____

21. The aggregate quantity of flammable, pyrophoric, toxic and highly toxic gases permitted in a single fabrication area in Group H-5 is _____.

    a. prohibited

    b. limited to 9,000 cubic feet total at NTP

    c. limited to 0.2 cubic feet per square foot

    d. b or c, whichever is greater

    Reference _____

22. Which of the following is not required for a pallet recycling facility with 15,000 square feet of outdoor pallet storage assuming maximum stack height?

    a. Operational permit

    b. Fire Prevention Plan

    c. Fire Safety and Evacuation Plan

    d. Cost analysis for extinguishment of the largest pile

    Reference _____

23. Carts and trucks used to transport HPM _____.

    a. are prohibited in exit enclosures

    b. are limited to electric power

    c. are prohibited

    d. shall be marked to indicate the contents

    Reference _____

24. Given: A composting facility has piles of agricultural products stored 25 feet high. What is the minimum separation distance between piles?

    a. 15 feet   b. 20 feet

    c. 37.5 feet   d. 50 feet

Reference _____

25. Materials used to seal off buildings during fumigation must meet the flame propagation criteria in:

    a. NFPA 701   b. NFPA 263

    c. ASTM E119   d. any of the above

Reference _____

26. What type of pressure relief device is required for organic coating process kettles?

    a. spring-loaded safety relief device

    b. fusible plug

    c. pilot-operated safety relief device

    d. rupture disc

Reference _____

27. What type of fire alarm is required at a plywood and veneer mill?

    a. fire alarm is not required

    b. automatic fire alarm system

    c. manual fire alarm system

    d. public address system that is audible throughout facility

Reference _____

28. What is the maximum electrical resistance for grounding metal buildings used for the manufacturing of organic coatings?

    a. 5 ohms   b. 10 ohms

    c. 1 megaohms   d. 5 megaohms

Reference _____

29. Given: A pallet recycling facility has wooden pallets stored 20 feet high. What is the minimum separation distance to an important building on the property?

    a. 25 feet

    b. 15 feet

    c. The distance specified in the alternative approach based on additional fire protection

    d. Either b or c

Reference _____

30. What size and classification of portable fire extinguisher is required at a composting facility with a pile 20 feet in height?

    a. Class 2-A:10-B:C within 100-foot travel distance

    b. Class 4-B:C at all processing equipment

    c. Class 4-A:60-B:C on all vehicles and processing equipment

    d. 2½ gallon pressurized water extinguishers within a 75-foot travel distance

Reference _____

31. The size of biomass feedstock pile can exceed 150 feet by 250 feet when a fire protection plan is approved. Which of the following is not required to be included in the fire protection plan?

    a. Factors that lead to spontaneous heating

    b. Material-handling equipment

    c. Method of early fire detection

    d. Cost recovery procedure for fire department response

Reference _____

32. Given: An exterior lumber storage covering 10 acres. What are the maximum dimensions of a single pile of lumber?

    a. 150 feet by 100 feet by 25 feet high

    b. 100 feet by 150 feet by 20 feet high

    c. 150 feet by 50 feet by 20 feet high

    d. 100 feet by 100 feet by 20 feet high

Reference _____

33. At an organic coating manufacturing plant, what is the minimum separation required between a tank vehicle loading/unloading station for Class I flammable liquids and the nearest lot line that can be built upon?

    a. 8 feet   b. 10 feet

    c. 20 feet   d. 25 feet

Reference _____

34. Cold decks at a timber mill shall not exceed _____ feet in length, _____ feet in width and _____ feet in height, unless specifically approved by the code official and additional fire protection is provided.

    a. 300; 100; 20   b. 500; 200; 30

    c. 500; 300; 20   d. 600; 200; 30

Reference _____

35. What is the minimum fire-flow required to protect the outdoor pallet storage area at a pallet recycling facility?

    a. 1,000 gpm for 2 hours

    b. 500 gpm per 10,000 square feet of storage pile

    c. 3,000 gpm for 4 hours

    d. as determined by the fire code official

Reference _____

2021 IFC Chapters 30 through 34

Special Occupancies and Operations, Part III: Industrial Ovens; Tents, Temporary Special Event Structures and Other Membrane Structures; High-piled Combustible Storage; Fire Safety During Construction and Demolition; and Tire Rebuilding and Tire Storage

OBJECTIVE: To provide a basic overview of the requirements of the *International Fire Code®* (IFC®) for industrial ovens, tents and structures for special events, buildings containing high-piled combustible storage, tire rebuilding and storage operations, and fire safety during construction and demolition.

REFERENCE: Chapters 30 through 34, 2021 IFC

KEY POINTS:
- How are industrial ovens classified?
- What interlocks are required for Class A furnaces?
- What are the building temperature limits for industrial ovens that are located in combustible buildings?
- Is fire protection required for industrial ovens? What types of fire protection are allowed?
- What are the requirements for fuel gas piping and valves supplying industrial ovens?
- What safety data is required on a Class A furnace nameplate?
- When is a permit required to erect or operate a tent or membrane structure?
- What is the maximum use period of a temporary tent or membrane structure?
- Given an occupant load, what are the minimum means of egress and egress widths for tents and membrane structures?
- How are the flammable characteristics of a tent or other membrane structure, including contents, evaluated?
- What is a special amusement area?
- What fire and life safety systems are required for special amusement areas? What if the special amusement area is temporary?
- How are outdoor assembly events regulated?

KEY POINTS:
(Cont'd)

- How are hazards such as combustible materials, liquefied petroleum gas, flammable and combustible liquids and their sources of ignition treated when utilized within a tent?
- What constitutes high-piled combustible storage?
- How does commodity classification influence the design of automatic sprinkler systems?
- What is a high-hazard commodity?
- How can a product containing Group A plastic be reduced to a lesser hazard commodity?
- When does a building containing high-piled storage require an automatic sprinkler system?
- What design basis is used where the stored products have different commodity classifications?
- What are the building access requirements for structures used for high-piled storage?
- What are the differences between solid pile, shelf, palletized and rack storage?
- Which nationally recognized standard may be used for items not specifically addressed by the IFC in regulating construction, alteration or demolition operations?
- What are the requirements for storage and handling of construction trash and debris that apply to all construction or demolition operations?
- Can flammable and combustible liquids, flammable gases and explosives be stored at a construction site?
- What are the owner's responsibilities for fire protection during construction or demolition?
- At what point during construction are water supplies, standpipes and sprinkler systems required?
- Where are portable fire extinguishers required on construction or demolition sites?
- What are the fire protection and mechanical ventilation requirements for tire rebuilding operations?
- What administrative controls are prescribed to control ignition sources during tire rebuilding operations?
- How are the hazards of exterior tire storage regulated?
- What are the requirements for pile volume, location, water supply and site security for exterior tire storage? Do the requirements change when the tires are stored inside?

2021 IFC Study Companion

Code Text: *An oven or furnace that has heat utilization equipment operating at approximately atmospheric pressure wherein there is a potential explosion or fire hazard that could be occasioned by the presence of flammable volatiles or combustible materials processed or heated in the furnace.*

Discussion and Commentary: Class A furnace is a designation assigned to industrial ovens as appliances that process materials that contain flammable or combustible liquids, combustible powders, plastics, wood or paper. The oven is designed to safely evaporate and exhaust solvents and vapors produced as a result of spray finishing or other flammable finishing operations before the components or parts enter the oven.

Flammable gases and vapors generated during the heating process must be ventilated out of the oven and ducted to the exterior of the building.

Code Text: *Safety data for Class A solvent atmosphere ovens shall be furnished on the manufacturer's nameplate. The nameplate shall provide the following design data: (1) The solvent used, (2) The number of gallons (L) used per batch or per hour of solvent entering the oven, (3) The required purge time, (4) The oven operating temperature, (5) The exhaust blower rating for the number of gallons (L) of solvent per hour or batch at the maximum operating temperature. **Exception:** For low-oxygen ovens, the maximum allowable oxygen concentration shall be included in place of the exhaust blower ratings.*

Discussion and Commentary: The nameplate explains the basic design of any Class A oven. It requires that the solvent be identified, the number of gallons that may be in the oven during its operation, the required prepurge before the oven is activated, the oven's operating temperature and the exhaust rate at the maximum operating temperature of the oven. If the oven is designed to operate in a reduced oxygen level, the maximum oxygen concentration shall also be included on the nameplate.

Smith & Klieff Industrial Appliances Company
Dickinson, Texas

Class A Solvent Atmosphere Oven

Approved Solvents: Methyl ethyl ketone: n-hexane

Maximum Solvent Load/Batch: 4.5 gallons/batch using acetone; 6.1 gallons/batch for other approved solvents

Minimum Purge Time: 90 seconds

Oven Operating Temperature: Minimum 240°F at the maximum solvent load/batch

Minimum exhaust flow rate: 45,600 CFM at 0.5 inch w.c. for specified maximum solvent load/batch and minimum oven temperature. Makeup air shall equal the exhaust flow rate.

To confirm that the required air exhaust rate is provided, consider requiring an air balance test report. This measurement will evaluate the exhaust fan and determine if the required exhaust flow is provided.

Code Text: *Tents and membrane structures having an area in excess of 400 square feet (37 m²) shall not be erected, operated or maintained for any purpose without first obtaining a permit and approval from the fire code official.*

(See IFC Section 3103.2 for exceptions.)

Discussion and Commentary: The IFC establishes low thresholds as to when a permit is required for tents and membrane structures. These low limits are in place because of the ease and flexibility with which these temporary structures can be set up. Two exceptions allow for residential camping tents and an unlimited number of tents when the individual tent area does not exceed 700 square feet, each tent is open on all sides and a minimum 12-foot separation distance is provided between each of the tents and between the tents and structures.

(Photograph courtesy of Fulton Cochran, Clark County Department of Building and Fire Prevention, NV.)

Section 3103.5 specifies the temporary use period as 180 days within a 12-month period. Tents and membrane structures that are intended to remain for more than this specified period are treated as permanent structures and must comply with the requirements in IFC Section 3104 and be granted a construction permit under the *International Building Code®* (IBC®).

Code Text: *A detailed site and floor plan for tents or membrane structures with an occupant load of 50 or more shall be provided with each application for approval. The tent or membrane structure floor plan shall indicate details of the means of egress facilities, seating capacity, arrangement of the seating and location and type of heating and electrical equipment. The construction documents shall include an analysis of structural stability.*

Discussion and Commentary: If the tent or membrane structure can accommodate an occupant load of 50 or more, Section 3103.6 requires that the permit applicant submit construction documents to the fire code official for review and approval. The calculation of the occupant load would be based on the function of the space beneath the tent or membrane structure and the required minimum floor area for each occupant as specified in Table 1004.5. Once the 50-person occupant threshold is exceeded, plans must be submitted to the fire code official with the required information necessary to confirm compliance with Section 3103.

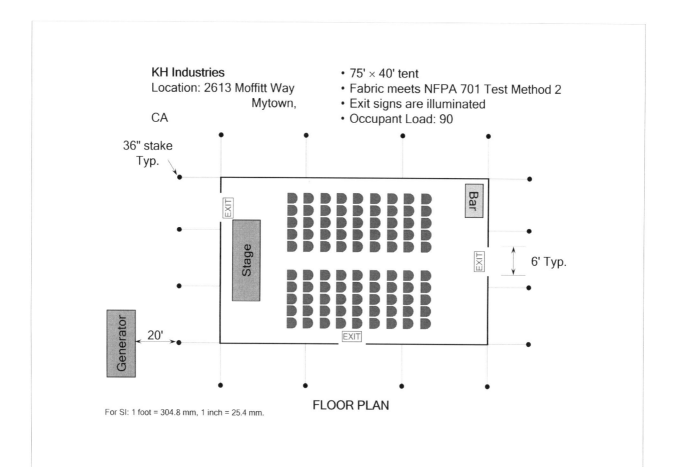

KH Industries
Location: 2613 Moffitt Way
Mytown,
CA

• 75' × 40' tent
• Fabric meets NFPA 701 Test Method 2
• Exit signs are illuminated
• Occupant Load: 90

36" stake Typ.

EXIT

Stage

Bar

EXIT

6' Typ.

Generator

20'

EXIT

For SI: 1 foot = 304.8 mm, 1 inch = 25.4 mm.

FLOOR PLAN

For example, assuming a concentrated assembly use without fixed seating: Table 1004.5 assigns an occupant net load factor area of 7 square feet/person. Section 3103.6 requires the submittal of construction documents when the tent, canopy or membrane structure will serve more than 50 persons. Therefore, construction documents would be required if the area was more than 350 square feet (7 ft²/person x 50 persons = 350 ft²).

Code Text: *Inspections. The entire tent, air-supported, air-inflated or tensioned membrane structure system shall be inspected at regular intervals, but not less than two times per permit use period, by the permittee, owner or agent to determine that the installation is maintained in accordance with this chapter. Exception: Permit use periods of less than 30 days.*

Inspection report. Where required by the fire code official, an inspection report shall be provided and shall consist of maintenance, anchors and fabric inspections.

Discussion and Commentary: This section requires that the temporary tent, air-supported or membrane structure is inspected during the time it is erected and used. Two inspections are required when the use period is 30 days or more. These inspections are to be conducted by the owner or permittee, or their authorized representative. These inspections are independent from the inspection conducted by the code official at the time of permit approval as provided in Section 105.3.3.

The inspection would consist of evaluating the stability of the structure, ensuring anchors are adequately attached, review of equipment or device location within the structure so that egress is maintained, and determining that fire and life safety equipment is still in place and operational.

Section 3103.7.1 authorizes the code official to require a report for each of these inspections.

This air-supported structure would require review of the power supply for the blowers, and an auxiliary inflation system if the occupant load exceeds 200 (IFC Section 3103.10.4).

Topic: Location	Category: Tents and Special Event Structures
Reference: IFC 3103.8.2	Subject: Temporary Tents and Membrane Structures

Code Text: *Tents or membrane structures shall not be located within 20 feet (6096 mm) of lot lines, buildings, other tents or membrane structures, parked vehicles or internal combustion engines. For the purpose of determining required distances, support ropes and guy wires shall be considered as part of the temporary membrane structure or tent.*

(See IFC Section 3103.8.2 for exceptions.)

Discussion and Commentary: Section 3103.8.1 requires fire department access in accordance with Section 503. This particular section specifies a minimum 20-foot separation between the temporary tent or membrane structure and the exposures specified in Section 3103.8.2, including other temporary or permanent tents or membranes structures, parked vehicles or internal combustion engines such as a temporary power generator. Exception 1 eliminates the separation distance if the tents or membrane structures are not used for cooking and the total area does not exceed 15,000 square feet. If cooking does occur, Exception 2 also allows for no separation but reduces the area limit to 10,000 square feet and requires an allowable area calculation in accordance with the IBC. The exception also requires that the means of egress from the building and the temporary structure comply with the IFC and that fire department access roads are provided.

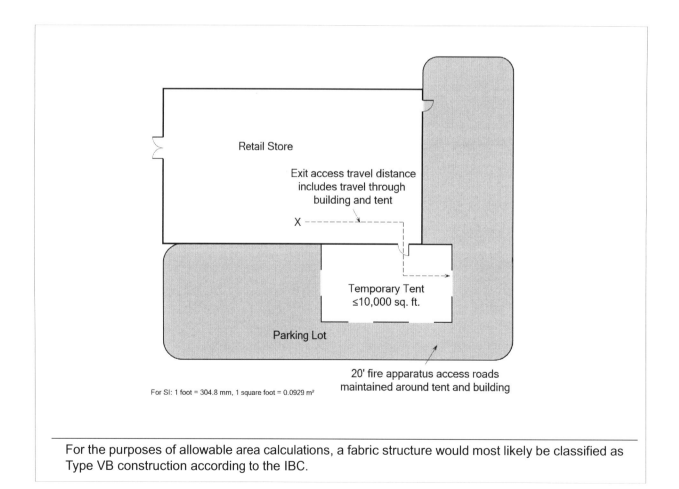

Retail Store

Exit access travel distance includes travel through building and tent

X

Temporary Tent
≤10,000 sq. ft.

Parking Lot

20' fire apparatus access roads maintained around tent and building

For SI: 1 foot = 304.8 mm, 1 square foot = 0.0929 m²

For the purposes of allowable area calculations, a fabric structure would most likely be classified as Type VB construction according to the IBC.

Code Text: *Tents and membrane structures exceeding one story shall be designed and constructed to comply with Sections 1606 through 1609 of the* International Building Code.

Discussion and Commentary: The IFC does not limit the size of tents or membrane structures. Because multi-story tents and membrane structures are often used at large events, the fire code official needs to confirm that the temporary tent or membrane structure can safely perform when subjected to wind loads, snow loads, dead loads and live loads. Section 3103.9 requires proper anchoring, and Section 3109.3.1 requires that multi-story tents and membrane structures meet the structural design criteria of specific sections in the IBC. Additionally, tents and membrane structures over 7,500 square feet or with an occupant load greater than 1,000 must also comply with these sections in the IBC (IFC Section 3103.9.2).

The referenced sections of the IBC contain design loads for wind and snow loads, in addition to dead loads and live loads on the elevated floor levels.

Code Text: *Storage of combustible materials in closely packed piles or combustible materials on pallets, in racks or on shelves where the top of storage is greater than 12 feet (3658 mm) in height. Where required by the fire code official, high-piled combustible storage also includes certain high-hazard commodities, such as rubber tires, Group A plastics, flammable liquids, idle pallets and similar commodities, where the top of storage is greater than 6 feet (1829 mm) in height.*

Discussion and Commentary: High-piled combustible storage is regulated because it arranges fuel into a configuration that can promote high burning rates. Many of the materials such as idle pallets, flammable liquids and Group A plastics can also exhibit high heat release rates and large volumes of smoke. Generally, combustible storage greater than 12 feet in height, regardless of the storage method, is classified as high-piled combustible storage. High-challenge commodities such as Group A plastics, rolled carpet, rubber tires and the like are classified as high-piled storage when the height of storage is more than 6 feet because of the greater hazard and fire-fighting challenge they present.

Pictured are solid blocks of expanded plastic which are classified as exposed, expanded Group A plastic and treated as high-hazard commodity in Chapter 32.

Code Text: *A combination of products, packing materials and containers.*

Discussion and Commentary: Before one can apply the requirements of Chapter 32, an analysis of the stored materials and goods must be performed. This analysis must evaluate the actual product, its packing materials and the shipping container. This analysis allows for the classification of the commodity. Once this analysis is completed, the designer can then review IFC Section 3203 and assign the appropriate classification to the commodity. In applying the fire protection requirements of IFC Chapter 32, there is no difference between assigning a commodity as a Class I or IV commodity. However, the commodity classification does make a significant difference in the design of the automatic sprinkler system if one is required to be installed. Note that when classifying a commodity, the pallet is not included in this analysis.

IFC Section 3201.3 requires the permit applicant to provide sufficient information demonstrating that the commodities are properly classified. Determining the commodity classification is based on the product, the container, the package, filler and any shrink wrap, but does not include the pallet.

Code Text: *Commodities shall be classified as Class I, II, III, IV or high hazard in accordance with Sections 3203.2 through 3203.10.3. Materials listed within each commodity classification are assumed to be unmodified for improved combustibility characteristics. Use of flame-retarding modifiers or the physical form of the material could change the classification.*

Discussion and Commentary: The classification system for Class I-IV commodities and plastics in the IFC is consistent with the requirements in NFPA 13. As the commodity number value rises, so does the relative heat release and burning rates. Simply stated, for equal storage conditions, a fire involving Class IV commodities will burn hotter and faster when compared to a Class I commodity. What is unique about the IFC is that certain materials or finished products are classified as high-hazard commodities. This commodity classification has a lower threshold for requiring automatic sprinklers. In addition, the design of the automatic sprinkler system may be governed by other standards. For example, consider a warehouse storing Level 3 aerosols. In this case, the stored commodity would be assigned a high-hazard classification, and IFC Table 3203.8 would also require compliance with the requirements of Chapter 51, including NFPA 30B.

This photograph illustrates encapsulated storage—where the pallet load is wrapped on all sides and the top with plastic causing fire sprinkler water to run off the pallet load. NFPA 13 has special design requirements for encapsulated storage.

Code Text: *Figures 3203.9(1) and 3203.9(2) shall be used to determine the commodity classification based on the quantity of Group A plastics in the following situations: (1) The product is not listed in Table 3203.8 and contains Group A plastics, (2) The commodity contains Group A plastics and is not classified as high-hazard in Table 3203.8, (3) The product listing in Table 3203.8 does not specifically include packaging, and the packaging material includes Group A plastics.*

Discussion and Commentary: The required discharge density can be significantly greater for an automatic sprinkler system protecting Group A plastics when compared to other less challenging commodities such as Class IV or III materials or products. Higher discharge densities can require the use of larger diameter pipe or the installation of a fire pump. FM Global determined that if a commodity is formulated with a limited amount of expanded or unexpanded plastic, it can be safely protected using an automatic sprinkler system designed for a Class IV or less commodity classification. Note that there are two figures for evaluating Group A plastics. Figure 3203.9(1) evaluates the *volume* of Group A plastics, and Figure 3203.9(2) evaluates the *weight* of Group A plastics. Both the volume and weight must be evaluated.

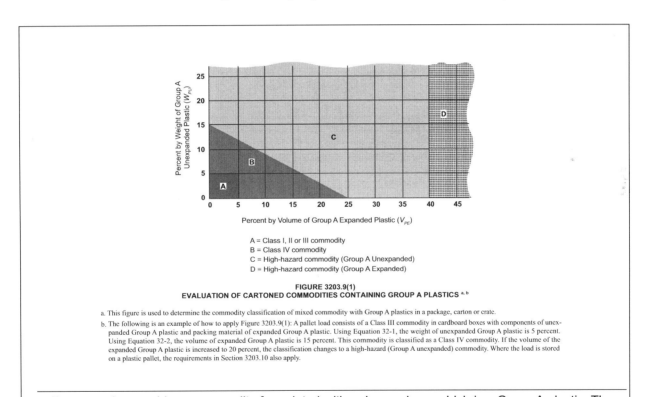

A = Class I, II or III commodity
B = Class IV commodity
C = High-hazard commodity (Group A Unexpanded)
D = High-hazard commodity (Group A Expanded)

FIGURE 3203.9(1)
EVALUATION OF CARTONED COMMODITIES CONTAINING GROUP A PLASTICS [a, b]

a. This figure is used to determine the commodity classification of mixed commodity with Group A plastics in a package, carton or crate.

b. The following is an example of how to apply Figure 3203.9(1): A pallet load consists of a Class III commodity in cardboard boxes with components of unexpanded Group A plastic and packing material of expanded Group A plastic. Using Equation 32-1, the weight of unexpanded Group A plastic is 5 percent. Using Equation 32-2, the volume of expanded Group A plastic is 15 percent. This commodity is classified as a Class IV commodity. If the volume of the expanded Group A plastic is increased to 20 percent, the classification changes to a high-hazard (Group A unexpanded) commodity. Where the load is stored on a plastic pallet, the requirements in Section 3203.10 also apply.

For example, consider a commodity formulated with polypropylene, which is a Group A plastic. The commodity contains 13 percent by weight of unexpanded plastic (P_{WU}) and 10 percent by volume of expanded plastic (P_{VE}). Application of IFC Figure 3203.9(1) would determine that the commodity classification based on volume is Class IV. Section 3203.9.1 requires that Figure 3203.9(2) also be used to evaluate the commodity based on weight of expanded plastic (P_{WE}) versus the weight of unexpanded plastic (P_{WU}). The higher of each classification would be the commodity classification. Assuming $P_{WE} > 5$ percent, evaluation with Figure 3203.9(2) identifies the commodity as high-hazard (Group A unexpanded).

Code Text: *High-piled storage areas, and portions of high-piled storage areas intended for storage of a different commodity class than adjacent areas, shall be designed and specifically designated to contain Class I, Class II, Class III, Class IV or high-hazard commodities. The designation of a high-piled combustible storage area, or portion thereof intended for storage of a different commodity class, shall be based on the highest hazard commodity class stored except as provided in Section 3204.2.*

Discussion and Commentary: This provision stipulates that when designing for high-piled combustible storage, the commodity designation must be declared. It also requires that the commodity designation be based on the highest hazard commodity that is being stored. If a new, more challenging commodity is introduced, the permit applicant can use the criteria in IFC Section 3204.2. This criteria allows for an engineering analysis of the sprinkler system to determine if it can safely protect the higher hazard commodity. This is commonly done by locating the higher challenge commodity near the fire sprinkler riser and performing hydraulic analysis to determine how much water the system will discharge.

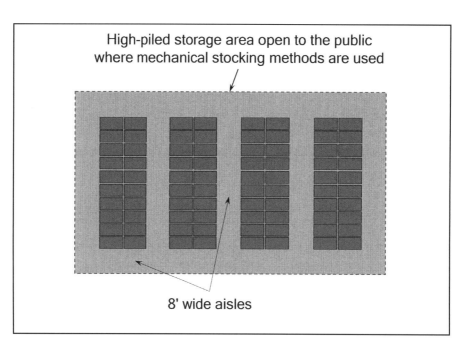

For SI: 1 foot = 304.8 mm.

The high-piled storage area includes aisles within the stacks and an equivalent operating aisle width around the perimeter of the stacks. Minimum aisle widths are based on the commodity classification, storage method and sprinkler system design. IFC Section 3206.10 specifies that aisles shall be not less than 96 inches wide in areas open to the public where mechanical stocking methods are used.

Topic: Extent of Protection   **Category:** High-Piled Combustible Storage

Reference: IFC 3206.2.1   **Subject:** General Fire Protection and Life Safety Features

Code Text: *The fire safety features required in Table 3206.2 shall extend to the lesser of 15 feet (4572 mm) beyond the high-piled storage area or a full height wall. Where portions of high-piled storage areas have different fire protection requirements because of commodity, method of storage or storage height, the fire protection features required by Table 3206.2 within this area shall be based on the most restrictive design requirements.*

Discussion and Commentary: In a mixed use occupancy such as a Group F-1 and S-1 occupancy, it is common for storage racks or palletized storage to be used. When high-piled storage is proposed or found during an inspection, the requirements for IFC Table 3206.2 must be applied. This table stipulates when either fire detection or automatic sprinkler protection is required, along with smoke and heat vents, draft curtains and fire department access doorways. This section stipulates that the fire protection features shall be based on the most restrictive design. The design will not only be influenced by the commodity but will also be influenced by storage heights and aisle widths, especially if the building is protected by an automatic sprinkler system.

Class III Commodity

Protection extended ≥15' on all sides of the Class IV Commodity Storage Area

Class IV Commodity

For SI: 1 foot = 304.8 mm.

If the fire protection design is modified for a higher hazard commodity, the higher level of protection must be extended a minimum of 15 feet beyond the perimeter of the designated high-piled storage area for the higher hazard commodity, unless limited areas of the higher hazard commodity are protected in accordance with Section 3204.2.

Code Text: *Where a building contains multiple high-piled storage areas, the aggregate of all high-piled storage areas shall be used for the application of Table 3206.2 unless the high-piled storage areas are separated in accordance with one of the following: (1) High-piled storage areas separated by fire barriers with a minimum fire-resistance-rating of 1 hour constructed in accordance with Section 707 of the* International Building Code, *(2) In buildings equipped throughout with an automatic sprinkler system in accordance with Section 903.3.1.1, high-piled storage areas separated by 100 feet (30 480 mm) or more. The area providing the separation shall not contain high-piled combustible storage.*

Discussion and Commentary: Frequently, facilities may have more than one high-piled storage area. Consider an assembly and packaging facility with product and packaging material stored on one side of the building and packaged product ready for shipment on the other side of the building. The two high-piled storage areas are separated by the assembly and packaging area consisting of conveyors and worktables. The high-piled storage area will be either the aggregate of the high-piled storage areas, or they can be considered separately if they are adequately separated. The required separation is either a 1-hour fire-resistance-rated wall, or a distance of 100 feet with no high-piled storage within the separation.

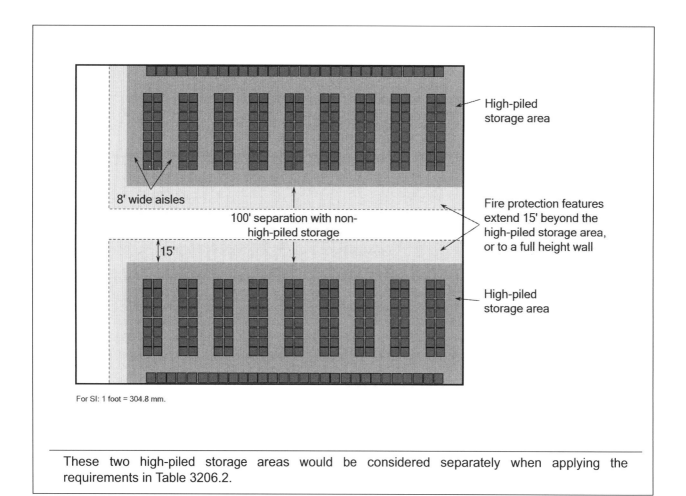

For SI: 1 foot = 304.8 mm.

These two high-piled storage areas would be considered separately when applying the requirements in Table 3206.2.

Code Text: ***Manual activated shutdown.*** *A manually activated switch shall be provided to initiate the approved automatic shutdown process. The switch shall be clearly identified and shall be in a location approved by the fire code official.*

Automatic shutdown. *Automatic shutdown shall be required for high-piled combustible storage areas greater than 500 square feet (46 m²). The approved automatic shutdown process shall commence upon any of the following events: (1) Water flow is detected in the automatic sprinkler system, if present, (2) Activation of the fire detection system, if present.*

Discussion and Commentary: High-piled storage areas with automated rack storage are to be provided with a manually operated emergency shutdown switch. When the automated rack storage area exceeds 500 square feet, an automatic shutdown is also required. Both sections refer to an "approved automatic shutdown process." This is an intentional term because an immediate ceasing of operations for the typical automated storage system is not always the best solution. Often, a phased shutdown is more appropriate. For example, assume a large facility with automated pallet movers and five fire sprinkler system zones. The fire sprinklers operate in Zone 1 and the Zone 1 water flow switch activates. The shutdown process could consist of: (1) automated movers in Zone 1 that are not carrying a load move out of the storage area and return to their home base. This allows for unobstructed aisles, (2) automated movers in Zone 1 carrying a load shall travel to the closest area out of the storage aisles. Once out of the storage area, the pallet mover stops. Again, the pallet mover does not obstruct the aisle, (3) automated movers in Zones 2 through 5 complete their task and then return to home base. This allows those aisles to be unobstructed and empty of product loads, rather than just stopping wherever they are located.

The shutdown process is specifically tailored to each facility but must meet the approval of the fire code official. The automated shutdown is to be initiated by either operation of the automatic sprinkler system or the fire detection system. Table 3206.2 will require either sprinklers or detection when the high-piled combustible storage area exceeds 500 square feet.

(Photograph courtesy of Getty Images.)

Automated storage systems can inadvertently move product into a fire, carry a burning product to uninvolved portions of the building. Their shutdown is critical to control the spread of fire.

Code Text: *The owner or owner's authorized agent shall be responsible for the development, implementation and maintenance of an approved, written site safety plan establishing a fire prevention program at the project site applicable throughout all phases of the construction, repair, alteration or demolition work. The plan addresses the requirements of this chapter and other applicable portions of this code, the duties of staff and staff training requirements. The plan shall be submitted and approved before a building permit is issued. Any changes to the plan shall be submitted for approval.*

Discussion and Commentary: The owner or the owner's authorized agent is accountable to maintain on-site safety and is responsible to develop and implement the site safety plan. The site safety plan is to be submitted for review and approval prior to issuance of the building permit.

The site safety plan addresses aspects of fire safety, fire department access, portable fire extinguisher locations, handling of debris and construction trash, hot work permit program, site security, generators and storage and handling of fuel for equipment.

All operations and storage of materials need to be handled in accordance with the site safety plan.

Code Text: *Temporary heating devices shall be listed and labeled. The installation, maintenance and use of temporary heating devices shall be in accordance with the terms of the listing and the manufacturer's instructions.*

Discussion and Commentary: Temporary heating equipment is commonly used on construction sites to prevent poured concrete, mortar for masonry construction or drywall finishing materials from freezing before they are cured. Leaking gas or liquid fuels can easily ignite when exposed to sparks or open flames from electrical equipment, welding or other construction activities on site. Chapter 33 establishes prescriptive requirements, such as set clearances from combustibles for heating appliances. The regulation of most appliances relies upon their listing or label for proper operation and clearances. The manufacturer's operating instructions, which are a part of the listing approval, are to be followed for proper installation, maintenance and use.

Section 3304 also refers to Section 605 for oil-fired heaters, Chapter 61 and the *International Fuel Gas Code* for LP-gas heaters and Section 5705 for refueling with flammable and combustible liquids.

Code Text: *In buildings where an automatic sprinkler system is required by this code or the* International Building Code, *it shall be unlawful to occupy any portion of a building or structure until the automatic sprinkler system installation has been tested and approved, except as provided in Section 105.3.3.*

Discussion and Commentary: The IBC and the IFC require certain occupancies, uses and fire areas to be protected by an automatic sprinkler system. Under certain circumstances, the IBC permits increases in building area, height, number of stories and exit travel distance, and reductions in fire-resistance ratings when an approved automatic sprinkler system is installed. The presence of a fully operational system is mandatory in these cases for the building or facility to meet the minimum life safety and property protection standards of the codes.

Section 3315.2 permits only authorized personnel to operate sprinkler control valves, and requires that designated parties are notified when valves are turned on or off and that sprinkler valves are checked at the end of each work period to make sure that automatic sprinkler protection is in service. Many fires can become uncontrolled in sprinklered buildings if sprinkler systems are not operational because of intentional or accidental shutoff of the water supply control valve.

Code Text: *Buffing operations shall be located in a room separated from the remainder of the building housing the tire rebuilding or tire recapping operations by a 1-hour fire barrier.* ***Exception:*** *Buffing operations are not required to be separated where all of the following conditions are met: (1) Buffing operations are equipped with an approved continuous automatic water-spray system directed at the point of cutting action, (2) Buffing machines are connected to particle-collecting systems providing a minimum air movement of 1,500 cubic feet per minute (cfm) (0.71 m³/s) in volume and 4,500 feet per minute (fpm) (23 m/s) in-line velocity, (3) The collecting system shall discharge the rubber particles to an approved outdoor noncombustible or fire-resistant container, which is emptied at frequent intervals to prevent overflow.*

Discussion and Commentary: The IFC requires tire buffing operations to be located in a room separated from the remainder of the building by a 1-hour fire barrier. If this is not desired, the exception allows for the elimination of the 1-hour fire barrier when all three criteria are satisfied. These criteria are designed to manage the hazard of crumb rubber. Crumb rubber is a byproduct of tire recycling and rebuilding and is used for a variety of uses including soil mulches and surfaces for childrens' playgrounds.

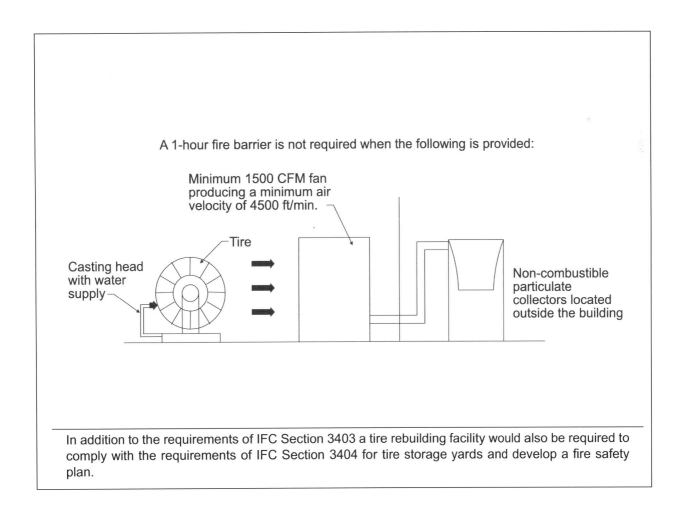

A 1-hour fire barrier is not required when the following is provided:

Minimum 1500 CFM fan producing a minimum air velocity of 4500 ft/min.

Tire

Casting head with water supply

Non-combustible particulate collectors located outside the building

In addition to the requirements of IFC Section 3403 a tire rebuilding facility would also be required to comply with the requirements of IFC Section 3404 for tire storage yards and develop a fire safety plan.

Code Text: *Outdoor waste tire storage shall not be located under bridges, elevated trestles, elevated roadways or elevated railroads.*

Discussion and Commentary: Tires generate a tremendous volume of heat and smoke when they burn. Because of this, the IFC does not permit waste tire storage to be located beneath pedestrian or vehicle roadways or railroad tracks. The provision is unique in that it only applies to waste tires rather than new tires. For other tire storage provisions, the IFC does not distinguish between waste versus new tires.

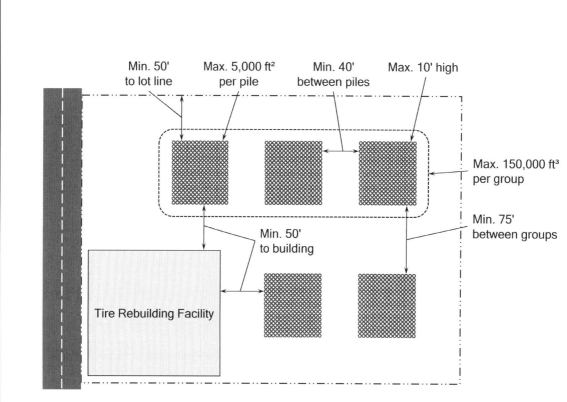

For SI: 1 foot = 304.8 mm; 1 cubic foot = 0.02832 m³.

Outdoor storage piles of tires are limited in size and height, and separations to other piles is intended to reduce fire spread (IFC Section 3405).

Study Session 11

IFC Chapters 30 through 34

1. Excluding the exception, what is the maximum dimension from a fuel gas valve to an industrial oven?

    a. 2 feet   b. 4 feet

    c. 6 feet   d. 8 feet

    Reference _____

2. What class of industrial oven requires an interlock that stops conveyors or other sources of flammable or combustible materials in the event of a ventilation failure?

    a. A   b. B

    c. C   d. D

    Reference _____

3. Which class of industrial oven requires an automatic fire-extinguishing system?

    a. Class C and D

    b. Class A and B

    c. All industrial ovens require it.

    d. Ovens do not require an automatic fire-extinguishing system.

    Reference _____

4. What is the minimum required separation distance between a membrane structure with an area of 17,200 square feet and a second membrane structure with an equal area?

    a. 15 feet   b. 25 feet

    c. 50 feet   d. Separation is not required.

    Reference _____

5. An air supported membrane structure with an occupant load of more than _____ and used as a place of public assembly requires a means of auxiliary power or an auxiliary blower powered by an internal combustion engine.

    a. 100   b. 200

    c. 300   d. 1,000

    Reference _____

6. Given: A membrane structure with an occupant load of 650 persons. What is the required number of egress openings and the minimum width of each egress opening?

    a. 1 opening; 36 inches   b. 3 openings; 72 inches

    c. 4 openings; 96 inches   d. 4 openings; 72 inches

    Reference _____

7. What is the maximum distance to an egress opening in a tent with an occupant load of 180?

    a. 50 feet   b. 100 feet

    c. 150 feet   d. 250 feet

    Reference _____

8. What is the maximum length of time a temporary special event structure can be erected and used?

    a. 6 weeks   b. 3 months

    c. 6 months   d. 1 year

    Reference _____

9. Given: A complex of five tents. One of the tents is used for cooking. What is the minimum required separation distance between the tent used for cooking and the other tents?

    a. 12 feet   b. 20 feet

    c. 50 feet   d. No separation is required

    Reference _____

10. An outdoor assembly event with an occupant load of 2,500 persons will require which of the following?

    a.   crowd managers

    b.   weather monitoring person, when required by the code official

    c.   public safety plan, when required by the code official

    d.   all of the above

Reference _____

11. Which of the following require a construction permit from the fire code official?

    a.   Temporary special event structure

    b.   Temporary tent with 725 square feet at a carnival

    c.   Temporary membrane structure covering 450 square feet at the fair

    d.   All of the above

Reference _____

12. Because of its occupant load, a tent contractor chooses to use a portable generator for a second source of power. The generator is fueled using gasoline. What is the minimum required separation between the generator and the tent?

    a.   10 feet   b.   20 feet

    c.   25 feet   d.   50 feet

Reference _____

13. What is the classification of an oven that operates at atmospheric pressure and does not contain flammable volatiles?

    a.   Furnace Class A   b.   Furnace Class B

    c.   Furnace Class C   d.   Furnace Class D

Reference _____

14. What is maximum temperature permitted at the roof or ceiling over an industrial oven?

    a.   160°F   b.   170°F

    c.   180°F   d.   160°C

Reference _____

15. By definition, the top of storage greater than _____ feet in height, but for high-hazard commodities, storage greater than _____ feet shall be regulated as high-piled combustible storage.

      a. 10; 6   b. 12; 4

      c. 12; 6   d. 12; 12

Reference _____

16. High-piled storage of Level 2 aerosols is classified as a _____ commodity.

      a. II   b. III

      c. IV   d. high-hazard

Reference _____

17. High-piled storage of rubber tires is classified as a _____ commodity.

      a. II   b. III

      c. IV   d. high-hazard

Reference _____

18. High-piled storage of frozen food in plastic trays is classified as a _____ commodity.

      a. II   b. III

      c. IV   d. high-hazard

Reference _____

19. An automatic shutdown is required for automated rack storage when the high-piled combustible storage area exceeds _____ square feet _____ .

      a. Any size

      b. 100, if high-hazard commodity

      c. 500, for any class commodity

      d. 1,000, if Class I–IV commodities

Reference _____

20. Given: A commodity contains 17 percent by weight of polystyrene. The commodity is constructed as an unexpanded plastic. What is the commodity classification?

    a. Group A plastic
    b. High-hazard commodity

    c. Class III commodity
    d. Class IV commodity

Reference _____

21. Given: A 9,000 square foot Group S-1 occupancy for the storage of Class IV commodities. The owner has elected not to install an automatic sprinkler system. The building is not open to the public. What is the maximum permissible storage height?

    a. 20 feet
    b. 30 feet

    c. 40 feet
    d. 50 feet

Reference _____

22. Given: A retail facility with high-piled combustible storage. The building is sprinklered with K-25.2 sprinklers in accordance with NFPA 13, and aisles nominally 8 feet wide. Displays and wing stacks are allowed within the aisle width provided they do not exceed _____ inches in height and a minimum clear aisle width of _____ is maintained.

    a. 24; 72

    b. 48; 48

    c. 48; 44

    d. Not permitted because it reduces aisle width

Reference _____

23. A storage rack is considered to have solid shelving when a solid surface such as a plywood panel is introduced and the area of the solid surface between flue spaces is greater than _____ square feet.

    a. 16
    b. 20

    c. 32
    d. 96

Reference _____

24. If an issue regarding fire safety during construction and demolition is not specifically addressed by IFC Chapter 33, compliance with _____ may be required.

    a.   16 CFR Part 1500.42—1984

    b.   16 CFR Part 1500.41—1984

    c.   18 USC Part 1, Chapter 40

    d.   NFPA 241

Reference _____

25. Given: A new building is being constructed. It will be 6 stories and is classified as Type IIIA construction. The building is located 50 feet from the closest lot line. What is the minimum fire flow required to be available during construction before construction on the second story is started?

    a.   Fire flow is not required until after construction is completed

    b.   25 percent of the required fire flow after construction is completed, with a minimum of 500 GPM

    c.   50 percent of the required fire flow after construction is completed, with a minimum of 500 GPM

    d.   100 percent of the required fire flow after construction is completed

Reference _____

26. Approved vehicle access for fire fighting shall be provided to all construction or demolition sites to within _____ feet of temporary or permanent fire department connections.

    a.   50   b.   100

    c.   150   d.   600

Reference _____

27. Where a building has been constructed to a height greater than _____ above the lowest level of fire department vehicle access, at least one temporary stairway shall be provided unless one or more of the permanent stairways are erected as the construction progresses.

    a.   30 feet   b.   40 feet

    c.   50 feet   d.   75 feet

Reference _____

28. An approved water supply for fire protection, either temporary or permanent, shall be made available at construction sites _____.

    a. before the first inspection

    b. as soon as the building permit is issued

    c. prior to commencement of grading

    d. when combustible building materials arrive on the site

    Reference _____

29. Where standpipes are required in a new building, they shall be installed prior to construction exceeding _____ feet in height above the lowest level of fire department access.

    a. 30   b. 40

    c. 50   d. 75

    Reference _____

30. Structures under construction, alteration or demolition are *not* required to have an approved portable fire extinguisher _____.

    a. at each stairway on all floor levels with accumulated combustible materials

    b. in every storage and construction shed

    c. where flammable liquids are stored

    d. at the temporary electrical service

    Reference _____

31. Assuming that a building does not comply with all of the requirements in the exception to IFC Section 3403.2, what is the required fire-resistance rating for the separation between the tire buffing room and the tire rebuilding operation?

    a. 1-hour   b. 2-hour

    c. 3-hour   d. 4-hour

    Reference _____

32. Given: An automotive repair shop stores new tires inside the building. The tires are stored on-tread in racks, two tiers high. The maximum dimension of the rack when looking in a direction parallel to the hole in the tires is _____ feet.

    a. 10   b. 25

    c. 50   d. 75

    Reference _____

33. The maximum volume of an individual pile of tires stored outside shall not exceed _____ cubic feet.

    a. 5,000   b. 50,000

    c. 100,000   d. 150,000

    Reference _____

34. Outdoor tire storage piles of 5,000 square feet each shall be separated by a clear space of at least _____ feet.

    a. 20   b. 25

    c. 30   d. 40

    Reference _____

35. What is the maximum hose lay distance allowed from a water supply to a pile of tires?

    a. 150 feet   b. 250 feet

    c. 400 feet   d. 500 feet

    Reference _____

2021 IFC Chapters 35 through 40

Special Occupancies and Operations, Part IV: Welding and Other Hot Work; Marinas; Combustible Fibers; Higher Education Laboratories; Processing and Extraction Facilities; and Storage of Distilled Spirits and Wines

OBJECTIVE: To gain a general understanding of the *International Fire Code®* (IFC®) requirements for welding and other forms of hot work, marinas, combustible fibers, laboratories in higher education facilities, plant processing and extraction operations and storage of distilled spirits and wines.

REFERENCE: Chapters 35 through 40, 2021 IFC

KEY POINTS:
- What administrative controls and general requirements regulate the hazards of welding and hot work?
- What are the prescribed controls for separating combustibles from hot work operations?
- Is it acceptable to disable an automatic sprinkler system during hot work or welding operations?
- What are the requirements for fire watches, including pre-hot work inspections?
- What is the Hot Work Permit Program and how does it work?
- What is the maximum pressure allowed for acetylene used for gas welding and cutting?
- When is a standpipe required at a marina?
- How is fire department apparatus access provided at a marina?
- Can fuels be dispensed at a marina, and if so, what are the requirements?
- What is an emergency operations staging area at a marina, and when is one required?
- Do the boat slips at a marina require an address or method of distinguishing one from another?
- What are combustible fibers and densely packed baled cotton?
- What type of combustible fibers represent a hazard?
- How are hazards that are created by combustible fibers addressed in facilities that generate or process combustible fibers?

KEY POINTS:
(Cont'd)

- What are the requirements for a given volume of stored loose fibers?
- What are the requirements for baled storage of combustible fibers?
- What is a "higher education laboratory"?
- How are laboratory suites different from control areas?
- What fire-resistance rating is required between laboratory suites?
- How is the maximum number of laboratory suites in a building determined?
- Is the code applied the same to existing laboratory suites as it is to new laboratory suites?
- When is an automatic sprinkler system required in a laboratory suite?
- Are hazardous materials limited in a laboratory suite? Are any hazardous materials prohibited?
- Can control areas be substituted for laboratory suites? Can laboratory suites and control areas be located on the same floor?
- What are the hazards of extracting oils from plants?
- What is the miscella?
- What is the process of desolventizing?
- How are existing plant extraction operations treated differently than new plant extraction operations?
- Is an operational permit required for plant extraction systems?
- Are flammable liquids or flammable gases used during the plant extraction process?
- What equipment must be listed for plant extraction processes?
- When is a technical report necessary to address the plant extraction process and equipment?
- What type of safety systems are required in a room containing a plant extraction process?
- Where are emergency shutoffs required in an extraction facility and what do they control?
- When is spill control required where distilled spirits are stored?
- Is an automatic sprinkler system required to protect storage of distilled spirits?
- Can distilled spirits be stored in the basement? Or, upper floors?
- Is the storage of distilled spirits considered a Group H occupancy?
- When is mechanical ventilation for storage rooms containing distilled spirits required?

Code Text: *Hot work shall only be conducted in areas designed or authorized for that purpose by the personnel responsible for a hot work program. Hot work shall not be conducted in the following areas unless approval has been obtained from the fire code official: (1) Areas where the sprinkler system is impaired, (2) Areas where there exists the potential of an explosive atmosphere, such as locations where flammable gases, liquids or vapors are present, (3) Areas with readily ignitable materials, such as storage of large quantities of bulk sulfur, baled paper, cotton, lint, dust or loose combustible materials, (4) On board ships at dock or ships under construction or repair, (5) At other locations as specified by the fire code official.*

Discussion and Commentary: The conventional application of IFC Chapter 35 is that a company or organization is responsible for the preparation and administration of a hot work permitting and work program. However, for certain hazardous operations such as hot work when a sprinkler system is disabled or when hot work is performed on maritime vessels, the IFC requires that the hot work management program be approved by the fire code official. IFC Section 3501.3 was developed to grant fire code officials broad authority when regulating hot work operations in hazardous locations or when the risk of ignition is increased. Item 5 in this section allows the fire code official to issue policies to address hazards unique to the jurisdiction.

My Fire Department

Fire Code Operational Permit

| **Hot Work Permit** |

Issued to: _____

Business Name: _____

Business Address: _____

Hot Work is permitted at the following location:

_____

All hot work activities shall be conducted using the Hot Work Permit Program approved by My Fire Department in accordance with IFC Section 3503.3.

_____ is designated as the Responsible Person by the permit applicant.

_____   _____
Fire Marshal   Date

A hot work permit can be issued for a specific job, or issued as an annual permit to a company that conducts multiple jobs throughout the year in a variety of locations (IFC Section 3503.3).

Code Text: *Approved special precautions shall be taken to avoid accidental operation of automatic fire detection systems.*

Discussion and Commentary: Hot work operations obviously generate heat, but they also generate light, sparks and smoke. Flame detectors will see the light spectrum of the hot work operation and react as it they would to a fire. Smoke detectors can be activated by the smoke if they are close to the hot work.

Precautions are necessary so that the hot work does not create nuisance alarms in the facility.

Topic: Fire Watch—When Required

Category: Welding and Other Hot Work

Reference: IFC 3504.2.1

Subject: Fire Safety Requirements

Code Text: *A fire watch shall be provided during hot work activities and shall continue for not less than 30 minutes after the conclusion of the work. The fire code official, or the responsible manager under a hot work program, is authorized to extend the fire watch based on the hazards or work being performed.* ***Exception:*** *Where the hot work area has no fire hazards or combustible exposures.*

Discussion and Commentary: Many times hot work may not immediately ignite adjacent combustible construction. But as hot particles fall undetected, they can eventually result in a fire. As a result, fire watch is required when the hot work area contains combustible materials or combustible construction. The fire watch is to remain vigilant for 30 minutes after the hot work is completed.

Fire watch personnel need to be prepared to take action during and up to 30 minutes after the conclusion of hot work action should a fire occur.

Topic: Scope	Category: Marinas
Reference: IFC 3601.1	Subject: General

Code Text: *Marina facilities shall be in accordance with this chapter.*

Discussion and Commentary: Chapter 36 establishes requirements for marinas. It contains minimum fire safety and fire protection requirements for fire department access, water supplies and Class I dry standpipe systems. Chapter 36 references NFPA 303, *Standard for Marinas*, and requires compliance with many portions of this standard. Motor fuel dispensing into marine craft is referenced to Chapter 23.

Marina motor vehicle fuel-dispensing stations must comply with requirements in IFC Section 2310.

Topic: Standpipes	**Category:** Marinas
Reference: IFC 3604.2	**Subject:** Fire Protection Equipment

Code Text: *Marinas and boatyards shall be equipped throughout with standpipe systems in accordance with NFPA 303. Systems shall be provided with hose connections located such that no point on the marina pier or float system exceeds 150 feet (15 240 mm) from a standpipe hose connection.*

Discussion and Commentary: Because of the difficulty of access to boat and marina fires, piers, marinas and wharves with facilities to moor five or more vessels are required to provide a standpipe system. The standpipe outlets must be located so that no portion of the marina, pier or float system are more than 150 feet from a hose connection. This provides fire fighters with the ability to drag hose to the outlet, make connection and approach the fire from that location.

Marinas and slips create significant exposure hazards when a fire occurs onboard.

Code Text: *Space shall be provided on all float systems for the staging of emergency equipment. Emergency operation staging areas shall provide a minimum of 4 feet wide by 10 feet long (1219 mm by 3048 mm) clear area exclusive of walkways and shall be located at each standpipe hose connection. Emergency operation staging areas shall be provided with a curb or barrier having a minimum height of 4 inches (102 mm) and maximum space between the bottom edge and the surface of the staging area of 2 inches (51 mm) on the outboard sides of the staging area.*

An approved sign reading FIRE EQUIPMENT STAGING AREA—KEEP CLEAR shall be provided at each staging area.

Discussion and   Float systems will move with the movement of the water. Fire fighters carrying gear and
Commentary: equipment out on the float need to be able to set down some of the equipment until it is needed. This provides a location where the fire department can place equipment securely so it does not roll off the float as it moves in the water. The staging area must be at least 4 inches in height with a gap at the bottom so water is not retained within the staging area.

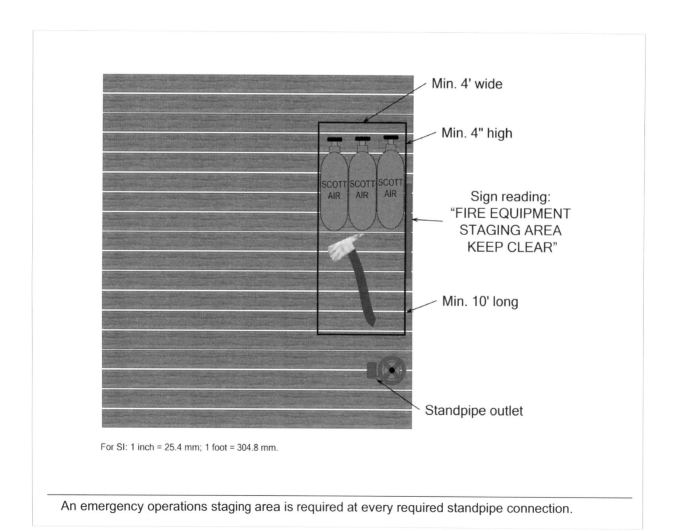

For SI: 1 inch = 25.4 mm; 1 foot = 304.8 mm.

An emergency operations staging area is required at every required standpipe connection.

Code Text: *Not more than 2,500 cubic feet (70 m³) of loose combustible fibers shall be stored in a detached structure suitably located, with openings protected against entrance of sparks. The structure shall not be occupied for any other purpose.*

Discussion and Commentary: Stored quantities of loose combustible fibers are permitted to be stored in a detached building. This building is often referred to as a "loose house." The detached building does not require fire-resistance-rated construction or fire sprinklers, but the maximum quantity of combustible fibers is limited to 2,500 cubic feet and can be used for no other purpose.

The option to the detached building is storing inside the main building. IFC Section 3704.5 allows indoor storage of loose combustible fibers with no maximum quantity threshold, but the storage room must be of 2-hour fire-resistance-rated construction and protected with an automatic sprinkler system.

Note that IFC Table 5003.1.1(1) Footnote q would also require a technical report to determine whether classification as a Group H-3 or S-1 is appropriate.

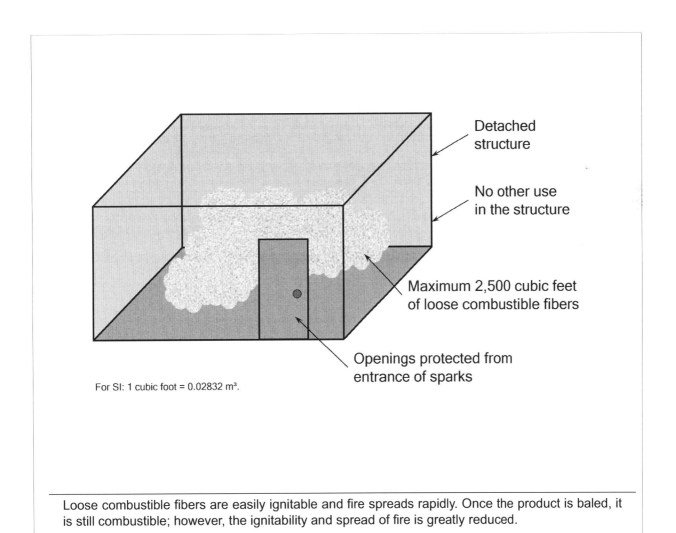

Detached
structure

No other use
in the structure

Maximum 2,500 cubic feet
of loose combustible fibers

Openings protected from
entrance of sparks

For SI: 1 cubic foot = 0.02832 m³.

Loose combustible fibers are easily ignitable and fire spreads rapidly. Once the product is baled, it is still combustible; however, the ignitability and spread of fire is greatly reduced.

Code Text: *Sisal and other fibers in bales bound with combustible tie ropes, jute and other fibers that swell when wet, shall be stored to allow for expansion in any direction without affecting building walls, ceilings or columns. A minimum clearance of 3 feet (914 mm) shall be required between walls and sides of piles, except that where the storage compartment is not more than 30 feet (9144 mm) wide, the minimum clearance at side walls shall be 1 foot (305 mm), provided that a center aisle not less than 5 feet (1524 mm) wide is maintained.*

Discussion and Commentary: Loose cotton is a combustible fiber. Consider when you are wearing cotton clothing that becomes wet. The fabric absorbs the water and becomes heavier. Baled fibers will react similarly when drenched with fire-fighting water. Baled fibers can absorb enough water to break out of the baling straps and expand to about five times its baled size. That is the reason that when combustible ties or ropes are used to strap the bale, the baled material cannot be placed adjacent to building walls. In a fire, if the tie burns, the baled product will expand as it absorbs the fire-fighting water and has the potential to damage the wall or structure, so clear space is required to allow expansion.

Baled storage in a retail facility with steel bands.

Code Text: *Higher education laboratories complying with the requirements of this chapter shall be permitted to exceed the maximum allowable quantities of hazardous materials in control areas set forth in Chapter 50 without requiring classification as a Group H occupancy. Except as specified in this chapter, such laboratories shall comply with all applicable provisions of this code and the* International Building Code.

Discussion and Commentary: Chapter 38 is designed to address unique needs of laboratories in higher education institutions, e.g., colleges and universities. These academic institutions often have chemistry, biology, medical, engineering and other laboratories where hazardous materials are used. There are often many small laboratories, each with small quantities of hazardous materials, but the aggregate quantity is over the maximum allowable quantity per control area. This chapter provides an alternative design and protection scheme which accommodates these uses in a safe manner.

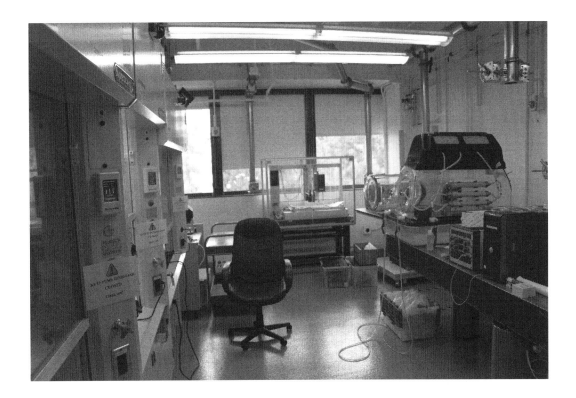

Multiple small labs typically exist at colleges and universities, and if they comply with Chapter 38, they are not classified as Group H occupancies.

Code Text: *New laboratories in new or existing buildings that increase maximum allowable quantities of hazardous materials based on the requirements in this chapter shall be equipped throughout with an approved automatic sprinkler system in accordance with Section 903.3.1.1.*

Discussion and Commentary: All new labs need to be provided with an automatic sprinkler system. Note that this requirement applies to a new operation, not necessarily a new building. In other words, if an existing building is going to have a new lab added under Chapter 38 provisions, and the new lab increases the amount of hazardous materials in the building, an automatic sprinkler system is required throughout the building.

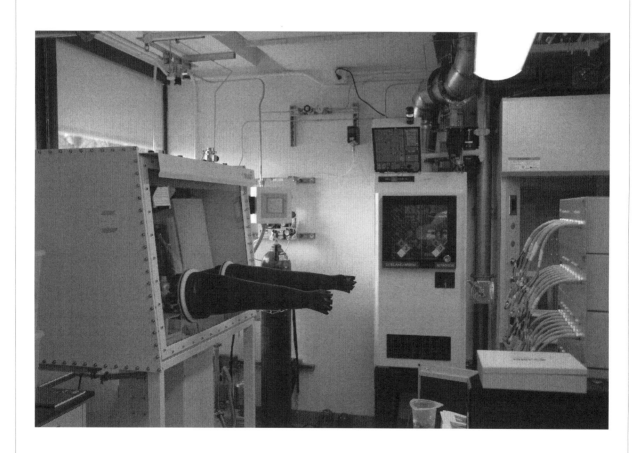

A new lab in an existing building creates a new operation, and based on IFC Section 102.1, Item 1 the lab is treated as new and must comply with the code.

Code Text: *Where laboratory suites are provided, they shall be constructed in accordance with this chapter and Section 428 of the* International Building Code.

Discussion and Commentary: Specific requirements apply to the construction of laboratory suites. The size of each laboratory suite is not limited other than by the *International Building Code®* (IBC®) based on building construction and occupancy classification. The IFC and Section 428 of the IBC require fire-resistance-rated separation between multiple laboratory suites, and between laboratory suites and nonlaboratory areas, such as offices, classrooms or lecture halls.

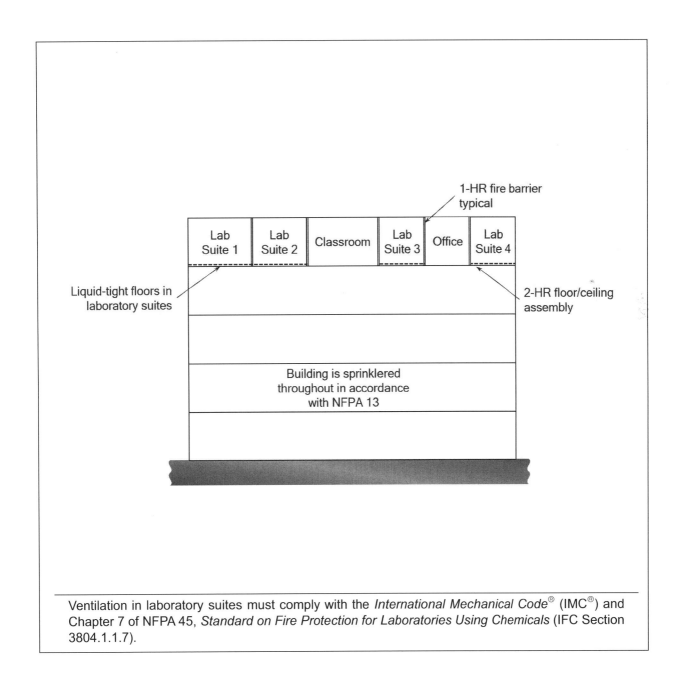

Ventilation in laboratory suites must comply with the *International Mechanical Code®* (IMC®) and Chapter 7 of NFPA 45, *Standard on Fire Protection for Laboratories Using Chemicals* (IFC Section 3804.1.1.7).

Code Text: *The number of laboratory suites and percentage of maximum allowable quantities of hazardous materials in laboratory suites shall be in accordance with Table 3804.1.1.*

Discussion and Commentary: Laboratory suites are similar in concept to control areas, but the actual requirements differ. For example, more laboratory suites are allowed within a building than control areas, and the maximum quantity of materials in laboratory suites exceeds that of a control area. But where control areas only need to be separated from one another, laboratory suites must be separated from nonlaboratory areas in addition to other laboratory suites.

The floor area of each laboratory suite is not regulated. But the limitation on the number of laboratory suites per floor in Table 3804.1.1, the maximum density of flammable liquids in Section 3803.2.2 and the limitation on the quantity of hazardous materials set the parameters for the size of each laboratory suite.

TABLE 3804.1.1
DESIGN AND NUMBER OF LABORATORY SUITES PER FLOOR

FLOOR LEVEL		PERCENTAGE OF THE MAXIMUM ALLOWABLE QUANTITY PER LAB SUITE[a]	NUMBER OF LAB SUITES PER FLOOR	FIRE-RESISTANCE RATING FOR FIRE BARRIERS IN HOURS[b]
Above grade plane	21+	Not Allowed	Not Allowed	Not Allowed
	16–20	25	1	2[c]
	11–15	50	1	2[c]
	7–10	50	2	2[c]
	4–6	75	4	1
	3	100	4	1
	1–2	100	6	1
Below grade plane	1	75	4	1
	2	50	2	1
	Lower than 2	Not Allowed	Not Allowed	Not Allowed

a. Percentages shall be of the maximum allowable quantity per control area shown in Table 5003.1.1(1) and Table 5003.1.1(2), with all increases allowed in the footnotes to those tables.
b. Fire barriers shall include walls, floors and ceilings necessary to provide separation from other portions of the building.
c. Vertical fire barriers separating laboratory suites from other spaces on the same floor are permitted to be 1-hour rated.

For example, the fifth floor of a building could have 4 laboratory suites, each separated by 1-hour fire-resistance-rated construction, each separated from nonlaboratory areas by 1-hour fire-resistance-rated construction, and each allowed to contain 75 percent of the maximum allowed quantity of hazardous materials in Tables 5003.1.1(1) and 5003.1.1(2).

Code Text: *An automatic fire detection system shall be installed in all existing laboratories in nonsprinklered buildings in accordance with this section. Detectors shall be connected to the building's fire alarm control unit where a fire alarm system is provided. Detector initiation shall activate the occupant notification system in accordance with Section 907.5 where connected to the building's fire alarm control unit. Activation of the detection system shall sound a local alarm in buildings not equipped with a fire alarm notification system.*

Discussion and Commentary: This section requires the installation of a fire detection system in existing laboratories that are located in nonsprinklered buildings. Similar to Chapter 11, this section applies whether any work is occurring in the building or not. This section acknowledges the increased hazard presented by the hazardous materials and requires this mitigation measure. New laboratories would be protected with a sprinkler system and a fire detection system is not required.

Existing labs have an option. The owner can choose to comply with Section 3805 for nonsprinklered laboratory suites, or with Chapter 50 for use of hazardous materials. Under Chapter 50, the quantities of materials are reduced; under Section 3805 a fire detection system is required. There are other fire and life safety characteristics that vary between the two options, but the owner must choose one or the other.

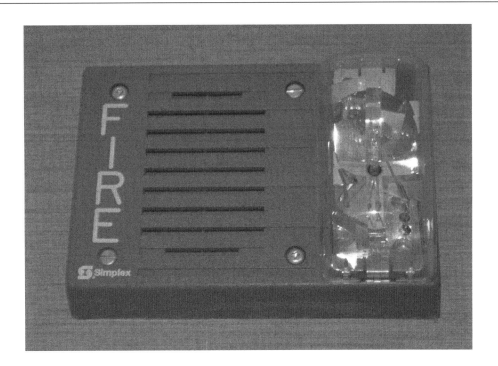

If a fire alarm is already provided within the building, the fire detection system is connected to that system and would activate the audible and visible notification appliances. If the building does not have a fire alarm, then the fire detection system is required to sound a local alarm.

Code Text: *Plant processing or extraction facilities shall comply with this chapter and the* International Building Code. *The extraction process includes the act of extraction of the oils and fats by use of a solvent, desolventizing of the raw material, production of the miscella, distillation of the solvent from the miscella and solvent recovery. The use, storage, transfilling and handling of hazardous materials in these facilities shall comply with this chapter, other applicable provisions of this code and the* International Building Code.

Discussion and Commentary: Chapter 39 is focused on the processing and extraction of oils and fats from various plants. This process includes extraction by use of a solvent, desolventizing the material, production of the miscella, distillation of the solvent from the miscella and solvent recovery. This chapter provides the tools to appropriately address the hazards while also meeting the unique needs of industry.

These processes are common to the cannabis industry; however, the chapter is not limited to that industry.

Code Text: ***Prohibited Occupancies.*** *Extraction processes utilizing flammable gases or flammable cryogenic fluids shall not be located in any building containing a Group A, E, I or R occupancy.*

Location. *The extraction equipment and extraction processes utilizing hydrocarbon solvents shall be located in a room or area dedicated to extraction.*

Discussion and Commentary: There are inherent hazards to the extraction process. As such, extraction processes utilizing flammable gas or flammable cryogenic fluids are prohibited in high life-hazard occupancies. Extraction processes cannot be located in a building containing a Group A, E, I or R occupancy. The extraction process is required to be located in a room separated from the remainder of the building where hydrocarbon solvents are utilized.

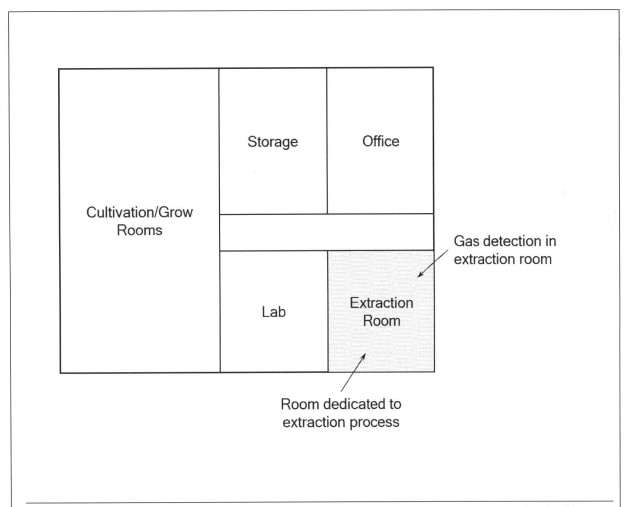

Extraction processes utilizing gaseous hydrocarbon-based solvents must be provided with an emergency shutoff system consisting of approved manual or automatic shutoff valves at the source and the point of use (IFC Section 3905.2).

Code Text: *Systems and equipment. Systems or equipment used for the extraction of oils from plant material shall comply with Section 3904.2.1 or 3904.2.2.*

Listings. Systems or equipment used for the extraction of oils from plant material shall be listed and labeled in accordance with UL 1389 and installed in accordance with the listing and the manufacturer's installation instructions.

Approvals. Systems or equipment used for the extraction of oils from plant material shall be approved for the specific use. The system shall be reviewed by a registered design professional. The registered design professional shall review and consider any information provided by the system's designer or manufacturer. A technical report in accordance with Section 3904.2.2.1 shall be prepared and submitted to the fire code official for review and approval. The firm or individual preparing the technical report shall be approved by the fire code official prior to performing the analysis.

Discussion and Commentary: The processes used are not necessarily typical hazardous material processes, and often the systems and equipment associated with such processes are not listed. These sections provide two routes for approval of the extraction equipment: (1) the equipment is listed, or (2) the systems and equipment obtain specific approvals for each installation. The approval path requires review of the equipment by a design professional, and the development of a technical report regarding the safety measures and operational restrictions of the equipment.

Many nonlisted extraction processes are one-of-a-kind. The design professional will evaluate the process and equipment to develop the technical report.

Code Text: *Activation of the gas detection system shall result in all the following: (1) Initiation of distinct audible and visual alarm signals in the extraction room, (2) Deactivation of all heating systems located in the extraction room, (3) Activation of the mechanical ventilation system, where the system is interlocked with gas detection, (4) De-energize all light switches and electrical outlets.*

Discussion and Commentary: A gas detection system is required where flammable gases are used as solvents for extraction processes. A flammable gas commonly utilized is liquefied petroleum gas. Activation of the gas detection system must provide an audible and visible alarm in the extraction room, deactivate all heating systems in the extraction room, start the ventilation system if it is interlocked with the gas detection, and disable all electrical lights, switches, outlets and other electrical components in the extraction room.

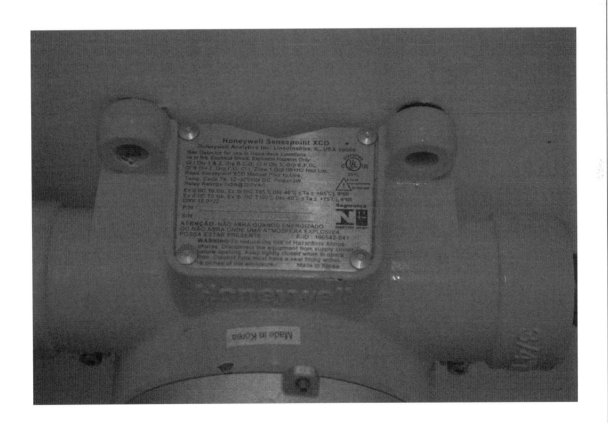

IFC Section 916 regulates the design and installation of the gas detection system.

Code Text: *Class I liquids shall be allowed to be stored in basements in amounts not exceeding the maximum allowable quantity per control area for use-open systems in Table 5003.1.1(1), provided that automatic suppression and other fire protection are provided in accordance with Chapter 9. Class II and IIIA liquids shall also be allowed to be stored in basements, provided that automatic suppression and other fire protection are provided in accordance with Chapter 9.*

Discussion and Commentary: Distilled spirits and wines with an alcohol concentration of 20 percent have a flash point of 97°F according to the *NFPA Fire Protection Guide to Hazardous Materials, 14th edition*. Based on that flash point, those alcoholic beverages are classified as a Class I flammable liquid. Storage of distilled spirits and wines which are Class I flammable liquids is prohibited in basements unless the basement is sprinklered and the aggregate quantity does not exceed the maximum allowable quantity for open-use in a control area.

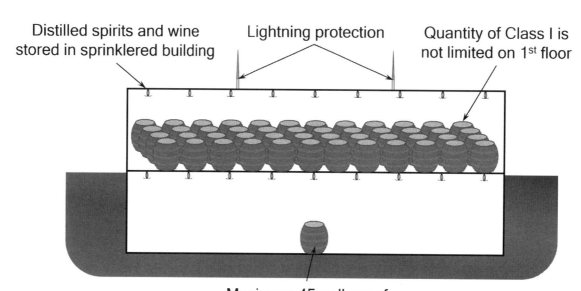

Distilled spirits and wine stored in sprinklered building   Lightning protection   Quantity of Class I is not limited on 1st floor

Maximum 45 gallons of Class IB and IC in basement

Allowed quantity of Class IB or IC in basement
- Class IB/IC open-use = 30 gallons [Table 5003.1.1(1)]
- Increase 100% for sprinklers throughout building = 60 gallons [Footnote d]
- Limited to 75% for location in basement = 45 gallons [Table 5003.8.3.2]

Smoking and use of open flames is prohibited in storage areas. Mechanical ventilation is required in all storage areas (IFC Section 4003).

Code Text: *Automatic sprinkler system. The storage of distilled spirits and wines shall be protected by an approved automatic sprinkler system as required by Chapter 9.*

Group S-1 distilled spirits or wine. An automatic sprinkler system shall be provided throughout a Group S-1 fire area used for the bulk storage of distilled spirits or wine.

Discussion and Commentary: The storage of distilled spirits and wines is classified as a Group S-1 occupancy. Even though the alcoholic beverages may be classified as flammable or combustible liquids, the storage facility is not classified as Group H. This classification is for storage only; it does not include the distilling, brewing or processing operations.

Section 4005.1 refers to Chapter 9 for the installation of an automatic sprinkler system in the storage facilities. Section 903.2.9.3 states that an automatic sprinkler system shall be installed where bulk storage of distilled spirits or wines occurs. This sprinkler provision only requires sprinklers in the fire area. The normal Group S-1 provisions for sprinklers require sprinklers throughout the building. However, if only the fire area is sprinklered, then most of the allowances or modifications in the IFC or IBC are not applicable.

(Photograph courtesy of Getty Images.)

Empty containers are treated the same as full containers, unless they have been rinsed and there are no explosive vapors remaining (IFC Section 4004.2).

Quiz

Study Session 12
IFC Chapters 35 through 40

1. Given: A facility is storing distilled spirits in barrels and a mechanical ventilation system is provided. Which of the following is the minimum design criteria for the ventilation system?

    a. Provide a minimum of 6 air changes per hour

    b. Provide a minimum of 1 cfm per square foot

    c. Provide ventilation adequate to maintain the vapor concentration below 25 percent of the lower flammable limit

    d. Either b or c

    Reference 4003.2

2. When must electrodes be removed from electrode holders used for electric arc hot work?

    a. When welding is discontinued.

    b. When welding or cutting is discontinued for 1 hour or more.

    c. At the end of the work shift.

    d. All of the above.

    Reference 3506.3

3. When are the requirements for fire protection equipment applicable at a marina?

    a. When the marina provides marine motor fuel-dispensing services.

    b. When a pier, marina or wharf can accommodate five or more vessels.

    c. Answers a and b are both correct.

    d. With the exception of a pier or wharf at a one- and two-family dwelling, fire protection is required for all marinas and floats.

    Reference 3604.1

4. Where are emergency operation staging areas required on floats?

    (a.) At each standpipe hose connection

    b. At every five-marine-vessel piers or slips

    c. At each berthing and storage area

    d. At the entrance of every marina

    Reference 3604.6

5. Trash containers at a marina shall have tight-fitting or self-closing lids and shall be constructed of _____.

    a. Metal

    b. Noncombustible materials

    c. Material with peak rate of heat release not exceeding 300 kW/m²

    (d.) Any of the above

    Reference 3603.4

6. Which of the following is not required as part of the pre-hot-work check?

    a. if fire watch is required, someone has been assigned to perform fire watch

    (b.) fire department has been notified of the hot work operation

    c. combustible material is removed or protected

    d. portable fire extinguishers are available

    Reference 3504.3.1

7. Given: An automatic sprinkler system is disabled and a request is submitted by a contractor to perform hot work inside a building. The company has an established hot work program. Can this work be performed?

    a. No, because the work is inside a building.

    b. Yes, because the work is inside a building.

    c. Yes, because the company has a hot work permit program.

    (d.) Yes, but the fire code official must specifically approve the permit for this condition.

    Reference 3501.3 #1

8. Given: Hot work is conducted at a building under a Hot Work Permit Program. After the hot work is completed, what is the length of time that the hot work permit must be available for review by the fire code official?

    a. 24 hours   b. 48 hours

    c. 3 years   d. such a record is not required

Reference 3503.3

9. When a fire watch is required, what is the minimum time period required after hot work is completed that a fire watch is required?

    a. 30 minutes   b. 45 minutes

    c. 60 minutes   d. until the end of the work shift

Reference 3504.2.1

10. Given: A hot work operation inside a building. What is the maximum travel distance from the operation to a portable fire extinguisher?

    a. 15 feet   b. 20 feet

    c. 25 feet   d. 30 feet

Reference 3504.2.6

11. When standpipes are required at a marina, hose connections must be located so they are no farther than _____ feet to any portion of the marina, pier or float.

    a. 50   b. 100

    c. 150   d. 200

Reference 3604.2

12. Which of the following is not required when performing hot work on a tank containing flammable liquids?

    a. the tank is to be filled completely so there is no vapor space which could be ignited

    b. on-site safety supervision is present

    c. test the surrounding area with a combustible gas detector

    d. hot work must conform to the IFC and the standard to which the tank was originally fabricated

Reference 3510.2

13. In an oxygen and fuel-gas welding operation, what is required when the welding operation is discontinued for one hour or more?

    a.   close the valve at the torch

    b.   close the valve at the gas supply

    c.   provide fire watch for 90 minutes

    d.   both a and b

Reference 3505.6

14. Given: A factory stores and uses combustible fibers in their operation and has a maximum of 90 cubic feet of combustible fibers in storage at any one time. Where can the loose combustible fibers be stored?

    a.   Metal bin with a self-closing cover

    b.   Double thickness cardboard boxes

    c.   Open top metal dumpster

    d.   Less than 100 cubic feet is not regulated

Reference 3704.2

15. Which of the following are required for a storage room containing 2,000 cubic feet of loose combustible fibers?

    a.   1-hour fire-resistance-rated construction separating the fiber storage room from the remainder of the building

    b.   sprinklers in the fiber storage room and 1-hour fire-resistance-rated construction separating the fiber storage room from the remainder of the building

    c.   sprinklers in the fiber storage room and 2-hour fire-resistance-rated construction separating the fiber storage room from the remainder of the building

    d.   sprinkler the entire building

Reference 3704.5

16. What is the maximum volume permitted for an individual storage pile of baled combustible fibers?

    a.   20,000 cubic feet   b.   25,000 cubic feet

    c.   50,000 cubic feet   d.   100,000 cubic feet

Reference 3705.1

17. What is the maximum volume in a nonsprinklered, detached storage building for loose combustible fibers?

    a. 500 cubic feet

    b. 1,000 cubic feet

    c. 2,000 cubic feet

    d. 2,500 cubic feet

    Reference 3704.6

18. In a sprinklered warehouse storing baled cotton fibers, what is the minimum clearance between the top of the storage piles and the sprinklers?

    a. 18 inches

    b. 24 inches

    c. 30 inches

    d. 36 inches

    Reference 3703.3

19. A stack of baled hay contains 100 tons and is stored outside at a Group M occupancy. What is the minimum separation distance required between the stack and the building?

    a. 10 feet

    b. 25 feet

    c. 50 feet

    d. distance equal to the height of the pile

    Reference 3703.4

20. A combustible fiber storage room is constructed of 1-hour fire-resistance-rated construction. What is the maximum quantity of combustible fibers allowed in the fiber storage room?

    a. 500 cubic feet

    b. 1,000 cubic feet

    c. 2,500 cubic feet

    d. loose combustible fire storage is not allowed in this room

    Reference 3704.3

21. A higher education laboratory can be located within buildings of which occupancy classification?

    a. Group A

    b. Group B

    c. Group E

    d. Group H

    Reference 3802.1
    Sec.202

22. A new single-story building will house a higher education laboratory. Which of the following fire protection systems are required?

    a. automatic sprinkler system

    b. automatic smoke detection system

    c. nothing is required provided the quantities do not exceed the maximum allowable quantity per laboratory suite

    d. both a and b

Reference _3803.1.7_

23. In a new building with multiple laboratory suites, how many laboratory suites are allowed on the third floor?

    a. 4

    b. 6

    c. 8

    d. unlimited provided they are separated with 1-hour fire-resistance-rated construction

Reference _3804.1.1_

24. In one laboratory suite on the third floor of a sprinklered building, what is the maximum allowable quantity of solid Class II organic peroxide when stored in hazardous materials storage cabinets?

    a. 50 pounds   b. 100 pounds

    c. 200 pounds   d. 400 pounds

Reference _3804.1.1_
               _5003.1.1 (1)_

25. In a sprinklered laboratory suite on the ground floor, what factors must be considered when determining the maximum allowable quantity per laboratory suite for Class IC flammable liquids?

    a. maximum percentage allowed in Table 3804.1.1

    b. maximum of 8 gallons per 100 square feet of the laboratory suite

    c. maximum allowable quantity in Table 5003.1.1(1)

    d. all of the above

Reference _3803.2.2_
              _3804.1.1_

26. What is the maximum container size for a liquid Class 2 oxidizer in a laboratory suite?

    a. ½ gallon
    b. 5.3 gallons
    c. 55-gallon drum
    d. 60 gallons

Reference 3803.2.1

27. Existing nonsprinklered higher education laboratories in existing buildings shall be retrofit with _____.

    a. an automatic sprinkler system in the laboratories

    b. an automatic sprinkler system throughout the building

    c. a gas detection system in the laboratories

    d. an automatic fire detection system in the laboratories

Reference 3805.3

28. In a facility storing distilled spirits, empty containers shall be _____.

    a. Treated the same as filled containers

    b. Treated the same as filled containers unless treated to remove all explosive vapors

    c. Discarded

    d. Stored only on the top tier

Reference 4004.2

29. A college has an existing nonsprinklered Group B building and they desire to add a laboratory suite on the second floor. Which of the following is correct about the automatic sprinkler system requirements?

    a. An automatic sprinkler system is not required.

    b. An automatic sprinkler system is required in the laboratory suite.

    c. An automatic sprinkler system is required throughout the story.

    d. An automatic sprinkler system is required throughout the building.

Reference 3803.1.7

30. In which of the following occupancies can a plant extraction process using flammable gas be located?

    a. Group A
    b. Group B
    c. Group I
    d. Group R

Reference 3903.2

31. Systems and equipment for plant extraction processes shall meet which of the following criteria?

    a.   listed equipment

    b.   reviewed and evaluated by a registered design professional

    c.   listing is not required if located in a room protected with an automatic sprinkler system

    d.   either a or b

Reference _3904.2 1_
_3404.8.2_

32. In a facility storing distilled spirits, the quantity of alcoholic beverages classified as Class IB stored in the basement cannot exceed the _____.

    a.   maximum allowable quantity for storage, provided the basement is sprinklered

    b.   maximum allowable quantity for use-open, provided the basement is sprinklered

    c.   maximum allowable quantity for storage, with or without sprinklers

    d.   storage in the basement is not permitted

Reference _4004.3_

33. Which of the following must occur when a gas concentration is detected above the threshold level in an extraction room?

    a.   activate the fire sprinklers in the extraction room

    b.   discharge the carbon dioxide extinguishing system to eliminate the possibility of ignition

    c.   deactivate all heating systems in the extraction room

    d.   lock the doors to the extraction room so no one can enter the contaminated atmosphere

Reference _3905.1.1_ #2

34. Failure of the gas detection system shall do all of the following except:

    a.   deactivate all heating systems

    b.   activate the mechanical ventilation system, if it is interlocked with the gas detection system

    c.   sound a trouble signal in an approved location

    d.   activate the fire alarm notification appliances

Reference _3905.1.2_

35. A technical report is submitted to justify the nonlisted extraction equipment. Which of the following is not required in the technical report?

    a.   signature of registered design professional performing the review

    b.   model number and serial numbers of equipment if provided

    c.   cost analysis for complying with the code

    d.   flow schematic or process flow diagram

Reference _3904.2.2.2_

2021 IFC Chapter 50
Hazardous Materials

OBJECTIVE: To gain a basic understanding of the *International Fire Code®* (IFC®) general provisions for hazardous materials in Sections 5001 through 5003 and the specific controls required when the maximum allowable quantity for hazardous materials is exceeded in Sections 5004 and 5005.

REFERENCE: Chapter 50, 2021 IFC

KEY POINTS:
- How does the IFC regulate the general versus specific hazards that various classes of hazardous materials present?
- What hazardous materials storage, use or transportation is exempt from Chapter 50?
- Hazardous materials are divided into two categories: physical and health hazards. What is the intent of this classification system?
- Can hazardous materials be stored or used in buildings other than Group H occupancies?
- When is the use of hazardous materials exceeding the maximum allowable quantity allowed in buildings without classifying the building as a Group H occupancy?
- Why do mixtures of hazardous materials deserve special treatment as it relates to their classification?
- How is the correct hazard classification determined?
- What three variables influence the maximum allowable quantity of a hazardous material?
- How is a Safety Data Sheet utilized? When are they required?
- What is the difference between use-open and use-closed systems?
- How can the maximum allowable quantity of hazardous materials be increased without creating a Group H (hazardous) occupancy?
- Given a hazardous material, what is the total amount of storage and use that is allowed in one indoor control area?
- How does the code address instances where the maximum allowable quantity is exceeded in one indoor control area?

KEY POINTS:
(Cont'd)

- What are the requirements for piping, tubing, valves and fittings?
- What are the requirements for testing hazardous materials equipment? What equipment requires testing and at what frequency?
- What controls are prescribed to ensure forklifts, motorized pallet jacks and similar material handling equipment do not constitute an ignition source in a hazardous (classified) location?
- What are the construction requirements for a control area?
- How many control areas can be located within a single building?
- When is detached storage of hazardous materials required?
- What are the requirements for storage of hazardous materials in mercantile (Group M) and storage (Group S) occupancies?
- What are the requirements for construction and ventilation of gas cabinets and exhausted enclosures?
- Can a single material fall into two or more hazard categories?
- If a material has more than one hazard classification, which category does installation and design comply with?
- What are incompatible hazardous materials, and how is this hazard managed?
- What are the requirements for storage of hazardous materials in amounts less than the maximum allowable quantity?
- What is spill control and secondary containment, and when are these controls required?
- What is the minimum design criterion for an automatic sprinkler system for the protection of hazardous materials?
- For certain chemical processes, what limit controls are prescribed for controlling liquid level, temperature and pressure?
- What are acceptable methods for the transfer of liquids when the amount being transferred exceeds the maximum allowable quantity?
- When is an emergency alarm required for hazardous materials storage and use?

Code Text: *Prevention, control and mitigation of dangerous conditions related to storage, dispensing, use and handling of hazardous materials shall be in accordance with this chapter.*

This chapter shall apply to all hazardous materials, including those materials regulated elsewhere in this code, except that when specific requirements are provided in other chapters, those specific requirements shall apply in accordance with the applicable chapter. Where a material has multiple hazards, all hazards shall be addressed.

(See IFC Section 5001.1 for 17 exceptions.)

Discussion and Commentary: IFC Chapter 50 addresses the regulation of storage, use and handling of hazardous materials. In applying IFC Section 5001.1, it is recognized that the IFC contains 16 material specific chapters for hazardous materials. Accordingly, the specific requirements for a given hazardous material will govern over any general provisions. The general provisions also specify that when a hazardous material has multiple hazards, all of the hazards must be addressed. For example, chlorine is classified as an Oxidizer Gas, Corrosive and Toxic Gas. When the maximum allowable quantity for each classification is exceeded, this section requires that all of the applicable requirements in Chapters 50, 60 and 63 must be complied with, in addition to Chapter 53 for compressed gases.

Of particular importance in the Scope is Exception 4. It states that the IFC does not have authority over transportation of hazardous materials. This is because hazardous materials transportation is regulated by the US Department of Transportation, Pipeline and Hazardous Materials Safety Administration.

Code Text: *Mixtures shall be classified in accordance with hazards of the mixture as a whole. Mixtures of hazardous materials shall be classified in accordance with nationally recognized reference standards; by an approved qualified organization, individual, or Safety Data Sheet (SDS); or by other approved methods.*

Discussion and Commentary: The hazards presented by a material that is a mixture of components does not always represent the hazards of each component individually. A good example for this is the mixture of hydrogen peroxide and water.

- Hydrogen peroxide in a mixture of 70% with water is classified as a Class 3 Oxidizer, Class 3 Unstable Reactive and Corrosive

- Hydrogen peroxide in a mixture of 50% with water is classified as a Class 2 Oxidizer, Class 1 Unstable Reactive and Corrosive

- Hydrogen peroxide in a mixture of 32% with water is classified as a Class 2 Oxidizer and Corrosive

- Hydrogen peroxide in a mixture of 8% with water is classified as a Class 1 Oxidizer

Each hazardous materials classification has different provisions for storage and handling. At a facility where raw materials are mixed or blended, the raw materials need to be classified as well as the finished product since the finished product is likely different.

The code official can require a technical report from a qualified person, under Section 104.8.2, classifying all of the chemicals and products at a facility.

The hazard classification for the finished product must be determined.

Code Text: *Piping, tubing, valves and fittings conveying hazardous materials shall be designed and installed in accordance with ASME B31.1 or other approved standards, and shall be in accordance with Sections 5003.2.2.1 and 5003.2.2.2.*

Discussion and Commentary: Piping, tubing, valves and fittings provide a means of supply to a desired use from a source. However, the design of these systems can involve extensive engineering. The selection of the correct materials of construction for the hazardous material in question along with adequately designing the pipe and valves based on system temperature and pressures requires an understanding of engineering principles. In addition, IFC Section 5003.2.2.2 has specific requirements for materials with a health, flammability or reactivity rating of 3 or 4 when classified using the NFPA 704 criteria. For piping operating at pressures above 15 PSIG, either an emergency shutoff valve or an excess flow control valve is required (IFC Section 5005.1.12). Additional controls are required in IFC Section 5003.2.2.2 for liquid and gas piping systems conveying health-hazard materials.

Piping systems designed to comply with the IFC for conveying hazardous materials should be designed to meet the requirements of ASME for conveying hazardous materials B31.1, *Power Piping* or B31.3, *Process Piping*.

Code Text: *In addition to the requirements of Section 5003.2.3, equipment, machinery and required detection and alarm systems associated with hazardous materials shall be maintained in an operable condition. Defective containers, cylinders and tanks shall be removed from service, repaired or disposed of in an approved manner. Defective equipment or machinery shall be removed from service and repaired or replaced. Required detection and alarm systems shall be replaced or repaired where defective.*

Discussion and Commentary: Processes that involve the use of hazardous materials vary greatly. Regardless of the type of storage vessel or the selected equipment, the vessels or equipment must be maintained to limit the potential of a release of hazardous material. This provision authorizes the code official to require equipment or machinery associated with the storage or use of hazardous materials to be maintained in an operable condition. If the equipment or machinery is defective, it is to be removed from service and repaired or replaced. Fire code officials should ensure that the selected component or element used in a repair or replacement is properly designed for the application. For example, changing piping materials can lead to serious consequences if the wrong material is used.

IFC Section 5003.2.9 contains specific criteria for the testing of certain equipment, devices and systems.

Topic: Control Areas	**Category:** Hazardous Materials
Reference: IFC 5003.8.3, 5003.8.3.1, 5003.8.3.2	**Subject:** Construction Requirements

Code Text: *Control areas. Control areas shall comply with Sections 5003.8.3.1 through 5003.8.3.5.3.*
Exception: *Higher education laboratories in accordance with Chapter 38 of this code and Section 428 of the* International Building Code.

Construction requirements. Control areas shall be separated from each other by fire barriers constructed in accordance with Section 707 of the International Building Code *or horizontal assemblies constructed in accordance with Section 711 of the* International Building Code, *or both.*

Percentage of maximum allowable quantities. The percentage of maximum allowable quantities of hazardous materials per control area allowed at each story within a building shall be in accordance with Table 5003.8.3.2.

Discussion and Commentary: The quantity of any hazardous material is limited within a single control area. The number, design and construction of control areas is stipulated in Table 5003.8.3.2. The concept of control areas is to allow additional hazardous materials in the building without classification as a Group H occupancy. Once a building is classified as Group H, there is no need for control areas.

Every building is at least one control area. Additional control areas can be created by separating areas of the building with fire-resistance-rated construction. The number of control areas per story is limited and the fire-resistance rating increases as the story moves away from grade. The quantity of hazardous materials in each control area decreases as the story moves away from grade.

TABLE 5003.8.3.2
DESIGN AND NUMBER OF CONTROL AREAS

STORY		PERCENTAGE OF THE MAXIMUM ALLOWABLE QUANTITY PER CONTROL AREA[a]	NUMBER OF CONTROL AREAS PER STORY	FIRE-RESISTANCE RATING FOR FIRE BARRIERS IN HOURS[b]
Above grade plane	Higher than 9	5	1	2
	7–9	5	2	2
	6	12.5	2	2
	5	12.5	2	2
	4	12.5	2	2
	3	50	2	1
	2	75	3	1
	1	100	4	1
Below grade plane	1	75	3	1
	2	50	2	1
	Lower than 2	Not Allowed	Not Allowed	Not Allowed

a. Percentages shall be of the maximum allowable quantity per control area shown in Tables 5003.1.1(1) and 5003.1.1(2), with all increases allowed in the footnotes to those tables.

b. Separation shall include fire barriers and horizontal assemblies as necessary to provide separation from other portions of the building.

Example: A two-story building would be allowed a maximum of four control areas on the first floor with a maximum of 100 percent of the maximum allowable quantity of hazardous materials in each control area, and a maximum of three control areas on the second floor with a maximum of 75 percent of the maximum allowable quantity of hazardous materials in each control area on the second floor.

Topic: Nonflammable Solids and Nonflammable and Noncombustible Liquids	Category: Hazardous Materials
Reference: IFC 5003.8.3.5.1	Subject: Hazardous Materials in Group M and S

Code Text: *The aggregate quantity of nonflammable solid and nonflammable or noncombustible liquid hazardous materials allowed within a single control area of a Group M display and storage area or a Group S storage area is allowed to exceed the maximum allowable quantities per control area specified in Tables 5003.1.1(1) and 5003.1.1(2) without classifying the building or use as a Group H occupancy, provided that the materials are displayed and stored in accordance with Section 5003.11.*

Discussion and Commentary: The code does not intend for every Group M occupancy to be reclassified as a Group H. This is not technically justified, because of the low fire loss history found in Group M occupancies. Accordingly, the maximum allowable quantity for retail uses is modified in Table 5003.11.1 (nonflammable solids, nonflammable liquids and noncombustible liquids), Table 5704.3.4.1 (flammable and combustible liquids) and Table 5104.7 (aerosols). Note that to permit these increased quantities, there are specific compliance requirements with regard to storage and display methods and maximum size of containers. The IFC also allows these increased quantities to occur in Group S occupancies provided that they also comply with the storage methods.

Quantities of flammable and combustible liquids are regulated in IFC Table 5704.3.4.1.

Code Text: *Where a gas cabinet is used to increase the maximum allowable quantity per control area or where the location of compressed gases in gas cabinets is provided to comply with the provisions of Chapter 60, the gas cabinet shall be in accordance with Sections 5003.8.6.1 through 5003.8.6.3.*

Discussion and Commentary: IFC Tables 5003.1.1(1) and 5003.1.1(2) allow a 100 percent increase in the MAQ for most compressed gases when stored in gas cabinets. Although there are specific requirements for highly toxic gases, the code generally permits the increase in quantity when gases are stored in an exhausted enclosure or gas cabinet. A gas cabinet is a noncombustible enclosure that has a means of accessing the cylinder valves and regulators without opening the cabinet door. The cabinet is ventilated and operates at a negative pressure in relation to the surrounding area. The air flow into the cabinet must provide a minimum velocity of 150 feet per minute at the face of any access port or window (IFC Sections 5306.2.3 and 6004.1.2).

A gas cabinet cannot contain more than three cylinders of a compressed or liquefied compressed gas, in accordance with Section 5003.8.6.3.

Code Text: *Responsible persons shall be designated and trained to be liaison personnel to the fire department. These persons shall aid the fire department in preplanning emergency responses and identifying the locations where hazardous materials are located, and shall have access to Safety Data Sheets and be knowledgeable in the site's emergency response procedures.*

Discussion and Commentary: A fire department liaison fills an important function and can be very beneficial to fire fighters. For large or complicated processes involving the storage and use of hazardous materials, this person can provide technical guidance to the fire code official on the hazards of the process. The individual will also have access to material safety data sheets and should be able to assist in the classification of the material.

A fire department liaison can prove useful during emergency response activities.

Code Text: *Incompatible materials in storage and storage of materials that are incompatible with materials in use shall be separated where the stored materials are in containers having a capacity of more than 5 pounds (2 kg), 0.5 gallon (2 L) or any amount of compressed gases. Separation shall be accomplished by . . .*

(See IFC Section 5003.9.8 for these requirements.)

Discussion and Commentary: Incompatible materials can create a significant problem without even being involved in fire. Two incompatible materials mixing can result in a reaction which gives off heat (exothermic reaction), creates toxic fumes, ignites or even explodes. For these reasons, incompatible materials must be separated at very small quantities, even when they are below the MAQ. Additionally, when they exceed the MAQ and secondary containment is required, they must be stored within separate containment areas.

(Photograph courtesy of Justrite Manufacturing Company)

Several methods are available to provide adequate separation for incompatible materials. Storing material within hazardous materials storage cabinets is one method of separating incompatible materials.

Code Text: *Safety cans shall be listed in accordance with UL 30 where used to increase the maximum allowable quantities per control area of flammable or combustible liquids in accordance with Table 5003.1.1(1). Safety cans listed in accordance with UL 1313 are allowed for flammable and combustible liquids where not used to increase the maximum allowable quantities per control area and for other hazardous material liquids in accordance with the listing.*

Discussion and Commentary: Footnote e to Tables 5003.1.1(1) and 5003.1.1(2) allows for a 100 percent increase in the maximum allowable quantity per control area when the liquids are stored in a safety can listed to UL 30. Section 5003.9.10 specifies that when safety cans are used to increase the MAQ, that the safety cans must be listed to UL 30, *Standard for Metal Safety Cans*. This section also states that other listed safety cans are allowed. There are other safety cans that are listed to UL 1313, *Standard for Nonmetallic Safety Cans for Petroleum Products*; however, these safety cans do not provide the same level of protection as safety cans listed to UL 30. Therefore, UL 1313 safety cans do not provide the benefit of increasing the MAQ, but they can be utilized without the MAQ increase.

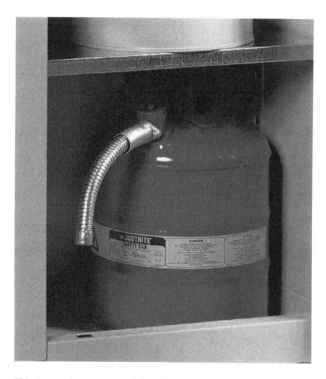

(Photograph courtesy of Justrite Manufacturing Company.)

This safety can is listed to UL 30 and is constructed of metal with welded seams.

Code Text: ***Outdoor control areas.*** *Outdoor control areas for hazardous materials shall be in accordance with the following general requirements...*

(See IFC Section 5003.12 for requirements.)

Outdoor storage location. *Outdoor storage areas for hazardous materials shall be located as required by Section 5003.12 except where material-specific requirements, including requirements in referenced standards, are provided in other chapters of this code.*

Outdoor location. *Outdoor handling areas for hazardous materials shall be located as required by Section 5003.12 except where material-specific requirements, including requirements in referenced standards, are provided in other chapters of this code.*

Discussion and Commentary: Hazardous materials are regulated in Chapter 50 and in the material-specific Chapters 51 through 67. These three sections in Chapter 50 reiterate the fact that specific provisions in the code supersede general requirements in the code, as stated in Section 102.10. The requirements in Chapter 50 for outdoor control areas are general requirements applicable to all hazardous materials. However, when a material-specific chapter has provisions that conflict with the general requirements, the material-specific provisions prevail. This rule holds true whether the specific requirements are more restrictive or less restrictive.

Normally, the language in the code prevails over the language in a referenced standard. When dealing with outdoor control areas for hazardous materials, if the referenced standard is specific to the material, the provisions in the standard will prevail over the general requirements for outdoor control areas in Section 5003.12.

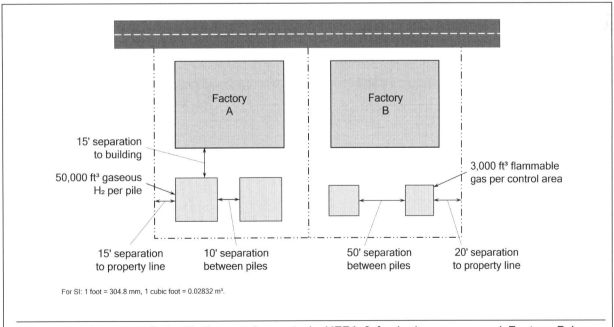

Factory A has complied with the requirements in NFPA 2 for hydrogen gas and Factory B has complied with the requirements in Chapter 50 for flammable gas in an outdoor control area.

Code Text: *Rooms, buildings or areas used for the storage of hazardous material liquids in individual vessels having a capacity of more than 55 gallons (208 L), or in which the aggregate capacity of multiple vessels exceeds 1,000 gallons (3785 L), shall be provided with spill control to prevent the flow of liquids to adjoining areas. Floors in indoor locations and similar surfaces in outdoor locations shall be constructed to contain a spill from the largest single vessel by one of the following methods . . .*

(See IFC Section 5004.2.1 for these requirements.)

Discussion and Commentary: When the MAQ is exceeded and the use of control areas and engineering controls such as automatic sprinklers and hazardous material cabinets still cannot accommodate the amount of storage, IFC Section 5004 prescribes additional engineering controls because the building use is now a Group H occupancy. If the room or area contains liquids, a means of spill control is required. Spill control is designed to contain and limit the spread of liquid spills. It is required when an individual container has a capacity of more than 55 gallons, or the aggregate volume of all the vessels is more than 1,000 gallons. The floor must be liquid tight. This can be accomplished by using containment curbs or trenches.

For new buildings, the foundation can be depressed to form the spill-control basin.

Code Text: *Secondary containment for outdoor storage areas shall be designed to contain a spill from the largest individual vessel. If the area is open to rainfall, secondary containment shall be designed to include the volume of a 24-hour rainfall as determined by a 25-year storm and provisions shall be made to drain accumulations of groundwater and rainwater.*

Discussion and Commentary: Once the outdoor MAQ is exceeded for the hazard class of the material, IFC Table 5004.2.2 should be reviewed based on the physical state of the material. If the table indicates that secondary containment is required, then the containment must be designed to contain a spill from the largest container. It also must be designed to contain the volume of rain produced in a 24-hour period based on a 25-year storm. A means for removing rainwater is also required.

Maps are available from the National Weather Service at https://hdsc.nws.noaa.gov/hdsc/pfds/pfds_map_cont.html which identify the 24-hour rainfall from a 25-year storm for each area of the United States.

Topic: Ventilation	**Category:** Hazardous Materials
Reference: IFC 5004.3	**Subject:** Storage

Code Text: *Indoor storage areas and storage buildings shall be provided with mechanical exhaust ventilation or natural ventilation where natural ventilation can be shown to be acceptable for the materials as stored.* **Exceptions:** *(1) Storage areas for flammable solids complying with Chapter 59. (2) Storage areas for medical gases complying with Chapter 53.*

Discussion and Commentary: Mechanical ventilation designed in accordance with the IFC and installed in accordance with the *International Mechanical Code®* (IMC®) provides a means for the removal of vapor resulting from a spill or gas release. IFC Section 5004.3.1 requires the mechanical ventilation system to have a minimum exhaust rate of one cubic foot of air per minute for each square foot of floor area serving the storage area. For example, consider a 3,800-square-foot Group H-3 occupancy for storage of flammable liquids. In this case: 1 CFM/ft² × 3,800 ft² = 3,800 CFM of required air flow. In addition, this section also requires that the density of the vapor be considered in the design. For heavier than air vapors, the exhaust duct must be terminated to within 12 inches of the floor. For lighter than air gases, the duct should be terminated to within 12 inches of the ceiling or roof.

All industrial liquids produce vapors that are heavier than air. Certain gases such as hydrogen, methane and ethane produce lighter than air gases. The photograph illustrates a 48-inch diameter exhaust duct designed to capture vapors from a 19-ton chlorine transport tanker at a water treatment plant.

Code Text: *Indoor storage areas and storage buildings shall be equipped throughout with an approved automatic sprinkler system in accordance with Section 903.3.1.1. The design of the sprinkler system shall be not less than that required for Ordinary Hazard Group 2 with a minimum design area of 3,000 square feet (279 m²). Where the materials or storage arrangement are required by other regulations to be provided with a higher level of sprinkler system protection, the higher level of sprinkler system protection shall be provided.*

Discussion and Commentary: All Group H occupancies require an automatic sprinkler system. This is because of the physical hazards that are stored, or to protect the health hazard from exposure resulting from a fire involving adjacent combustible materials stored in the Group H-4 occupancy. This section specifies a minimum discharge density of 0.17 GPM/ft² over a minimum 3,000 ft² design area. The IFC does not specify if the system is required to be a wet-pipe or dry-pipe sprinkler system. If a more demanding design is required, such as for flammable gases or oxidizer storage, the appropriate NFPA requirements from the applicable standard should be applied.

The IFC provides a minimum sprinkler design criteria, but products such as flammable liquids, explosives and pyrophorics often require a higher sprinkler density.

Code Text: ***Standby or emergency power.*** *Where mechanical ventilation, treatment systems, temperature control, alarm, detection or other electrically operated systems are required, such systems shall be provided with an emergency or standby power in accordance with Section 1203.*

    For storage areas for highly toxic or toxic materials, see Sections 6004.2.2.8 and 6004.3.4.2.

    Exempt applications. *Standby or emergency power is not required for mechanical ventilation systems for any of the following: (1) Storage of Class 1B and Class 1C flammable liquids and Class II and III combustible liquids in closed containers not exceeding a capacity of $6^1/_2$ gallons (25 L), (2) Storage of Class 1 and 2 oxidizers, (3) Storage of Class II, III, IV and V organic peroxides, (4) Storage areas for asphyxiant, irritant and radioactive gases.*

Discussion and Commentary: When standby or emergency power is provided, IFC Section 5004.7 states that the required loads or other electrically operated systems shall be connected to these branch circuits. Certain classes of oxidizers, gases and organic peroxides are exempt.

The design and construction of standby and emergency power systems shall comply with NFPA 110 and the requirements of NFPA 70 for legally required standby power systems.

Code Text: *Materials that must be kept at temperatures other than normal ambient temperatures to prevent a hazardous reaction shall be provided with an approved means to maintain the temperature within a safe range. Redundant temperature control equipment that will operate on failure of the primary temperature control system shall be provided. Where approved, alternative means that prevent a hazardous reaction are allowed.*

Discussion and Commentary: Certain hazardous materials require temperature controls to prevent a hazardous reaction from occurring. Most notable of these are organic peroxides. Depending on their manufacturer recommended storage temperature and their US DOT control and self-accelerating decomposition temperature (SADT), a means of temperature control may be required. If an organic peroxide reaches its SADT, it will autodecompose and produce a fire and possibly a deflagration. When temperature control is provided, the means of providing the refrigeration must be redundant in design so that the secondary system engages in the event the primary temperature control fails.

In certain processes, liquid that is either heated or cooled is necessary for proper process safety. Certain industrial processes must remain heated within safe limits so that the reaction rate is controlled.

Code Text: *Where overhead noncombustible construction is provided for sheltering outdoor hazardous material storage areas, such storage shall not be considered indoor storage when the area is constructed in accordance with the requirements for weather protection as required by the* International Building Code. ***Exception:*** *Storage of explosive materials shall be considered as indoor storage.*

Discussion and Commentary: Weather protection offers an inexpensive option when compared to the cost of a Group H occupancy. When the storage is moved to the exterior, the costs associated with the type of construction, fire-resistive separation (if located inside a mixed occupancy building), mechanical ventilation and automatic sprinklers are avoided. The requirements of *International Building Code*® (IBC®) Section 414.6.1 are applicable to the construction of the weather protection. The IBC section requires that the overhead structure is limited to an area of 1,500 ft² and constructed of noncombustible materials. The referenced IBC section does allow an increase beyond the 1,500 ft² when allowed by an area increase calculation performed in accordance with IBC Section 506. The IFC also specifies that the storage of explosives shall be classified as indoor storage, which ensures that the requirements of Chapters 50 and 56 are satisfied.

Note that automatic sprinklers cannot be eliminated for outdoor storage in all cases. See the requirements of Chapter 64 for storage of pyrophoric materials and Chapter 60 for highly toxic materials.

Code Text: *Use, dispensing and handling of hazardous materials in amounts exceeding the maximum allowable quantity per control area set forth in Section 5003.1 shall be in accordance with Sections 5001, 5003 and 5005. Use, dispensing and handling of hazardous materials in amounts not exceeding the maximum allowable quantity per control area set forth in Section 5003.1 shall be in accordance with Sections 5001 and 5003.*

Discussion and Commentary: Footnote b in IFC Tables 5003.1.1(1), 5003.1.1(2), 5003.1.1(3) and 5003.1.1(4) states that the amount in storage plus the amount in use cannot exceed the amount allowed for storage. This simply means that the hazardous material being used is deducted from the amount that was in storage. When the amount in use exceeds either the MAQ for an open or closed system, this section requires that the use provisions in IFC Section 5005.1 become applicable. The specific requirements will be based on the type of use (either a use-closed or use-open system).

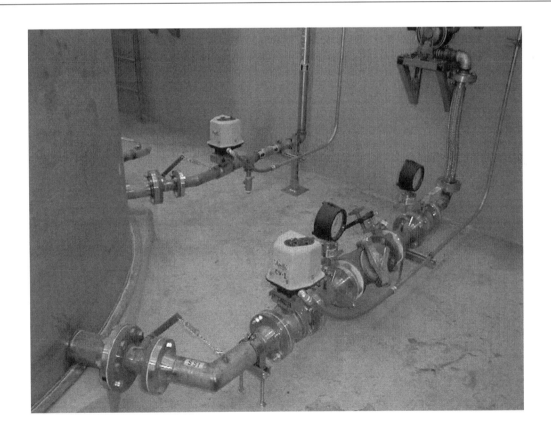

Reviewing IFC Table 5003.1.1(1) reveals that use-open systems have MAQs reduced by at least 75 percent when compared to use-closed systems. This is because use-open systems discharge vapor to the atmosphere, which increases the potential for a chemical exposure if it involves health hazard materials, or a fire or explosion if the open system involves the use of physical hazard hazardous materials.

Code Text: *Liquids having a hazard ranking of 3 or 4 in accordance with NFPA 704 shall be transferred by one of the following methods: (1) From safety cans complying with UL 30, (2) Through an approved closed piping system, (3) From containers or tanks by an approved pump taking suction through an opening in the top of the container or tank, (4) From containers or tanks by gravity through an approved self-closing or automatic-closing valve where the container or tank and dispensing operations are provided with spill control and secondary containment in accordance with Section 5004.2. Highly toxic liquids shall not be dispensed by gravity from tanks, (5) Approved engineered liquid transfer systems.*

(See IFC Section 5005.1.10 for exceptions.)

Discussion and Commentary: Liquid transfer operations have an increased potential for spills or releases because of the inherent hazard of moving liquid from one source to another. The IFC allows liquid dispensing, but the method must be approved and meet the requirements of IFC Section 5005.1.10 when a liquid has an NFPA 704 hazard ranking of 3 or 4. This would include liquids classified as corrosive, Class IA and IB flammable liquids, oxidizers, pyrophoric, toxic and highly toxic. Gravity dispensing is approved when the container or tank is equipped with an approved self- or automatic-closing valve and the area or room has spill control and secondary containment.

Gravity dispensing of highly toxic liquids is prohibited (IFC Section 5005.1.10, Item 4).

Code Text: *Where gases, liquids or solids having a hazard ranking of 3 or 4 in accordance with NFPA 704 are dispensed or used, mechanical exhaust ventilation shall be provided to capture gases, fumes, mists or vapors at the point of generation.* ***Exception:*** *Gases, liquids or solids that can be demonstrated not to create harmful gases, fumes, mists or vapors.*

Discussion and Commentary: Use-open systems constitute a greater hazard when compared to closed systems because the process is open to the atmosphere, liberating vapors or mists. Accordingly, the IFC requires mechanical ventilation at the point of generation when the material has an NFPA 704 health, flammability or reactivity rating of 3 or 4. If it can be demonstrated that the used hazardous material cannot create a harmful discharge, the fire code official can exempt the process from the required mechanical ventilation system. If this arises, an important question is . . . what is harmful? The word harmful is not defined. Monitoring of the atmosphere near the tanks or process and confirming that exposure limits are below permissible exposure limits or threshold limit values is one method of ensuring compliance.

Materials that are not heated and exhibit low vapor pressures are possible candidates for exemption from the required mechanical ventilation system. This would include sulfuric acid and phosphoric acid.

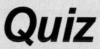

Study Session 13

IFC Chapter 50

1. How are the hazards of a mixture classified?

   (a.) as a whole

   b. The most hazardous constituent is used as the basis for classification.

   c. none of the above

   d. all of the above

   Reference 5001.7.1

2. Hazardous materials in quantities less than the maximum allowable quantity and located within a Group F-1 occupancy must comply with which portions of IFC Chapter 50?

   a. None, they are below the MAQ

   b. Sections 5001 and 5002

   (c) Sections 5001 and 5003

   d. All of Chapter 50

   Reference 5003.1.3

3. What is the maximum allowable quantity for a business seeking to store a Class II combustible liquid? The one-story building is classified as a Group F-1 occupancy, is equipped with an automatic sprinkler system and is constructed as one control area and the storage is in approved flammable liquid storage cabinets.

   a. 120 gallons   b. 240 gallons

   c. 360 gallons   (d.) 480 gallons

   Reference 5003.1.1(1)
              Footnote D/E

4. SDC Industries sent the fire code official a letter indicating the company will soon store tertiary butyl peroxide, a liquid Class III organic peroxide. The one-story building is not sprinklered but is subdivided into two control areas. The organic peroxide will also be stored in an approved hazardous material storage cabinet in each control area. What is the total amount of this material that can be stored in the building?

    a. 125 pounds   b. 250 pounds

    c. 500 pounds   d. 1,000 pounds

Reference 5003. 1.1(1)
             Footnote e

5. What is the occupancy classification for a building storing over the maximum allowable quantity of Xylianatonl, a Class II organic peroxide?

    a. H-1   b. H-2

    c. H-3   d. H-4

Reference 5003.1.1

6. A 10-percent concentration of sulfuric acid is classified as a corrosive liquid. What is the maximum allowable quantity for this material stored in a one-story Group S-1 occupancy that is one control area? The building is protected throughout by an automatic sprinkler system.

    a. 500 gallons   b. 1,000 gallons

    c. 2,000 gallons   d. 4,000 gallons

Reference 5003.1.1
             Footnote D

7. What is the maximum allowable quantity for the storage of compressed flammable gas in one outdoor control area?

    a. 2,000 cubic feet @ NTP   b. 3,000 cubic feet @ NTP

    c. 4,000 cubic feet @ NTP   d. 5,000 cubic feet @ NTP

Reference 5003.1.1 (3)

8. Given: A flammable gas piping system operating at a pressure of 145 PSIG. The gas has a NFPA 704 flammability rating of 4. Which of the following engineering controls are required for the piping system?

    a. emergency shutoff valve   b. excess flow valve

    c. diaphragm valve   d. either a or b

Reference 5005.1.12

9. After what time period of non-use are hazardous material tanks required to be safe-guarded?

    a. 30 days   b. 60 days

    c. 90 days   d. 120 days

    Reference 5003.2.6.1

10. Where exceeding _____ atmospheric hazardous material storage tanks are required to be equipped with a liquid-level limit control?

    a. 500 gallons   b. 750 gallons

    c. 1,000 gallons   d. No such system is required

    Reference 5003.2.9

11. Acetylene is classified as a compressed flammable and unstable (reactive) Class 2 gas. At what volume (at NTP) is a detached storage building required for this gas?

    a. 2,000 cubic feet   b. 5,000 cubic feet

    c. 7,500 cubic feet   d. 10,000 cubic feet

    Reference 5003.8.2

12. How many control areas are permitted on the fourth floor of a Group B/F-1/S-1 mixed occupancy?

    a. 1   b. 2

    c. 3   d. 4

    Reference 5003.1.1

13. Given: Storage of Class IC flammable liquids on the third floor of a five-story build-ing. The building is fully sprinklered. The liquids are not stored in cabinets. The third floor is constructed as a single control area. What is the MAQ?

    a. 120 gallons   b. 240 gallons

    c. 480 gallons   d. 960 gallons

    Reference 5003.1.1

14. Calculate the MAQ per control area for the storage of a solid Class II Organic Peroxide located two levels below the grade plane. The material is stored in hazardous material storage cabinets. Only the levels of the building located below grade plane are protected by an automatic sprinkler system in accordance with Section 903.3.1.1.

    a. 25 pounds   (b.) 50 pounds

    c. 100 pounds   d. 200 pounds

Reference _5003.1.1 (1)_
Footnote E

15. Which of the following components or systems does not operate at a negative pressure and is not permitted for the storage of compressed and liquefied compressed gases?

    a. gas rooms   b. exhausted enclosures

    c. gas cabinets   (d.) hazardous material storage cabinets

Reference _5003.8.7.1_

16. In a semiconductor facility, liquids transported in an exit enclosure or corridor are required to be transported using a cart or truck when exceeding _____ gallons.

    a. 1   (b.) 5

    c. 10   d. 55

Reference _5003.10.2_

17. What is the minimum container weight and volume that is applicable for separation of incompatible hazardous materials?

    a. $\frac{1}{2}$ pound; $\frac{1}{2}$ gallon; $\frac{1}{2}$ cubic foot of compressed gas

    b. 1 pound; 1 gallon; 1 cubic foot of compressed gas

    c. 5 pounds; 5 gallons; any amount of compressed gas

    (d.) 5 pounds; $\frac{1}{2}$ gallon; any amount of compressed gas

Reference _5003.9.8_

18. In a semiconductor facility, liquids transported in an exit enclosure or corridor are permitted to be transported in not more than ____ drums not exceeding ____ gallons each that are transported by suitable drum trucks.

    a. 10, 5 gallons   b. 4, 25 gallons

    (c.) 4, 55 gallons   d. 6, 100 gallons

Reference _5003.10.2_

19. What is the maximum allowable quantity of Class 3 solid oxidizers in 20-pound plastic buckets allowed in a one-story Group M occupancy that is equipped with an automatic sprinkler system and is designed as one control area? Each individual container contains 20 pounds of Class 3 oxidizers.

    a. 250 pounds   b. 1,350 pounds

    c. 2,250 pounds   (d.) 2,700 pounds

    Reference 5003.11.1

20. What is the maximum allowable quantity of toxic liquids allowed in a one-story Group M occupancy that is equipped with an automatic sprinkler system and is constructed using two control areas? The liquids are not stored in hazardous material cabinets.

    a. 100 gallons   b. 200 gallons

    c. 300 gallons   (d) 400 gallons

    Reference 5003. 11.1
                  Footnote B

21. The maximum height of storage in the stock room for hazardous materials in a Group M occupancy is _____ feet.

    a. 5   b. 6

    (c) 8   d. Not allowed

    Reference 5003.11.3.2

22. Given: Two outdoor control areas on a property with an area of 21,000 square feet. What is the minimum required separation distance between each control area?

    a. 20 feet   (b.) 50 feet

    c. 75 feet   d. 300 feet

    Reference 5003. 12 #3

23. Spill control of Class 2 oxidizer liquids is required when the aggregate volume of the stored containers indoors exceeds _____ gallons.

    a. 55   b. 100

    c. 500   (d.) 1,000

    Reference 5004.2.1

24. Secondary containment is required when the aggregate amount of solid Class 3 organic peroxide materials stored outdoors exceeds _____ pounds.

    a. 100   b. 1,000

    c. 10,000   (d.) not required

    Reference 5004.2.2

25. Outdoor secondary containment shall be designed to contain the contents of the largest individual vessel and must include the volume of a _____ rainfall based on a 25-year storm.

    a. 8-hour   b. 12-hour

    c. 16-hour   d. 24-hour

    Reference 5004.2.2.4

26. Which of the following hazardous materials does not require mechanical ventilation when stored indoors?

    a. toxic solids   b. Class 3 oxidizers

    (c.) flammable solids   d. Class II organic peroxides

    Reference 5004.3 Exc.1

27. What is the minimum air flow exhaust rate required for a mechanical ventilation system used for a Hazardous occupancy?

    a. 0.75 cubic foot/minute/square foot

    b. 1 square foot/minute/square foot

    (c.) 1 cubic foot/minute/square foot

    d. either b or c

    Reference 5004.3.1 #2

28. What is the minimum discharge density and design area for the automatic sprinkler system in a Group H occupancy?

    a. Light Hazard/1,500 ft² if the materials are not flammable or combustible

    b. Ordinary Hazard Group 2/3,000 ft²

    c. Extra Hazard Group 1/3,000 ft²

    d. Extra Hazard Group 2/3,000 ft²

    Reference 5004.5

29. Which of the following hazardous materials cannot be dispensed using a gravity dispensing system from a storage tank?

    a. Class IB flammable liquids   b. highly toxic liquids

    c. corrosive liquids   d. toxic liquids

    Reference 5005.1.10 #4

30. Regardless of volume, what type of tank requires a means of high-level liquid control when the quantity of use exceeds the maximum allowable quantity?

    a. portable tanks   b. stationary tanks

    c. use-closed tanks   d. use-open tanks

    Reference 5005.1.4.1

31. When safety cans are used to increase the maximum allowable quantity of flammable and combustible liquids they must be listed in accordance with _____.

    a. UL 30   b. UL 142

    c. UL 1313   d. UL 2085

    Reference 5003.9.10

32. What is the maximum allowable quantity of compressed nitrogen (a simple asphyxiant and inert gas) in a one-story building treated as a single control area?

    a. 810 cubic feet   b. 1,000 cubic feet

    c. 6,000 cubic feet   d. not limited

    Reference 5003.1.1(1)

33. Given: A sprinklered one-story building is storing liquefied highly toxic gas in exhausted enclosures. What is the maximum allowable quantity per control area for indoor storage?

    a. 4 pounds   b. 8 pounds

    c. 16 pounds   d. Not allowed

    Reference 5003.1.1(2)
    Footnote B and G

34. Piperidine is classified as a corrosive liquid and a Class IB flammable liquid. What is the maximum allowable quantity for this material stored in a one-story Group S-1 occupancy that is one control area? The building is protected throughout by an automatic sprinkler system and the piperidine is in approved storage cabinets.

a. 480 gallons

b. 960 gallons

c. 1,000 gallons

d. 2,000 gallons

Reference 5003.1.1(1)
Footnote D and E
5003.1.1(2) D and E
Footnote

35. Which of the following is incorrect about periodic testing for gas detection systems, limit control systems and emergency alarm systems?

a. Periodic testing shall not be required where approved written documentation is provided stating that testing will damage the equipment, device or system and the equipment is maintained as required by the manufacturer.

b. Periodic testing shall not be required for equipment, devices and systems that self-diagnose and report trouble.

c. Periodic testing shall not be required if system activation occurs during the required testing period and the components activated properly.

d. If all the equipment and systems passed the acceptance testing, then periodic testing is not required.

Reference 5003.2.9
5003.2.9.1

Study Session

14

2021 IFC Chapters 51 through 55
Aerosols, Compressed Gases, Corrosive Materials and Cryogenic Fluids

OBJECTIVE: To gain a basic understanding of the *International Fire Code®* (IFC®) requirements for aerosols, compressed gases, solid and liquid corrosive materials and cryogenic fluids.

REFERENCE: Chapters 51 through 55, 2021 IFC

KEY POINTS:
- What is an aerosol container, and how are aerosols classified?
- What are the quantity limits for Level 2 and 3 aerosols in Assembly, Business, Education, Factory, Institutional and Residential occupancies?
- What are the quantity limits for Level 2 and 3 aerosols in a nonsegregated warehouse? Segregated warehouse?
- Can aerosol products be stored in plastic or glass containers? Are they treated differently from metal containers?
- What methods can be utilized to create a segregated aerosol warehouse?
- Can flammable and combustible liquids be stored in an aerosol warehouse?
- What is the maximum amount of aerosols that can be stored and displayed in mercantile occupancies?
- What are the display height limits for aerosols in mercantile occupancies?
- What specific requirements apply for the display of aerosols adjacent to flammable and combustible liquids?
- Can the aerosol container be constructed of material other than metal?
- What is an aerosol cooking spray product?
- Is an automatic sprinkler system required to protect all aerosol storage arrangements?
- Does Chapter 53 regulate the physical or health hazards of compressed gases or the potential energy of gases compressed into cylinders and systems?
- What are the requirements for design and construction of gas containers, cylinders and tanks?

KEY POINTS:
(Cont'd)

- Why are pressure relief devices required on compressed gas cylinders, containers and tanks?
- Is the storage of medical gas different than storage of other gases?
- What is the difference between an interior medical gas storage room and an exterior medical gas storage room?
- Are permits required for the use of carbon dioxide in a building?
- What methods are recognized for securing compressed gas containers, cylinders and tanks?
- Does the IFC regulate irritant, asphyxiant or radioactive gases?
- What is a carbon dioxide enrichment system?
- What safety features are required in the IFC?
- What is the required separation distance between compressed gas cylinders and elevated platforms, ledges or mezzanines?
- What is the maximum temperature limit for heating compressed gas cylinders, and what are the requirements for this activity?
- What controls are required to control flow and pressure in a compressed gas system?
- What is the scope of Chapter 54, "Corrosive Materials"?
- What is a corrosive material?
- What are the requirements for indoor storage of corrosive materials that exceed the maximum allowable quantity in a single control area?
- What is the scope of Chapter 55, "Cryogenic Fluids"?
- What is a cryogenic fluid and a cryogenic vessel?
- Why are pressure relief devices specified for conditions where a cryogenic fluid could be trapped in piping or a container?
- How does a fire code official determine if a cryogenic vessel is properly constructed?
- What are the minimum separation distances for stationary cryogenic containers?
- What are the requirements for the construction of a cryogenic fluid piping system?
- What are the requirements for indoor dispensing and filling of cryogenic fluids?

Code Text: *The provisions of this chapter, the* International Building Code *and NFPA 30B shall apply to the manufacturing, storage and display of aerosol products, aerosol cooking spray products and plastic aerosol 3 products. Manufacturing of aerosol products, aerosol cooking spray products and plastic aerosol 3 products using hazardous materials shall also comply with Chapter 50.*

Discussion and Commentary: Aerosol containers are treated as their own class of hazardous material because they present specific fire hazards. Many aerosols contain hazardous materials that could be regulated by Chapter 50; however, they are not because of the limited amount of hazardous materials within each container. Fire protection requirements for the protection of aerosols is based on full- and intermediate-scale fire tests that were sponsored by the Society of Chemical Manufacturers & Affiliates and performed at the FM Global Fire Technology Laboratory. These fire tests served as the basis for the development of NFPA 30B and Chapter 51.

The manufacturing process for aerosols may involve the use of hazardous materials. Accordingly, the scope of the chapter requires that aerosol manufacturing facilities also comply with the requirements in Chapter 50.

Code Text: *Aerosol products shall be classified as Level 1, 2 or 3 in accordance with Table 5103.1 and NFPA 30B. Aerosol products in cartons which are not identified in accordance with this section shall be classified as Level 3.*

Discussion and Commentary: The classification criteria are based on the heat of combustion of the base product and the propellant. This also directly correlates to the design of the automatic sprinkler system used to protect the stored products. Essentially, Level 1 aerosols are water-based products and, for the purposes of fire protection, are treated as a Class III commodity using the classification criteria in Chapter 32. Level 2 aerosols are typically alcohol based products. Level 3 aerosols are formulated using nonwater miscible hydrocarbons such as alkanes, alkenes and ketones. These represent the most challenging fire problem and have very specific fire protection design criteria. IFC Section 5103.2 requires that the classification be identified on the shipping carton.

TABLE 5103.1
CLASSIFICATION OF AEROSOL PRODUCTS

CHEMICAL HEAT OF COMBUSTION		AEROSOL CLASSIFICATION
GREATER THAN (BTU/LB)	LESS THAN OR EQUAL TO (BTU/LB)	
0	8,600	1
8,600	13,000	2
13,000	—	3

For SI: 1 British thermal unit per pound = 0.002326 kJ/g.

NFPA 30B contains detailed information addressing the chemical heat of combustion for a variety of components and stipulates detailed methodology for classification of aerosols.

Code Text: *Solid pile, palletized or rack storage of aerosol cooking spray products in a general purpose warehouse shall not be more than 2,500 pounds (1135 kg) net weight, unless protected in accordance with NFPA 30B.*

Discussion and Commentary: Based on all initial testing by FM Global, it was determined that materials with a flash point over 500°F could be ignored regarding their contribution to an aerosol product fire. However, some aerosol products are designed to deliver a vegetable oil, or similar substance, to reduce sticking on cooking or baking surfaces. These products have very high levels of oils with flash points over 500°F. Fire testing of this type of product showed that it is a higher hazard than a Class III commodity. These materials are specifically addressed as a separate aerosol classification and quantities are limited in the IFC and NFPA 30B. Essentially, this section provides two options: (1) protect the product according to NFPA 30B, or (2) limit the quantity to 2,500 pounds.

This photograph indicates that the product is an aerosol cooking spray and requires protection as such.

Code Text: *Aerosol product warehouses shall be protected by an approved wet-pipe automatic sprinkler system in accordance with NFPA 30B. Sprinkler protection shall be designed based on the highest classification level of aerosol product present.*

Discussion and Commentary: FM Global's criteria for the design of automatic sprinkler systems used for the protection of Level 2 and 3 aerosols begins with the following statement: *The protection of Level 2 and 3 aerosols is an either/or proposition. Either the sprinklers control the fire or the building will be destroyed by the fire.* This is a powerful statement and confirms the challenge of providing adequate fire protection for Level 2 and 3 aerosols. Fortunately, NFPA 30B requirements are based on the results of successful fire tests. However, the design criteria is dependent on the proper selection of the correct sprinklers and is further dependent on building height, the type of storage and the proximity of other hazardous materials such as flammable liquids. Fire code officials should closely verify compliance with NFPA 30B for the design of automatic sprinklers used for the protection of Level 2 and 3 aerosols.

NFPA 30B was the first standard to recognize the use of early suppression fast response (ESFR) sprinklers for the protection of buildings storing aerosols.

Code Text: *Aerosol products, aerosol cooking spray products and plastic aerosol 3 products in retail display areas shall not exceed quantities needed for display and normal merchandising and shall not exceed the quantities in Table 5106.2.1.*

Discussion and Commentary: This section provides several limitations on the quantity of Level 2 and 3 aerosols in retail display areas. (1) There is a limitation as to no more than is needed for display and normal merchandising. This statement is requiring that additional replacement stock be located in the stock room or store room rather than out on the display floor. If every product on the merchandising floor is on display and available for purchase, it would be difficult to require it to be relocated to the store room, (2) The quantity does have an upper limit in Table 5106.2.1. For example, a single-story sprinklered retail store with a typical fire sprinkler system design of Ordinary Hazard Group 2 will be allowed 10,000 pounds, (3) Footnote a also provides a maximum density of aerosols at 1,000 pounds net weight within a 100-square-foot display area, which equates to 10 pounds per square foot.

TABLE 5106.2.1
MAXIMUM QUANTITIES OF LEVEL 2 AND 3 AEROSOL PRODUCTS, AEROSOL COOKING SPRAY PRODUCTS AND PLASTIC AEROSOL 3 PRODUCTS IN RETAIL DISPLAY AREAS

	MAXIMUM NET WEIGHT PER FLOOR (pounds)[b]		
Floor	Unprotected[a]	Protected in accordance with Section 5106.2[a,c]	Protected in accordance with Section 5106.3[c]
Basement	Not allowed	500	500
Ground	2,500	10,000	10,000
Upper	500	2,000	Not allowed

For SI: 1 pound = 0.454 kg, 1 square foot = 0.0929 m².
a. The total quantity shall not exceed 1,000 pounds net weight in any one 100-square-foot retail display area.
b. Per 25,000-square-foot retail display area.
c. Minimum Ordinary Hazard Group 2 wet-pipe automatic sprinkler system throughout the retail sales occupancy.

Table 5106.2.1 allows the elimination of the density requirement in Footnote a when the fire sprinkler system is designed in accordance with Section 5106.3. Section 5106.3.2 specifies the sprinkler design must be in accordance with NFPA 30B.

Topic: Pressure Relief Devices—Where Required **Category:** Compressed Gases
Reference: IFC 5303.3.1 **Subject:** General Requirements

Code Text: *Pressure relief devices shall be provided to protect containers, cylinders and tanks containing compressed gases from rupture in the event of overpressure.* ***Exception:*** *Cylinders, containers and tanks where exempt from the requirements for pressure relief devices specified by the standards of design listed in Section 5303.3.2.*

Discussion and Commentary: Pressure relief devices are provided to protect containers, cylinders and tanks from a catastrophic failure in the event the vessel is overheated. For cylinders, the requirements of Compressed Gas Association (CGA) Standard S1.1, *Pressure Relief Device Standards-Part 1-Cylinders for Compressed Gases*, are referenced in IFC Section 5303.3.2. CGA Standard S1.1 allows the use of spring-loaded safety relief valves, fusible plugs or burst disks. A spring-loaded safety relief valve is designed to open at a preset pressure to relieve excess pressure. This set pressure is usually at or below the maximum allowable working pressure of the cylinder. Once the pressure is reduced below the safety relief valve's set point, the valve closes. Burst disks and fusible plugs are sacrificial relief devices. A sacrificial relief device is replaced after it has operated. When a sacrificial device operates, it releases all of the contents of the cylinder, container or tank. A fusible plug is activated by heating a low melt point temperature metal, whereas a burst disk is activated by pressure.

Pressure relief devices for ASME pressure vessels are limited to spring-loaded safety relief valves or burst disks. There are several different types of spring-loaded safety relief valves. Fusible plugs generally are not used on ASME vessels, because the large surface area can require relief devices with a cross-sectional relief area measured in inches or feet.

Topic: Marking of Piping Systems	**Category:** Compressed Gases
Reference: IFC 5303.4.3	**Subject:** General Requirements

Code Text: *Piping systems shall be marked in accordance with ASME A13.1. Markings used for piping systems shall consist of the content's name and include a direction-of-flow arrow. Markings shall be provided at each valve; at wall, floor or ceiling penetrations; at each change of direction; and at not less than every 20 feet (6096 mm) or fraction thereof throughout the piping run.* **Exceptions:** *(1) Piping that is designed or intended to carry more than one gas at various times shall have appropriate signs or markings posted at the manifold, along the piping and at each point of use to provide clear identification and warning, (2) Piping within gas manufacturing plants, gas processing plants, refineries and similar occupancies shall be marked in an approved manner.*

Discussion and Commentary: Piping identification is necessary for several reasons. First, in facilities that distribute multiple gases via piping systems, it is important that a supply source of one gas not be accidentally connected to another gas supply source. Consider the potential consequences of a flammable gas such as ethane being accidentally connected to piping that was conveying oxygen. Second, identification of the piping allows fire fighters and other emergency responders to identify the contents of the piping system in the event the pipe or tubing (or more likely, valves or fittings) were to leak. By identifying the direction of flow it also provides a means of following the piping to its source so that the flow of gas can be stopped.

The photograph illustrates numerous tubing runs. Note that the tubing is identified by its contents and the direction of flow.

Code Text: *Compressed gas containers, cylinders and tanks shall be secured to prevent falling caused by contact, vibration or seismic activity. Securing of compressed gas containers, cylinders and tanks shall be by one of the following methods: (1) Securing containers, cylinders and tanks to a fixed object with one or more restraints, (2) Securing containers, cylinders and tanks on a cart or other mobile device designed for the movement of compressed gas containers, cylinders or tanks, (3) Nesting of compressed gas containers, cylinders and tanks at container filling or servicing facilities or in sellers' warehouses not open to the public. Nesting shall be allowed provided the nested containers, cylinders or tanks, if dislodged, do not obstruct the required means of egress, (4) Securing of compressed gas containers, cylinders and tanks to or within a rack, framework, cabinet or similar assembly designed for such use.* **Exception:** *Compressed gas containers, cylinders and tanks in the process of examination, filling, transport or servicing.*

Discussion and Commentary: An unsecured compressed gas cylinder can contain a large amount of potential energy. If the valve is sheared from the cylinder head, it can propel the cylinder through walls of buildings. There have been numerous reports of compressed gas cylinders passing through 8-inch block walls. If the cylinder impacted a human it could easily injure or kill. Accordingly, the IFC requires that cylinders be secured using one of four identified methods.

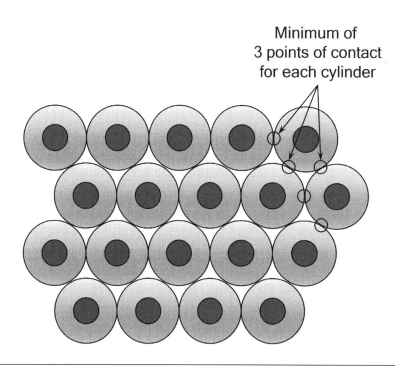

Minimum of
3 points of contact
for each cylinder

This graphic illustrates the concept of nesting. Nesting is defined as a method of securing flat-bottomed compressed gas cylinders upright in a tight mass using a contiguous three-point contact system whereby all cylinders within a group have not less than three points of contact with other cylinders, walls or bracing (IFC Section 202).

Code Text: *Medical gases shall be located in areas dedicated to the storage of such gases without other storage or uses. Where containers of medical gases in quantities greater than the permit amount are located inside buildings, they shall be in a 1-hour exterior room, a 1-hour interior room or a gas cabinet in accordance with Section 5306.2.1, 5306.2.2 or 5306.2.3, respectively. Rooms or areas where medical gases are stored or used in quantities exceeding the maximum allowable quantity per control area as set forth in Section 5003.1 shall be in accordance with the* International Building Code *for high-hazard Group H occupancies.*

Discussion and Commentary: Medical gases are not exempt from regulation and present the same hazards as other gases. In addition to the hazards associated with high pressure cylinders, these gases can also be oxidizers or flammable gases. Section 5306 deals with medical gases at health care facilities and requires the storage of medical gas to be in a storage area that has no other storage or use. When the quantity exceeds the permit amount, as specified in Table 105.5.9, the storage must be in a gas cabinet, 1-hour interior storage room or 1-hour exterior storage room. When the quantity exceeds the maximum allowable quantity per control area, then the storage must be in a Group H occupancy.

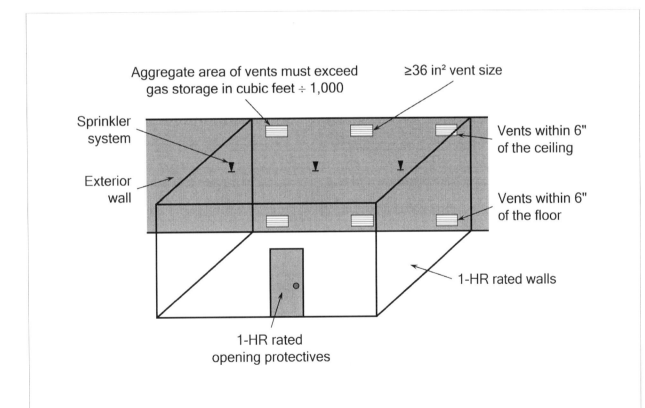

A 1-hour exterior medical gas storage room is not exterior to the building, rather at least one wall of the room is an exterior wall. This allows for natural ventilation to provide ventilation for the room. A 1-hour interior medical gas storage room is required to have mechanical ventilation (IFC Sections 5306.2.1 and 5306.2.2).

Code Text: *General. Compressed gases in storage or use not regulated by the material-specific provisions of Chapters 6, 54, 55, and 60 through 67, including asphyxiant, irritant and radioactive gases, shall comply with this section in addition to other requirements of this chapter.*

Ventilation. Indoor storage and use areas and storage buildings shall be provided with ventilation in accordance with Section 5004.3. Where mechanical ventilation is provided, the systems shall be operational during such time as the building or space is occupied.
Exceptions: *(1) A gas detection system complying with Section 5307.2.1 shall be permitted in lieu of mechanical ventilation, (2) Areas containing insulated liquid carbon dioxide systems used in beverage dispensing applications shall comply with Section 5307.3.*

Discussion and Commentary: This section addresses other health hazard gases that are not regulated in the IFC. These gases can be asphyxiants, irritants or radioactive. These gases are not classified as hazardous materials, but they do present hazards to life and health. The requirements are fairly simple—provide ventilation. The two exceptions provide for facilities where gas detection is utilized and for facilities with specific application of CO_2. Insulated liquid CO_2 systems for beverage dispensing and CO_2 enrichment systems have specific requirements.

Section 5004.3.1 requires the exhaust ventilation system to:

1. Be installed in accordance with the *International Mechanical Code*.

2. Provide a ventilation rate of not less than 1 cubic foot per minute per square foot of floor area over the storage area.

3. Operate continuously unless alternative designs are approved.

4. Be provided with a manual shutoff control outside of the room in a position adjacent to the access door to the room or in an approved location.

5. Be designed to consider the density of the potential fumes or vapors released. For fumes or vapors that are heavier than air, exhaust shall be taken from a point within 12 inches of the floor. For fumes or vapors that are lighter than air, exhaust shall be taken from a point within 12 inches of the highest point of the room.

6. Location the exhaust and inlet air openings to provide air movement across all portions of the floor or room to prevent the accumulation of vapors.

7. Be designed so as not recirculate air to occupied areas.

Mechanical ventilation is designed to capture released gases and exhaust them to the outside of the building.

Topic: Insulated Liquid CO_2 Systems Used in Beverage Dispensing Applications   **Category:** Compressed Gases

Reference: IFC 5307.3   **Subject:** Compressed Gases Not Otherwise Regulated

Code Text: *Insulated liquid carbon dioxide systems with more than 100 pounds (45.4 kg) of carbon dioxide used in beverage dispensing applications shall comply with Section 5307.3.1.*

Discussion and Commentary: A common occurrence in restaurant and fast food facilities is the use of carbon dioxide (CO_2) bulk tanks for created carbonated beverages. A CO_2 release in an enclosed space will displace the oxygen creating an asphyxiation hazard. CO_2 systems exceeding 100 pounds must comply with Section 5307.3 and obtain a permit to operate. Section 5307.3.1 requires a mechanical ventilation system that exhausts to the exterior at a minimum rate of 1 cfm per square foot [0.00508 m³/(s × m²)]. An exception allows the use of an emergency alarm system consisting of gas detectors and a local alarm within the room where the CO_2 system is located in lieu of the continuous ventilation system. A supervisory alarm is required at 5,000 ppm (9000 mg/m³), which is the 8-hour time-weighted average exposure limit, and a proximity alarm must occur if the concentration reaches 30,000 ppm (54 000 mg/m³).

The bulk tank for CO_2 can often be located in the basement of food establishments. This can create a serious problem since CO_2 is odorless, colorless and heavier than air.

Code Text: *Activation of the low-level gas detection system alarm shall automatically: (1) Stop the flow of carbon dioxide to the piping system, (2) Activate the mechanical exhaust ventilation system, (3) Activate an audible and visible supervisory alarm signal at an approved location within the building.*

Activation of the high-level gas detection system alarm shall automatically: (1) Stop the flow of carbon dioxide to the piping system, (2) Activate the mechanical exhaust ventilation system, (3) Activate an audible and visible evacuation alarm both inside and outside of the carbon dioxide enrichment area, and the area in which the carbon dioxide containers are located.

Discussion and Commentary: Increasing the carbon dioxide (CO_2) concentration is one method that is used to enhance plant growth. These systems are commonly used in the cannabis industry. The CO_2 detection levels are the same as those used for beverage dispensing operations, however additional operations are required in this case because the room already has an increased level of CO_2. This system must also shut off the flow of CO_2 and activate the mechanical exhaust ventilation system. It should be noted that liquid CO_2 is not a cryogenic fluid because its boiling point is -109°F and therefore is not regulated under IFC Chapter 55.

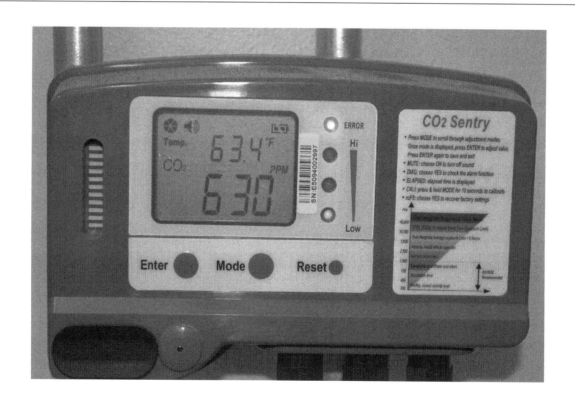

This CO_2 gas detector constantly monitors the concentration levels within the room.

Code Text: *A chemical that causes visible destruction of, or irreversible alterations in, living tissue by chemical action at the point of contact. A chemical shall be considered corrosive if, when tested on the intact skin of albino rabbits by the method described in DOTn 49 CFR173.137, such chemical destroys or changes irreversibly the structure of the tissue at the point of contact following an exposure period of 4 hours. This term does not refer to action on inanimate surfaces.*

Discussion and Commentary: Chemicals that are classified as corrosive are essential materials in the manufacturing environment. Corrosives are materials that chemically are defined as either acids or bases. Their classification is heavily dependent on their pH, which is a measure of certain types of molecules that contain positive or negative charges of oxygen-hydrogen (OH). Purified water has a pH of 7. Materials with a pH less than 7 are considered acids, whereas materials with a pH greater than 7 are considered bases. The pH scale has a range of 1 to 14. The lower the pH, the more it is considered an acid. The higher the pH, the more the material is considered to be a base. Generally speaking, a material that has a pH of 2 or less or 12.5 or more is considered to be a corrosive material as defined in the IFC.

The IFC definition does not consider materials that are corrosive to inanimate materials. Ferric chloride is a common chemical used in wastewater treatment. It is generally not considered corrosive to skin but can easily attack and destroy carbon steel.

Code Text: *Indoor storage of corrosive materials in amounts exceeding the maximum allowable quantity per control area indicated in Table 5003.1.1(2), shall be in accordance with Sections 5001, 5003 and 5004 and this chapter.*

Discussion and Commentary: When the MAQ for one or more control areas has been exceeded, and additional engineering controls such as automatic sprinkler protection and storage cabinets cannot accommodate the desired amount of storage, then reclassification of the occupancy as a Group H-4 occupancy is appropriate and meets the requirements of the IFC and *International Building Code*® (IBC®). A Group H-4 occupancy for corrosive materials requires spill control and secondary containment if the stored materials are liquid, mechanical ventilation, automatic sprinkler protection and a liquid tight floor. If the room is in a mixed occupancy building, a fire barrier with the appropriate fire-resistance rating specified in IBC Chapter 5 is also required, along with compliance with the IBC Chapter 10 requirements for means of egress.

If the stored corrosive materials can liberate corrosive vapors, such as hydrochloric acid, the automatic sprinkler system should be designed to be resistant to a corrosive atmosphere.

Code Text: *Storage, use and handling of cryogenic fluids shall comply with this chapter and NFPA 55. Cryogenic fluids classified as hazardous materials shall also comply with Chapter 50. Partially full containers containing residual cryogenic fluids shall be considered as full for the purposes of the controls required.* **Exceptions:** *(1) Fluids used as refrigerants in refrigeration systems (see Section 608), (2) Liquefied natural gas (LNG), which shall comply with NFPA 59A.*

Oxidizing cryogenic fluids, including oxygen, shall comply with Chapter 63, as applicable.

Flammable cryogenic fluids, including hydrogen, methane and carbon monoxide, shall comply with Chapters 23 and 58, as applicable.

Inert cryogenic fluids, including argon, helium and nitrogen, shall comply with ANSI/CGA P-18.

Discussion and Commentary: Cryogenic fluids are compressed gases that have been refrigerated and compressed into a liquid state. Cryogenic fluids are a safe and efficient method of storing and using these gases. By definition, cryogenic fluids have a boiling point temperature of -130°F or lower at 1 atmosphere (14.7 PSIA). IFC Chapter 55 is very similar in format and use to IFC Chapter 53 in that it regulates the storage and use of the cryogenic fluid itself and defers the management of the inherent hazard of the cryogenic fluid to the appropriate NFPA or CGA standard.

Cryogenic fluids are found in a variety of settings including motor fuels, health care, metal manufacturing and semiconductors.

Code Text: *A fluid having a boiling point lower than -130°F (-89.9°C) at 14.7 pounds per square inch atmosphere (psia) (an absolute pressure of 101.3 kPa).*

Discussion and Commentary: The primary hazards with cryogenic fluids are: (1) The hazard of the gas does not change by refrigerating the gas and converting it to a liquid. Methane, when refrigerated, still is a flammable gas and if it is released as a cryogenic fluid can create a large flammable vapor cloud, (2) Cryogenic fluids have tremendous expansion ratios. Liquid nitrogen has an expansion ratio of 1:696. This means one cubic foot of liquid nitrogen expands into 696 cubic feet of nitrogen gas. In a closed delivery system this equates to a tremendous volume of pressure that must be safely relieved, especially if the liquid is trapped, such as liquid argon in a pipe between two closed valves, (3) Their cold temperature can cause thermal burns to human flesh and cause spalling in concrete.

It should be noted that liquid carbon dioxide is not a cryogenic fluid because its boiling temperature is -109°F and therefore is not regulated under IFC Chapter 55.

Another safety issue for cryogenic fluids is the use of proper materials for construction. Because of their low temperatures, metals that exhibit low temperature stress fracturing, such as plastics and certain carbon steels are not acceptable for cryogenic fluid service.

Code Text: *Shutoff valves shall not be installed between pressure relief devices and containers.* ***Exceptions:*** *(1) A shutoff valve is allowed on containers equipped with multiple pressure-relief device installations where the arrangement of the valves provides the full required flow through the minimum number of required relief devices at all times, (2) A locking-type shutoff valve is allowed to be used upstream of the pressure relief device for service-related work performed by the supplier when in accordance with the requirements of the ASME Boiler and Pressure Vessel Code.*

Discussion and Commentary: A pressure relief device is designed to protect a pressure vessel in the event that the pressure exceeds the maximum allowable working pressure. This can occur if liquids are trapped in the vessel and the vessel is heated by solar radiation. It can also occur if the vessel is subjected to fire exposure. Therefore, the IFC requires that the pressure vessel be equipped with a pressure relief device. A shutoff valve is not permitted between the pressure vessel and the pressure relief valve. However, when two or more relief valves are provided, a shutoff valve is permitted so that maintenance can be performed. The cross-sectional area of the valve must equal or exceed the required cross-sectional area of the pressure relief device.

The photograph illustrates two spring-loaded safety pressure relief valves on a cryogenic vessel. One of the relief valves is isolated from use by the shutoff valve.

Code Text: *Piping systems shall be suitable for the use intended through the full range of pressure and temperature to which they will be subjected. Piping systems shall be designed and constructed to provide adequate allowance for expansion, contraction, vibration, settlement and fire exposure.*

Discussion and Commentary: Cryogenic piping systems that use a vaporizer to convert the fluid into a gas commonly have different piping materials. The piping supplying the fluid from the pressure vessel to the vaporizer must be constructed of materials that can resist the low temperatures of the cryogenic fluid. Once the fluid enters the vaporizer it is converted into a gas. This allows the use of a piping material that is compatible with gas rather than cryogenic fluids.

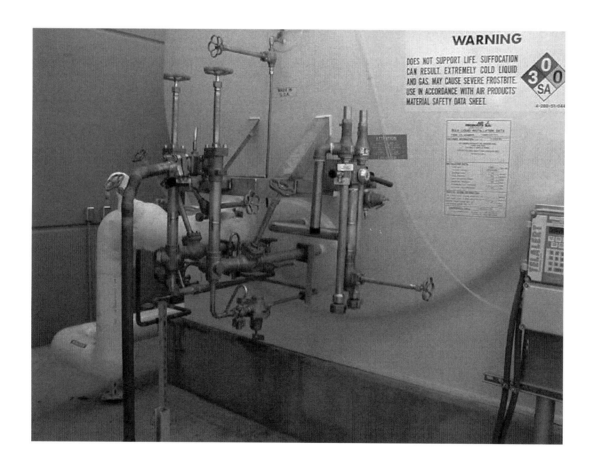

Given that these systems involve cryogenic fluids that also present one or more physical or health hazards when converted to gas, and given their expansion ratios, the IFC requires a construction permit and operational permit for these systems (IFC Sections 105.5.11 and 105.6.3).

Code Text: *Manual or automatic emergency shutoff valves shall be provided to shut off the cryogenic fluid supply in case of emergency. An emergency shutoff valve shall be located at the source of supply and at the point where the system enters the building.*

Discussion and Commentary: Given the expansion ratio of cryogenic fluids and that their physical or health hazard does not change upon release to the atmosphere, either a manual or automatic shutoff valve is required to prevent the accidental release of either a cryogenic fluid or a gas produced by the cryogenic container. The valve is required to be located at the point of connection to the cryogenic vessel and at the point where the piping enters into the building.

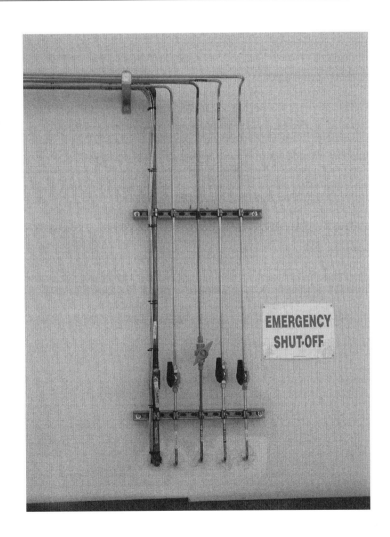

IFC Section 5003.2.2.1, Items 3 and 4 require that the valves be clearly visible, identified in an approved manner and provided with ready access.

Quiz

Study Session 14
IFC Chapters 51 through 55

1. Given: An aerosol container that contains a base product and a propellant with a chemical heat of combustion of 22,700 Btu/lb. What is the correct classification of this aerosol?

    a. Level 1   b. Level 2

    c. Level 3   d. Aerosol Cooking Spray

    Reference Table 5163.1

2. What is the total net weight of Level 2 and 3 aerosols permitted in a Group I-2 occupancy?

    a. 500 pounds   b. 1,000 pounds

    c. 5,000 pounds   d. 12,000 pounds

    Reference 5164.2 #3

3. Given: A single story, general purpose warehouse is classified as Group S-1. The 150,000 square-foot building is protected throughout with an automatic sprinkler system which complies with NFPA 30B. What is the net weight of Level 3 aerosols that can be stored in a solid-pile configuration using the nonsegregated storage method?

    a. 1,000 pounds   b. 2,000 pounds

    c. 12,000 pounds   d. 36,000 pounds

    Reference 51043.1
                       Footnote B

4. The maximum amount of aerosol cooking spray products in a general-purpose warehouse is _____ unless the storage is protected in accordance with NFPA 30B.

    a. 1,000 pounds   b. 2,500 pounds

    c. 5,000 pounds   d. 12,000 pounds

    Reference 5104.3.3

5. Which class or classes of commodities are not permitted in a chain-link fence enclosure used for the containment of aerosols in segregated storage?

   a. Class III

   b. Class IV

   c. High hazard

   d. both b and c

   Reference 5104.3.2.1 #3

6. In a general purpose warehouse with segregated method of storage for Level 2 and 3 aerosols, what is the maximum area of storage permitted in a 100,000-square-foot Group S-1 occupancy that is sprinklered and has a two-hour fire-resistance-rated fire barrier separating the aerosol storage?

   a. 20,000 square feet

   b. 25,000 square feet

   c. 30,000 square feet

   d. 40,000 square feet

   Reference 5104.3.2
   Footnote A

7. What is the minimum NFPA 13 design density required for an automatic sprinkler system protecting Level 2 and Level 3 aerosols in a retail display?

   a. Light Hazard

   b. Ordinary Hazard Group 1

   c. Ordinary Hazard Group 2

   d. Extra Hazard Group 1

   Reference 5106.2.5

8. What is the maximum net weight of Level 2 and 3 aerosols that can be displayed on the ground floor of a Group M occupancy that is provided with an NFPA 30B compliant automatic sprinkler system?

   a. 500 pounds

   b. 2,000 pounds

   c. 2,500 pounds

   d. 10,000 pounds

   Reference 5106.2.1

9. The maximum height for the retail display of Level 2 and 3 aerosols on shelves in a Group M occupancy equipped with an automatic sprinkler system designed to Ordinary Hazard Group 2 is _____ .

   a. 4

   b. 6

   c. 8

   d. 12

   Reference 5106.2.3

10. Given: Retail display of Level 2 and 3 aerosols stored and displayed in double-row racks in a building protected with an automatic sprinkler system designed in accordance with NFPA 30B. What is the maximum volume of containers containing Class I, II or III liquids that are permitted to be stored adjacent to the aerosol products?

    a.   1.06-gallon glass containers

    b.   1.06-gallon plastic containers

    c.   2.1-gallon nonrelieving containers

    (d.) 5.3-gallon metal-relieving containers

Reference 5106.5.8 #1

11. Given: A restaurant using an insulated liquid CO_2 system for beverage dispensing with a bulk tank containing 250 pounds of liquid CO_2 with mechanical ventilation to handle a leak. What is the minimum ventilation rate required in the room containing the CO_2 tank?

    a.   No minimum ventilation rate is specified since the tank size is less than 300 pounds

    b.   1 air change per minute based on the size of the room

    (c.) 1 cfm per square foot based on the size of the room

    d.   6 air changes per hour based on the size of the room

Reference 5307.3.1

12. Given: A mini-mart uses an insulated liquid CO_2 system for beverage dispensing. The bulk tank is located inside the building and contains 200 pounds of CO_2 with an emergency alarm to respond to a CO_2 leak. Which of the following is not correct?

    a.   The gas sensors must be provided in areas where CO_2 will accumulate.

    (b.) When the gas detection system is activated, the CO_2 container must dump its contents directly to the exterior.

    c.   Mechanical ventilation designed to exhaust released CO_2 is not required.

    d.   The alarm must sound a supervisory alarm at a normally attended location when the concentration reaches 5,000 parts per million.

Reference 5307.3.2

13. Containers for aerosol products are limited in size, and the maximum size glass container is _____ fluid ounces.

    a. 3   b. 33.8

    (c.) 4   d. Glass is not allowed

Reference 5101.4

14. What is the required information for marking of compressed gas piping?

    a. direction of flow

    b. name of the pipe contents

    c. the piping design pressure and temperature

    d. both a and b

    Reference 5303.4.3

15. What is the minimum separation distance required between compressed gas cylinder storage areas and combustible waste?

    a. 5 feet   b. 10 feet

    c. 20 feet   d. 30 feet

    Reference 5303.7.2

16. Compressed gas cylinders shall not be placed near platform edges where the distance exceeds_____.

    a. two times the height of the cylinder

    b. the height of the cylinder

    c. $^{1}/_{2}$ the height of the cylinder

    d. 30 inches

    Reference 5303.7.3

17. What is the minimum ventilation rate requirement for a vault containing compressed gases?

    a. $^{1}/_{2}$ CFM/square foot

    b. 1 CFM/square foot

    c. not less than 150 CFM of air flow

    d. both b and c are required

    Reference 5303.16.9

18. At what concentration is the vapor detection system inside of a gas vault required to activate when the vault is not used for the storage, handling or dispensing of toxic gases?

    a. 25 percent of the LEL value   b. 50 percent of the LEL value

    c. 50 percent of the IDLH value   d. Either a or c

    Reference 5303.16.10

19. What type of safety system is required for a room or building that contains compressed gases that are classified as simple asphyxiants?

    a. gas detection system

    b. one-hour fire barrier

    c. mechanical ventilation system

    d. either a or c

Reference 5307.2

20. Secondary containment is required for outdoor above-ground storage tanks containing corrosive liquids when the aggregate volume exceeds _____.

    a. 500 gallons   b. 1,000 gallons

    c. 2,000 gallons   d. when the outdoor MAQ is exceeded

Reference 5404.2.1

21. What is the minimum separation distance required for a 3,000-gallon outdoor above-ground storage tank containing 23 percent hydrochloric acid, a corrosive liquid, from a public way? The tank is not associated with the manufacturing or distribution of hydrochloric acid.

    a. 10 feet   b. 20 feet

    c. $\frac{1}{2}$ the diameter of the tank   d. Separation is not required.

Reference 5404.2.2

22. In addition to the provisions of Section 5004.12, floors in storage areas for corrosive liquids shall be _____.

    a. Liquid-tight construction

    b. Elevated

    c. Provided with stepping stones

    d. Polished so a leak is readily noticeable

Reference 5404.1.1

23. At atmospheric pressure (14.7 PSIA), at what temperature is a gas classified as a cryogenic fluid?

    a.   When its triple point is lower than 130°F.

    b.   When its boiling point is lower than -130°F.

    c.   When its boiling point is lower than 130°F.

    d.   When its freezing point is lower than -130°F.

Reference _202_

24. A pressure relief device on a cryogenic vessel must have sufficient capacity to prevent the container's maximum _____ from being exceeded.

    a.   volume   b.   design pressure

    c.   design temperature   d.   design flow rate

Reference _5503.2.3_

25. Given: A 3,000-gallon stationary pressure vessel is used for the storage of liquid nitrogen, a simple asphyxiant, inert, cryogenic fluid. What is the minimum required separation distance from the pressure vessel to a building air intake?

    a.   1 foot   b.   5 feet

    c.   10 feet   d.   15 feet

Reference _5504.3.1.1_

26. Given: A 60-gallon DOT container is used for the storage of liquid argon, a simple asphyxiant, inert, cryogenic fluid. The container is located outside of a building. What is the minimum required separation distance of the DOT container from an exit?

    a.   1 foot   b.   5 feet

    c.   10 feet   d.   15 feet

Reference _5504.3.1.7.1_

27. Cryogenic fluid containers are prohibited from being installed in _____.

    a.   Indoors

    b.   Areas subject to wind speeds exceeding 120 miles per hour

    c.   Areas subject to freezing

    d.   Diked areas containing other hazardous materials

Reference _5504.3.1.1.3_

28. What type of device is required in a cryogenic fluid piping system where cryogenic fluid can become trapped between two shutoff valves?

    a. pressure relief valve   b. check valve

    c. butterfly valve   d. full port ball valve

Reference 5505.1.2.3.2

29. What is the minimum test pressure required for pneumatically testing cryogenic piping systems?

    a. the working pressure of the piping system

    b. 110 percent of the working pressure

    c. 150 percent of the working pressure

    d. 1.1 times the pipe yield strength

Reference 5505.1.2.6

30. At what location is an emergency shutoff valve required for outdoor cryogenic fluid storage and use system?

    a. at the source of the supply   b. where the system enters the building

    c. at the point of use   d. both a and b are required locations

Reference 5505.3.2

31. What is the minimum clear space required for maintenance, access and inspection around compressed gas tube trailers?

    a. 1 foot

    b. 3 feet

    c. 5 feet

    d. No clearance dimension is specified in the IFC

Reference 5303.7.11

32. Which of the following safety features is not required for a 1-hour interior medical gas storage room?

    a. Fire sprinklers

    b. Gas detection system

    c. Mechanical ventilation

    d. 1-hour separation from the remainder of the building

Reference 5306.7.2

33. When are aerosol products in plastic containers protected as Class III commodities?

    (a.) The base product has no fire point, and the propellant is nonflammable.

    b. The base product is flammable, but the propellant is nonflammable.

    c. The base product contains no more than 30 percent ethanol or isopropyl alcohol, and the propellant is nonflammable.

    d. Never; they are always treated as high-hazard commodities.

    Reference 5104.1.1 #1

34. Medical gases are required to be stored in gas cabinets, 1-hour interior medical gas storage room or 1-hour exterior medical gas storage room when the aggregate quantity exceeds _____.

    a. the maximum allowable quantity per control area

    (b.) the amount requiring a permit

    c. twice the maximum allowable quantity per control area if the building is sprinklered

    d. any amount

    Reference 5306.2

35. Which of the following features is not required for a gas cabinet storing medical gases?

    a. mechanical ventilation which exhausts to the exterior

    (b.) must be located in a 1-hour exterior room

    c. fire sprinklers inside the gas cabinet

    d. can contain no more than three cylinders

    Reference 5003.8.6.3
    5306.2.3

2021 IFC Chapter 56
Explosives and Fireworks

OBJECTIVE: To gain a basic understanding of the *International Fire Code®* (IFC®) requirements for the storage, manufacturing and use of explosives, fireworks and small arms ammunition.

REFERENCE: Chapter 56, 2021 IFC

KEY POINTS:
- What steps are required before permits for storage and use of explosives or fireworks can be issued?
- What restrictions can be invoked when issuing a permit for explosives or fireworks?
- How is a jurisdiction indemnified from inspection or plan review errors that may have contributed to an incident involving explosives or fireworks?
- How are explosives and fireworks classified? What is the difference between fireworks and pyrotechnic special effects?
- What notifications are required when a new explosives storage site is established?
- What are operating buildings, inhabited buildings and public traffic routes?
- How are the quantity-distance tables applied when determining required separation distances?
- What types of magazines are acceptable for the storage of high and low explosives?
- What are the requirements for indoor storage magazines?
- What is the maximum allowable quantity for Divisions 1.1 through 1.6 explosives?
- Given an explosive with a known net explosive weight (net weight) and classification, what are the required separation distances from inhabited buildings, public traffic routes, other magazines or other operating buildings?
- What are the requirements for maintenance of explosive magazines?
- What is the inspection frequency and elements for explosive magazines?
- How is the net weight used to determine intraline separation distances?
- What are the quantity limits for manufacturing operations involving explosives?

KEY POINTS:
(Cont'd)

- When is remote controlled equipment required for manufacturing operations involving explosives?
- What are the quantity limits and requirements for the display and storage of smokeless propellant, black powder and small arms primers in Group M occupancies?
- Where retail sale of fireworks is allowed, what are the applicable requirements?
- Is the operation of loading or reloading ammunition in a commercial facility regulated?
- What are the requirements for a fireworks display permit?
- What classes of explosives are allowed for fireworks displays?
- What are the requirements for proper installation of mortars?
- Following a fireworks display, what kind of inspection is required and what steps must be performed?
- What are the requirements for the disposal of fireworks?
- Are the requirements different for permanent storage and temporary storage facilities?
- What limitations apply to pyrotechnic special effects?

Code Text: *The possession, manufacture, storage, sale, handling and use of fireworks are prohibited. **Exceptions:** (1) Storage and handling of fireworks as allowed in Section 5604, (2) Manufacture, assembly and testing of fireworks as allowed in Section 5605, (3) The use of fireworks for fireworks displays as allowed in Section 5608, (4) The possession, storage, sale, handling and use of specific types of Division 1.4G fireworks where allowed by applicable laws, ordinances and regulations, provided such fireworks comply with the 2006 edition of NFPA 1124, CPSC 16 CFR Parts 1500 and 1507, and DOTn 49 CFR, Parts 100–185, as applicable for consumer fireworks.*

Discussion and Commentary: With the exceptions of fireworks storage in accordance with NFPA 1124 *Code for the Manufacture, Transportation, and Storage of Fireworks and Pyrotechnic Articles*; or fireworks manufactured in accordance with IFC Section 5605; or where consumer possession, storage and use of Division 1.4G fireworks is permitted by the jurisdiction, fireworks are prohibited by the IFC. According to the Consumer Products Safety Commission, fireworks used by consumers caused an estimated 11,400 injuries that were treated in a emergency rooms in the US in 2013[1]. Because of these injuries and the potential for ignition of wood shake roofs or wildland-urban interface areas, many fire code officials prohibit the possession, storage or use of these materials within their jurisdictions.

Exception 4 states that the 2006 edition of NFPA 1124 is applicable for retail display in areas where retail sale of consumer fireworks is allowed. NFPA 1124 limits the height of storage areas in public retail areas to 6 feet.

[1]Tu, Tongling and Demar V. Granados, *Fireworks-Related Deaths, Emergency Department-Treated Injuries, and Enforcement Activities During* 2013, US Consumer Product Safety Commission, June 2014, Page 1.

Code Text: *The storage and handling of ammonium nitrate shall comply with the requirements of NFPA 400 and Chapter 63. **Exception:** Storage of ammonium nitrate in magazines with blasting agents shall comply with the requirements of NFPA 495.*

Discussion and Commentary: Ammonium nitrate is commonly used as a blasting agent. It is classified as a Class 4 Oxidizer by the IFC and as a Division 1.5 explosive using the criteria found in UN/DOTn when the particle size is greater than 80 microns. For particle sizes between 15 and 80 microns, it is classified as a UN/DOTn Division 1.3 explosive (mass fire) material, and for particle sizes less than 15 microns, UN/DOTn classifies ammonium nitrate as a Division 1.1 explosive (mass detonating) material. For industrial blasting operations used for the removal of natural resources, ammonium nitrate particles are greater than 80 microns. Because it is a powerful oxidizer, it must be mixed with a fuel such as diesel fuel, carbon black or nut hulls. For it to perform as a blasting agent, a blasting cap must be used to detonate the fuel and oxidizer mixture.

The storage of ammonium nitrate shall comply with NFPA 400, *Hazardous Materials Code*. If it is stored in magazines with other blasting agents, the requirements of NFPA 495, *Explosive Materials Code* apply (IFC Section 5601.1.5).

Code Text: *Persons shall not keep or store, nor shall any permit be issued to keep or store, any explosives at any place of habitation, or within 100 feet (30 480 mm) thereof.* **Exception:** *Storage of smokeless propellant, black powder, and small arms primers for personal use and not for resale in accordance with Section 5606.*

Discussion and Commentary: Because of the hazards of possible mass detonation, mass fragmentation and mass fire associated with the improper storage or handling of explosives and Division 1.3G fireworks, IFC Section 5601.2.1 prohibits the storage of explosive materials at any place of habitation. This includes single-family and multi-family dwellings constructed under the IRC and Groups R-1, R-2, R-3 and R-4 occupancies as defined in the IBC. Individual storage of smokeless propellant, black powder and small arms ammunition for personal use and not for resale is permitted when the storage is in compliance with IFC Section 5606.

See IFC Section 5606.4 for storage requirements of small arms ammunition components in places of habitation. This IFC requirement is an operational provision, not a construction provision, so even though a dwelling may be constructed under the *International Residential Code*® (IRC®), this requirement still applies to the residential building.

Code Text: *The quantity-distance (Q-D) tables in Sections 5604.5 and 5605.3 shall be used to provide the minimum separation distances from potential explosion sites as set forth in Tables 5601.8.1(1) through 5601.8.1(3). The classification and the weight of the explosives are primary characteristics governing the use of these tables. The net explosive weight shall be determined in accordance with Sections 5601.8.1.1 through 5601.8.1.4.*

Discussion and Commentary: The separation distances are based on the UN/DOTn hazard explosive classification system and the net explosive weight of the stored materials. Three tables serve as an index for each Table of Distance (located in Sections 5604 and 5605) based on the hazard classification of the explosive. Table 5601.8.1(1) applies to Division 1.1, 1.2 and 1.5 explosives. Table 5601.8.1(2) applies to Division 1.3 explosives, and Table 5601.8.1(3) applies to Division 1.4 materials. Each column identifies the applicable exposure for the applicable item and stipulates the applicable table and appropriate separation distances based on the distance specified in the table referenced to the exposure by hazard classification.

TABLE 5601.8.1(2)
APPLICATION OF QUANTITY-DISTANCE (Q-D) TABLES—DIVISION 1.3 EXPLOSIVES [a,b,c]

ITEM	MAGAZINE	OPERATING BUILDING	INHABITED BUILDING	PUBLIC TRAFFIC ROUTE
Inhabited building	IBD in Table 5604.5.2(2)	IBD in Table 5604.5.2(2)	Not Applicable	Not Applicable
Magazine	IMD in Table 5604.5.2(2)	ILD or IPD in Table 5604.5.2(2)	IBD in Table 5604.5.2(2)	PTR in Table 5604.5.2(2)
Operating building	ILD or IPD in Table 5604.5.2(2)	ILD or IPD in Table 5604.5.2(2)	IBD in Table Q-5604.5.2(2)	PTR in Table 5604.5.2(2)
Public traffic route	PTR in Table 5604.5.2(2)	PTR in Table 5604.5.2(2)	Not Applicable	Not Applicable

For SI: 1 foot = 304.8 mm.

a. The minimum separation distance shall be not less than 50 feet.

b. Linear interpolation between tabular values in the referenced Q-D table shall be allowed.

c. For definitions of Quantity-Distance abbreviations IBD, ILD, IMD, IPD and PTR, see Chapter 2.

Example 1: What is the minimum required separation distance of 1,200 pounds (net explosive weight) of Division 1.3 material stored in a magazine adjacent to an Inhabited Building (IBD)?

Example 1 answer: Using the left column titled ITEM, the magazine must meet the inhabited building distance (IBD) specified in Table 5604.5.2(2) for Division 1.3 materials. The value in Table 5604.5.2(2) specifies a minimum separation distance of 115 feet for inhabited buildings.

Example 2: What is the minimum required separation distance of 1,200 pounds (net explosive weight) of Division 1.3 material stored in a magazine adjacent to another magazine (IMD)?

Example 2 answer: Using the left column titled ITEM, the magazine must meet the intermagazine distance (IMD) specified in Table 5604.5.2(2) for Division 1.3 materials. The value in Table 5604.5.2(2) specifies a minimum separation distance of 75 feet from other magazines containing explosives.

Code Text: *The effective screening of a building containing explosive materials from the magazine or other building, railway or highway by a natural or an artificial barrier. A straight line from the top of any sidewall of the building containing explosive materials to the eave line of any magazine or other building or to a point 12 feet (3658 mm) above the center of a railway or highway shall pass through such barrier.*

Discussion and Commentary: When an explosion occurs, the blast force spreads in all directions. The blast force will travel across the ground surface until it is interrupted or redirected. The intent of a barricade is to disrupt the blast force. Throughout Chapter 56 several separation distances are reduced in cases where barricades are provided. The barricade reduces the blast force for structures on the other side of the barricade.

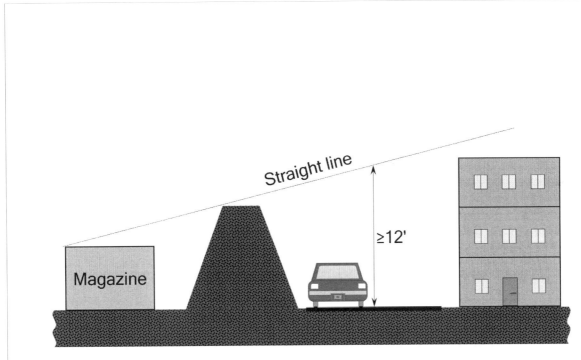

For SI: 1 foot = 304.8 mm.

This drawing depicts an adequately barricaded building and roadway.

Code Text: *The quantity of explosive material and separation distance relationships providing protection. These relationships are based on levels of risk considered acceptable for the stipulated exposures and are tabulated in the appropriate Q-D tables. The separation distances specified afford less than absolute safety . . .*

(See IFC Section 202 for definitions of the various separation distances.)

Discussion and Commentary: The tables in IFC Section 5601.8.1 introduce the requirements for Q-D. Proper application of Q-D requires that the correct separation distances be applied based on the exposure being protected. Five different exposures are evaluated using Q-D. The exposures are minimum separation distance, Intraline or Intraplant Distance (ILD or IPD), the Inhabited Building Distance (IBD), the Intermagazine Distance (IMD) and the minimum separation from Public Traffic Routes (PTR). Proper application of these distances ensure that a minimum level of safety is provided in the case of a mass detonation or mass fire even involving explosives.

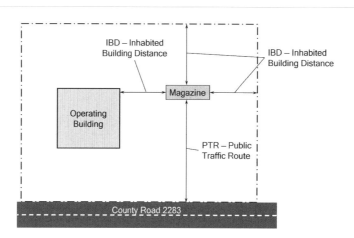

Given: A magazine containing 12,800 pounds of Division 1.2 explosives. The magazine is not barricaded. The daily traffic count for County Road 2283 is 900 vehicles. Determine the following distances:
- Distance to the operating building (IBD)
- Distance to the property line (IBD)
- Distance to the roadway (PTR)

Answer: Application of Table 5601.8.1(1) is appropriate because of the explosive classification. The separation distance to the property lines will be based on the IBD (inhabited building distance) in Table 5604.5.2(1). The separation distance to County Road 2283 is PTR in Table 5604.5.2(1). The separation between the magazine the operating building will be based on the IPD (intraplant distance) in Table 5605.3.

Table 5604.5.2(1) is referenced to determine the IBD and PTR. In the column titled "Quantity of Explosive Materials" review the values for the range of 12,000 to 14,000 pounds. Based on the values in this table IBD = 1,770 feet and PTR = 550 feet.

Table 5605.3 is referenced to determine the IPD. In this table we find that for the value range of 12,000 to 14,000 pounds, a distance of 225 feet is required where the two items are barricaded, per footnote a, 450 feet where not barricaded.

Code Text: *Explosives and explosive materials, and Division 1.3G fireworks shall be stored in magazines constructed, located, operated and maintained in accordance with the provisions of Section 5604 and NFPA 495 or NFPA 1124.* **Exceptions:** *(1) Storage of fireworks at display sites in accordance with Section 5608.5 and NFPA 1123 or NFPA 1126. (2) Portable or mobile magazines not exceeding 120 square feet (11 m²) in area shall not be required to comply with the requirements of the* International Building Code.

Discussion and Commentary: To ensure that explosives and Division 1.3G fireworks are properly protected from fire exposure, theft, and in certain cases, bullets fired from weapons, the IFC requires that explosives and Division 1.3 fireworks be stored in magazines. Magazines can be located outdoors or may be located indoors in accordance with IFC Section 5604.5.1. Magazines can be permanent, such as a Type 1 magazine, or they may be portable, such as a Type 3 magazine, known as a day box.

(Photograph courtesy of Getty Images.)

The photograph illustrates a Type 1 magazine. Construction requirements for all magazines are contained in NFPA 495, NFPA 1124 and Bureau of Alcohol, Tobacco, Firearms and Explosives regulations in DOTy 27 CFR Part 555, *Commerce in Explosives* (IFC Section 5604.6).

Code Text: *The storage of explosives and explosive materials in magazines shall comply with Table 5604.3.*

Discussion and Commentary: Table 5604.3 establishes the maximum allowable quantity for one control area for explosives and Division 1.3G fireworks. The maximum allowable quantity is based on level of fire protection and fire resistive isolation provided. Note that the Table does not permit the indoor storage of explosives in a nonsprinklered building. This is consistent with the requirement in Table 5003.1.1(1), Footnote g. Depending on the amount of storage, the explosive's classification and the protection that the magazine is provided, Table 5604.3 allows one to select the magazine type for the given application. For example, consider 100 pounds of Division 1.1 material stored in an outdoor magazine. Because day boxes (Type 3 magazine) have a limited capacity, either a Type 1 or 2 magazine can be used, based on the requirements of this table for the storage of Division 1.1 explosive.

TABLE 5604.3
STORAGE AMOUNTS AND MAGAZINE REQUIREMENTS FOR EXPLOSIVES, EXPLOSIVE MATERIALS AND FIREWORKS, 1.3G MAXIMUM ALLOWABLE QUANTITY PER CONTROL AREA

NEW UN/ DOTN DIVISION	OLD DOTN CLASS	ATF/OSHA CLASS	INDOOR[A] (POUNDS)				OUTDOOR (POUNDS)	MAGAZINE TYPE REQUIRED				
			UNPRO-TECTED	CABINET	SPRIN-KLERS	SPRIN-KLERS & CABINET		1	2	3	4	5
1.1[b]	A	High	0	0	1	2	1	X	X	X	—	—
1.2	A	High	0	0	1	2	1	X	X	X	—	—
1.2	B	Low	0	0	1	1	1	X	X	X	X	—
1.3	B	Low	0	0	5	10	1	X	X	X	X	—
1.4	B	Low	0	0	50	100	1	X	X	X	X	—
1.5	C	Low	0	0	1	2	1	X	X	X	X	—
1.5	Blasting Agent	Blasting Agent	0	0	1	2	1	X	X	X	X	X
1.6	Not Applicable	Not Applicable	0	0	1	2	1	X	X	X	X	X

For SI: 1 pound = 0.454 kg, 1 pound per gallon = 0.12 kg per liter, 1 ounce = 28.35 g.

a. A factor of 10 pounds per gallon shall be used for converting pounds (solid) to gallons (liquid) in accordance with Section 5003.1.2.

b. Black powder shall be stored in a Type 1, 2, 3 or 4 magazine as provided for in Section 5604.3.1.

Note that a Type 5 magazine can only be used for Division 1.5 (blasting agent) and Division 1.6 (extremely insensitive) explosives.

Code Text: *Outdoor magazines other than Type 3 shall be located so as to comply with Table 5604.5.2(2) or Table 5604.5.2(3) as set forth in Tables 5601.8.1(1) through 5601.8.1(3). Where a magazine or group of magazines, as described in Section 5604.5.2.2, contains different classes of explosive materials, and Division 1.1 materials are present, the required separations for the magazine or magazine group as a whole shall comply with Table 5604.5.2(2).*

Discussion and Commentary: This provision requires that the separation distances be maintained in accordance with the requirements of IFC Section 5601.8.1. When two or more magazines are located adjacently, and the separation distances prescribed for their given hazard classification are not satisfied, the net explosive weights of the magazines must be summed and used as the basis for calculation of the separation distance in the quantity-distance tables. This section also requires that when two classes of explosives are present, and one of those stored classes is designated as a Division 1.1 material, then the separation distances must be based on the presence of the mass detonating (Division 1.1) explosive.

Note that the separation distance requirements for Division 1.1 materials are based on the magazines either being barricaded or not being barricaded. The definition of barricade in Section 202 provides the criteria for the construction of barricades.

Code Text: *Where two or more magazines are separated from each other by less than the intermagazine distances (IMD), such magazines as a group shall be considered as one magazine and the total quantity of explosive materials stored in the group shall be treated as if stored in a single magazine. The location of the group of magazines shall comply with the intermagazine distances (IMD) specified from other magazines or magazine groups, inhabited buildings (IBD), public transportation routes (PTR) and operating buildings (ILD or IPD) as required.*

Discussion and Commentary: If the minimum required separation is not provided between magazines, a detonation in one magazine can cause sympathetic detonations in the other adjacent magazine. For explosives classified as producing a mass fire (Division 1.3), a fire in one magazine can extend into the adjacent magazine. This section specifies that if adequate separation is not provided between two or more magazines, the aggregate net explosive weight is used for the purpose of determining the required separation distance between the group of magazines and other magazines, inhabited buildings, public transportation routes and operating buildings.

The photograph shows a location with five magazines. In this case, each magazine was authorized to contain 10,000 pounds of Division 1.3 material. Applying IFC Table 5604.5.2(2), a minimum separation distance of 100 feet is required between each magazine. As is illustrated, 100 foot separation is not provided between each magazine. Therefore, the aggregate net explosive weight is used, and the distances to inhabited buildings, other magazines outside of this group, operating buildings and public transportation routes must be verified to ensure adequate separation.

Code Text: *Not more than two Type 3 magazines shall be located at the same blasting site. Where two Type 3 magazines are located at the same blasting site, one magazine shall be used solely for the storage of detonators.*

Discussion and Commentary: A Type 3 magazine is commonly referred to as a day box. These magazines are only allowed for the temporary storage of explosives, essentially enough explosives for one day of operation. They are required to be resistant to fire, theft and weather. Like other magazines they are required to meet the Table of Distances based on the quantity of explosives stored. A maximum of two Type 3 magazines are permitted at an explosive site—one for the explosive and one for the detonators. Detonators are used to initiate the main explosion, therefore the detonators are stored in a separate magazine from the explosive material.

(Photograph courtesy of Armag Corporation.)

The photograph illustrates two Type 3 magazines. A Type 3 magazine is portable, fire resistant, theft resistant and weather resistant.

Code Text: *Magazines shall be constructed in accordance with Sections 5604.6.1 through 5604.6.5.2.*

Discussion and Commentary: In addition to the magazine construction requirements contained in NFPA 495, IFC Section 5604.6 contains requirements relating to access road signs leading to magazines and identification of the magazine. If lighting or heat is required inside of the magazine, the design of the lighting or heating system must meet the requirements of NFPA 495. In addition, the interior of the magazine must be constructed so that ferrous metal is not exposed. The concerns are with regard to an exposed nail tip or nail head cutting a box containing explosives or detonators and creating a source of spark.

NFPA 495 also contains requirements for securing of magazines, such as this shroud illustrated in this photograph that covers the latch and lock.

Code Text: *Magazines containing explosive materials shall be opened and inspected at maximum seven-day intervals. The inspection shall determine whether there has been an unauthorized or attempted entry into a magazine or an unauthorized removal of a magazine or its contents.*

Discussion and Commentary: The purpose of the weekly inspection is to verify that magazines have not been tampered with, to ensure that theft or undocumented loss of explosives has not occurred and to ensure that the authorized net explosive weight has not been exceeded. These inspections should also document if any repairs to the magazine are required. Note that if theft, loss or unauthorized removal occurs, the notification requirements in IFC Section 5603.3 must be satisfied. The nitro-glycerine in dynamite can leak out of the dynamite stick when the material is left in a magazine for extended periods of time, creating a very hazardous situation. Inspections should include evaluating this occurrence and remediating it in accordance with IFC Section 5604.10.2.

Magazines must be secured from theft, tampering and misuse, and the inspections are intended to monitor these items and ensure that the explosives are not contaminated or degrading.

Topic: Separation of Manufacturing Operating Buildings	**Category:** Explosives and Fireworks
Reference: IFC 5605.4	**Subject:** Manufacture, Assembly and Testing

Code Text: *Where an operating building on an explosive materials plant site is designed to contain explosive materials, such a building shall be located away from inhabited buildings, public traffic routes and magazines in accordance with Table 5604.5.2(2) or 5604.5.2(3) as appropriate, based on the maximum quantity of explosive materials permitted to be in the building at one time (see Section 5601.8).* **Exception:** *Fireworks manufacturing buildings constructed and operated in accordance with NFPA 1124.*

Discussion and Commentary: An operating building is defined in IFC Section 202 as *a building occupied in conjunction with the manufacture, transportation, or use of explosive materials. Operating buildings are separated from one another with the use of intraplant or intraline distances.* For Division 1.3 materials, the requirements in IFC Table 5604.5.2(2) will specify the ILD or IPD based on the net explosive weight of explosives in the operating building. Table 5604.5.2(3) contains the same requirements for Division 1.4 explosives. For Division 1.1, 1.2 or 1.5 materials, Footnote c in Table 5604.5.2(1) specifies that the operating building be located with respect to its proximity to inhabited buildings, public highways and passenger railroads based on the maximum quantity of explosive authorized in the building.

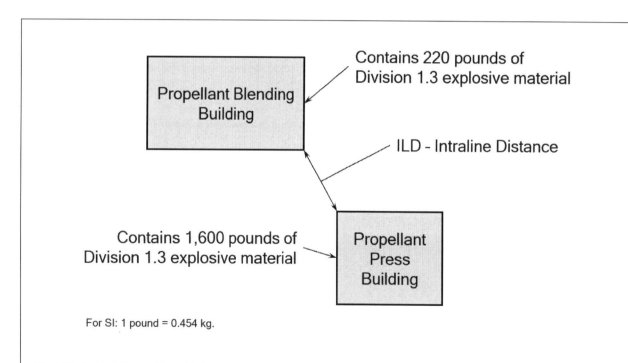

Contains 220 pounds of Division 1.3 explosive material

Propellant Blending Building

ILD - Intraline Distance

Contains 1,600 pounds of Division 1.3 explosive material

Propellant Press Building

For SI: 1 pound = 0.454 kg.

Example: Two operating buildings at a propellant manufacturing facility. The propellant blending building has an authorized net explosive weight of 220 pounds of Division 1.3 explosive material. The propellant press building has an authorized net weight of 1,600 pounds of Division 1.3 material. What is the required separation distance between the two operating buildings (ILD)?

Answer: The press building contains the greatest net weight of the two buildings. Application of IFC Table 5604.5.2(2) finds that the ILD must be at least 75 feet.

Code Text: *Where the type of material and processing warrants, mechanical operations involving explosives in excess of 1 pound (0.454 kg) shall be carried on at isolated stations or at intraplant distances, and machinery shall be controlled from remote locations behind barricades or at separations so that workers will be at a safe distance while machinery is operating.*

Discussion and Commentary: Explosive and energetic manufacturing operations commonly involve the blending of oxidizers and metals, shaping or extruding the explosive material and packaging the finished products. Because of the hazards of handling explosives, especially when other materials are blended, the IFC requires that the handling process be isolated from plant personnel when the amount of explosives exceeds one pound. The IFC requires that the equipment be controlled remotely or that adequate barricading be provided so that in the event of ignition, plant personnel are protected from the explosion and fire.

Most manufacturers of energetic materials will perform small scale detonation tests. This facility has provided earthen barricades for shielding of personnel and adjacent properties.

Code Text: *The display and storage of small arms ammunition in Group M occupancies shall comply with Sections 5606.5.1 through 5606.5.2.3.*

Discussion and Commentary: The provisions in IFC Section 5606.5 regulate the retail display and storage of black powder, smokeless propellant and small arms primers. These provisions are divided into two parts. Section 5606.5.1 limits the amount of smokeless propellant, black powder and primers that can be displayed. Section 5606.5.2 sets the limits for storage. The IFC permits progressively increased storage amounts of smokeless propellant based on the level of protection provided. For amounts between 100 to 800 pounds, wooden cabinets constructed of nominal 1-inch wood that are separated by a 1-hour fire partition or 25 feet are permitted.

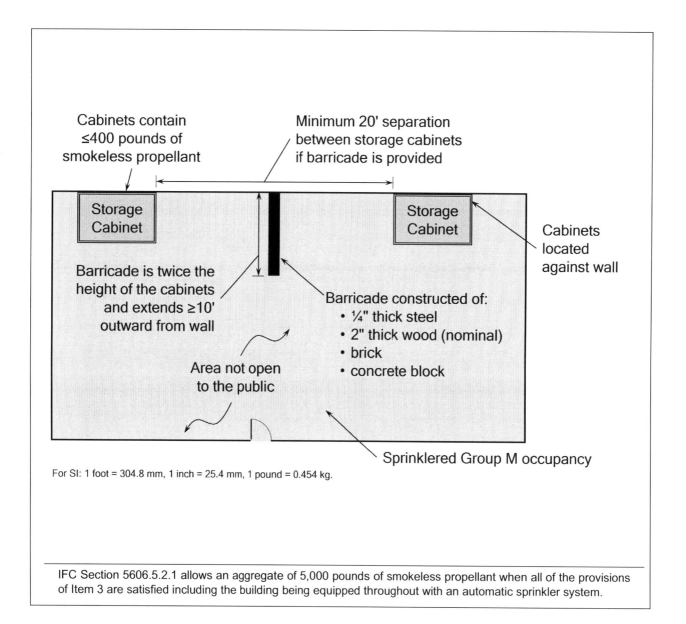

For SI: 1 foot = 304.8 mm, 1 inch = 25.4 mm, 1 pound = 0.454 kg.

IFC Section 5606.5.2.1 allows an aggregate of 5,000 pounds of smokeless propellant when all of the provisions of Item 3 are satisfied including the building being equipped throughout with an automatic sprinkler system.

Code Text: *Commercial reloading of small arms ammunition shall comply with Sections 5606.6.1 through 5606.6.8.*

Discussion and Commentary: Commercial ammunition reloading operations handle black powder or smokeless powder and must comply with specific safety criteria. The electrical wiring and equipment within 3 feet of the reloading equipment must be Class I, Division 2, Group A, and the work area must be provided with static electricity controls. The number of personnel in the reloading building is limited to the number necessary to conduct operations.

(Photograph courtesy of Getty Images.)

Reloading machines may be automated, and smokeless powder must be stored in the original shipping container until it is loaded into the reloading machine (IFC Section 5606.6.5).

Code Text: *Prior to issuing permits for a fireworks display, plans for the fireworks display, inspections of the display site and demonstrations of the display operations shall be approved. A plan establishing procedures to follow and actions to be taken in the event that a shell fails to ignite in, or discharge from, a mortar or fails to function over the fallout area or other malfunctions shall be provided to the fire code official.*

Discussion and Commentary: Prior to a permit being issued for fireworks or pyrotechnic displays, plans must be submitted to the fire code official for review and approval. If the permit application is for a fireworks display, NFPA 1123, *Code for Fireworks Displays*, is applicable; for pyrotechnic displays, see NFPA 1126, *Standard for the Use of Pyrotechnics Before a Proximate Audience.* For fireworks, Chapter 5 of NFPA 1123 requires that the site plan indicate the dimensions of the discharge area as well as spectator and fallout areas and that the required separation distances are provided.

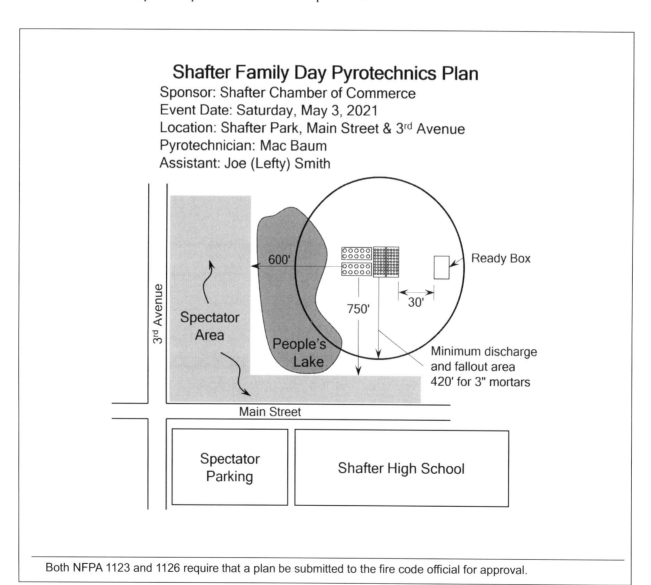

Both NFPA 1123 and 1126 require that a plan be submitted to the fire code official for approval.

Quiz

Study Session 15
IFC Chapter 56

1. Which National Fire Protection Association standard contains requirements for the storage of ammonium nitrate?

    a. NFPA 400   b. NFPA 480

    c. NFPA 1122   d. NFPA 1125

    Reference 5601.1.5

2. When explosive material is removed from a magazine, the material _____ is to be used first.

    a. On the top of a stack

    b. On the bottom of a stack

    c. Which can be accessed in the shortest amount of time

    d. Which is oldest and usable

    Reference 5604.7.9

3. Which of the following classifications is not assigned to mass detonating explosives?

    a. Division 1.1   b. Division 1.2

    c. Division 1.3   d. Division 1.5

    Reference 202

4. Which type of permanent magazine requires a means of ventilation?

    a. Type 1   b. Type 2

    c. Type 4   d. Type 5

    Reference 202

5. What type of magazine is prohibited for the storage of Division 1.2 explosive materials?

    a. Type 1   b. Type 2

    c. Type 3   (d.) Type 5

    Reference 5604.3

6. In which occupancy is the storage of explosives in an indoor magazine prohibited?

    (a.) Group A   b. Group F

    c. Group H   d. Group S

    Reference 5604.5.1.1

7. Given: A Type 1 magazine containing 5,500 pounds of a Division 1.1 explosive material. The magazine is not barricaded. What is the minimum separation distance required between the magazine and inhabited buildings?

    a. 130 feet   b. 730 feet

    c. 1,092 feet   (d.) 1,460 feet

    Reference 5604.5.2(1)

8. Without interpolation, what is the minimum unbarricaded separation distance between two Type 2 magazines, each storing 4,000 pounds of Division 1.3 explosives?

    (a.) 75   b. 100

    c. 115   d. 150

    Reference 5604.5.2 (2)

9. Given: Two magazines, each containing 32,000 pounds of Division 1.3 explosives. The intermagazine separation distance between the two magazines does not comply with IFC Section 5604.5.2.1. What is the required separation distance, without interpolating, from the two magazines to inhabited buildings?

    a. 260 feet   (b.) 270 feet

    c. 280 feet   d. 290 feet

    Reference 5604.5.2(2)

10. What is the maximum number of Type 3 magazines allowed at a single blasting site?

    a. one   b. two

    c. three   d. four

    Reference 5605.3.3

11. What type of magazine is permitted to have exposed ferrous metal on the interior of the magazine?

    a. Type 2 magazine   b. Type 3 magazine

    c. Type 4 magazine   d. Type 5 magazine

    Reference 5604.6.4

12. What is the minimum clearance required between an explosives magazine and vegetative growth?

    a. 20 feet   b. 25 feet

    c. 50 feet   d. 100 feet

    Reference 5604.2.3

13. What is the maximum storage height for explosives inside of a magazine?

    a. 6 feet   b. 8 feet

    c. 10 feet   d. 2 feet from the top of the magazine

    Reference 5604.7.8

14. What is the maximum interval for the inspection of explosion magazines?

    a. 2 days   b. 3 days

    c. 5 days   d. 7 days

    Reference 5604.9

15. Given: A propellant classified as a Division 1.2 explosive is manufactured in each of two operating buildings, which are not barricaded. One of the buildings has an authorized net explosive weight of 1,800 pounds. The second building has an authorized net explosive weight of 2,300 pounds. What is the minimum required intraline distance (ILD) for these?

    a. 115 feet   b. 130 feet

    c. 260 feet   d. None of the above

    Reference 5605.3

16. Given: A Type 2 magazine is located outdoors adjacent to an operating building at a fireworks manufacturing facility. The intraline distance between the magazine and the operating building is 25 feet. What is the maximum permitted net explosive weight allowed in the magazine? A barricade is not provided.

    a. 50 pounds   b. 75 pounds

    c. 100 pounds   d. 200 pounds

Reference 5605.4.2

17. Which of the following is not required when a suspected misfire occurs in a blasting operation?

    a. search for unexploded charges

    b. personnel shall be excluded from the blast area when a misfire is found

    c. misfires shall be transported to the local fire department

    d. misfires shall be reported to the blasting supervisor

Reference 5607.15

18. What is the quantity limit for the storage of salute powder in an operating building used for the manufacturing of pyrotechnic materials?

    a. 1 pound   b. 5 pounds

    c. 10 pounds   d. 500 pounds

Reference 5605.6.8

19. What is the maximum number of small arms primers allowed to be displayed in a Group M occupancy?

    a. 1,000

    b. 10,000

    c. 20,000 if the building is sprinklered

    d. The quantity is not limited.

Reference 5606.5.1.3

20. When smokeless propellant is stored inside of a wooden box with minimum 1-inch nominal wall thickness, what is the maximum permitted amount in a Group R-3 occupancy?

    a. 20 pounds   b. 50 pounds

    c. 100 pounds   d. The quantity is not limited

Reference 5606.4.2

21. The maximum amount of smokeless propellants displayed in a Group M occupancy is _____ pounds.

    a. 1
    b. 5
    c. 10
    d. 20

Reference _5605.1.1_

22. What is the maximum amount of black powder that is allowed to be displayed in a Group M occupancy?

    a. 1 pound
    b. 20 pounds
    c. 100 pounds
    d. 800 pounds

Reference _5606.5.1.2_

23. When nonportable storage cabinets are used to increase the amount of smokeless propellants inside of a Group M occupancy, what is the maximum amount permitted in each cabinet?

    a. 100 pounds
    b. 400 pounds
    c. 800 pounds
    d. 5,000 pounds

Reference _5606.5.2.1 (2)_

24. What is the maximum amount of black powder that is allowed to be stored inside of a Group M occupancy?

    a. 50 pounds
    b. 100 pounds
    c. 800 pounds
    d. 5,000 pounds

Reference _5606.5.2.2_

25. When more than 750,000 small arms primers are stored in a Group M occupancy, what is the maximum number of primers permitted in a single storage cabinet?

    a. 100,000
    b. 200,000
    c. 500,000
    d. 750,000

Reference _5606.5.2.3_

26. In a Group M occupancy, what is the minimum separation required between small arms primers and oxidizers?

    a. 20 feet
    b. 25 feet
    c. 1-hour fire partition
    d. either b or c

Reference _5606.5.2.3(2.5)_

27. In jurisdictions where the retail sale of consumer fireworks is permitted, what is the standard containing the provisions for display of the product?

    a. NFPA 13 2019 edition

    (b.) NFPA 1124 2006 edition

    c. NFPA 400 2019 edition

    d. NFPA 1124 2017 edition

    Reference 5601.1.3
    Ex.4

28. Which of the following standards specify the requirements for the storage of fireworks at the display site?

    a. NFPA 1123

    b. NFPA 1126

    c. NFPA 495

    (d.) either a or b

    Reference 5608.5

29. What is the minimum required separation distance between mortars and ready boxes for display fireworks, 1.3G?

    a. 15 feet

    (b.) 25 feet

    c. 50 feet

    d. 100 feet

    Reference 5608.5.5

30. If unfired shells are found during a post-fireworks display inspection, what is the minimum duration that is required before the shell can be handled?

    a. 15 minutes after the start of the display

    (b.) 15 minutes after that particular shell was fired

    c. 15 minutes after the end of the show

    d. there is no minimum time, since it took a while to find the shell

    Reference 5608.10

31. For the purpose of determining minimum separation based on the quantity-distance (Q-D) tables, a detonating cord with a charge of 50 grains/foot equals _____ pounds of explosives per 1,000 feet of cord.

    a. 2

    b. 4

    c. 6

    (d.) 8

    Reference 5604.3.3

32. What is the intraline distance (ILD) for a Type I magazine built using noncombustible materials (IBC Type IIB construction) storing 63,400 pounds of Division 1.4 explosives?

     (a.) 50 feet   b. 100 feet

     c. 185 feet   d. 2,000 feet

     Reference _5604.5.2(3)_

33. An artificial barricade constructed to reduce the required separation distance between magazines and buildings must have a minimum thickness of _____.

     a. 6 inches   b. 1 foot

     (c.) 3 feet   d. 6 feet

     Reference _5602.1_

34. Using interpolation, what is the minimum separation distance between an inhabited building and a Type 1 magazine with 35,000 pounds of Division 1.3 explosives?

     a. 155 feet   b. 160 feet

     c. 215 feet   (d.) 225 feet

     Reference _5604.5.2(2)_

35. At a Group M occupancy, quantities of black powder exceeding _____ pounds must be stored in an outdoor magazine.

     a. 20   (b.) 50

     c. 100   d. 800

     Reference _5606.5.2.2_

2021 IFC Chapter 57
Flammable and Combustible Liquids

OBJECTIVE: To gain a basic understanding of the *International Fire Code®* (IFC®) general provision requirements and requirements for the storage, use, handling and dispensing of flammable and combustible liquids

REFERENCE: Chapter 57, 2021 IFC

KEY POINTS:
- What specific types or uses of flammable and combustible liquids are exempt from the requirements of Chapter 57?
- How are flammable and combustible liquids classified?
- How is the flash point temperature of a flammable or combustible liquid determined?
- What is the difference between a container and a portable tank?
- What are the requirements for hazardous (classified) location electrical equipment in areas using flammable liquids or heated combustible liquids?
- What are the requirements for the design and construction of flammable and combustible liquid piping systems?
- What are the requirements for the protection of piping supports for flammable and combustible liquids?
- What types of tanks can be used for storing flammable and combustible liquids?
- What are the requirements for the design, construction and installation of flammable and combustible liquid storage tanks?
- What is a normal vent on a tank? What is an emergency vent on a tank? What are the requirements for their proper design and installation?
- When is overfill protection required for above-ground storage tanks?
- What are vaulted storage tanks?
- When is foam fire protection required for above-ground storage tanks?
- What are the requirements for above-ground storage tanks installed inside of buildings?

- How are the separation distances between above-ground storage tanks and exposures including property lines, important buildings and public ways determined?

- What is a protected above-ground storage tank?

- What is the purpose of drainage and diking? When diking is used a means of containment, what is the minimum required volume of the dike?

- What are the requirements for locating underground storage tanks?

- What are the requirements for the removal or abandonment of underground and aboveground storage tanks?

- What are the requirements for liquid storage cabinets? Are these cabinets required to be listed?

- What are the requirements for rack, palletized and solid-pile storage of flammable and combustible liquids inside of buildings?

- What are the quantity limits for flammable and combustible liquids in one control area? Are Group M occupancies different?

- What methods are approved for the transfer of Class I, II and III liquids?

- What specific limitations are applied to activities involving the use of flammable and combustible liquids for cleaning?

- What are the general requirements for use, dispensing and mixing of liquids inside of a building?

- What are the requirements for use, dispensing and mixing of liquids outside of buildings?

- What is a solvent distillation unit and the requirements for their location and operation?

- What are alcohol-based hand rubs and the requirements for their storage and use inside of buildings?

- What is on-demand mobile fueling?

- What requirements are applicable to on-demand mobile fueling?

Code Text: *This chapter shall not apply to liquids as otherwise provided in other laws or regulations or chapters of this code, including. . .*

(See IFC Section 5701.2 for 13 items.)

Discussion and Commentary: Chapter 57 contains the minimum requirements for the storage, use, dispensing and handling of flammable and combustible liquids. Note that dispensing of these liquids into motor vehicles is also regulated by Chapter 23. Certain liquids that are classified as either flammable or combustible are exempt from the requirements of Chapter 57. Many of the exceptions apply because the liquids are regulated elsewhere in the IFC. For example, home heating oil systems are regulated in accordance with IFC Section 605. Liquids that do not have a "fire point" are exempted from Chapter 57 requirements. In this case, the liquid has a flash point. However, once the liquid has flashed in the test apparatus, it no longer sustains combustion for at least 5 seconds, a requirement of ASTM D92, *Test Method for Flash and Fire Points by Cleveland Open Cup Tester*. If the liquid does not continue to burn, the hazard is gone, and therefore, these liquids are exempt. These liquids are typically water-based paints.

Off-site transportation of flammable and combustible liquids is not regulated by the IFC. See IFC Section 5701.2, Item 13.

Code Text: *Flammable and combustible liquids shall be classified in accordance with the definitions in Chapter 2.*

When mixed with lower flash-point liquids, Class II or III liquids are capable of assuming the characteristics of the lower flash-point liquids. Under such conditions the appropriate provisions of this chapter for the actual flash point of the mixed liquid shall apply.

When heated above their flash points, Class II and III liquids assume the characteristics of Class I liquids. Under such conditions, the appropriate provisions of this chapter for flammable liquids shall apply.

Discussion and Commentary: Liquids are classified as either being flammable or combustible as the result of flash point and boiling point temperature testing. All of the flash point tests specified in the IFC are closed cup tests. Closed cup tests for determining flash point are specified because they have a greater degree of reproducibility. For a given liquid sample, the closed cup test results must be reproducible within a plus or minus tolerance of 3°F. Open cup test results are allowed a tolerance of plus or minus 9°F. Note that when combustible liquids are heated above their flash points, the IFC correctly indicates that these liquids are to be treated as Class I liquids. Heating a liquid increases its ability to vaporize. It is the vapors that burn; liquids themselves do not burn.

Flammable and Combustible Liquids Classified by Flash Point and Boiling Point

CLASSIFICATION	FLASH POINT	BOILING POINT
FLAMMABLE LIQUIDS		
Class IA	< 73°F	< 100°F
Class IB	< 73°F	≥ 100°F
Class IC	≥ 73°F and < 100°F	Not applicable
COMBUSTIBLE LIQUIDS		
Class II	≥ 100°F and < 140°F	Not applicable
Class IIIA	≥ 140°F and < 200°F	Not applicable
Class IIIB	≥ 200°F	Not applicable

Vapor pressure is used to measure the volatility of a liquid. Generally speaking, the higher a liquid's vapor pressure the lower its flash point and boiling point temperature.

Code Text: *Areas where flammable liquids are stored, handled, dispensed or mixed shall be in accordance with Table 5703.1.1. A classified area shall not extend beyond an unpierced floor, roof or other solid partition.*

The extent of the classified area is allowed to be reduced, or eliminated, where sufficient technical justification is provided to the fire code official that a concentration in the area in excess of 25 percent of the lower flammable limit (LFL) cannot be generated.

Discussion and Commentary: Classified locations are areas where electrical equipment must be designed so as not to constitute a source of ignition. There are a number of systems available for electrical equipment to be designed to so as not to constitute a source of ignition, including explosion proof fixtures, hermetically sealed equipment, the use of pressurization or purging of equipment, oil immersed equipment, or intrinsically safe electrical equipment. Whatever method is used, it must also meet the requirements of NFPA 70, *National Electrical Code.* The *National Electrical Code* requires that a classified electrical location be determined based on the Class of the material, the appropriate classification for the material (Group) and the design condition that may make the electrical equipment either a source of ignition or a potential source of ignition (division). Ventilation is often provided to reduce any released flammable vapors. In areas where adequate ventilation is provided, and the lower flammable limit is maintained below 25 percent, the size of the classified area can be reduced.

EXPLANATION OF *NATIONAL ELECTRICAL CODE* CLASSIFIED (HAZARDOUS) LOCATION TERMS

CLASS	
Class	**Explanation**
I	Vapors of flammable liquids or flammable gases
II	Carbon based or metal combustible dusts
III	Combustible fibers or flyings
GROUP	
Class	**Explanation**
A	Acetylene
B	Materials such as hydrogen
C	Materials such as ethylene, ethylene oxide or propylene
D	Materials such as gasoline, propane or methyl ethyl ketone
E	Combustible metal dusts such as aluminum
F	Carbon based dusts such as coal or carbon black
G	Combustible dusts such as flour, plastics, grains or wood
DIVISION	
Division	**Explanation**
1	An atmosphere where flammable vapors or gases, combustible dusts or ignitable fibers or flyings are present
2	An atmosphere where flammable vapors or gases, combustible dusts or ignitable fibers or flyings may be present

The *National Electrical Code* also permits the use of a zone classification system in lieu of the division system. This system is based on the European Union's hazardous location classification system.

Code Text: *The fire code official is authorized to require warning signs for the purpose of identifying the hazards of storing or using flammable liquids. Signage for identification and warning such as for the inherent hazard of flammable liquids or smoking shall be provided in accordance with this chapter and Sections 5003.5 and 5003.6.*

Discussion and Commentary: Proper identification of the presence of flammable or combustible liquids is important to facility employees and emergency responders. Accordingly, IFC Section 5703.5 requires that flammable and combustible liquid storage and use locations be identified. This includes identifying that the hazard is present, providing warning statements as to the inherent hazards of the stored liquids and controlling ignition sources such as smoking.

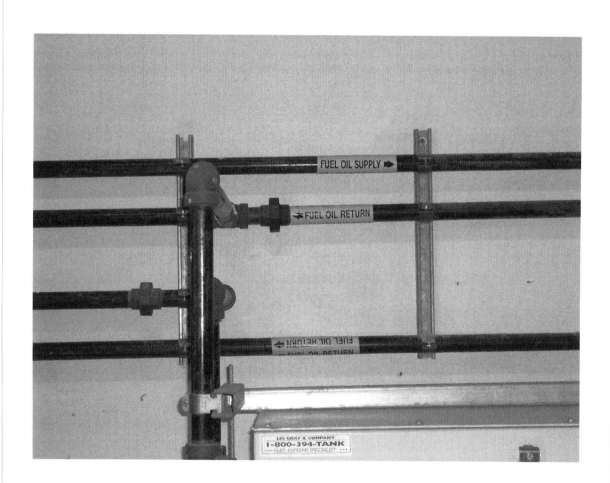

Piping containing flammable or combustible liquids must also be identified. The photograph illustrates labeling on the piping connected to the diesel tank, as required by IFC Section 5703.5.2.

Topic: Protection from External Corrosion and Galvanic Action	**Category:** Flammable and Combustible Liquids
Reference: IFC 5703.6.5	**Subject:** General Requirements

Code Text: *Where subject to external corrosion, piping, related fluid-handling components and supports for both underground and above-ground applications shall be fabricated from non-corrosive materials, and coated or provided with corrosion protection. Dissimilar metallic parts that promote galvanic action shall not be joined.*

Discussion and Commentary: Leaks or total failures of pressure-containing components such as piping, supports and fittings have resulted from internal or external corrosion. Internal corrosion can result from the material being conveyed in the system. Consider the hazardous material acetic acid. It is classified as a Corrosive and Class II Combustible liquid. Acetic acid will rapidly attack and destroy 304 series stainless steel and carbon steel but can be safely handled using 316 series stainless steel. Proper selection of materials that will be wetted by the liquid in the piping system is important to ensuring that piping systems remain liquid tight.

Although proper selection of the pipe and fitting materials of construction is important, it is equally important that gaskets, pump seals and other materials wetted by the stored liquid also be chemically compatible.

Code Text: *Above-ground tanks with connections located below normal liquid level shall be provided with internal or external isolation valves located as close as practical to the shell of the tank. Except for liquids whose chemical characteristics are incompatible with steel, such valves, when external, and their connections to the tank shall be of steel.*

Discussion and Commentary: Valves are critical in the control and direction of liquid flow. Because of their importance, any connection or tank nozzle requires a valve that is located as close as practical to the tank's shell. The type of valve selected is also important. Valves must be designed to the specific application and the design pressure and flow of the system. The IFC requires that all valves that are installed externally be constructed of steel. An issue with this language is that the types of steel allowed or prohibited are not indicated. Cast iron is a form of steel, but it should never be used for flammable or combustible liquids valves and piping systems, because it is very susceptible to fracturing if heated. The concern is water or foam-water from a fire stream impacting the cast iron. This can cause it to fail catastrophically.

This photograph illustrates a 3-inch gate valve installed on the nozzle of a storage tank. Outlets on storage tanks are commonly identified and referred to as nozzles rather than outlets.

Code Text: *Joints shall be liquid tight and shall be welded, flanged or threaded except that listed flexible connectors are allowed in accordance with Section 5703.6.9. Threaded or flanged joints shall fit tightly by using approved methods and materials for the type of joint. Joints in piping systems used for Class I liquids shall be welded when located in concealed spaces within buildings.*

Nonmetallic joints shall be approved and shall be installed in accordance with the manufacturer's instructions.

Pipe joints that are dependent on the friction characteristics or resiliency of combustible materials for liquid tightness of piping shall not be used in buildings. Piping shall be secured to prevent disengagement at the fitting.

Discussion and Commentary: Typical failures in piping occur at joints and fittings rather than the pipe itself. The reason that the predominance of failures occurs at joints and fittings is that these components cannot carry the same amount of pressure when compared to the pressure containment ability of the pipe. The IFC recognizes three assembly methods: welding, flanged assembly or threaded assembly. Nonmetallic pipe and joints are also permitted; however, NFPA 30 *Flammable and Combustible Liquids Code* listings specifically limit them to underground uses. It is possible to use nonmetallic pipe and joints in above-ground applications. However, these generally involve the use of plastics lining the interior of a carbon steel pipe.

Piping assembled using welded and flange construction methods.

Topic: Use of Tank Vehicles as Storage Tanks	**Category:** Flammable and Combustible Liquids
Reference: IFC 5704.2.2	**Subject:** Storage

Code Text: *Tank cars and tank vehicles shall not be used as storage tanks.*

Discussion and Commentary: This is an important provision because it prohibits the use of DOT approved tank vehicles and tank cars as permanent storage tanks. Although railroad tank cars are required by DOT to be constructed of carbon steel, DOT tank vehicles are permitted to be constructed of aluminum. Aluminum exhibits a lower melting point when compared to carbon steel. In addition, certain DOT cargo tankers (such as those used for milk) do not require a means of emergency venting. Accordingly, IFC Section 5704.2.2 does not permit the use of DOT tank vehicles or tank cars as permanent storage tanks.

An 8,000 gallon DOT MC-307 cargo tanker improperly used as a permanent storage tank. Note the hose connected to the piping system, the cargo tanker's proximity to the building wall and the lack of secondary containment.

Topic: Construction Requirements for Tanks	**Category:** Flammable and Combustible Liquids
Reference: IFC 5704.2.7	**Subject:** Storage

Code Text: *The design, fabrication and construction of tanks shall comply with NFPA 30. Each tank shall bear a permanent nameplate or marking indicating the standard used as the basis of design.*

Discussion and Commentary: NFPA 30, *Flammable and Combustible Liquids Code* recognizes two methods of constructing underground storage tanks (UST) or above-ground storage tanks (AST): either a shop-fabricated tank or a field-erected tank. Shop-fabricated tanks are always used for USTs and for ASTs with a nominal volume of 50,000 gallons or less. These tanks are normally listed by a third-party testing laboratory such as UL or Southwest Research Institute. Shop-fabricated tanks are constructed and assembled inside of a manufacturing building and are shipped as a completed storage tank, minus any of the desired end use components such as valves and piping. A field-erected tank is fabricated in pieces and is assembled on site. These tanks are not listed, but they are constructed to the design standards and requirements of the American Petroleum Institute. Their volume or diameter is not limited by the IFC or NFPA 30.

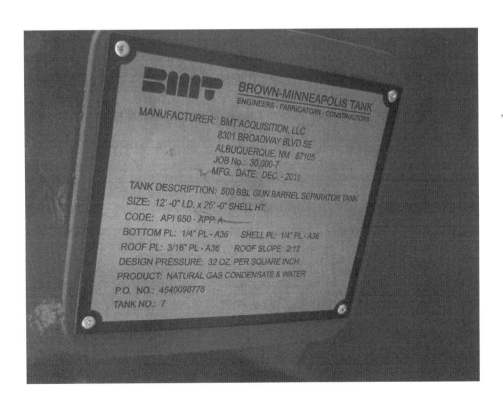

All tanks require a nameplate. The nameplate indicates the standard of construction and the design conditions for the storage tank. This photograph illustrates the nameplate for a 500 barrel storage tank. The tank was constructed and erected in accordance with API Standard 650.

Topic: Vent Pipe Outlets	Category: Flammable and Combustible Liquids
Reference: IFC 5704.2.7.3.3	Subject: Storage

Code Text: *Vent pipe outlets for tanks storing Class I, II or IIIA liquids shall be located such that the vapors are released at a safe point outside of buildings and not less than 12 feet (3658 mm) above the finished ground level. Vapors shall be discharged upward or horizontally away from adjacent walls to assist in vapor dispersion. Vent outlets shall be located such that flammable vapors will not be trapped by eaves or other obstructions and shall be not less than 5 feet (1524 mm) from building openings or lot lines of properties that can be built upon. Vent outlets on atmospheric tanks storing Class IIIB liquids are allowed to discharge inside a building where the vent is a normally closed vent.* **Exception:** *Vent pipe outlets on tanks storing Class IIIB liquid inside buildings and connected to fuel-burning equipment shall be located such that the vapors are released to a safe location outside of buildings.*

Discussion and Commentary: As product leaves a tank from dispensing or use, the tank needs to be vented to prevent collapsing the tank. When the tank is refilled, the tank also needs to be vented to avoid overpressure and rupture. This routine venting operation occurs through the normal vent. The outlet of the normal vent is required to be twelve feet above the ground. At the point of vapor release, the vapor concentration is very high and most likely at or above the lower flammable limit (LFL). Releasing the vapors at this height allows the vapors to mix with air as they fall to the ground, diluting the concentration to below the LFL. The design allows for a safe release of flammable vapors.

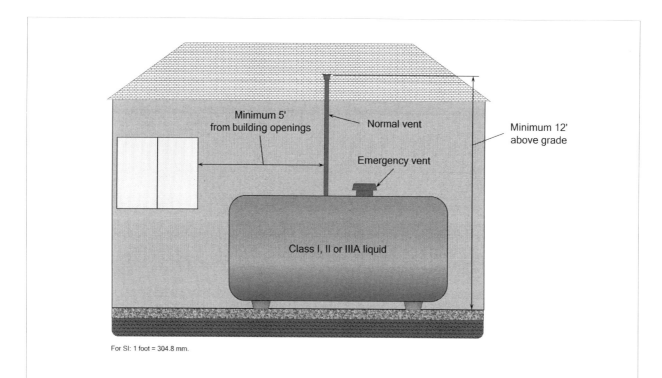

For SI: 1 foot = 304.8 mm.

The normal vent on a tank containing a Class IIIB liquid can terminate inside the building provided it is a normally closed vent. Vents that are not normally closed must terminate outdoors in a safe location.

2021 IFC Study Companion

Topic: Emergency Venting

Reference: IFC 5704.2.7.4

Category: Flammable and Combustible Liquids

Subject: Storage

Code Text: *Stationary, above-ground tanks shall be equipped with additional venting that will relieve excessive internal pressure caused by exposure to fires. Emergency vents for Class I, II and IIIA liquids shall not discharge inside buildings. The venting shall be installed and maintained in accordance with Section 22.7 of NFPA 30.* **Exceptions:** *(1) Tanks larger than 12,000 gallons (45 420 L) in capacity storing Class IIIB liquids which are not within the diked area or the drainage path of Class I or II liquids do not require emergency relief venting, (2) Emergency vents on protected above-ground tanks complying with UL 2085 containing Class II or IIIA liquids are allowed to discharge inside the building.*

Discussion and Commentary: Except for tanks larger than 12,000 gallons storing Class IIIB liquids that are not within the dike or drainage of Class I or II liquids, all above-ground storage tanks require an emergency vent. An emergency vent is designed to vent the vapor produced when an AST is heated by either a pool or exposure fire. Failing to provide an emergency vent can result in fire fighter and civilian deaths. Nineteen fire fighters were killed in 1962 in an incident involving a low pressure storage tank in Sunray, Texas. Six Kansas City fire fighters died because of a tank explosion in 1959. In 1967, three fire fighters were killed and 67 civilians were injured when a tank without an emergency vent exploded in Kennadale, Texas. Emergency vents may be direct action type, or the tank may vent by construction.

A direct action emergency vent. The spring loaded vent cover is secured by a graphite pin that will break when the tank's internal pressure reaches 8 psi of pressure. Emergency vents are sized based on the tank's orientation (horizontal or vertical), it's geometry (rectangular or cylindrical) and the stored liquid's heat of vaporization.

Code Text: *An approved means or method in accordance with Section 5704.2.9.7.5 shall be provided to prevent the overfill of all Class I, II and IIIA liquid storage tanks. Storage tanks in refineries, bulk plants or terminals regulated by Sections 5706.4 or 5706.7 shall have overfill protection in accordance with API 2350.*

An approved means or method in accordance with Section 5704.2.9.7.5 shall be provided to prevent the overfilling of Class IIIB liquid storage tanks connected to fuel-burning equipment inside buildings. **Exception:** *Outside above-ground tanks with a capacity of 1,320 gallons (5000 L) or less.*

Discussion and Commentary: All tanks storing Class I, II or IIIA liquids and Class IIIB liquids where connected to fuel-burning equipment are required to have an approved method of overfill protection, unless the tank is above ground, located outside and not more than 1,320 gallons. The method of overfill protection must comply with one of the two prescribed methods in IFC Section 5704.2.9.7.5. A system designed to indicate when the liquid level is at 90 percent of the tank volume and to stop the delivery of fuel at 95 percent may be used, or a flow limiting valve may be provided in the tank fill connection. For storage tanks at bulk plants or terminals, the overfill protection system must comply with API 2350 *Overfill Protection for Storage Tanks in Petroleum Facilities.*

The photograph illustrates a variable liquid level gauge. The gauge is calibrated in feet and inches and is equipped with high and high-high level alarms. Note the electrical conduit in the bottom of the gauge. It contains conductors terminated into the tank's control panel and the pipeline operations center. Activation of the high-high alarm stops the transfer pump supplying the storage tank and alerts bulk terminal personnel of the potential for a tank overfill.

Code Text: *Where required by the fire code official, foam fire protection shall be provided for above-ground tanks, other than pressure tanks operating at or above 1 pound per square inch gauge (psig) (6.89 kPa) where such tank, or group of tanks spaced less than 50 feet (15 240 mm) apart measured shell to shell, has a liquid surface area in excess of 1,500 square feet (139 m²), and is in accordance with one of the following . . .*

(See IFC Section 5704.2.9.2.1 for Items 1 through 4.)

Discussion and Commentary: Petroleum terminals can be required to provide foam fire protection based on this section. However, these requirements are based on the construction of storage tanks and potential exposed surface area of liquid. For example, pressure tanks operating above 1 PSIG are not atmospheric tanks. These are low pressure tanks and are used for the storage of natural gas and liquefied petroleum gases. To attempt to provide foam fire protection on these tanks is futile because the vapor from the stored liquid could leak through the foam chambers and cause a fire or explosion. For atmospheric tanks, the IFC does allow the fire code official to require foam fire protection when tanks are located less than 50 feet apart (measured from one tank shell to another) and the aggregate liquid surface area exceeds 1,500 square feet.

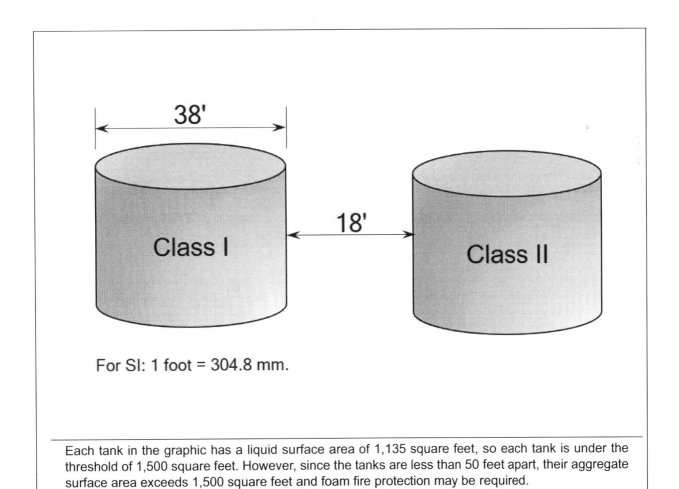

For SI: 1 foot = 304.8 mm.

Each tank in the graphic has a liquid surface area of 1,135 square feet, so each tank is under the threshold of 1,500 square feet. However, since the tanks are less than 50 feet apart, their aggregate surface area exceeds 1,500 square feet and foam fire protection may be required.

Topic: Fire Protection of Supports	**Category:** Flammable and Combustible Liquids
Reference: IFC 5704.2.9.2.3	**Subject:** Storage

Code Text: *Supports or pilings for above-ground tanks storing Class I, II or IIIA liquids elevated more than 12 inches (305 mm) above grade shall have a fire-resistance rating of not less than 2 hours in accordance with the fire exposure criteria specified in ASTM E1529.*
Exceptions: (1) Structural supports tested as part of a protected above-ground tank in accordance with UL 2085, (2) Stationary tanks located outside of buildings when protected by an approved water-spray system designed in accordance with Chapter 9 and NFPA 15, (3) Stationary tanks located inside of buildings equipped throughout with an approved automatic sprinkler system designed in accordance with Section 903.3.1.1.

Discussion and Commentary: The purpose of this provision is to ensure that tanks supported by columns are protected in the event the columns are exposed to a pool fire. If a column collapses, the contents of the tank could be released and create a much larger (and more difficult) fire to manage. The requirements in ASTM E1529, *Standard Test Method for Determining Effects of Large Hydrocarbon Pool Fires on Structural Members and Assemblies* are based on the heat release and burning rate of hexane and are intended to protect vessels used for hydrocarbon processing applications.

The photograph illustrates columns coated with an FM Global-approved fire-resistant assembly for the protection of atmospheric storage tanks containing flammable liquids.

Code Text: *The area surrounding a tank or group of tanks shall be provided with drainage control or shall be diked to prevent accidental discharge of liquid from endangering adjacent tanks, adjoining property or reaching waterways.* ***Exceptions:*** *(1) The fire code official is authorized to alter or waive these requirements based on a technical report which demonstrates that such tank or group of tanks does not constitute a hazard to other tanks, waterways or adjoining property, after consideration of special features such as topographical conditions, nature of occupancy and proximity to buildings on the same or adjacent property, capacity, and construction of proposed tanks and character of liquids to be stored, and nature and quantity of private and public fire protection provided, (2) Drainage control and diking is not required for listed secondary containment tanks.*

Discussion and Commentary: All above-ground storage tanks require a means of containment, often referred to as diking. The dike is designed to contain the contents of the largest tank within the dike. Dikes are designed to protect and limit the spread of liquid in the event of a tank overfill or worse—failure of the storage tank. Dikes must be designed to withstand the hydrostatic force of the liquid against the dike wall. The IFC allows the fire code official to waive or alter the requirements based on an analysis prepared as a technical report. Tanks that are listed as being constructed with integral secondary containment do not require diking.

The photograph shows a containment dike for an above-ground storage tank. The containment dike must contain the contents of the largest release from a single tank within the containment area.

Code Text: *The design, construction and capacity of containers for the storage of Class I, II and IIIA liquids shall be in accordance with this section and Section 9.4 of NFPA 30.*

Discussion and Commentary: NFPA 30 contains very detailed requirements for the construction of containers and portable tanks storing flammable and combustible liquids. Containers can be constructed of glass, metal or plastic. Most important are containers constructed of plastics. Plastic containers have a very low reliability under fire exposure and can rapidly fail and result in a large pool fire that may not be controlled by an automatic sprinkler system. NFPA 30 establishes the maximum container or portable tank volumes based on the material of construction and the classification of the liquid.

Maximum Allowable Size – Containers, Intermediate Bulk Containers (IBCs) and Portable Tanks

CONTAINER TYPE	FLAMMABLE LIQUIDS			COMBUSTIBLE LIQUIDS	
	CLASS IA	CLASS IB	CLASS IC	CLASS II	CLASS IIIA
Glass	1 pint	1 quart	1.3 gallons	1.3 gallons	5.3 gallons
Metal (other than drums)	1.3 gallons	5.3 gallons	5.3 gallons	5.3 gallons	5.3 gallons
Approved plastic	1.3 gallons	5.3 gallons	5.3 gallons	5.3 gallons	5.3 gallons
Safety cans (listed)	2.6 gallons	5.3 gallons	5.3 gallons	5.3 gallons	5.3 gallons
Metal drums	119 gallons	119 gallons	119 gallons	119 gallons	119 gallons
Approved metal portable tanks and IBCs	793 gallons	793 gallons	793 gallons	793 gallons	793 gallons
Rigid plastic IBCs	NP	NP	NP	793 gallons	793 gallons
Composite IBCs with rigid inner receptacle	NP	NP	NP	793 gallons	793 gallons
Composite IBCs with flexible inner receptacle	NP	NP	NP	331 gallons	331 gallons
UN approved IBCs	NP	NP	NP	331 gallons	331 gallons
Non-bulk bag-in-box	NP	NP	NP	NP	NP
Polyethylene UN1H1, or UN1H2, or under DOTn exemption	1.3 gallon	5.3 gallons	5.3 gallons	119 gallons	119 gallons
Fiber drum	NP	NP	NP	119 gallons	119 gallons

NP = Not permitted

NFPA 30 limits the size of containers and portable tanks based on the construction of the container.

Code Text: *For occupancies other than Group M wholesale and retail sales uses, indoor storage of flammable and combustible liquids shall not exceed the maximum allowable quantities per control area indicated in Table 5003.1.1(1) and shall not exceed the additional limitations set forth in this section.*

For Group M occupancy wholesale and retail sales uses, indoor storage of flammable and combustible liquids shall not exceed the maximum allowable quantities per control area indicated in Table 5704.3.4.1.

Storage of hazardous production material flammable and combustible liquids in Group H-5 occupancies shall be in accordance with Chapter 27.

Discussion and Commentary: As with other regulated hazardous materials, the IFC establishes quantity limits for flammable and combustible liquids. The maximum allowable quantity per control area (MAQ) is based on the classification of the liquid, the number and location of the control areas, and any additional protection features such as automatic sprinkler protection or the use of storage cabinets. As a result of fire testing and differences in packaging, the MAQ for Group M occupancies has been increased to accommodate the display and storage of liquids in large retail home improvement stores. Finally, because of the unique nature of semiconductor fabrication facilities, the IFC refers the user to Chapter 27 when determining the MAQ for liquids.

Flammable and combustible liquids in retail occupancies can have larger allowable quantities, but have additional restrictions on container size and storage arrangements.

Code Text: *The following limits for quantities of stored flammable or combustible liquids shall not be exceeded: (1) Group A occupancies: Quantities in Group A occupancies shall not exceed that necessary for demonstration, treatment, laboratory work, maintenance purposes and operation of equipment, and shall not exceed quantities set forth in Table 5003.1.1(1).*

(See IFC Section 5704.3.4.2 for Items 2 through 8 for other occupancy limitations.)

Discussion and Commentary: The allowable quantity in certain occupancies is further restricted based on the life hazard in the building. For example, Item 1 limits the quantity of flammable and combustible liquids to only what is necessary for demonstration, treatment, lab work, maintenance or operation of equipment. These quantities are all that is allowed even though the MAQ could allow larger quantities. This section is intended to eliminate unnecessary storage in buildings where the product is not needed.

The quantity in rooms for drinking, dining, office and school use are limited to the amount necessary for demonstration, treatment, lab work, maintenance or operation of equipment in this Group B occupancy.

Code Text: *Piles shall be separated from each other by not less than 4-foot (1219 mm) aisles. Aisles shall be provided so that all containers are 20 feet (6096 mm) or less from an aisle. Where the storage of liquids is on racks, a minimum 4-foot-wide (1219 mm) aisle shall be provided between adjacent rows of racks and adjacent storage of liquids. Main aisles shall be not less than 8 feet (2438 mm) wide.*

Additional aisles shall be provided for access to doors, required windows and ventilation openings, standpipe connections, mechanical equipment and switches. Such aisles shall be not less than 3 feet (914 mm) in width, unless greater widths are required for separation of piles or racks, in which case the greater width shall be provided.

Discussion and Commentary: Once the MAQ is exceeded and additional controls such as more control areas, automatic sprinkler protection or storage cabinets cannot accommodate the required storage amounts, the permit holder has three options: (1) Move the material outside of the building, (2) Limit quantities to the MAQ as allowed when the building is sprinklered or the liquids are stored in cabinets or (3) Construct a liquid storage room. A liquid storage room is generally a Group H-3 occupancy designed for the storage of Class I, II and IIIA liquids. In a mixed occupancy building it is separated by a minimum 1-hour or greater fire barrier, depending on the classification of the adjacent occupancy. The room is also provided with either spill control or secondary containment, as well as mechanical ventilation and a properly designed automatic sprinkler system. Pile separation and aisle arrangements provide clearance for personnel to access the flammable and combustible liquids without interference with other piles. Egress from the room for evacuation and access to fire protection and other facilities within the room must be maintained.

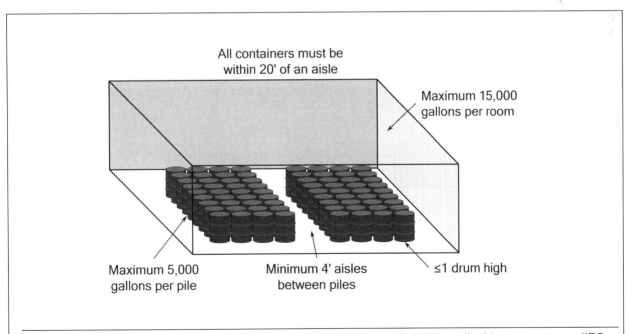

All containers must be within 20' of an aisle

Maximum 15,000 gallons per room

Maximum 5,000 gallons per pile

Minimum 4' aisles between piles

≤1 drum high

The aggregate quantity flammable and combustible liquids is limited in a liquid storage room (IFC Section 5704.3.7). The quantities in a liquid storage warehouse are unlimited (IFC Section 5704.3.8).

Topic: Outdoor Storage of Containers and Portable Tanks	**Category:** Flammable and Combustible Liquids
Reference: IFC 5704.4	**Subject:** Container and Portable Tank Storage

Code Text: *Storage of flammable and combustible liquids in closed containers and portable tanks outside of buildings shall be in accordance with Section 5703 and Sections 5704.4.1 through 5704.4.8. Capacity limits for containers and portable tanks shall be in accordance with Section 5704.3.*

Discussion and Commentary: Outdoor storage of flammable and combustible liquids is a common method used to avoid the requirements of the IFC and *International Building Code®* (IBC®) for the construction of liquid storage rooms and warehouses. But, outdoor storage is not exempt from all requirements. There are several requirements that still apply, including compliance with Table 5704.4.2, which sets forth quantity and height limits per pile based on whether the storage is in containers or portable tanks. In addition, requirements for spill control and secondary containment, protection from vehicles, security of the storage area and quantity limits for storage adjacent to buildings are also set forth in this section.

Footnote c in IFC Table 5704.4.2 requires separation distances to be doubled when a public fire department or private fire brigade is not available to apply cooling water.

Code Text: *Class I liquids or, when heated to or above their flash points, Class II and III liquids, shall be transferred by one of the following methods: (1) From safety cans complying with UL 30, (2) Through an approved closed piping system, (3) From containers or tanks by an approved pump taking suction through an opening in the top of the container or tank, (4) For Class IB, IC, II and III liquids, from containers or tanks by gravity through an approved self-closing or automatic-closing valve when the container or tank and dispensing operations are provided with spill control and secondary containment in accordance with Section 5703.4. Class IA liquids shall not be dispensed by gravity from tanks, (5) Approved engineered liquid transfer systems.* **Exception:** *Liquids in original shipping containers not exceeding a 5.3-gallon (20 L) capacity.*

Discussion and Commentary: Because of the hazards associated with the dispensing of liquids, the IFC establishes minimum controls for this activity. The preferred method for liquid transfer is to pump the liquid. This offers the best method of flow control. However, gravity dispensing can be safely performed when the appropriate controls are provided. This includes an approved self- or automatic-closing valve and a means of spill control and secondary containment. The IFC does not allow gravity dispensing of Class IA liquids unless the container volume is less than 5.3 gallons.

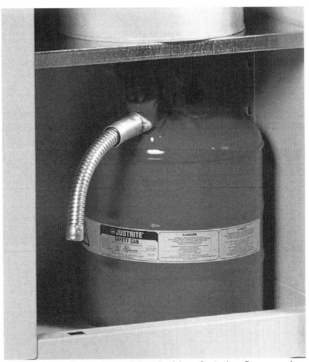

(Photograph courtesy of Justrite Manufacturing Company.)

Class I liquids can be stored and dispensed from a safety can listed to UL 30.

Code Text: *Vessels used for mixing or blending of Class I liquids and Class II or III liquids heated up to or above their flash points shall be provided with self-closing, tight-fitting, noncombustible lids that will control a fire within such vessel. **Exception:** Where such devices are impractical, approved automatic or manually controlled fire-extinguishing devices shall be provided.*

Discussion and Commentary: One of the main hazards with flammable liquids is vapors released to the atmosphere. These vapors create a flammable cloud when mixture with air is within the flammable range. Many Class I flammable liquids release vapors to the atmosphere at normal room temperatures. For that reason, mixing or blending vessels containing Class I flammable liquids must be protected either with a noncombustible lid or a fire-extinguishing appliance.

Class II and III combustibles present an identical hazard when those liquids are heated above their flash point. Therefore, mixing and blending vessels containing Class II or III combustible liquids must be protected in a similar manner to Class I flammable liquids.

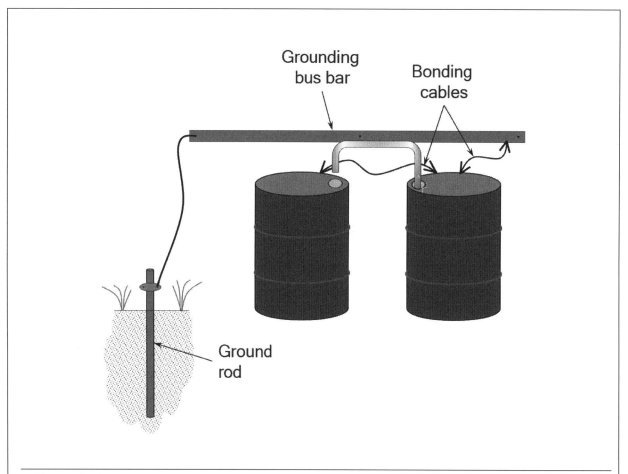

The static charge that is accumulated when transferring flammable and combustible liquids needs to be dissipated back to ground via electrically conductive material.

Code Text: *The use of wall-mounted dispensers containing alcohol-based hand rubs classified as Class I or II liquids shall be in accordance with all of the following . . .*

(See IFC Section 5705.5 for Items 1 through 7.)

Discussion and Commentary: Alcohol-based hand rubs (ABHR) are very common in health care occupancies because of their importance for control of infections. Studies by the American Hospital Association and the American Society of Hospital Engineers confirmed that ABHRs reduce infection and that their convenient location also contributed to frequency of use, thereby reducing the potential for infection caused by lack of adequate sanitation. The IFC allows ABHRs in all occupancies, not just Group I occupancies. The requirements are based on fire modeling of spill fires as well as quantity limits for each ABHR dispenser and the total amount of alcohol permitted within the corridors of control areas. Alcohol-based hand rubs typically contain Class I flammable liquids. Footnote p in Table 5003.1.1(1) states that the quantities contained in ABHRs is not counted when the units are installed and mounted in accordance with this section.

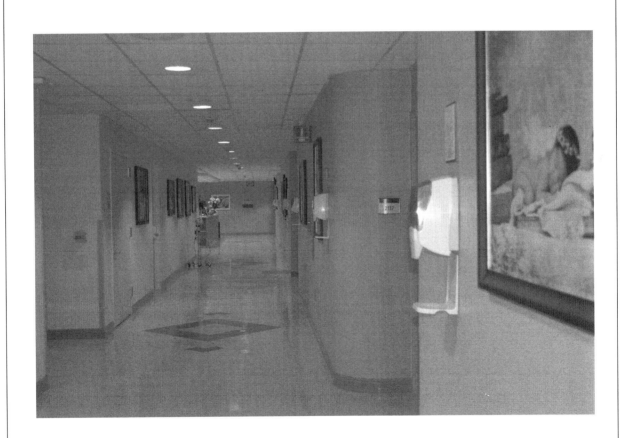

IFC Section 5705.5.1 specifies requirements for installation of ABHR in corridors. These requirements are more restrictive when compared to ABHRs in patient rooms.

Code Text: *Each mobile fueling vehicle shall comply with all local, state and federal requirements, as well as the following: (1) Mobile fueling vehicles with a chassis-mounted tank in excess of 110 gallons (416 L) shall also comply with the requirements of Section 5706.6 and NFPA 385, (2) The mobile fueling vehicle and its equipment shall be maintained in good repair, (3) Safety cans and approved metal containers shall be secured to the mobile fueling vehicle except when in use, (4) Fueling a motor vehicle from tanks or containers mounted in a trailer connected to a mobile fueling vehicle shall be prohibited.*

Discussion and Commentary: On-demand mobile fueling is not defined in the IFC, but it is becoming a common practice in many locations. With current technology, customers can now place an order to have their vehicle refueled. The on-demand mobile fueling vehicle brings the fuel to the vehicle, rather than the vehicle being driven to the service station. The on-demand mobile fueling operator is required to obtain a permit to conduct this operation. These requirements place the responsibility on the on-demand mobile fueling operator to take safety precautions at the site of fueling. Mobile fueling can only occur at locations which have been approved by the fire code official, but once the site is approved, fueling can occur at the site repeatedly.

A site plan for a mobile fueling operation should indicate the following:

1. All buildings and structures.
2. Lot lines or property lines.
3. Electric car chargers.
4. Solar photovoltaic parking lot canopies.
5. Appurtenances on-site and their use or function.
6. All uses adjacent to the lot lines of the site.
7. Fueling locations.
8. Locations of all storm drain openings and adjacent waterways or wetlands.
9. Information regarding slope, natural drainage, curbing and impounding.
10. How a spill will be kept on the site property.
11. Scale of the site plan.

A site plan is not required unless the fire code official requires it. The plan should include adequate information to evaluate the hazards and exposures (IFC Section 5707.3.3).

Quiz

Study Session 16

IFC Chapter 57

1. What is the maximum allowable quantity of Class IB flammable liquids in retail display in a nonsprinklered 40,000-square-foot Group M occupancy?

   a. 30 gallons

   b. 120 gallons

   c. 1,600 gallons

   d. 7,500 gallons

   Reference 5704.34.1

2. What is the total combined quantity of flammable and combustible liquids that can be stored in a liquid storage cabinet?

   a. 60 gallons

   b. 90 gallons

   c. 120 gallons

   d. It is established by the listing organization.

   Reference 5704.3.2.2

3. Which of the following is exempt from the requirements of Chapter 57?

   a. liquids with a flash point above 450°F

   b. liquids with an ignition temperature above 600°F

   c. low volatility liquids

   d. liquids with a flash point, but no fire point

   Reference 5701.2 Exc.7

4. Given: A liquid with a boiling point temperature of 134°F and a closed cup flash point temperature of 86°F. What is the classification of the liquid?

   a. Class IA flammable

   b. Class IB flammable

   c. Class IC combustible

   d. Class II combustible

   Reference 5702.1

5. At what quantity limit is a liquid storage cabinet required when flammable and combustible liquids are used for operations and maintenance of equipment?

    a. 10 gallons   b. 30 gallons

    c. when the MAQ is exceeded   d. none of the above

Reference 5704.3.4.4

6. What is the maximum allowable quantity of Class IC flammable liquids permitted for storage and use in the basement laboratory of a Group I-1 occupancy? The basement is one level below grade plane. The basement is one control area and is protected throughout by an automatic sprinkler system.

    a. 30 gallons   b. 45 gallons

    c. 60 gallons   d. 120 gallons

Reference 5704.3.5.1

7. What classified location division is assigned to the area within 3 feet of the normal vent for a 10,000 gallon above-ground storage tank storing a Class I liquid?

    a. Division 1   b. Division 2

    c. Division 3   d. Ordinary

Reference 5703.1.1

8. A new 60-foot section of $2^1/_2$-inch pipe is installed at a manufacturing plant. The pipe will contain a Class IC flammable liquid that is transferred from an outdoor storage tank to a new machine. The system is designed to operate a maximum pressure of 140 PSIG at 70°F. The contractor for the piping system requested a fire department inspection for the hydrostatic pressure test. What is the minimum test pressure for this new pipe section?

    a. 140 PSIG   b. 154 PSIG

    c. 210 PSIG   d. 250 PSIG

Reference 5703.6.3

9. Given: A Group H-3 liquid storage room. The room contains Class II liquids, the building is one story in height and the liquid is stored in portable tanks. Excluding the footnotes, what is the maximum pile height and quantity of liquid for each pile?

    a. 7 feet and 20,000 gallons   b. 10 feet and 40,000 gallons

    c. 14 feet and 40,000 gallons   d. 14 feet and 80,000 gallons

Reference 5704.3.6.3(2)

10. Which of the following methods is not a permitted method of pipe assembly for flammable and combustible liquid piping inside of a building?

    a. threaded   b. flanged

    c. welded   d. grooved joint with a rubber seal

Reference 5703.6.10

11. Given: Class IC flammable liquids stored outdoors in 55-gallon metal containers. A total volume of 2,100 gallons will be stored in one pile. The site is protected by a public fire department. What is the minimum separation distance required between the storage and the property line?

    a. 10 feet   b. 25 feet

    c. 50 feet   d. 100 feet

Reference 5704.4.2 Footnote D

12. What is the maximum height of storage for portable metal containers containing Class IIB liquid located in an outdoor storage area?

    a. 10 feet   b. 12 feet

    c. 14 feet   d. 18 feet

Reference 5704.4.2

13. What class of flammable or combustible liquid is allowed to have its tank vent discharge inside of a building?

    a. Class IC   b. Class II

    c. Class IIIA   d. Class IIIB

Reference 5704.2.7.3.3 Exc. 3

14. Which class of flammable liquids cannot be dispensed using the gravity method from tanks into containers?

    a. Class IA   b. Class IB

    c. Class IC   d. all of the above

Reference 5705.2.4 #4

15. Outdoor above-ground storage tanks containing Class II combustible liquids require overfill protection when the tank capacity exceeds _____ gallons?

    a. 660

    b. 1,320

    c. 5,000

    d. 10,000

    Reference 5704.2.7.5.8

16. Which class of flammable or combustible liquid is prohibited for use in cleaning operations?

    a. Class IA

    b. Class IB

    c. Class IC

    d. Class II

    Reference 5705.3.6.1

17. At what elevation is column protection required for elevated storage tanks located in a sprinklered building?

    a. 6 inches

    b. 12 inches

    c. 24 inches

    d. not required

    Reference 5704.2.9.2.3

18. Given: A Group H-2 occupancy using a Class II combustible liquid in an open system. At what threshold is spill control required?

    a. dispensing into containers exceeding 1.3 gallons

    b. the open system exceeds 5.3 gallons

    c. the aggregate container volume exceeds 55 gallons

    d. either a or b

    Reference 5705.3.7.5.3

19. Given: A Group H-3 occupancy using a Class II combustible liquid in a closed dispensing system. At what volume is secondary containment required?

    a. dispensing into containers exceeding 3 gallons

    b. the closed system exceeds 5.3 gallons

    c. the individual container volume exceeds 30 gallons

    d. the aggregate container volume exceeds 1,000 gallons

    Reference 5705.3.7.6.3

20. What is the maximum allowable quantity for dispensing of Class II combustible liquids in an outdoor control area?

    a. 10 gallons   b. 15 gallons

    c. 20 gallons   d. 30 gallons

Reference 5705.3.8.2

21. Which of the following overflow prevention devices are acceptable for a storage tank containing a Class II liquid located inside of a building?

    a. a float valve

    b. a preset meter on the fill line

    c. a valve actuated by the weight of the tank's contents

    d. all of the above

Reference 5704.2.9.5.1

22. What is the maximum size tank for a Tier 1 on-demand mobile fueling vehicle?

    a. 60 gallons   b. 110 gallons

    c. 1,600 gallons   d. tank size is not limited

Reference 5707.2.1 #1

23. What is the minimum separation distance required between two alcohol-based hand rub (ABHR) dispensers located in a corridor?

    a. 24 inches   b. 48 inches

    c. 72 inches   d. 96 inches

Reference 5705.5 #2
5705.5.1

24. What type of device is required on a protected above-ground storage tank when the external piping extends below the level of the top of the storage tank?

    a. an antisiphon device   b. a check valve

    c. an excess flow valve   d. a diverter valve

Reference 5704.2.9.7.9

25. An above-ground tank containing a Class IIIA liquid has a nozzle below the liquid level. What is the maximum distance between the tank shell and a shut off valve in the piping connected to the nozzle?

    a.   must be internal to the tank shell

    b.   as close as practical to the shell of the tank

    c.   before the first pipe joint or fitting

    d.   not required

Reference _5703.6.7_

26. What is the maximum allowable quantity permitted for non-aerosol ABHR dispensers located in a corridor? (The corridor is one control area.)

    a.   10 gallons   b.   20 gallons

    c.   30 gallons   d.   120 gallons

Reference _5705.5.1 #3_

27. What is the maximum capacity for a temporary above-ground storage tank used for the storage of a Class II liquid at a construction site?

    a.   1,100 gallons   b.   10,000 gallons

    c.   12,000 gallons   d.   20,000 gallons

Reference _5706.2.4_

28. Given: A permanent above-ground tank with a capacity of 1,000 gallons is used on a farm for dispensing gasoline. What type of valve is required on the tank because it is dispensing via gravity discharge?

    a.   manual shutoff valve

    b.   automatic shutoff valve that is heat activated

    c.   excess flow valve

    d.   both a and b

Reference _5706.2.5.2 #2_

29. The fire code official can require foam fire protection for which of the following tank configurations?

    a. A single above-ground storage tank with a diameter of 50 feet, containing a Class II liquid

    b. Two above-ground storage tanks located 30 feet apart, each with a diameter of 40 feet and containing Class I liquids

    c. A single above-ground storage tank with a diameter of 15 feet, containing a Class I liquid, where the fire code official determines that the tank represents an unusual fire exposure hazard

    (d.) All of the above

Reference 5704.29.2.1

30. Drainage control or diking is required for which of the following tanks?

    (a.) 12,000 gallon above-ground storage tank containing a Class IIIB liquid

    b. 1,000 gallon protected above-ground storage tank with listed secondary containment

    c. 2,000 gallon above-ground storage tank with an approved technical report indicating that the tank does not constitute a hazard

    d. All of the above

Reference 5704.2.10

31. Bulk transfer and process transfer operations for Class I liquids shall be separated from buildings, above-ground tanks, combustible materials, lot lines, public streets, public alleys or public ways by a distance of _____ feet.

    a. 15   b. 20

    (c.) 25   d. 50

Reference 5706.5.1.1

32. A Group H-3 use, dispensing and mixing room cannot be located _____ .

    a. in a building with other occupancies

    b. on a story above the grade plane

    (c.) in a basement

    d. none of the above

Reference 5705.3.7.2

33. Given: A Group B occupancy that has 25 gallons of fuel for lawn maintenance equipment. Where must the fuel be stored?

    a.   this quantity is not allowed   b.   in the janitor's closet

    c.   in a liquid storage cabinet   d.   in a detached shed

Reference 5704.3.4.9

34. When located inside buildings, which of the following tanks are allowed to have the emergency vent discharge inside the building?

    a.   protected above-ground tank containing a Class II liquid

    b.   UL 142 tank containing a Class IIIA liquid

    c.   any approved tank containing a Class IIIB liquid

    d.   both a and c

Reference 5704.2.7.4

35. Which of the following are correct for on-demand mobile fueling operations?

    a.   fire code official must be notified prior to every fuel delivery

    b.   when dispensing within 15 feet of a storm drain a method to keep a spill from reaching the storm drain is required

    c.   a fuel limit switch is required to limit a single delivery to 30 gallons

    d.   both b and c

Reference 5707.4.1
5707.5.3

2021 IFC Chapters 58 through 61

Flammable Gases and Flammable Cryogenic Fluids; Flammable Solids; Highly Toxic and Toxic Materials; and Liquefied Petroleum Gases

OBJECTIVE: To gain a basic understanding of the *International Fire Code®* (IFC®) requirements for flammable gases and solids, highly toxic and toxic materials, and liquefied petroleum gases.

REFERENCE: Chapters 58 through 61, 2021 IFC

KEY POINTS:
- What is a flammable gas? What is the scope of Chapter 58?
- What special limitations are applicable to flammable gases in Group A, B, E, I and R occupancies?
- Where and what types of shutoff valves are required for flammable compressed gases?
- What is the maximum allowable quantity for flammable gases?
- What is a hydrogen fuel gas room and what are the requirements?
- Given a specified volume of flammable gas, what are the minimum separation distances from regulated exposures such as property lines, public ways and buildings?
- Is gas detection required for flammable gas storage or use areas?
- What is a flammable solid?
- What is the maximum allowable quantity for flammable solids in a control area?
- What are the requirements for indoor storage of flammable solids in quantities exceeding the maximum allowable quantity in a single control area?
- What are the requirements for the storage of fine magnesium scrap?
- What is the cleaning and removal frequency for magnesium chips, turnings and fines?
- What are highly toxic or toxic materials?
- What is the maximum allowable quantity for highly toxic or toxic materials?
- When is a treatment system required for highly toxic liquids?

KEY POINTS:
(Cont'd)

- What special provisions apply to highly toxic or toxic solids or liquids stored beneath weather protection?

- What special limitations are applicable to highly toxic and toxic gases in certain occupancies?

- What are the requirements and options for highly toxic and toxic material treatment systems?

- What are the performance requirements for highly toxic and toxic material treatment systems?

- When is a gas detection system required for highly toxic or toxic compressed gases?

- What are the minimum separation distances for highly toxic or toxic compressed gases?

- What is required for an ozone gas generator?

- When are construction plans required for liquefied petroleum gas (LP-gas) installations?

- What are the separation requirements between an LP-gas tank and a building or property line?

- What is required when an LP-gas tank is no longer used?

- What are the requirements for the use of LP-gas in Group F occupancies?

- What are the requirements for the use of LP-gas in Group E and I occupancies?

- What is an overfill prevention device for LP-gas storage, and when is one required?

- Are there special requirements for the LP-gas cylinder exchange program?

- What quantity of LP-gas is permitted inside of buildings that are accessible to the public? What is the maximum cylinder volume allowed?

- What quantity of LP-gas is permitted inside of buildings that are not accessible to the public? What is the maximum cylinder volume allowed?

- Given a given amount of LP-gas, what are the minimum separation distances from exposures for outside storage of cylinders awaiting use, resale or exchange?

Topic: Flammable Gas and
     Flammable Liquefied Gas
Reference: IFC 5802.1, 202

Category: Flammable Gases and Flammable
     Cryogenic Fluids
Subject: Definitions

Code Text: ***Flammable Gas.*** *A material which is a gas at 68°F (20°C) or less at 14.7 pounds per square inch atmosphere (psia) (101 kPa) of pressure [a material that has a boiling point of 68°F (20°C) or less at 14.7 psia (101 kPa)] which: (1) Is ignitable at 14.7 psia (101 ka) when in a mixture of 13 percent or less by volume with air; or (2) Has a flammable range at 14.7 psia (101 kPa) with air of not less than 12 percent, regardless of the lower limit.*

    The limits specified shall be determined at 14.7 psi (101 kPa) of pressure and a temperature of 68°F (20°C) in accordance with ASTM E681.

   Flammable Liquefied Gas. *A liquefied compressed gas which, under a charged pressure, is partially liquid at a temperature of 68°F (20°C) and which is flammable.*

Discussion and Commentary: Gases are stored in cylinders by compressing the molecules, or they are stored as a liquid. Gases are considered flammable if they have a flammable range of at least 12 percent in air, regardless of the lower flammable limit or when it is ignitable in a mixture of 13 percent or less by volume in air. Compressed flammable gases include hydrogen and methane. Liquefied flammable gases include butane and ethane. Certain gases may exhibit flammable characteristics but may not be classified as flammable. For example, anhydrous ammonia exhibits a flammable range of 15.5 to 27 percent. Even though ammonia does have a limited flammability hazard, it is not classified as a flammable gas based on its flammable range.

A third method for storage of gases is to refrigerate the gas and condense it into a liquid. Flammable gases that are refrigerated into a liquid at temperatures below -130°F are defined as flammable cryogenic fluids.

Topic: Special Limitations	**Category:** Flammable Gases and Flammable Cryogenic Fluids
Reference: IFC 5803.1.1	**Subject:** Quantities below the MAQ

Code Text: *Flammable gases shall not be stored or used in Group A, E, I or R occupancies or in offices in Group B occupancies.* ***Exceptions:*** *(1) Cylinders of nonliquefied compressed gases not exceeding a capacity of 250 cubic feet (7.08 m³) or liquefied gases not exceeding a capacity of 40 pounds (18 kg) each at normal temperature and pressure (NTP) used for maintenance purposes, patient care or operation of equipment, (2) Food service operations in accordance with Section 6103.2.1.7, (3) Hydrogen gas systems located in a hydrogen fuel gas room constructed in accordance with Section 421 of the* International Building Code.

Discussion and Commentary: Storage in quantities below the maximum allowable quantity (MAQ) are still regulated by the IFC. The general hazardous material provisions in IFC Sections 5001 and 5003 and general provisions for flammable gases in IFC Section 5803 are applicable. Additional limitations apply to specific occupancies where the potential life hazard justifies a further reduction in the allowed quantities. Flammable gases are prohibited in Group A, E, I and R occupancies along with office spaces in Group B occupancies, even though they are below the MAQ. Some exceptions provide for limited use of flammable gases when in compliance with additional regulations.

The maximum allowable quantity for compressed flammable gases in one nonsprinklered control area is 1,000 cubic feet. The maximum allowable quantity for liquefied flammable gases is 150 pounds in one nonsprinklered control area. [IFC Table 5003.1.1(1)].

Topic: Emergency Shutoff	**Category:** Flammable Gases and Flammable Cryogenic Fluids
Reference: IFC 5803.1.3, 5803.1.3.1, 5803.1.3.2	**Subject:** General Requirements

Code Text: *Emergency shutoff. Compressed gas systems conveying flammable gases shall be provided with approved manual or automatic emergency shutoff valves that can be activated at each point of use and at each source.*

Shutoff at source. A manual or automatic fail-safe emergency shutoff valve shall be installed on supply piping at the cylinder or bulk source. Manual or automatic cylinder valves are allowed to be used as the required emergency shutoff valve where the source of supply is limited to unmanifolded cylinder sources.

Shutoff at point of use. A manual or automatic emergency shutoff valve shall be installed on the supply piping at the point of use or at a point where the equipment using the gas is connected to the supply system.

Discussion and Commentary: In the event of a flammable gas release, the priority is to control and stop the release of the gas. If the gas is ignited, the strategy is to either allow the fire to consume the gas or stop the flow of gas. Flammable gas fires should never be extinguished unless the flow of gas can be stopped. The IFC requires that either a manual or automatic shutoff valve be provided so that the flow of gas can be stopped in the event of a leak or fire. The valves can be manual or automatic. The cylinder valve can serve as the manual shutoff at the source if cylinders are not manifolded. A separate manual or automatic shutoff valve is required at the gas source if cylinders are manifolded.

(Photograph courtesy of Getty Images.)

Valves, along with other devices and piping, must be compatible with the flammable gas handled (IFC Section 5003.2.2.1).

Topic: Bonding of Electrically
           Conductive Material and Equipment

Reference: IFC 5803.1.5.1

Category: Flammable Gases and
           Flammable Cryogenic Fluids

Subject: General Requirements

Code Text: *Exposed noncurrent-carrying metal parts, including metal gas piping systems, that are part of flammable gas supply systems located in a hazardous (electrically classified) location shall be bonded to a grounded conductor in accordance with the provisions of NFPA 70.*

Discussion and Commentary: Any flammable gas piping that is located within a hazardous atmosphere must be bonded to an electrical ground. To determine if a room or area is classified as a hazardous location, inspect the installed electrical equipment to determine if it is listed for Class I, II or III locations and if the equipment is designed for use in a Division 1 or 2 atmosphere.

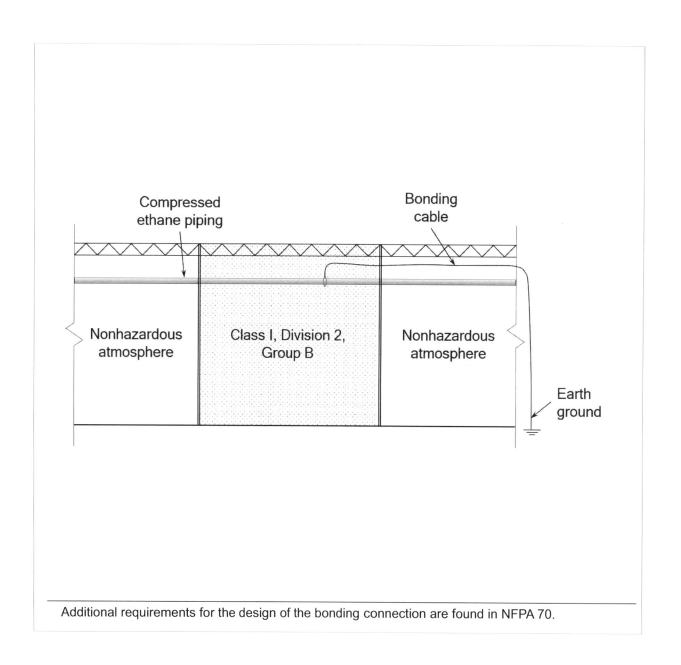

Additional requirements for the design of the bonding connection are found in NFPA 70.

Topic: Limitations	**Category:** Flammable Gases and Flammable Cryogenic Fluids
Reference: IFC 5806.2	**Subject:** Flammable Cryogenic Fluids

Code Text: *Storage of flammable cryogenic fluids in stationary containers outside of buildings is prohibited within the limits established by law as the limits of districts in which such storage is prohibited [JURISDICTION TO SPECIFY].*

Discussion and Commentary: Flammable cryogenic fluids include hydrogen and methane. Although the loss history is extremely low for releases, some communities may not allow flammable cryogenic installations because of land use issues. Section 5806.2 gives the code official the authority to limit the location of these flammable cryogenic fluids. The code official must establish and publish the boundary limits during the code adoption process. There are several sections of the IFC which are formatted similarly. These sections are identified on page vii of the IFC.

Refrigerated methane and hydrogen both have expansion ratios over 600:1, meaning that small release of a cryogenic fluid can create a large volume of flammable gas.

Code Text: *Hydrogen fuel gas rooms not exceeding the maximum allowable quantity per control area in Table 5003.1.1(1) shall be separated from other areas of the building in accordance with Section 509.1 of the* International Building Code.

Discussion and Commentary: A hydrogen fuel gas room could be classified as a Group H-2, or it could be an incidental use area within the building, depending on the quantity of gas. The MAQ is 1,000 cubic feet. This volume can be doubled when the building has a fire sprinkler system and doubled again when the gas is stored in gas cabinets or a gas room. The hydrogen fuel gas room qualifies as a gas room since it is required to have a separate ventilation system; therefore, the MAQ is 4,000 cubic feet. As an incidental use area, IBC Table 509.1 requires a 1-hour separation from Group B, F, M, S and U occupancies, and a 2-hour separation from Group A, E, I and R occupancies. When exceeding the MAQ, it would be classified as a Group H-2 occupancy and separated from the remainder of the building according to IBC Table 508.4, which could be up to a 4-hour requirement.

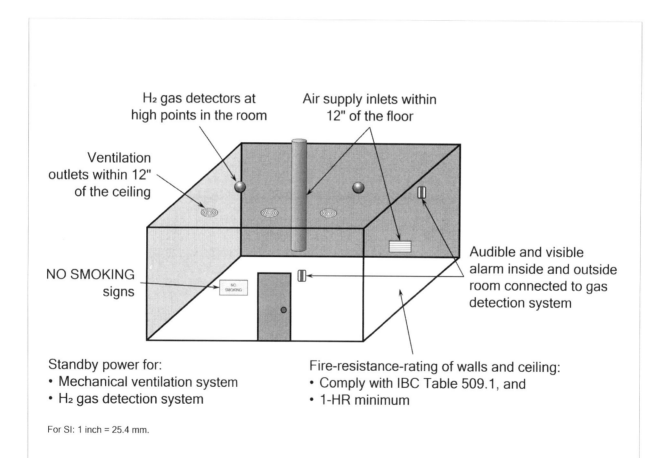

H_2 gas detectors at
high points in the room

Air supply inlets within
12" of the floor

Ventilation
outlets within 12"
of the ceiling

Audible and visible
alarm inside and outside
room connected to gas
detection system

NO SMOKING
signs

Standby power for:
• Mechanical ventilation system
• H_2 gas detection system

Fire-resistance-rating of walls and ceiling:
• Comply with IBC Table 509.1, and
• 1-HR minimum

For SI: 1 inch = 25.4 mm.

IFC Section 5808 contains several requirements for hydrogen fuel gas rooms, such as ventilation, gas detection, alarm system and standby power.

Topic: Flammable Solid

Reference: IFC 5902.1, 202

Category: Flammable Solids

Subject: Definitions

Code Text: *A solid, other than a blasting agent or explosive, that is capable of causing fire through friction, absorption of moisture, spontaneous chemical change, or retained heat from manufacturing or processing, or which has an ignition temperature below 212°F (100°C) or which burns so vigorously and persistently when ignited as to create a serious hazard. A chemical shall be considered a flammable solid as determined in accordance with the test method of CPSC 16 CFR Part 1500.44, if it ignites and burns with a self-sustained flame at a rate greater than 0.0866 inch (2.2 mm) per second along its major axis.*

Discussion and Commentary: Flammable solids are materials that have an ignition temperature less than 212°F or are capable of igniting through friction with other materials, absorption of other chemicals or moisture, or through a self-induced chemical change. Combustible metals such as titanium, magnesium or tantalum are examples of flammable solids. Flammable solids generally result in very luminescent fires that cannot be controlled using water. Their combustion byproducts are metal fumes, which are generally toxic, and which in small doses can cause damage to the liver or kidneys.

Many flammable solids are also classified as water reactive materials because they can liberate hydrogen gas when mixed with water.

Code Text: ***Indoor storage.*** *Indoor storage of flammable solids in amounts exceeding the maximum allowable quantity per control area indicated in Table 5003.1.1(1) shall be in accordance with Sections 5001, 5003, 5004 and this chapter.*

    Pile size limits and location. *Flammable solids stored in quantities greater than 1,000 cubic feet (28 m³) shall be separated into piles each not larger than 1,000 cubic feet (28 m³).*

    Aisles. *Aisle widths between piles shall not be less than the height of the piles or 4 feet (1219 mm), whichever is greater.*

    Basement storage. *Flammable solids shall not be stored in basements.*

Discussion and Commentary: When the storage amount of flammable solids exceeds the MAQ, the provisions in IFC Section 5904 are applicable. This section limits where the flammable solids may be stored and the maximum volume per pile or array of flammable solids. Whenever multiple storage arrays of flammable solids exist, the IFC also establishes minimum aisle dimensions between each storage array.

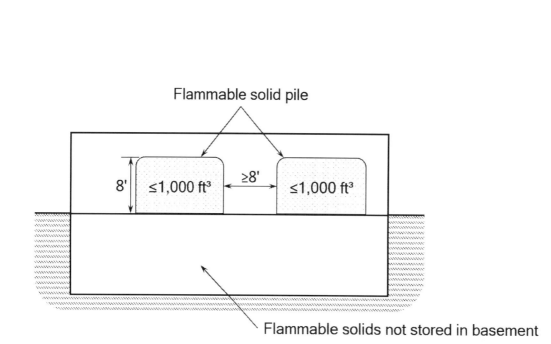

Flammable solid pile

8'   ≤1,000 ft³   ≥8'   ≤1,000 ft³

Flammable solids not stored in basement

For SI: 1 foot = 304.8 mm, 1 cubic foot = 0.2832 m³.

The pile volumes are intended to limit the available amount of fuel in each storage array and provide a separation to the adjacent pile to slow fire spread.

Code Text: *Outdoor storage of flammable solids shall not be located within 20 feet (6096 mm) of a building, lot line, public street, public alley, public way or means of egress. A 2-hour fire barrier without openings or penetrations and extending 30 inches (762 mm) above and to the sides of the storage area is allowed in lieu of such distance. The wall shall either be an independent structure, or the exterior wall of the building adjacent to the storage area.*

Discussion and Commentary: Flammable solids stored outdoors must comply with the outdoor control area requirements in Chapter 50 and the additional, or modified, requirements in Section 5904.2. Section 5904.2.1 specifies the separation to exposures and allows for a reduction to buildings or property lines when protected with 2-hour construction. The quantity in each pile is limited to 5,000 cubic feet (IFC Section 5904.2.2).

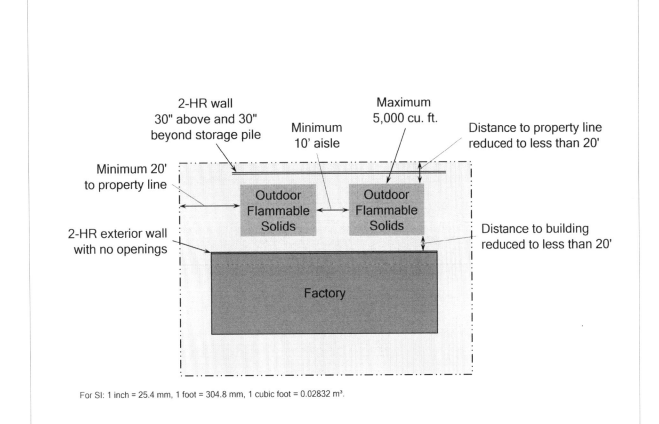

For SI: 1 inch = 25.4 mm, 1 foot = 304.8 mm, 1 cubic foot = 0.02832 m³.

Outdoor storage piles of flammable solids must be separated by an aisle which is a minimum width of one-half the storage height or 10 feet, whichever is greater (IFC Section 5904.2.2).

Code Text: *A material which produces a lethal dose or lethal concentration which falls within any of the following categories: (1) A chemical that has a median lethal dose (LD_{50}) of 50 milligrams or less per kilogram of body weight when administered orally to albino rats weighing between 200 and 300 grams each, (2) A chemical that has a median lethal dose (LD_{50}) of 200 milligrams or less per kilogram of body weight when administered by continuous contact for 24 hours (or less if death occurs within 24 hours) with the bare skin of albino rabbits weighing between 2 and 3 kilograms each, (3) A chemical that has a median lethal concentration (LC_{50}) in air of 200 parts per million by volume or less of gas or vapor, or 2 milligrams per liter or less of mist, fume or dust, when administered by continuous inhalation for one hour (or less if death occurs within 1 hour) to albino rats weighing between 200 and 300 grams each.*

Mixtures of these materials with ordinary materials, such as water, might not warrant classification as highly toxic. While this system is basically simple in application, any hazard evaluation that is required for the precise categorization of this type of material shall be performed by experienced, technically competent persons.

Discussion and Commentary: The measurement of toxicity used in the IFC is either median lethal concentration or median lethal dose. The terms LC_{50} and LD_{50} mean that at a given dosage of a chemical, 50 percent of the test animals died during the toxicology experiment. Inhalation hazards of lethal concentrations are measured in parts per million or milligrams per liter. Absorption hazards are measured using milligrams of toxin per kilogram of body weight administered onto the skin of the test animal. Ingestion hazards are measured using the mass of the toxic material orally administered to the test animals.

(Photograph courtesy of Getty Images.)

Source information for toxicity data includes the *Registry of Toxic Effects of Chemical Substances* and *Sax's Handbook of Dangerous Industrial Chemicals*. An excellent source of information is HMEx: the *Hazardous Materials Expert Assistant* software, which is an electronic database of more than 9,000 chemical names and synonyms. This program is available through the ICC Store at shop.iccsafe.org/catalogsearch/result/?cat=&q=hmex

Code Text: *Where overhead weather protection is provided for outdoor storage or use of highly toxic liquids or solids, and the weather protection is attached to a building, the storage or use area shall either be equipped throughout with an approved automatic sprinkler system in accordance with Section 903.3.1.1, or storage or use vessels shall be fire resistive. Weather protection shall be provided in accordance with Section 5004.13 for storage and Section 5005.3.9 for use.*

Discussion and Commentary: Highly toxic solids and liquids present the greatest health hazard to emergency responders and facility personnel. If these materials are stored outdoors underneath a weather protection canopy, the IFC has specific requirements for their protection. The section is applicable to use and storage areas which have exceeded the maximum allowable quantity in an outdoor storage area found in Table 5003.1.1(4). Therefore, when a weather protection canopy is attached to a building, either an approved automatic sprinkler system or fire-resistive vessels shall be provided. Note that the IFC does not specify a fire-resistance duration or the appropriate test method for determining a vessel's fire resistance.

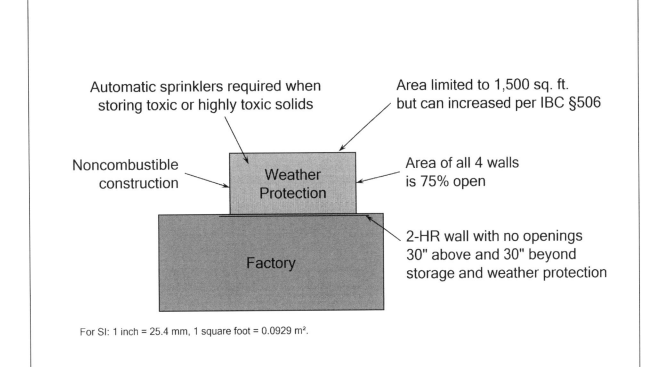

For SI: 1 inch = 25.4 mm, 1 square foot = 0.0929 m².

This provision applies only to highly toxic solids and liquids. The requirement for sprinklers or fire-resistant vessels does not apply to toxic solids and liquids. Weather protection for toxic and highly toxic gases must comply with Section 6004.3.3 and *International Building Code*® (IBC®) Section 414.6.1.

Code Text: *Gas cabinets containing highly toxic or toxic compressed gases shall comply with Section 5003.8.6 and the following requirements: (1) The average ventilation velocity at the face of gas cabinet access ports or windows shall be not less than 200 feet per minute (1.02 m/s) with not less than of 150 feet per minute (0.76 m/s) at any point of the access port or window, (2) Gas cabinets shall be connected to an exhaust system, (3) Gas cabinets shall not be used as the sole means of exhaust for any room or area, (4) The maximum number of cylinders located in a single gas cabinet shall not exceed three, except that cabinets containing cylinders not over 1 pound (0.454 kg) net contents are allowed to contain up to 100 cylinders, (5) Gas cabinets required by Section 6004.2 or 6004.3 shall be equipped with an approved automatic sprinkler system in accordance with Section 903.3.1.1. Alternative fire-extinguishing systems shall not be used.*

Discussion and Commentary: IFC Section 202 defines a gas cabinet as a fully enclosed, ventilated, noncombustible enclosure used to provide an isolated environment for compressed gas cylinders in storage or use. Doors and access ports for exchanging cylinders and accessing pressure-regulating controls are allowed to be included. When used for the storage and use of toxic or highly toxic gases, the IFC requires the cabinet to be connected to an exhaust system and have a minimum air velocity of 200 feet per minute at the face of any windows or access ports.

The IFC also permits the use of exhausted enclosures for the storage and use of highly toxic or toxic compressed gases (IFC Section 6004.1.3).

Topic: Leaking Cylinders and Tanks

Category: Highly Toxic and Toxic Materials

Reference: IFC 6004.2.2.3

Subject: Compressed Gases

Code Text: *One or more gas cabinets or exhausted enclosures shall be provided to handle leaking cylinders, containers or tanks.* **Exceptions:** *(1) Where cylinders, containers or tanks are located within gas cabinets or exhausted enclosures, (2) Where approved containment vessels or containment systems are provided in accordance with all of the following: (2.1) Containment vessels or containment systems shall be capable of fully containing or terminating a release, (2.2) Trained personnel shall be available at an approved location, (2.3) Containment vessels or containment systems shall be capable of being transported to the leaking cylinder, container or tank.*

Discussion and Commentary: The IFC requires that a gas cabinet or exhausted enclosure be provided for leaking cylinders. This cabinet or exhausted enclosure is connected to a treatment system designed to meet the requirements of IFC Section 6004.2.2.7. Because of the expense associated with designing and constructing such a system, the IFC allows the use of containment vessels or systems so that a leaking cylinder can be rendered safe and transported to a location for treatment and disposal of its contents.

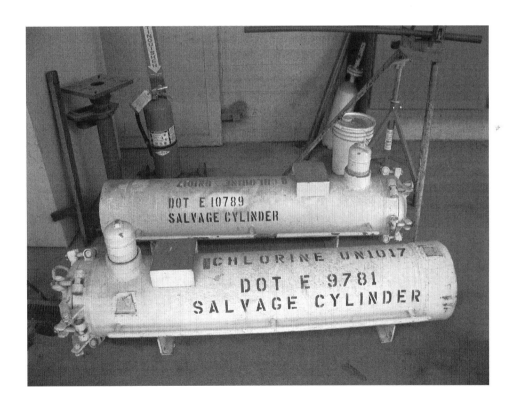

The use of containment vessels or systems in lieu of gas cabinets or exhausted enclosures must be approved by the fire code official. A critical element is to ensure that sufficient staffing is available to deploy the containment vessel or system and that the appropriate protective clothing and respiratory protection equipment is available.

Code Text:　*The exhaust ventilation from gas cabinets, exhausted enclosures and gas rooms, and local exhaust systems required in Sections 6004.2.2.4 and 6004.2.2.5 shall be directed to a treatment system. The treatment system shall be utilized to handle the accidental release of gas and to process exhaust ventilation. The treatment system shall be designed in accordance with Sections 6004.2.2.7.1 through 6004.2.2.7.5 and Section 510 of the* International Mechanical Code.

(See IFC Section 6004.2.2.7 Exceptions 1 and 2.)

Discussion and Commentary:　The IFC requires a system to reduce the hazard of a compressed or liquefied compressed toxic or highly toxic gas that is accidentally released. Note that Exception 1 provides an alternative for highly toxic and toxic gases in storage, and Exception 2 provides an alternative to the treatment system for toxic gases in use. When a treatment system is required, the system must be designed to reduce the gas to 50 percent of its immediately dangerous to life and health (IDLH) value at the point of discharge (IFC Section 6004.2.2.7.2).

IDLH values are available on the internet by using the *NIOSH Pocket Guide to Chemical Hazards* at http://www.cdc.gov/niosh/npg/.

Topic: Gas Detection System

Category: Highly Toxic and Toxic Materials

Reference: IFC 6004.2.2.10

Subject: Compressed Gases

Code Text: *A gas detection system complying with Section 916 shall be provided to detect the presence of gas at or below the PEL or ceiling limit of the gas for which detection is provided. The system shall be capable of monitoring the discharge from the treatment system at or below one-half the IDLH limit and shall initiate a response in accordance with Sections 6004.2.2.10.1 through 6004.2.2.10.3 if the gas detection alarm is activated.* **Exception:** *A gas detection system is not required for toxic gases when the physiological warning threshold level for the gas is at a level below the accepted PEL for the gas.*

Discussion and Commentary: Gas detection systems are required to provide early warning and notification in the event of a leak in a cylinder, piping or at other portions of the system. These systems are designed to activate at or below either the permissible exposure limit or the ceiling exposure limit. The permissible exposure and ceiling detection limits are below the IDLH value and allow individuals without respiratory protection to safely egress from the area. For toxic gases, the IFC does not require gas detection when the physiological warning threshold level is below the PEL for the gas.

Chlorine has a TWA PEL (time-weighted average permissible exposure limit) of 0.50 ppm. Its odor threshold can range from 0.02 to 0.31 ppm. However, odor thresholds have certain ranges. For chlorine, one source reported a high odor threshold level of 3.4 ppm. Because of this, gas detection should be required.

Code Text: *Weather protection in accordance with Section 5004.13 shall be provided for portable tanks and cylinders located outdoors and not within gas cabinets or exhausted enclosures. The storage area shall be equipped with an approved automatic sprinkler system in accordance with Section 903.3.1.1.* **Exception:** *An automatic sprinkler system is not required when: (1) All materials under the weather protection structure, including hazardous materials and the containers in which they are stored, are noncombustible. (2) The weather protection structure is located not less than 30 feet (9144 mm) from combustible materials or structures or is separated from such materials or structures using a fire barrier complying with Section 6004.3.2.1.1.*

Discussion and Commentary: This provision requires an automatic sprinkler system to be provided when highly toxic or toxic gases are stored beneath a weather protection structure, the quantities exceed the outdoor MAQ and the gases are not within gas cabinets or exhausted enclosures. The exception provides an alternative to the requirement via the installation of an automatic sprinkler system. To meet the requirement, the stored hazardous material must not be combustible, the packaging must be noncombustible, and the weather protection structure must be located at least 30 feet from combustible materials or structures. If the separation distance cannot be satisfied, a 2-hour fire barrier can be constructed that interrupts the line of sight from the storage to the exposure.

Chlorine is classified as a liquefied compressed gas, an oxidizing gas and a toxic gas. Because it is not a flammable gas, it could be stored beneath an unsprinklered weather protection structure so long as the structure meets all of the requirements set forth in the exception in IFC Section 6004.3.3.

Topic: Construction Documents

Category: Liquefied Petroleum Gases

Reference: IFC 6101.3

Subject: General

Code Text: *Where a single LP-gas container is more than 2,000 gallons (7570 L) in water capacity or the aggregate water capacity of LP-gas containers is more than 4,000 gallons (15 140 L), the installer shall submit construction documents for such installation.*

Discussion and Commentary: The IFC does not require construction plans for LP-gas installations when a single container has a water capacity of 2,000 gallons or less, or where multiple containers are installed, the aggregate is 4,000 gallons or less. This is because most installations for single users, or single businesses, do not require large LP-gas containers. Also, these installations are typically designed for vapor service, which make them relatively simple fuel gas storage and supply systems. Fire code officials should recognize that systems intended for liquid service such as those used for cylinder filling or vehicle fuel dispensing are more complicated installations.

The requirements in NFPA 58 for LP-gas containers over 2,000 gallons water capacity are more detailed when compared to smaller installations.

Code Text: *LP-gas containers shall not be filled or maintained with LP-gas in excess of either the volume determined using the fixed liquid-level gauge installed in accordance with the manufacturer's specifications and in accordance with Section 5.9.5 of NFPA 58 or the weight determined by the required percentage of the water capacity marked on the container. Portable LP-gas containers shall not be refilled unless equipped with an overfilling prevention device (OPD) where required by Section 5.9.3 of NFPA 58.*

Discussion and Commentary: A portable LP-gas cylinder is typically filled while weighing the cylinder or using a fixed liquid level gauge. Both methods provide a safe and reliable means of preventing overfilled cylinders. An OPD is a mechanical valve that is designed to prevent cylinders from being overfilled. They are required on cylinders with a propane capacity of 4 to 40 pounds used for vapor service. They are not required on cylinders used for industrial trucks (forklifts) or industrial welding and cutting.

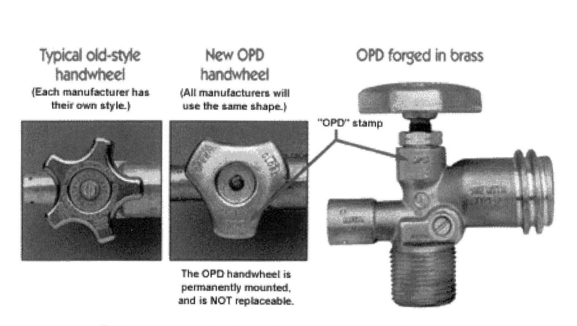

Typical old-style handwheel
(Each manufacturer has their own style.)

New OPD handwheel
(All manufacturers will use the same shape.)

OPD forged in brass

"OPD" stamp

The OPD handwheel is permanently mounted, and is NOT replaceable.

(Photograph courtesy of the National Propane Gas Association, Washington, DC.)

NFPA 58 Section 5.9.3 requires that cylinders shall not be refilled unless equipped with an overfill prevention device. The cylinder exchange program is designed to retrofit existing cylinders that are still serviceable with an OPD. The photograph above shows the industry changes to the visible portions of the valve to identify retrofit cylinders.

Code Text: *Storage outside of buildings of LP-gas containers awaiting use, resale or part of a cylinder exchange program shall be located in accordance with Table 6109.12.*

Discussion and Commentary: Cylinder exchange programs are popular for consumers because of the ease of fuel availability. They also offer a safer method for consumers to use LP-gas because the cylinders are examined each time they are refilled. The IFC requirements specify where cylinder exchange cabinets could be located based on the number and location of egress doors and their separation distances from exposures such as combustible materials and motor vehicle fuel dispensers.

The requirements are based on the low loss history presented by cylinder exchange cabinets and on the fact that cylinders sold at exchange cabinets have a maximum water capacity of 20 pounds. The cylinder exchange location in the photograph is designed and approved for self-service.

Quiz

Study Session 17
IFC Chapters 58 through 61

1. In a Group B occupancy, what is the maximum permitted volume of a cylinder that contains a compressed flammable gas used for operation of equipment?

   (a.) 250 ft³ @ NTP   b. 500 ft³ @ NTP

   c. 750 ft³ @ NTP   d. 1,000 ft³ @ NTP

   Reference 5803.1.1
             EXC. 1

2. Diethyl ether has a lower flammable limit of 1.9 percent by volume in air and upper flammable limit of 36 percent by volume in air. Based on these flammability characteristics, is it classified as a flammable gas?

   (a) Yes

   b. No

   c. Only if it is heated

   d. Unknown without further testing in accordance with NFPA 400

   Reference 5602.1
             Def. 202

3. Given: A ¹/₂-inch diameter carbon steel pipe that contains compressed isobutane. Isobutane is a flammable gas. In what areas is the pipe required to be bonded to a grounded conductor?

   a. all areas

   b. no such requirement exist

   (c.) in hazardous (electrically classified) locations

   d. the piping is noncurrent carrying, so it is not required to be bonded

   Reference 5803.1.5.1

4. When a flammable gas detection system activates in a hydrogen fuel gas room, which of the following shall occur?

    a. Activate the mechanical exhaust system

    b. Activate an audible and visual alarm inside the room

    c. Activate an audible and visual alarm outside the room

    d. All of the above

Reference 5808.51

5. What type of valve is required in the piping at the source of supply for a flammable gas?

    a. automatic emergency shutoff valve

    b. manual emergency shutoff valve

    c. thermal activated shutoff valve

    d. either a or b

Reference 5803.1.3.1

6. What is the frequency for requalification of metal hydride storage system containers?

    a. every 3 years   b. every 5 years

    c. every 12 years   d. annually

Reference 5607.1.4

7. Given: A building contains 1,000 pounds of a flammable solid and is classified as a Group H-3 occupancy. What percentage of the flammable solids are allowed to be stored in the basement?

    a. 50 percent   b. 75 percent

    c. 100 percent   d. Basement storage is prohibited.

Reference 5904.1.3

8. Which of the following building construction types can be used for a storage building to contain magnesium in combustible containers?

    a. Nonsprinklered Type I   b. Nonsprinklered Type III

    c. Nonsprinklered Type IV   d. Nonsprinklered Type V

Reference 5906.2.3

9. Given: A property processes magnesium scrap. What is the minimum required separation distance from the Group B administrative building to the building used for storage of more than 1,000 cubic feet of fine magnesium scrap?

    a. no minimum requirement   b. 75 feet

    c. 100 feet   d. 150 feet

Reference 5906.4.3

10. What is the classification of a liquid that has a median lethal dose (LD_{50}) of 484 mg/kg when administered by continuous contact for 24 hours (or less if death occurs within 24 hours) with the bare skin of albino rabbits weighing between 2 and 3 kilograms each?

    a. highly toxic   b. toxic

    c. irritant   d. nonhazardous

Reference 6002.1
               Def. 202

11. Toxic gas stored outdoors must be 75 feet from a lot line unless _____ .

    a. weather protection is provided

    b. stored in exhausted enclosures

    c. shielded by a 2-hour fire barrier

    d. stored in a below-grade pit

Reference 6004.3.2.1.1

12. What is the maximum amount of toxic gas allowed in Group R occupancies?

    a. 20 ft³ @ NTP

    b. 810 ft³ @ NTP

    c. 20 ft³ @ NTP when stored in a gas cabinet

    d. It is not allowed.

Reference 6004.1.1.2

13. What type of automatic fire-extinguishing system is allowed inside of a gas cabinet containing three cylinders of toxic gas?

    a. clean agent

    b. wet-chemical

    c. approved automatic sprinkler system

    d. any type of system is allowed

Reference 6004.1.2 #5

14. Treatment systems for toxic and highly toxic gases shall be designed to reduce the maximum concentrations of gas to _____ IDLH at the point of discharge to the atmosphere.

    a. $^1/_4$ (b.) $^1/_2$

    c. $^3/_4$ d. $^1/_{10}$

Reference 6004.2.2.7.2

15. Which of the following require an automatic fire detection system when the maximum allowable quantity is exceeded?

    a. flammable solids

    b. toxic gases

    c. highly toxic compressed gases

    d. all hazardous materials require a fire detection system

Reference 6004.2.2.9

16. Gas detection systems for toxic gases shall activate when the presence of gas is at a concentration that is at or below the _____ of the gas for which detection is provided.

    a. TWA or IDLH   b. STEL or ceiling limit

    c. PEL or ceiling limit   d. ceiling limit or LC_{50}

Reference 6004.2.2.10

17. Where an ozone gas generator is installed in a room, manual shutdown controls shall be provided at the generator and within _____ of the main exit or exit access door.

    a. 30 inches   b. 5 feet

    c. 10 feet   d. 20 feet

Reference 6005.6

18. When not installed in an exhausted enclosure, piping for an ozone gas generator shall be _____.

    a. Welded stainless steel

    b. Flanged stainless steel

    c. Double-walled piping

    d. Either a or c

Reference 6005.4.1

19. At what capacity are construction documents required for a single container of LP-gas?

    a. 1,000 gallons water capacity

    b. 2,000 gallons water capacity

    c. more than 2,000 gallons water capacity

    d. 4,000 gallons water capacity

Reference 6101.3

20. For research and experimentation in Group F occupancies, an aggregate water capacity of _____ pounds shall not be exceeded for a single manifolded group of portable LP-gas containers.

    a. 20   b. 50

    c. 125   d. 735

Reference 6103.7.1.3

21. For LP-gas containers with an individual water capacity of more than 2.7 pounds, how should the cylinders be stored?

    a. upright

    b. with the pressure relief valve in direct communication with the vapor space

    c. inverted so that the relief valve will function

    d. all pressure relief valves are designed to discharge either liquid or vapor

Reference 6109.3

22. What is the required separation distance between a cylinder exchange cabinet containing 1,420 pounds of LP-gas and the closest motor vehicle fuel dispenser?

    a. 0 feet   b. 10 feet

    c. 20 feet   d. 25 feet

Reference 6109.12

23. Given: One LP-gas cylinder exchange cabinet located near the front egress door for a 2,300-square-foot Group M retail store. The cabinet contains 600 pounds of LP-gas. The Group M occupancy has one exit. What is the required separation distance between the cylinder exchange cabinet and the egress door?

    a. 0 feet   b. 5 feet

    c. 10 feet   d. 20 feet

Reference 6109.12

24. A cylinder exchange cabinet is installed near the front of a large Group M occupancy. The cabinet contains 3,460 pounds of LP-gas. The building has more than two exits. What is the required separation distance between the exchange cabinets and the building?

   a.   0 feet   b.   5 feet

   c.   10 feet   d.   20 feet

   Reference 6109.12

25. Given: A gasoline service station has one LP-gas cylinder exchange cabinet with a capacity of 1,500 pounds. The cylinder exchange cabinet must be a minimum distance of _____ from the gasoline dispensers.

   a.   5   b.   10

   c.   20   d.   25

   Reference 6109.12

26. When determining the capacity of a treatment system, what is maximum total release time prescribed by the IFC for the release of a highly toxic liquefied gas stored in a cylinder?

   a.   5 minutes   b.   30 minutes

   c.   40 minutes   d.   240 minutes

   Reference 6004.2.2.7.5

27. What type of valve is designed to reduce the maximum flow of compressed gas under full-flow conditions?

   a.   reduced flow valve   b.   check valve

   c.   excess flow valve   d.   minimum flow valve

   Reference 6002.1
                   Def. 202

28. What is the minimum separation distance between property that can be built upon and one 18,000-gallon above-ground LP-gas container?

   a.   10 feet   b.   50 feet

   c.   75 feet   d.   100 feet

   Reference 6104.3

29. Given: An LP-gas distribution facility with three 30,000 gallon water capacity LP-gas storage containers. What is the minimum separation distance between the LP-gas containers?

    a.   3 feet

    (b.) 5 feet

    c.   10 feet

    d. $^1/_4$ the sum of the diameters of the adjacent containers

    Reference 6104.3

30. What is the minimum separation distance prescribed by the IFC for unattended parking of an LP-gas tank vehicle and an apartment complex?

    a.   150 feet   b.   300 feet

    (c.) 500 feet   d.   750 feet

    Reference 6111.2.1

31. Metal hydride storage systems are used to store what material?

    (a.) Hydrogen   b.   Hydrogen peroxide

    c.   Hydrated iron   d.   Ferrous Bueller

    Reference 5807.1

32. Smoking is prohibited within _____ of an LP-gas point of transfer.

    a.   15 feet   b.   20 feet

    (c.) 25 feet   d.   50 feet

    Reference 6107.2

33. Given: A building contains a hydrogen fuel gas room where the MAQ is not exceeded. Which of the following is not required in the hydrogen fuel gas room?

    a.   Automatic sprinkler system   b.   Mechanical ventilation

    c.   Gas detection system   (d.) Standby power

    Reference 5003.1.4

34. When is a gas detection system required for highly toxic gases?

    a.   always required for storage or use inside a building

    (b.) when the quantity exceeds the maximum allowable quantity per control area and the physiological warning threshold is above the permissible exposure limit

    c.   only required if the gas does not have an odor

    d.   whenever required by the fire code official

Reference 6004.2.2.10

35. Underground tanks for the storage of liquid hydrogen must be separated a minimum of _____ feet from a property line.

    a.   1   (b.) 3

    c.   5   d. 10

Reference 5806.4.2

2021 IFC Chapters 62 through 67
Organic Peroxides; Oxidizers, Oxidizing Gases and Oxidizing Cryogenic Fluids; Pyrophoric Materials; Pyroxylin (Cellulose Nitrate) Plastics; Unstable (Reactive) Materials; and Water-Reactive Solids and Liquids

OBJECTIVE: To obtain a basic understanding of the *International Fire Code*® (IFC®) requirements for organic peroxides, oxidizers, pyrophorics, pyroxylin plastics, unstable (reactive) materials, and water-reactive solids and liquids.

REFERENCE: Chapters 62 through 67, 2021 IFC

KEY POINTS:
- What is an organic peroxide?
- What special limitations are applicable to organic peroxides stored or used in Group A, B, E, I, F, M or S occupancies?
- When is detached storage of organic peroxides required?
- Given a hazard class and quantity of an organic peroxide, what are the minimum separation distances from exposures?
- For storage over the maximum allowable quantity, what are the requirements for smoke detection, allowed indoor storage locations and standby power for certain classes of organic peroxides?
- When quantities are greater than the maximum allowable quantity in a single control area, what controls are prescribed to prevent the contamination of organic peroxides?
- When is standby power required for systems and equipment required to protect organic peroxides?
- What is an oxidizer?
- What special limitations are applicable to oxidizers stored or used in Group A, B, E, I, F, M or S occupancies?
- What is the design criteria for an automatic sprinkler system in an oxidizer storage area?
- Given a specific class and physical state of an oxidizer, determine the storage conditions using the IFC.
- When is a detached building required for storage of oxidizers?

KEY POINTS:
(Cont'd)

- What are the limitations on the use of liquid oxygen (LOX) in home health care?
- When is explosion control required for oxidizers?
- What is a pyrophoric material?
- What is the maximum allowable quantity of pyrophoric material in a single control area?
- What is silane? How is it regulated?
- Does the code prescribe special requirements for storage or use of pyrophoric material inside a building?
- Does the IFC prescribe special requirements for the storage of pyrophoric material beneath a weather protection structure?
- When is explosion control required for pyrophoric materials?
- What hazards are characteristic of pyroxylin (cellulose nitrate) plastics?
- When is an automatic sprinkler system required for the manufacture or storage of pyroxylin plastics?
- When is pyroxylin plastic required to be stored in a cabinet? What is the maximum capacity of a cabinet?
- What is an unstable (reactive) material?
- What special limitations are applicable to unstable (reactive) materials stored or used in Group A, B, E, I, F, M or S occupancies?
- When is explosion control required for (unstable reactive) materials?
- What are the requirements for determining required separation distances for outdoor storage of Class 3 and 4 unstable (reactive) materials?
- When is explosion control required for unstable (reactive) materials?
- What is a water-reactive material?
- When the amount of water-reactive material exceeds the maximum allowable quantity in one control area, what are the construction requirements for rooms or areas containing this class of hazardous material?
- When is explosion control required for water-reactive materials?

Code Text: *An organic compound that contains the bivalent -O-O- structure and which may be considered to be a structural derivative of hydrogen peroxide where one or both of the hydrogen atoms have been replaced by an organic radical. Organic peroxides can present an explosion hazard (detonation or deflagration) or they can be shock sensitive. They can also decompose into various unstable compounds over an extended period of time.*

(See IFC Section 202 for definitions of Classes I through V and Unclassified Detonable.)

Discussion and Commentary: An organic peroxide is a derivative of hydrogen peroxide, an inorganic peroxide. An organic peroxide requires a carbon and hydrogen molecule and two oxygen molecules that are bivalent, or connected together. Organic peroxides are a challenging hazardous material because they contain carbon, hydrogen and oxygen, meaning that the chemical itself contains fuel and oxygen, although they are not oxidizers. The -O-O- bond can be broken producing free radicals, making organic peroxides useful as initiators in epoxy resin and fiberglass operations. Many classes of organic peroxides require temperature controls, and all are very sensitive to any contaminants. Many organic peroxides are shipped with a chemical stabilizer that can be either a flammable or combustible liquid. The category of Unclassified Detonable does not mean that it has not been classified. These materials do not fit into the Class I through IV definitions, and they can detonate.

Examples of Organic Peroxides and Their Classification

CHEMICAL	CONCENTRATION	CLASSIFICATION
Benzoyl peroxide	>98 percent	Organic Peroxide Class I
	78 percent	Organic Peroxide Class III
	70 percent	Organic Peroxide Class IV
	35 percent	Organic Peroxide Class V
Butyl hydroperoxide	90 percent	Organic Peroxide Class I
	80 percent	Organic Peroxide Class II
	72 percent	Organic Peroxide Class III
Methyl ethyl ketone peroxide	52 percent	Organic Peroxide Class I
	45 percent	Organic Peroxide Class II
	30 percent	Organic Peroxide Class III

Like most chemicals, the percentage of concentration affects the characteristics of the material. Additional changes occur depending on what the chemical is diluted with.

Code Text: *In Group A, E, I or U occupancies, any amount of unclassified detonable and Class I organic peroxides shall be stored in accordance with the following: (1) Unclassified detonable and Class I organic peroxides shall be stored in hazardous materials storage cabinets complying with Section 5003.8.7. (2) The hazardous materials storage cabinets shall not contain other storage.*

Discussion and Commentary: Depending on its classification, an Unclassified Detonable or Class I organic peroxide is capable of either detonation or deflagration. Even with their low maximum allowable quantities (1 pound and 5 pounds, respectively), the hazards of the materials warrant additional controls because of the life safety challenges in A, E and I occupancies. For Group U occupancies, emergency responders would not anticipate encountering these classes of hazardous materials in this occupancy, and they are completely prohibited in Group R occupancies. Accordingly, the IFC prescribes that these particular organic peroxides be separated by storage in an approved hazardous material storage cabinet, and that the storage be limited to these hazardous materials. IFC Sections 6203.1.1.3 and 6203.1.1.4 contain similar restrictions for Groups B, F, M and S occupancies and classrooms.

IFC Table 5003.1.1(1) Footnote g does not permit the storage or use of Unclassified Detonable organic peroxides in an unsprinklered building.

	Topic: Distance from Detached Buildings to Exposures	Category: Organic Peroxides
	Reference: IFC 6204.1.2	Subject: Storage

Code Text: *In addition to the requirements of the* International Building Code, *detached storage buildings for Class I, II, III, IV and V organic peroxides shall be located in accordance with Table 6204.1.2. Detached buildings containing quantities of unclassified detonable organic peroxides in excess of those set forth in Table 5003.8.2 shall be located in accordance with Table 5604.5.2(1).*

Discussion and Commentary: Detached buildings are required when the quantity of hazardous materials create a hazard of such magnitude to preclude other occupancies being in the same building or even attached to the storage building. Table 5003.8.2 provides the thresholds where detached storage buildings are required. Class I and Unclassified Detonable (UD) organic peroxides require detached storage when quantities exceed the maximum allowable quantity per control area (5 pounds and 1 pound respectively in Table 5003.8.2). Unclassified Detonable organic peroxides are capable of detonation. Accordingly, detached storage for

TABLE 6204.1.2
ORGANIC PEROXIDES—DISTANCE TO EXPOSURES FROM
DETACHED STORAGE BUILDINGS OR OUTDOOR STORAGE AREAS

ORGANIC PEROXIDE CLASS	MAXIMUM STORAGE QUANTITY (POUNDS) AT MINIMUM SEPARATION DISTANCE					
	DISTANCE TO BUILDINGS, LOT LINES, PUBLIC STREETS, PUBLIC ALLEYS, PUBLIC WAYS OR MEANS OF EGRESS			DISTANCE BETWEEN INDIVIDUAL DETACHED STORAGE BUILDINGS OR INDIVIDUAL OUTDOOR STORAGE AREAS		
	50 feet	100 feet	150 feet	20 feet	75 feet	100 feet
I	2,000	2,000	175,000	2,000	20,000	175,000
II	100,000	200,000	No Limit	100,000[a]	No Limit	No Limit
III	200,000	No Limit	No Limit	200,000[a]	No Limit	No Limit
IV	No Limit	No Limit	No Limit	No Limit	No Limit	No Limit
V	No Limit	No Limit	No Limit	No Limit	No Limit	No Limit

For SI: 1 foot = 304.8 mm, 1 pound = 0.454 kg.
a. Where the amount of organic peroxide stored exceeds this amount, the minimum separation shall be 50 feet.

UD organic peroxides must comply with separation distances in Chapter 56 for explosives.

Code Text: *An approved supervised smoke detection system in accordance with Section 907 shall be provided in rooms or areas where Class I, II or III organic peroxides are stored. Activation of the smoke detection system shall sound a local alarm.* **Exception:** *A smoke detection system shall not be required in detached storage buildings equipped throughout with an approved automatic fire-extinguishing system complying with Chapter 9.*

Discussion and Commentary: A smoke detection system that transmits a local alarm signal and a fire alarm signal to a supervisory station is required where Class I, II or III organic peroxides are stored in a building, unless it is a detached storage building. By definition, Class II organic peroxides burn very rapidly, whereas Class III organic peroxides burn rapidly. Accordingly, smoke detection is required because any localized heating of these classes of organic peroxides is a clear indication that this material is undergoing auto-decomposition.

Because of the storage condition specified in IFC Section 6204.1, a smoke detection system is required only when the amount of storage exceeds the maximum allowable quantity per control area.

Code Text: *Maximum allowable quantities per building in a mixed occupancy building shall not exceed the amounts set forth in Table 5003.8.2. Maximum allowable quantities per building in a detached storage building shall not exceed the amounts specified in Table 6204.1.2.*

Discussion and Commentary: IFC Table 5003.8.2 defines the quantity of organic peroxide allowed in a building before a detached building is required. IFC Section 202 defines a detached building as *a separate single-story building, without a basement or crawl space, used for the storage or use of hazardous materials and located an approved distance from all structures.* Therefore, once the code prescribed quantity limits are exceeded, detached storage is required.

TABLE 5003.8.2 (*excerpts*)
DETACHED BUILDING REQUIRED

A DETACHED BUILDING IS REQUIRED WHERE THE QUANTITY OF MATERIAL EXCEEDS THAT LISTED HEREIN			
Material	**Class**	**Solids and liquids (tons)[a, b]**	**Gases (cubic feet)[a, b]**
Organic peroxides	Detonable Class I Class II Class III	Maximum Allowable Quantity Maximum Allowable Quantity 25 50	Not Applicable

For SI: 1 pound = 0.454 kg, 1 cubic foot = 0.02832 m^3, 1 ton = 2000 lbs. – 907.2 kg.

a. For materials that are detonable, the distance to other buildings or lot lines shall be in accordance with Section 415.6 of the *International Building Code* or Chapter 56 based on the trinitrotoluene (TNT) equivalence of the material, whichever is greater.

b. "Maximum Allowable Quantity" means the maximum allowable quantity per control area set forth in Table 5003.1.1(1).

A detached storage building would be classified as Group H-1, H-2 or H-3 depending on the class of organic peroxide.

Topic: Location in Building	**Category:** Organic Peroxides
Reference: IFC 6204.1.8	**Subject:** Storage

Code Text: *The storage of Class I or II organic peroxides shall be on the ground floor. Class III organic peroxides shall not be stored in basements.*

Discussion and Commentary: Organic peroxides commonly contain stabilizers to ensure that the material can be safely stored and used. Some of these stabilizers are flammable or Class II combustible liquids. For example, methyl ethyl ketone, a Class IB flammable liquid, and odorless mineral spirits, a Class II combustible liquid, are common stabilizers found in organic peroxides. Given the hazard classification of these materials, storage in basements can create very difficult fire-fighting operations. Storage of Class I or II organic peroxides in amounts greater than the maximum allowable quantity in a multistory building also introduces the potential for fireground complications. As a result, IFC Section 6204.1.8 limits the locations where these materials can be stored.

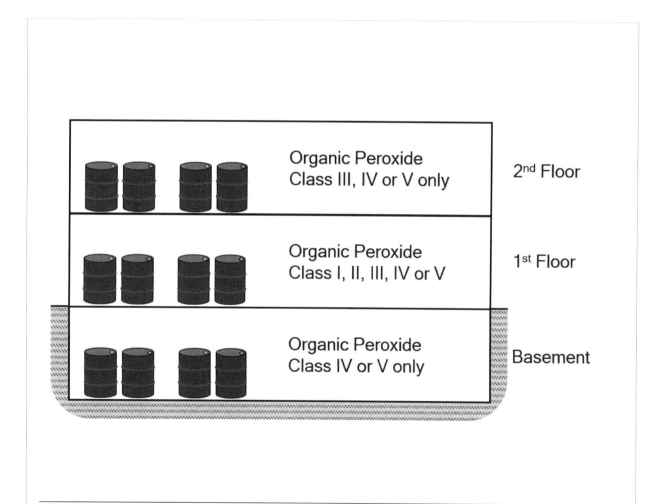

Class I organic peroxides are capable of deflagrations, whereas Class II and III organic peroxides burn very rapidly or rapidly. Because of these hazards, the IFC limits the floor level where these materials can be stored.

Topic: Standby Power

Category: Organic Peroxides

Reference: IFC 6204.1.11

Subject: Storage

Code Text: *Standby power shall be provided in accordance with Section 1203 for the following systems used to protect Class I and unclassified detonable organic peroxide: (1) Exhaust ventilation system, (2) Treatment system, (3) Smoke detection system, (4) Temperature control system, (5) Fire alarm system, (6) Emergency alarm system.*

Discussion and Commentary: Standby power is required for safety equipment when it protects Class I and unclassified detonable organic peroxides. The standby power system provides continued operation of the safety provisions for these higher hazard organic peroxides.

The self-accelerating decomposition temperature (SADT) is the temperature that will cause auto-ignition of the organic peroxide. If an organic peroxide is heated to its SADT, fire code officials can expect a working fire involving hazardous materials. Organic peroxides are available that have an SADT of 32°F, therefore, the refrigeration systems and temperature controls must be provided with standby power.

Code Text: *A material that readily yields oxygen or other oxidizing gas, or that readily reacts to promote or initiate combustion of combustible materials and, if heated or contaminated, can result in vigorous self-sustained decomposition.*

(See IFC Section 202 for definitions of Classes 1 through 4.)

Discussion and Commentary: An oxidizer accelerates burning, but the material itself does not burn. Oxidizers can be found in all three physical states: solid, liquid or gas. They are commonly used for disinfecting water [anhydrous chlorine, an oxidizing, corrosive and toxic gas, or calcium hypochlorite, a Class 3 oxidizer, Class 2 unstable (reactive), Class 1 water-reactive and corrosive solid] or in the manufacturing of plastics (hydrogen peroxide, a Class 3 or 2 liquid oxidizer, depending on its concentration). Oxidizers are generally very stable chemicals and normally do not need temperature controls. However, they are very sensitive to any contamination or mixing with incompatible materials.

Examples of Solid and Liquid Oxidizers and Their Classification

CLASSIFICATION	CHEMICAL
Oxidizer Class 1	Hydrogen peroxide (>8% and ≤27.5%)
	Nitric acid (≤40%)
	Potassium percarbonate
	Sodium carbonate peroxide
Oxidizer Class 2	Hydrogen peroxide (>27.5% and ≤52%)
	Nitric acid (>40% and <86%)
	Potassium peroxide
	Sodium dichloro-s-triazinetrione anhydrous (sodium dichloroisocyanurate anhydrous)
	Sodium permanganate
Oxidizer Class 3	Hydrogen peroxide (>52% and ≤91%)
	Nitric acid (>86%)
	Potassium chlorate
	Sodium chlorate
Oxidizer Class 4	Ammonium perchlorate
	Ammonium permanganate
	Hydrogen peroxide (>91%)

Hydrogen peroxide is in the table above as an oxidizing material (IFC Section E102.1.7.1). Based on its concentration, the level of hazard changes. Hydrogen peroxide is also available in retail, but its typical concentration in those formulations is 3 percent.

Code Text: *The storage configuration of Class 1, 2 and 3 liquid and solid oxidizers shall be as set forth in Table 6303.1.4.*

TABLE 6303.1.4
STORAGE OF CLASS 1, 2 AND 3
OXIDIZER LIQUIDS AND SOLIDS

STORAGE CONFIGURATION	LIMITS (feet)		
	CLASS 1	CLASS 2	CLASS 2
Piles			
Maximum width	24	16	12
Maximum height	20	Note c	Note c
Maximum distance to aisle	12	8	8
Minimum distance to next pile	4[a]	Note a	Note a
Minimum distance to walls	2[b]	2	4
Maximum quantity per pile	200 tons	MAQ	NA
Maximum quantity per building	No limit	Note d	Note d

For SI: 1 foot = 304.8 mm, 1 pound = 0.454 kg, 1 ton = 0.907185 metric ton

MAQ = Maximum Allowable Quantity

NA = Not Applicable

a. The minimum aisle width shall be equal to the pile height, but not less than 4 feet and not greater than 8 feet.
b. There shall not be a minimum distance from the pile to a wall for amounts less than 9,000 pounds.
c. Maximum storage height in nonsprinklered buildings is limited to 6 feet. In sprinklered buildings see NFPA 400 for storage heights based on ceiling sprinkler protection.
d. Maximum quantity per building varies. See Chapter 50 for control areas and MAQs.

Discussion and Commentary: The storage configuration and the maximum quantity of oxidizing solids and liquids is regulated in Table 6303.1.4. The pile height, width, aisles and even distance to walls is specified based on the material classification. Footnote c refers to NFPA 400, *Hazardous Materials Code*, for allowable storage heights of Class 2 and 3 oxidizers in a sprinklered building. The storage height limits are based on the sprinkler design.

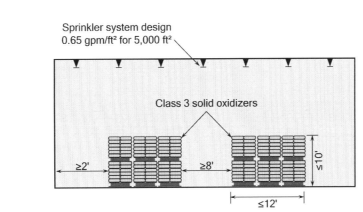

For SI: 1 foot = 305.4 mm, 1 square foot = 0.0929 m², 1 gpm/square foot = 40.8 L/min/m².

The storage arrangement of solid Class 3 solid oxidizers in a sprinklered building with a sprinkler system density of 0.65 gallons per minute per square foot and a design area of 5,000 square feet is shown in the graphic. If the sprinkler design is different, the storage height will change accordingly.

Code Text: *In addition to Section 5004.12, floors of storage areas for liquid and solid oxidizers shall be of liquid-tight construction.*

Discussion and Commentary: Oxidizing materials stored indoors can complicate fire situations in the building. Solid and liquid oxidizers stored indoors must be on a liquid-tight floor when the MAQ is exceeded. This section refers to Section 5004.12 which requires that the floor be of non-combustible construction.

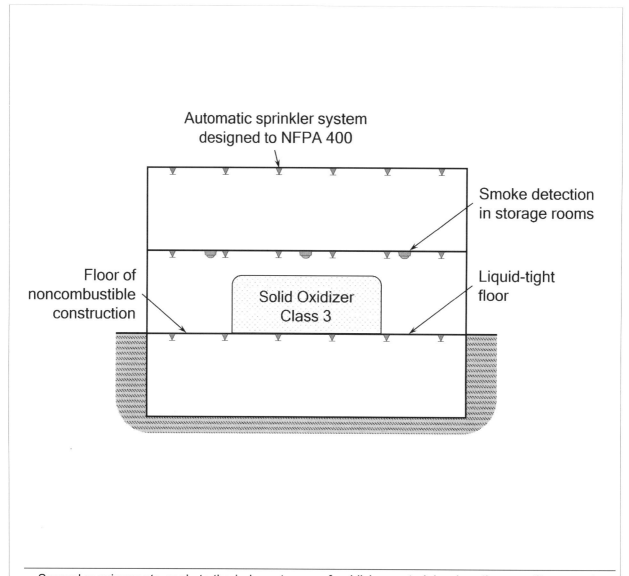

Several requirements apply to the indoor storage of oxidizing materials when the quantity exceeds the MAQ and the building is a Group H occupancy. Class 3 and 4 oxidizers can only be stored on the ground floor (IFC Section 6304.1.5).

Code Text: *An approved supervised smoke detection system in accordance with Section 907 shall be installed in liquid and solid oxidizer storage areas. Activation of the smoke detection system shall sound a local alarm.* **Exception:** *Detached storage buildings protected by an approved automatic fire-extinguishing system.*

Discussion and Commentary: A smoke detection system is required in storage rooms containing oxidizing solids or liquids exceeding the maximum allowable quantity per control area. Even though the oxidizer does not burn, it can increase the magnitude of a fire exponentially. The smoke detection system is in addition to the automatic sprinkler system—it does not replace the sprinkler system.

The smoke detection system is intended to detect a fire before it reaches the oxidizers. The system will sound a local alarm and will also be monitored as required in IFC Section 907.6.6.

Smoke detection provides early warning of a fire. The smoke detection system must be installed in accordance with IFC Section 907.

Code Text: *The maximum quantity of oxidizers per building in storage buildings shall not exceed those quantities set forth in Tables 6304.1.5(1) through 6304.1.5(3).*

The storage configuration for liquid and solid oxidizers shall be as set forth in Table 6303.1.4 and Tables 6304.1.5(1) through 6304.1.5(3).

Class 2 oxidizers shall not be stored in basements except when such storage is in stationary tanks.

Class 3 and 4 oxidizers in amounts exceeding the maximum allowable quantity per control area set forth in Section 5003.1 shall be stored on the ground floor only.

Discussion and Commentary: This provision establishes the requirements for storage locations, heights and pile volumes for each class of oxidizing solids and liquids. For Class 2 and 3 oxidizers, IFC Tables 6304.1.5(1) and (2) establish the quantity limits based on the storage being in a control area, a storage area classified as a Group H occupancy or a detached building. Footnote a in both tables limits the storage height to 6 feet, but allows increases in that height based on the sprinkler system design. Chapter 15 in NFPA 400 contains the criteria for sprinkler design allowing an increase in the storage height. Table 5003.8.2 sets the thresholds when a detached building is required for oxidizers Classes 2, 3 and 4 at 2,000 tons, 1,200 tons and the MAQ, respectively.

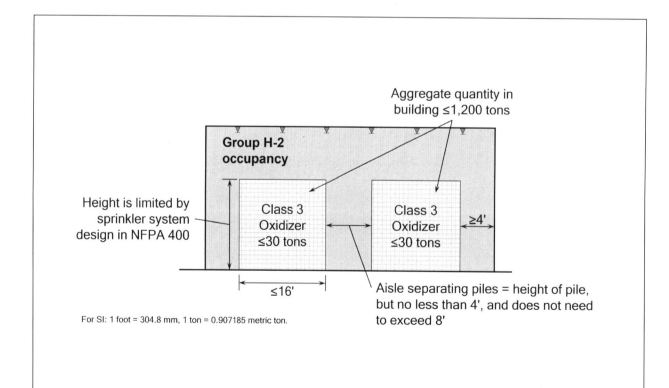

Even in a Group H occupancy there are requirements for minimum pile separation and aisle widths, maximum pile size and minimum separation to building walls [IFC Table 6304.1.5(2)].

Code Text: *An automatic emergency shutoff valve shall be installed on supply piping at the cylinder or bulk source. The shutoff valve shall be operated by a remotely located manually activated shutdown control located not less than 15 feet (4572 mm) from the source of supply. Manual or automatic cylinder valves are allowed to be used as the required emergency shutoff valve where the source of supply is limited to unmanifolded cylinder sources.*

Discussion and Commentary: The IFC requires an emergency shutoff valve for pyrophoric gas systems at the supply source. The manual cylinder valve can fulfill this requirement provided the cylinder is not connected to a manifold. A shutoff valve is also required at the point of use. The valve at the point of use can be either manual or an automatic emergency shutoff valve.

Fire code officials should understand that pyrophoric gases are classified as Flammable Gases by the US Department of Transportation. Therefore, it is important that the permit applicant provide sufficient information to the code official so that the hazardous material can be properly classified.

Code Text: *Where overhead construction is provided for sheltering outdoor storage areas of pyrophoric materials, the storage areas shall be provided with approved automatic fire-extinguishing system protection.*

Discussion and Commentary: Because of the inherent auto-ignition hazard of pyrophoric materials, weather protection canopies sheltering pyrophoric materials must be protected with an approved automatic fire-extinguishing system. IFC Section 6405.2 contains a similar requirement for weather protection over outdoor use areas handling pyrophoric materials to be equipped with a fire-extinguishing system. Some pyrophoric materials can also be very water reactive, such as triethyl-aluminum, which is classified as a pyrophoric, Class 3 water reactive, highly toxic and corrosive liquid (IFC Section E102). Therefore, selection and approval of the appropriate fire-extinguishing agent is important when protecting these materials.

For pyrophoric compressed gases such as silane and diborane, NFPA 55 specifies that an Extra Hazard Group I discharge density over a 2,500 square foot design area be specified for the automatic sprinkler system. Unless the area increases allowed by *International Building Code*® (IBC®) Section 506 are applied, IBC Section 414.6.1.3 limits the area of weather protection canopies to 1,500 ft².

Code Text: *The manufacture or storage of articles of cellulose nitrate (pyroxylin) plastic in quantities exceeding 100 pounds (45 kg) shall be located in a building or portion thereof equipped throughout with an approved automatic sprinkler system in accordance with Section 903.3.1.1.*

Discussion and Commentary: Pyroxylin (cellulose nitrate) plastic is formulated from a combination of cellulose, nitric acid and sulfuric acid. The resulting compound, also known as pyroxylin or nitrocellulose, is an unstable and extremely combustible plastic. Once exposed to elevated temperatures, pyroxylin (cellulose nitrate) plastic is subject to spontaneous ignition. Pyroxylin (cellulose nitrate) plastic is especially susceptible to ignition, burns vigorously once ignited, produces toxic nitrogen oxides and will burn in the absence of oxygen. Accordingly, buildings or rooms where pyroxylin is used or stored in quantities exceeding 100 pounds are required to be protected with an automatic sprinkler system. Additional storage limits of IFC Section 6504 are shown in the graphic below.

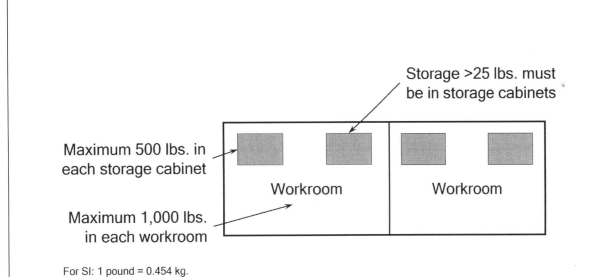

Storage >25 lbs. must be in storage cabinets

Maximum 500 lbs. in each storage cabinet

Maximum 1,000 lbs. in each workroom

Workroom   Workroom

For SI: 1 pound = 0.454 kg.

Pyroxylin plastics burn at a rate approximately 15 times that of a comparable mass of paper. IFC Section 1103.5.5 requires existing buildings with more than 100 pounds in storage or use to be protected with sprinklers.

Code Text: *A material, other than an explosive, which in the pure state or as commercially produced, will vigorously polymerize, decompose, condense or become self-reactive and undergo other violent chemical changes, including explosion, when exposed to heat, friction or shock, or in the absence of an inhibitor, or in the presence of contaminants, or in contact with incompatible materials. Unstable (reactive) materials are subdivided as follows ...*

(See IFC Section 202 for definitions of Classes 1 through 4.)

Discussion and Commentary: Unstable (reactive) materials are probably the most improperly classified group of hazardous materials because their reactivity can be dependent on the manufacturing process. In other cases, the actual chemistry of the molecule lends itself to being an unstable (reactive) material. These hazardous materials can polymerize, decompose, condense or undergo other violent chemical reactions if temperature, flow and pressure are not controlled. Introduction of a contaminant can also cause a reaction. Accordingly, many organic peroxides and oxidizers are also classified as a certain class of unstable (reactive) material.

Acetylene is a Class 2 unstable (reactive) gas. To maintain it in a stable state, cylinders contain acetone that acts as a stabilizer.

Code Text: *Indoor storage rooms, areas and buildings containing Class 3 or 4 unstable (reactive) materials shall be provided with explosion control in accordance with Section 911.*

Discussion and Commentary: By definition, Class 4 and 3 unstable (reactive) materials are capable of detonation or explosive decomposition. This section prescribes that explosion control be provided when the amount in storage exceeds the maximum allowable quantity in Table 5003.1.1(1). The type of explosion control that is required depends on the hazard classification of the unstable (reactive) material.

Class 4 and Class 3 detonable unstable (reactive) materials require explosion control using barricades constructed in accordance with NFPA 495, *Explosive Materials Code.* Class 3 nondetonable unstable (reactive) materials require deflagration venting in accordance with the requirements of IFC Section 911 and NFPA 69, *Standard on Explosion Prevention Systems.*

Code Text: *Rooms or areas used for the storage of water-reactive solids and liquids shall be constructed in a manner which resists the penetration of water through the use of waterproof materials. Piping carrying water for other than approved automatic sprinkler systems shall not be within such rooms or areas.*

Discussion and Commentary: Because water-reactive materials can have an adverse reaction with water, IFC Section 6704.1.3 requires that Group H occupancies storing these materials be constructed in a manner that resists the penetration of water. This includes routing domestic water or steam lines around the room and ensuring that roof drain openings or pipes are not routed through these rooms. Piping supplying the automatic sprinkler system is allowed in the room. In fact, fire sprinklers are not eliminated in rooms containing water-reactive materials; instead, IFC Section 6704.1.4 requires that Class 3 water-reactive materials are stored in water-tight containers where located in a sprinklered room.

Sprinkler piping can leak. Therefore, if possible, it is suggested that the sprinkler piping be located outside of the room. One method of accomplishing this is to use sidewall sprinklers in these occupancies.

Code Text: *Outdoor storage of water-reactive solids and liquids shall be within tanks or closed water-tight containers and shall be in accordance with Sections 6704.2.2 through 6704.2.5.*

Discussion and Commentary: Water-reactive materials can be stored outside provided that Class 2 and 3 materials are in tanks or water-tight containers. Outdoor storage areas either must comply with Table 5003.1.1(3) for outdoor control areas, or can comply with these requirements. Outdoor control areas for Class 2 and 3 water-reactive solids are limited to 200 pounds and 20 pounds respectively. The provisions in Section 6704.2 allow the quantities to increase to 1,000 and 500 cubic feet per pile respectively. Class 1 water-reactive materials are not limited.

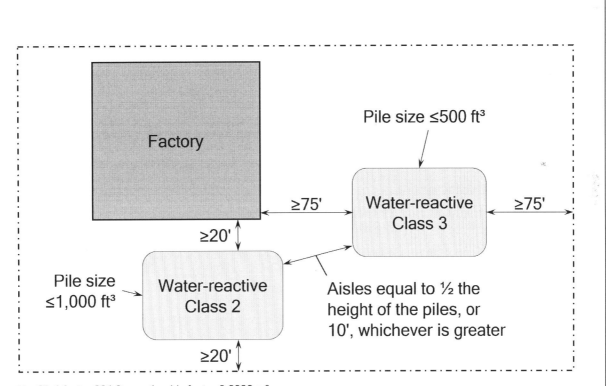

For SI: 1 foot = 304.8 mm, 1 cubic foot = 0.2832 m³.

The graphic depicts the required storage configuration for water-reactive solids and liquids when quantities exceed the maximum allowable quantity per outdoor control area. Secondary containment is required for Class 2 and 3 water-reactive materials (IFC Section 6704.2).

Quiz

Study Session 18

IFC Chapters 62 through 67

1. Given: A warehouse storing 3,000 pounds of solid Class 2 oxidizers. Each square storage pile is surrounded by aisles. The maximum width of each pile is _____ feet and the minimum separation to another pile is _____ feet?

    a. 12, 2

    b. 16, 4

    c. 25, 0

    d. 25, 4

    Reference _____

2. Given: Storage of a solid Class I organic peroxide in a Group F-1 occupancy. The building is protected throughout by an automatic sprinkler system. The organic peroxide is stored in an approved hazardous materials storage cabinet. What is the maximum allowable quantity in one control area?

    a. 5 pounds

    b. 10 pounds

    c. 20 pounds

    d. Not permitted

    Reference _____

3. A building contains 2,300 pounds of Class III liquid organic peroxides, and the room is classified as a Group H-3 occupancy. The building also contains a Group F-1, S-1 and B occupancy. Is a smoke detection system required?

    a. yes

    b. yes, and detached storage is also required

    c. no, it is not required when the building is sprinklered

    d. no, Class III organic peroxides do not require smoke detection

    Reference _____

4. Given: A detached storage building containing 200,000 pounds of a liquid Class II organic peroxide. What is the required separation distance of this detached building to a public way?

   a. 50 feet

   b. 100 feet

   c. 150 feet

   d. Detached storage is not required.

   Reference _____

5. The classification of hazardous (classified) location electrical equipment for a Group H-2 occupancy storing Class II organic peroxides is _____.

   a. Class I, Division 1

   b. Class I, Division 2

   c. Class II, Division 1

   d. Class II, Division 2

   Reference _____

6. What is the required clearance between uninsulated metal walls and organic peroxide storage?

   a. 6 inches

   b. 1 foot

   c. 2 feet

   d. 5 feet

   Reference _____

7. Which of the following classes of organic peroxide can be stored in the basement of a building?

   a. I

   b. II

   c. III

   d. IV

   Reference _____

8. What class of organic peroxides requires a means of standby power?

   a. I

   b. II

   c. III

   d. IV

   Reference _____

9. A Group I-2 hospital is storing 3 pounds of a material classified as a Class I organic peroxide solid. Which of the following requirements apply?

    a. The material must be stored in a hazardous material storage cabinet.

    b. The material is not permitted in a Group I-2 occupancy.

    c. The material must be stored in separate containers which do not exceed 12 ounces each.

    d. The quantity is below the maximum allowable quantity therefore no requirements apply.

    Reference _____

10. What are the requirements for the storage of Class 4 liquid and solid oxidizers in retail sales areas of Group M occupancies?

    a. Must be stored in a hazardous materials cabinet.

    b. The storage cabinet cannot contain other storage.

    c. Class 4 liquid and solid oxidizers are not allowed.

    d. Both a and b are required.

    Reference _____

11. What NFPA standard governs the design of automatic sprinkler systems for solid and liquid oxidizers?

    a. 30   b. 30A

    c. 400   d. 750

    Reference _____

12. When the maximum allowable quantity has been exceeded, what class(es) of oxidizers are restricted to storage on the ground floor of any building?

    a. Class 2   b. Class 3

    c. Class 4   d. Class 3 and 4

    Reference _____

13. Storage in a high school lab of any quantity of materials classified as solid Class 4 oxidizers shall be _____.

    a. Not permitted

    b. In a hazardous materials storage cabinet

    c. Allowed in classrooms with openable windows

    d. Storage with combustible liquids, but not flammable liquids

    Reference _____

14. Given: Outdoor storage of compressed oxygen, which is classified as an oxidizing gas. The amount in storage is 37,400 cubic feet at normal temperature and pressure. What is the minimum required separation distance between the oxygen storage and the closest lot line?

    a. 5 feet   b. 10 feet

    c. 15 feet   d. No separation is required.

Reference _____

15. A chemical with an auto-ignition temperature in air at or below 130°F is classified as _____.

    a. unstable (reactive)   b. a flammable liquid

    c. pyrophoric   d. organic peroxide

Reference _____

16. What is the maximum allowable quantity of pyrophoric liquid allowed in a single control area of an unsprinklered building when the material is stored in an approved hazardous material cabinet?

    a. 0 pounds   b. 4 pounds

    c. 8 pounds   d. 16 pounds

Reference _____

17. What is the maximum tank size permitted for an indoor storage tank containing a pyrophoric liquid?

    a. 100 gallons   b. diameter of 10 feet

    c. 500 gallons   d. 1,000 gallons

Reference _____

18. Storage of unstable (reactive) materials is prohibited on the _____ of a building.

    a. Basement levels   b. Ground floor

    c. Upper floors   d. Roof top

Reference _____

19. Class _____ unstable (reactive) materials are sensitive to thermal or mechanical shock at elevated temperature and pressure.

    a. 1   b. 2

    c. 3   d. 4

Reference _____

20. Class 4 unstable (reactive) materials are prohibited in Group _____ occupancies.

    a. A   b. E

    c. I   d. R

Reference _____

21. What is the minimum aisle width between four piles of unstable (reactive) material storage? Each pile has a maximum volume of 500 cubic feet.

    a. the width of the pile

    b. 4 feet

    c. 4 feet or the height of the pile, whichever is less

    d. 4 feet or the height of the pile, whichever is greater

Reference _____

22. Liquid oxygen home care containers must be filled _____.

    a. In a room with open windows or mechanical exhaust ventilation

    b. Outdoors, or indoors if the container is specifically designed for indoor filling

    c. Outdoors, or indoors if the building is sprinklered

    d. At the distributor's facility

Reference _____

23. What is the classification of a material that reacts with water, with some release of energy, but not violently?

    a. Class 3 water-reactive   b. Class 2 water-reactive

    c. Class 1 water-reactive   d. Class 2 unstable (reactive)

Reference _____

24. Given: an outdoor storage vessel contains 100,000 cubic feet of an oxidizing cryogenic fluid. The minimum distance to from the vessel to the property line?

    a. 5 feet   b. 10 feet

    c. 15 feet   d. 25 feet

Reference _____

25. A Group H-3 occupancy is proposed for the storage of Class 2 water-reactive materials. Which of the following piping carrying water is allowed in the room where the water-reactive materials are stored?

    a. domestic water piping

    b. roof drain piping

    c. automatic sprinkler system piping

    d. no piping containing water is allowed

Reference _____

26. Which class of water-reactive materials can be stored with flammable liquids?

    a. Class 1

    b. Class 2

    c. Class 3

    d. Water-reactive solids and liquids shall not be stored with flammable liquids.

Reference _____

27. Storage of solid Class 2 water-reactive solids exceeding _____ shall be in a detached building.

    a. 50 pounds   b. 100 pounds

    c. 125 pounds   d. 125 tons

Reference _____

28. In Group I-1, I-4 and R occupancies, liquid oxygen home care containers shall not exceed an individual capacity of _____.

    a. 1,000 cubic feet   b. 40 liters

    c. 500 cubic feet   d. 15.8 gallons

Reference _____

29. When liquid oxygen is used for home health care, the maximum aggregate quantity of liquid oxygen that can be stored and used in each dwelling unit is _____.

    a. 500 cubic feet   b. 100 liters

    c. 31.6 gallons   d. 1,000 cubic feet

    Reference _____

30. A material that reacts violently with water or has the ability to boil water is classified as a _____ water-reactive solid or liquid.

    a. Class 1   b. Class 2

    c. Class 3   d. Class 4

    Reference _____

31. Indoor storage of pyroxylin (cellulose nitrate) plastics exceeding _____ pounds requires an automatic sprinkler protection system.

    a. 50 pounds   b. 100 pounds

    c. 250 pounds   d. 500 pounds

    Reference _____

32. What is the minimum separation distance required between outdoor storage of solid Class 3 water-reactive materials and buildings?

    a. 20 feet   b. 50 feet

    c. 75 feet   d. 100 feet

    Reference _____

33. Given: A Group F manufacturing facility using pyroxylin plastics. What is the maximum quantity allowed in a storage cabinet within a workroom?

    a. 25 pounds   b. 100 pounds

    c. 500 pounds   d. 1,000 pounds

    Reference _____

34. What standard is referenced for the storage of silane gas?

    a. NFPA 13

    b. CGA G-13

    c. ASME *Boiler and Pressure Vessel Code*

    d. NFPA 58

Reference _____

35. Given: A Group H occupancy storing unstable (reactive) material. Which classes of unstable (reactive) material require explosion control?

    a. Class 4

    b. Class 3 and 4

    c. Class 2, 3 and 4

    d. All classes require explosion control.

Reference _____

Answer Keys

Study Session 1
2021 *International Fire Code*

1.	d	Sec. 101.2.1
2.	d	Sec. 102.1
3.	c	Sec. 108.2
4.	c	Sec. 102.10
5.	a	Sec. 104.1
6.	d	Sec. 104.3
7.	b	Sec. 104.6
8.	b	Sec. 104.8.2
9.	d	Sec. 106.1
10.	a	Sec. 104.9
11.	c	Sec. 105.5.16, 105.5.18, 105.5.38
12.	d	Sec. 105.5.9
13.	c	Table 105.5.22
14.	d	Table 105.5.22
15.	d	Table 105.5.22
16.	a	Sec. 105.6.24
17.	b	Sec. 114.1, 114.2, 114.4
18.	b	Sec. 112.3
19.	b	Chapter 80
20.	c	Sec. 102.7
21.	d	Chapter 80
22.	d	Sec. 101.3
23.	b	Sec. 105.3.1
24.	d	Sec. 110.1
25.	d	Sec. 1103.5
26.	b	Sec. A101.3
27.	b	Sec. A101.5
28.	b	Sec. A101.3.6
29.	d	Sec. 108.2, 108.3
30.	c	Sec. 105.5.2
31.	c	Sec. 105.5.18, # 3
32.	b	Sec. 104.10.2
33.	c	Sec. 1103.1.1
34.	d	Sec. 107.2
35.	d	Sec. 1103.4.2

Study Session 2

2021 *International Fire Code*

1.	a	Sec. 201.1
2.	a	Sec. 201.4
3.	b	Sec. 202, IBC Ch. 3
4.	d	Sec. 202, IBC Sec. 303.1.2, # 1
5.	b	Sec. 202, IBC Sec. 303.3
6.	b	Sec. 202, IBC Sec. 304.1
7.	a	Sec. 202, IBC Sec. 305.2
8.	d	Sec. 202, IBC Sec. 308.3
9.	c	Sec. 202, IBC Sec. 309.1
10.	a	Sec. 202, IBC Sec. 310.3
11.	d	Sec. 202, IBC Sec. 312.1
12.	d	Sec. 202, IBC Sec. 311.3
13.	b	Sec. 202, IBC Sec. 303.1.2, # 2
14.	d	Sec. 202, IBC Sec. 303.6
15.	c	Sec. 202, IBC Sec. 307.3
16.	a	Sec. 202, IBC Sec. 308.2
17.	b	Sec. 202, IBC Sec. 309.1
18.	b	Sec. 202, IBC Sec. 303.1.2, #1
19.	b	Sec. 202, IBC Sec. 307.1.1
20.	a	Sec. 202, IBC Sec. 312.1
21.	b	Sec. 202
22.	c	Sec. 202, IBC Sec. 307.6
23.	d	Sec. 202, IBC Sec. 305
24.	c	Sec. 202, IBC Sec. 311.1
25.	a	Sec. 202, IBC Sec. 306.2
26.	a	Sec. 202, IBC Sec. 303.1.4, 305.1.1
27.	c	Sec. 202, IBC Sec. 306.3
28.	c	Sec. 202, IBC Sec. 308.4
29.	d	Sec. 202, IBC Sec. 311.3
30.	b	IBC Table 508.4
31.	c	IBC Sec. 508.1
32.	b	IBC Sec. 509.4.2
33.	a	IBC Table 508.4
34.	d	IBC Sec. 304.1
35.	d	IBC Sec. 509.1, 509.4.2

Study Session 3

2021 *International Fire Code*

1.	d	Sec. 310.2, 310.2.1
2.	a	Sec. 202
3.	d	Sec. 303.4
4.	c	Sec. 304.3.2
5.	b	Sec. 305.2
6.	a	Sec. 307.4.2
7.	d	Sec. 308.3
8.	b	Sec. 309.5
9.	c	Sec. 312.2, # 4
10.	c	Sec. 314.4
11.	b	Sec. 315.3.1, Exc. 2
12.	b	Sec. 317.2
13.	c	Sec. 403.2
14.	c	Sec. 404.2.2, # 3
15.	a	Sec. 405.3, Table 405.3
16.	d	Sec. 403.4.1
17.	c	Sec. 403.6.1.4
18.	b	Sec. 405.2, Exc 1
19.	b	Sec. 403.9.2.2.3
20.	c	Sec. 403.9.3.4
21.	a	Sec. 311.6, # 2
22.	c	Sec. 315.4.2
23.	c	Sec. 312.2
24.	b	Sec. 315.7.2
25.	d	Table 315.7.6(2)
26.	d	Sec. 315.7.7
27.	c	Sec. 316.1
28.	a	Sec. 105.5.32
29.	b	Sec. 319.8.1
30.	a	Sec. 317.2
31.	c	Sec. 315.3.4
32.	d	Sec. 318.1
33.	b	Sec. 320.3.12
34.	a	Sec. 321.1
35.	d	Table 405.3

Study Session 4

2021 *International Fire Code*

1.	c	Appendix B, Tables B105.1(2), B105.2
2.	a	Appendix C, Table C102.1
3.	d	Sec. 507.5.1
4.	b	Sec. 507.5.1.1
5.	a	Sec. 503.1.1
6.	b	Sec. 105.6.11
7.	b	Sec. 504.3
8.	d	Sec. 507.2
9.	a	Sec. 508.1.6
10.	b	Sec. 508.1.2
11.	c	Sec. 510.4.1.1
12.	d	Sec. L101.1
13.	d	Sec. 510.4
14.	c	Appendix B, Sec. B104.3
15.	b	Appendix B, Tables B105.1(1), B105.1(2)
16.	b	Appendix B, Tables B105.2, B105.1(2)
17.	c	Appendix C, Table C102.1, Footnote b
18.	b	Appendix D, Sec. D103.2
19.	c	Appendix D, Sec. D103.6.1
20.	d	Appendix D, Sec. D106.1
21.	c	Sec. 503.2.1
22.	b	Sec. 503.1.1
23.	c	Sec. 503.2.1
24.	b	Sec. 503.2.5

25.	a	Sec. 508.1
26.	b	Sec. 505.1
27.	b	Sec. 510.5.3
28.	b	Sec. 507.5.1
29.	c	Sec. 507.5.5
30.	a	Sec. 509.1
31.	a	Sec. 506.1
32.	d	Sec. 501.4
33.	d	Sec. L106.1
34.	a	Sec. 509.2
35.	a	Sec. 507.4

Study Session 5

2021 *International Fire Code*

1.	a	Sec. 202
2.	b	Sec. 605.1.3
3.	c	Sec. 605.4.1
4.	c	Sec. 605.4.2.2
5.	d	Sec. 605.5, Exc. 1
6.	d	Sec. 604.5.4, IBC Sec. 3007.3, 3008.3
7.	b	Sec. 1203.2
8.	c	Sec. 1203.1.4, 1203.2.18
9.	d	Sec. 603.5.2
10.	c	Sec. 603.8
11.	a	Sec. 608.13.4
12.	a	Sec. 608.6, 608.7, 608.8
13.	b	Sec. 604.6.1
14.	c	Sec. 1207.4.3, 1207.7.4
15.	d	Sec. 1207.6.1, Table 1207.6
16.	d	Table 1207.6
17.	d	Sec. 701.2.1
18.	d	Sec. 1205.3.1, 1205.3.2
19.	b	Sec. 1205.2.1, Exc. 2
20.	d	Sec. 604.6.2
21.	b	Sec. 704.3
22.	c	Sec. 806.1
23.	c	Sec. 807.5.2.2
24.	d	Sec. 805.2.1.1, Exc.;
25.	d	Sec. 808.1
26.	c	Sec. 806.1.1, Exc. 1
27.	a	Sec. 807.5.4
28.	a	Sec. 803.1.2
29.	b	Sec. 803.14
30.	c	Table 803.3, Footnote h
31.	d	Sec. 605.4.2.2, # 3
32.	a	Sec. 605.5.2.1.1
33.	c	Table 606.3.3.1
34.	a	Sec. 1207.1.1
35.	d	Table 1207.6

Study Session 6

2021 *International Fire Code*

1.	b	Sec. 903.2.10.2
2.	b	Sec. 901.7
3.	a	Sec. 903.2.1.2
4.	a	Sec. 903.2.4
5.	c	Sec. 903.2.7
6.	d	Sec. 903.2.9.1, # 1, 3
7.	b	Sec. 903.2.7.2
8.	d	Sec. 903.2.4.2, 903.2.4, # 1
9.	d	Sec. 903.4, Exc.
10.	d	Sec. 903.6, 1103.5.1, 1103.5.4 # 1, 1105.9
11.	b	Sec. 901.8.2
12.	d	Sec. 905.3.1, 905.3.3
13.	d	Sec. 905.12, 1103.6.1
14.	d	Sec. 905.4.2
15.	c	Sec. 910.2, Exc. 2
16.	b	Sec. 903.2.1.2
17.	a	Sec. 903.2.4.1
18.	d	Sec. 913
19.	c	Table 903.2.5.2
20.	b	Sec. 910.4.3;
		$100,000 \times 27 = 2,700,000$ cubic feet
		$2,700,000 \times 2 = 5,400,000$ cubic feet in 2 air changes
		$5,400,000/60 = 90,000$ cubic feet per minute
		$90,000/30,000 = 3$ fans
21.	d	Sec. 910.2, Exc. 1
22.	b	Sec. 910.2.1

23.	d	Sec. 910.3.2
24.	b	Sec. 910.3.3;
		$60,000 \times 24 = 1,440,000$ cubic feet
		$1,440,000/9,000 = 160$ square feet of vent area
25.	c	Sec. 903.3.8.4
26.	d	Sec. 910.4.6
27.	c	Sec. 910.4.4
28.	b	Table 914.8.3
29.	d	Sec. 914.3.2
30.	c	Sec. 914.3.1.1
31.	c	Sec. 909.5
32.	d	Sec. 905.3.4
33.	c	Sec. 905.4.1, IBC Sec. 713.4
34.	c	Sec. 914.3.1
35.	b	Sec. 912.2.2

Study Session 7

2021 *International Fire Code*

1.	c	Sec. 911.2, # 5		29.	b	Sec. 902.1, 202
2.	b	Sec. 916.7, # 2, 916.8, # 2		30.	b	Sec. 909.4
3.	c	Sec. 904.2.1		31.	d	Sec. 904.13.5.3
4.	d	Sec. 907.5.2.1.1		32.	c	Sec. 904.11.1.4
5.	d	Sec. 917.1		33.	a	Sec. 904.13.1
6.	d	Sec. 904.13.2		34.	b	Sec. 907.2.11.2
7.	d	Sec. 904.3.4		35.	d	Sec. 907.2.11.3
8.	c	Sec. 911.2, # 1				
9.	c	Sec. 907.2.1.1				
10.	d	Sec. 907.2.13.1.2, # 1				
11.	c	Sec. 907.3.1				
12.	d	Sec. 915.1.1				
13.	b	Table 907.5.2.3.2				
14.	b	Sec. 907.9, 1103.7.5.1				
15.	b	Sec. 907.2.11.2, 907.2.11.3, 907.2.11.4				
16.	a	Sec. 907.2.14				
17.	c	Sec. 904.14.1.1, # 1				
18.	b	Sec. 907.2.2, # 1				
19.	d	Table 906.3(1)				
20.	c	Table 906.3(2)				
21.	d	Sec. 906.9.1				
22.	d	Sec. 904.13.1				
23.	b	Sec. 906.4.2, # 1				
24.	b	Sec. 907.2.4, # 1				
25.	a	Sec. 908.3				
26.	d	Sec. 907.2.20				
27.	c	Sec. 916.8				
28.	c	Sec. 902.1, 202				

Study Session 8

2021 *International Fire Code*

1.	b	Sec. 1002.1, 202
2.	d	Sec. 1002.1, 202
3.	c	Sec. 1002.1, 202
4.	b	Table 1004.5
5.	b	Table 1004.5; 1500/50 = 30
6.	b	Sec. 1004.6
7.	c	Sec. 1005.3.2; $3200 \times 0.2 = 640$
8.	a	Sec. 1005.3.1; $200 \times 0.3 = 60$
9.	d	Sec. 1005.5
10.	d	Sec. 1005.7.1
11.	b	Sec. 1003.3.1
12.	b	Sec. 1003.3.1, Exc.
13.	c	Table 1006.2.1
14.	b	Sec. 1010.1.1
15.	c	Sec. 1010.1.1
16.	a	Sec. 1010.1.1, Exc. 3
17.	a	Sec. 1010.1.1.1
18.	b	Sec. 1010.1, 2nd paragraph
19.	d	Sec. 1010.1.2.1
20.	d	Sec. 1013.2
21.	b	Sec. 1013.6.2
22.	d	Sec. 1013.6.3
23.	c	Table 1017.2
24.	a	Table 1017.2
25.	d	Table 1020.3

26.	c	Table 1020.2
27.	a	Table 1006.3.4(2)
28.	b	Sec. 1006.2.2.1
29.	d	Sec. 1006.2.2.2
30.	b	Sec. 1030.2
31.	d	Sec. 1020.5, Exc. 2
32.	c	Sec. 1025.1
33.	d	Sec. 1032.8
34.	a	Sec. 1007.1.1, Exc. 2 $(60 \times 60) + (80 \times 80) = 10{,}000$ $\sqrt{10{,}000} = 100$ $100 \times {}^{1}/_{3} = 33.3$
35.	d	Sec. 1032.10.1, 1032.10.2

Study Session 9
2021 *International Fire Code*

1.	c	Sec. 2405.3.1
2.	a	Sec. 2004.3
3.	a	Sec. 2006.1
4.	d	Sec. 2405.9.4
5.	a	Sec. 2004.6
6.	d	Sec. 2005.6, # 3
7.	c	Sec. 2410.1
8.	d	Sec. 2006.4.3
9.	d	Sec. 2006.5.1, 2006.5.2
10.	d	Sec. 2006.15
11.	c	Sec. 2006.17.1
12.	d	Sec. 2409.1, 2409.3
13.	b	Sec. 2106.3, Table 5003.1.1(1)
14.	b	Sec. 2007.5
15.	d	Sec. 2409.3
16.	c	Sec. 2104.1
17.	a	Sec. 2105.3
18.	d	Sec. 2106.2
19.	a	Sec. 2203.1, Table 2203.1
20.	c	Sec. 2108.2, Exc. 2
21.	b	Sec. 2202.1, 202
22.	c	Sec. 2203.4, 2203.5
23.	a	Sec. 2203.1, # 2
24.	d	Sec. 2303.1, # 5
25.	b	Sec. 2407.2
26.	a	Sec. 2305.2.3, # 4
27.	d	Table 2306.2.3
28.	a	Sec. 2306.2.3, # 3
29.	c	Sec. 2306.5

30.	d	Sec. 2107.3
31.	d	Sec. 2203.3.2
32.	b	Sec. 2404.9.1
33.	d	Sec. 2404.7.6
34.	b	Sec. 2403.2.1.3
35.	a	Sec. 2404.3.3.4, Exc.

Study Session 10

2021 *International Fire Code*

1.	c	Sec. 105.5.27
2.	b	Sec. 2804.3
3.	c	Sec. 2809.2
4.	a	Sec. 2809.3, 2809.4, 2809.5
5.	a	Sec. 2904.2, # 3
6.	b	Sec. 2905.5
7.	b	Sec. 2907.5
8.	c	Sec. 2503.2
9.	d	Sec. 2506.2
10.	c	Sec. 2504.2
11.	d	Sec. 2603.4, 202; only combustible liquids have a flash point $\geq 100°F$
12.	c	Sec. 2702.1, 202
13.	b	Sec. 2703.7.2
14.	c	Sec. 2703.10.4.4.1
15.	b	Sec. 2703.13.2, # 3
16.	d	Sec. 2703.14.2
17.	c	Sec. 2703.15.2
18.	d	Sec. 2704.2.1
19.	d	Sec. 2704.3.1
20.	d	Table 2705.2.2, Footnotes a and b
21.	d	Table 2704.2.2.1, Footnote d
22.	d	Sec. 105.5.31, 2810.3, 2810.4
23.	d	Sec. 2705.3.4.1
24.	c	Sec. 2808.4; $1.5 \times 25 = 37.5$ feet
25.	a	Sec. 2603.5

26.	d	Sec. 2906.5
27.	c	Sec. 2804.2.1
28.	a	Sec. 2904.4
29.	d	Sec. 2810.7, 2810.11
30.	c	Sec. 2808.8
31.	d	Sec. 2808.3.1
32.	c	Sec. 2809.2, 2809.3
33.	d	Sec. 2909.3
34.	c	Sec. 2806.2
35.	d	Sec. 2810.9

Study Session 11
2021 *International Fire Code*

1.	c	Sec. 3004.2.1		29.	b	Sec. 3314.1
2.	a	Sec. 3005.1		30.	d	Sec. 3316.1
3.	b	Sec. 3006.1		31.	a	Sec. 3403.2
4.	c	Sec. 3103.8.3		32.	c	Sec. 3409.1
5.	b	Sec. 3103.10.4		33.	b	Sec. 3405.1
6.	d	Table 3103.12.2		34.	d	Sec. 3405.2
7.	b	Sec. 3103.12.1		35.	d	Sec. 3408.1
8.	a	Sec. 3105.4				
9.	b	Sec. 3107.12.5				
10.	d	Sec. 3106.4				
11.	d	Sec. 105.6.21, 105.6.24				
12.	b	Sec. 3107.16				
13.	b	Sec. 3002.1, 202				
14.	a	Sec. 3003.4				
15.	c	Sec. 3202.1, 202				
16.	c	Table 3203.8				
17.	d	Table 3203.8				
18.	b	Table 3203.8				
19.	c	Sec. 3209.4.2				
20.	b	Figure 3203.9(1), Figure 3203.9(2)				
21.	b	Table 3206.2				
22.	b	Sec. 3205.5, Exc.				
23.	b	Sec. 3208.2.2				
24.	d	Sec. 3301.1				
25.	c	Sec. 3313.3.3.2				
26.	b	Sec. 3311.1				
27.	b	Sec. 3312.1				
28.	d	Sec. 3313.1				

Study Session 12

2021 *International Fire Code*

1.	d	Sec. 4003.2
2.	b	Sec. 3506.3
3.	c	Sec. 3604.1
4.	a	Sec. 3604.6
5.	d	Sec. 3603.4
6.	b	Sec. 3504.3.1
7.	d	Sec. 3501.3, # 1
8.	b	Sec. 3503.3
9.	a	Sec. 3504.2.1
10.	d	Sec. 3504.2.6
11.	c	Sec. 3604.2
12.	a	Sec. 3510.2
13.	d	Sec. 3505.6
14.	a	Sec. 3704.2
15.	c	Sec. 3704.5
16.	b	Sec. 3705.1
17.	d	Sec. 3704.6
18.	d	Sec. 3703.3
19.	d	Sec. 3703.4
20.	a	Sec. 3704.3
21.	b	Sec. 3802.1, 202
22.	a	Sec. 3803.1.7
23.	a	Table 3804.1.1
24.	c	Tables 3804.1.1, 5003.1.1(1) with Footnotes d and e
25.	d	Sec. 3803.2.2, 3804.1.1; Table 3804.1.1
26.	b	Sec. 3803.2.1

27.	d	Sec. 3805.3
28.	b	Sec. 4004.2
29.	d	Sec. 3803.1.7
30.	b	Sec. 3903.2
31.	d	Sec. 3904.2.1, 3904.2.2
32.	b	Sec. 4004.3
33.	c	Sec. 3905.1.1, # 2
34.	d	Sec. 3905.1.2
35.	c	Sec. 3904.2.2.2

Study Session 13

2021 *International Fire Code*

1.	a	Sec. 5001.2.1
2.	c	Sec. 5003.1.3
3.	d	Table 5003.1.1(1), Footnotes d and e
4.	c	Table 5003.1.1(1), Footnote e
5.	c	Table 5003.1.1(1)
6.	b	Table 5003.1.1(2), Footnote d
7.	b	Table 5003.1.1(3)
8.	d	Sec. 5005.1.12
9.	c	Sec. 5003.2.6.1
10.	a	Sec. 5003.2.7
11.	d	Table 5003.8.2
12.	b	Table 5003.8.3.2
13.	a	Tables 5003.1.1(1), Footnote d, 5003.8.3.2
14.	b	Tables 5003.1.1(1), Footnote e, 5003.8.3.2
15.	d	Sec. 5003.8.7.1
16.	b	Sec. 5003.10.2
17.	d	Sec. 5003.9.8
18.	c	Sec. 5003.10.2
19.	d	Table 5003.11.1, Footnote b
20.	d	Table 5003.11.1, Footnote b; 200 gallons in each control area
21.	c	Sec. 5003.11.3.2
22.	b	Sec. 5003.12, # 3
23.	d	Sec. 5004.2.1
24.	d	Sec. 5004.2.2, Table 5004.2.2
25.	d	Sec. 5004.2.2.4
26.	c	Sec. 5004.3, Exc.
27.	c	Sec. 5004.3.1, # 2
28.	b	Sec. 5004.5
29.	b	Sec. 5005.1.10, # 4
30.	d	Sec. 5005.1.4.1
31.	a	Sec. 5003.9.10
32.	d	Table 5003.1.1(1)
33.	b	Table 5003.1.1(2), Footnotes b and g
34.	a	Table 5003.1.1(1), Footnotes d and e, Table 5003.1.1(2), Footnotes d and e
35.	d	Sec. 5003.2.9 and 5003.2.9.1

Study Session 14
2021 *International Fire Code*

1.	c	Table 5103.1		29.	b	Sec. 5505.1.2.6
2.	b	Sec. 5104.2, # 3		30.	d	Sec. 5505.3.2
3.	d	Table 5104.3.1, Footnote b		31.	b	Sec. 5303.7.11
4.	b	Sec. 5104.3.3		32.	b	Sec. 5306.2.2
5.	d	Sec. 5104.3.2.1, # 3		33.	a	Sec. 5104.1.1, # 1
6.	b	Table 5104.3.2, Footnote a		34.	b	Sec. 5306.2
7.	c	Sec. 5106.2.5		35.	b	Sec. 5003.8.6.3, 5306.2.3
8.	d	Table 5106.2.1				
9.	c	Sec. 5106.2.3				
10.	d	Sec. 5106.5.8, # 1				
11.	c	Sec. 5307.3.1, 5004.3				
12.	b	Sec. 5307.3.2				
13.	c	Sec. 5101.4				
14.	d	Sec. 5303.4.3				
15.	b	Sec. 5303.7.2				
16.	c	Sec. 5303.7.3				
17.	d	Sec. 5303.16.9				
18.	a	Sec. 5303.16.10				
19.	c	Sec. 5307.2				
20.	b	Sec. 5404.2.1				
21.	b	Sec. 5404.2.2				
22.	a	Sec. 5404.1.1				
23.	b	Sec. 202				
24.	b	Sec. 5503.2.3				
25.	c	Table 5504.3.1.1				
26.	c	Table 5504.3.1.2.1				
27.	d	Sec. 5504.3.1.1.3				
28.	a	Sec. 5505.1.2.3.2				

Study Session 15

2021 *International Fire Code*

1.	a	Sec. 5601.1.5	28.	d	Sec. 5608.5
2.	d	Sec. 5604.7.9	29.	b	Sec. 5608.5.5
3.	c	Sec. 5602.1, 202	30.	b	Sec. 5608.10
4.	a	Sec. 5602.1, 202	31.	d	Sec. 5604.3.3
5.	d	Table 5604.3	32.	a	Table 5604.5.2(3)
6.	a	Sec. 5604.5.1.1	33.	c	Sec. 5602.1, 202
7.	d	Tables 5601.8.1(1), 5604.5.2(1)	34.	d	Tables 5601.8.1(2), 5604.5.2(2)
8.	a	Tables 5601.8.1(2), 5604.5.2(2)	35.	b	Sec. 5606.5.2.2
9.	b	Sec. 5604.5.2.2, Tables 5601.8.1(2), 5604.5.2(2)			
10.	b	Sec. 5604.5.3.3			
11.	d	Sec. 5604.6.4			
12.	b	Sec. 5604.7.3			
13.	b	Sec. 5604.7.8			
14.	d	Sec. 5604.9			
15.	c	Table 5605.3, Footnote a			
16.	a	Sec. 5605.4.1.2			
17.	c	Sec. 5607.15			
18.	c	Sec. 5605.6.8			
19.	b	Sec. 5606.5.1.3			
20.	b	Sec. 5606.4.2			
21.	d	Sec. 5606.5.1.1			
22.	a	Sec. 5606.5.1.2			
23.	b	Sec. 5606.5.2.1, # 2			
24.	a	Sec. 5606.5.2.2			
25.	b	Sec. 5606.5.2.3, # 2.2			
26.	d	Sec. 5606.5.2.3, # 2.5			
27.	b	Sec. 5601.1.3, Exc. 4			

Study Session 16

2021 *International Fire Code*

1.	c	Table 5704.3.4.1
2.	c	Sec. 5704.3.2.2
3.	d	Sec. 5701.2, Exc. 7
4.	c	Sec. 5702.1, 202
5.	a	Sec. 5704.3.4.4
6.	b	Sec. 5704.3.5.1, Table 5003.1.1(1), Footnote d, Table 5003.8.3.2
7.	a	Table 5703.1.1
8.	c	Sec. 5703.6.3
9.	c	Table 5704.3.6.3(2)
10.	d	Sec. 5703.6.10
11.	b	Sec. 5704.4.2, Table 5704.4.2, Footnote d
12.	c	Table 5704.4.2
13.	d	Sec. 5704.2.7.3.3, Exc. 3
14.	a	Sec. 5705.2.4, # 4
15.	b	Sec. 5704.2.7.5.8, Exc.
16.	a	Sec. 5705.3.6.1
17.	d	Sec. 5704.2.9.2.3, Exc.
18.	d	Sec. 5705.3.7.5.3
19.	d	Sec. 5705.3.7.6.3
20.	d	Table 5705.3.8.2
21.	d	Sec. 5704.2.9.5.1
22.	c	Sec. 5707.2.1, # 1
23.	b	Sec. 5705.5, # 2, 5705.5.1
24.	a	Sec. 5704.2.9.7.9
25.	b	Sec. 5703.6.7
26.	a	Sec. 5705.5.1, # 3

27.	b	Sec. 5706.2.4
28.	d	Sec. 5706.2.5.2, # 2
29.	d	Sec. 5704.2.9.2.1
30.	a	Sec. 5704.2.10
31.	c	Sec. 5706.5.1.1
32.	c	Sec. 5705.3.7.2
33.	c	Sec. 5704.3.4.4
34.	a	Sec. 5704.2.7.4
35.	d	Sec. 5707.4.1, 5707.5.3

Study Session 17

2021 *International Fire Code*

1.	a	Sec. 5803.1.1, Exc. 1
2.	a	Sec. 5802.1, 202
3.	c	Sec. 5803.1.5.1
4.	d	Sec. 5808.5.1
5.	d	Sec. 5803.1.3.1
6.	b	Sec. 5807.1.4
7.	d	Sec. 5904.1.3
8.	a	Sec. 5906.2.3
9.	c	Sec. 5906.4.3
10.	b	Sec. 6002.1, 202
11.	c	Sec. 6004.3.2.1.1
12.	d	Sec. 6004.1.1.2
13.	c	Sec. 6004.1.2, # 5
14.	b	Sec. 6004.2.2.7.2
15.	c	Sec. 6004.2.2.9
16.	c	Sec. 6004.2.2.10
17.	c	Sec. 6005.6
18.	d	Sec. 6005.4.1
19.	c	Sec. 6101.3
20.	d	Sec. 6103.2.1.3
21.	b	Sec. 6109.3
22.	c	Table 6109.12
23.	c	Table 6109.12
24.	c	Table 6109.12
25.	c	Table 6109.12
26.	b	Table 6004.2.2.7.5
27.	a	Sec. 6002.1, 202
28.	b	Table 6104.3

29.	b	Table 6104.3
30.	c	Sec. 6111.2.1
31.	a	Sec. 5802.1, 202
32.	c	Sec. 6107.2
33.	a	Sec. 5808
34.	b	Sec. 6004.2.1.2, 6004.2.2.10
35.	b	Sec. 5806.4.2, # 2

Study Session 18

2021 *International Fire Code*

1.	d	Table 5003.1.1(1), Table 6304.1.5(1)
2.	c	Table 5003.1.1(1), Footnotes d and e
3.	a	Sec. 6204.1.5
4.	b	Table 6204.1.2
5.	b	Sec. 6204.1.4
6.	c	Sec. 6204.1.7, # 3
7.	d	Sec. 6204.1.8
8.	a	Sec. 6204.1.11
9.	a	Table 5003.1.1(1), 6203.1, 6203.1.1.1
10.	c	Sec. 6303.1.1.1.3
11.	c	Sec. 6304.1.2
12.	d	Sec. 6304.1.5
13.	b	Sec. 6303.1.1.1.1, # 1
14.	a	Table 6304.2.1
15.	c	Sec. 6402.1, 202
16.	a	Table 5003.1.1(1), Footnote g
17.	c	Sec. 6404.1.2
18.	a	Sec. 6604.1.5
19.	c	Sec. 6602.1, 202
20.	d	Sec. 6603.1.2.2
21.	d	Sec. 6604.1.4
22.	b	Sec. 6306.3.6.1
23.	c	Sec. 6702.1, 202
24.	b	Table 6304.2.1
25.	c	Sec. 6704.1.3

26.	a	Sec. 6704.1.5
27.	d	Sec. 6704.1.1, 5003.8.2
28.	d	Sec. 6306.3.1
29.	c	Sec. 6306.4
30.	b	Sec. 6702.1, 202
31.	b	Sec. 6504.2
32.	c	Sec. 6704.2.2
33.	c	Sec. 6504.1.2
34.	b	Sec. 6404.1
35.	b	Sec. 6604.1.2

ICC INTERNATIONAL CODE COUNCIL®

Building Confidence, Building Community

Additional Code Resources from ICC
Tools to help you learn, interpret and apply the I-Codes®

Significant Changes to the 2021 International Codes®
Practical resources that offer a comprehensive analysis of the critical changes since the previous edition

Authored by code experts, these useful tools are "must-have" guides to the many important changes in the 2021 International Codes. Key changes are identified then followed by in-depth, expert discussion of how the change affects real world application. A full-color photo, table or illustration is included for each change to further clarify application.

Significant Changes to the International Building Code, 2021 Edition	Search #7024S21
Significant Changes to the International Residential Code, 2021 Edition	Search #7101S21
Significant Changes to the International Fire Code, 2021 Edition	Search #7404S21
Significant Changes to the International Energy Conservation Code, 2021 Edition	Search #7808S21
Significant Changes to the International Plumbing Code/ International Mechanical Code/International Fuel Gas Code, 2021 Edition	Search #7202S21

2021 Code Essentials
A straightforward, focused approach to code fundamentals using non-code language

A user-friendly, concise approach that facilitates understanding of the essential code provisions. These invaluable companion guides contain detailed full-color illustrations to enhance comprehension, references to corresponding code sections, and a glossary of code and construction terms that clarify their meaning in the context of the code.

Building Code Essentials: Based on the 2021 IBC	Search #4031S21
Residential Code Essentials: Based on the 2021 IRC	Search #4131S21
Fire Code Essentials: Based on the 2021 IFC	Search #4431S21
Energy Code Essentials: Based on the 2021 IECC	Search #4831S21
Existing Building Code Essentials: Based on the 2021 IEBC	Search #4552S21
Plumbing Code Essentials: Based on the 2021 IPC	Search #4231S21
Mechanical Code Essentials: Based on the 2021 IMC	Search #4031S21

Study Companions
The ideal learning tool for exam prep or everyday application

These comprehensive study guides provide practical learning assignments helpful for independent study or instructor-led programs in the workplace, college courses, or vocational training programs. Each book is organized into study sessions with clear learning objectives, key points for review, code text and commentary applicable to the specific topic, and hundreds of illustrations. A helpful practice quiz at the end of each session allows you to measure your progress along the way. The answer key lists the code section referenced in each question for further information.

2021 International Building Code Study Companion	Search #4017S21
2021 International Residential Code Study Companion	Search #4117S21
2021 International Fire Code Study Companion	Search #4407S21
2021 International Plumbing Code Study Companion	Search #4217S21
2021 International Mechanical Code Study Companion	Search #4317S21
2021 International Fuel Gas Code Study Companion	Search #4607S21
2021 International Energy Conservation Code Study Companion	Search #4807S21
2021 Permit Technician Study Companion	Search #4027S21
2021 Special Inspection Study Companion	Search #4032S21
2021 Accessibility Study Companion	Search #4123S21

Browse the latest code tools at shop.iccsafe.org

ICC
EVALUATION
SERVICE®

☑ **Specify** and
☑ **Approve** *with* **Confidence**

When facing new or unfamiliar materials, look for an ICC-ES Evaluation Report or Listing before approving for installation.

ICC-ES® **Evaluation Reports** are the most widely accepted and trusted technical reports for code compliance.

ICC-ES **Building Product Listings** and **PMG Listings** show product compliance with applicable standard(s) referenced in the building and plumbing codes as well as other applicable codes.

When you specify or approve products or materials with an ICC-ES report, building product listing or PMG listing, you avoid delays on projects and improve your bottom line.

ICC-ES is a subsidiary of ICC®, the publisher of the codes used throughout the U.S. and many global markets, so you can be confident in their code expertise.

www.icc-es.org | 800-423-6587

Proctored Remote Online Testing Option (PRONTO™)

Convenient, Reliable, and Secure Certification Exams

Take the Test at Your Location

Take advantage of ICC PRONTO, an industry leading, secure online exam delivery service. PRONTO allows you to take ICC Certification exams at your convenience in the privacy of your own home, office or other secure location. Plus, you'll know your pass/fail status immediately upon completion.

 With PRONTO, ICC's Proctored Remote Online Testing Option, take your ICC Certification exam from any location with high-speed internet access.

 With online proctoring and exam security features you can be confident in the integrity of the testing process and exam results.

 Plan your exam for the day and time most convenient for you. PRONTO is available 24/7.

 Eliminate the waiting period and get your results in private immediately upon exam completion.

 #1 ICC was the first model code organization to offer secured online proctored exams—part of our commitment to offering the latest technology-based solutions to help building and code professionals succeed and advance. We continue to expand our catalog of PRONTO exam offerings.

Discover ICC PRONTO and the wealth of certification opportunities available to advance your career: www.iccsafe.org/MeetPRONTO

ISO/IEC 17065
Product Certification Body
#1000

20-18842